CATHOLIC PARTICULARITY IN SEVENTEENTH-CENTURY FRENCH WRITING

CATHOLIC PARTICULARITY IN SEVENTEENTH-CENTURY FRENCH WRITING

'Christianity is Strange'

RICHARD PARISH

OXFORD
UNIVERSITY PRESS

UNIVERSITY PRESS

Great Clarendon Street, Oxford OX2 6DP

Oxford University Press is a department of the University of Oxford.
It furthers the University's objective of excellence in research, scholarship,
and education by publishing worldwide in

Oxford New York

Auckland Cape Town Dar es Salaam Hong Kong Karachi
Kuala Lumpur Madrid Melbourne Mexico City Nairobi
New Delhi Shanghai Taipei Toronto

With offices in

Argentina Austria Brazil Chile Czech Republic France Greece
Guatemala Hungary Italy Japan Poland Portugal Singapore
South Korea Switzerland Thailand Turkey Ukraine Vietnam

Oxford is a registered trade mark of Oxford University Press
in the UK and in certain other countries

Published in the United States
by Oxford University Press Inc., New York

First published 2011

British Library Cataloguing in Publication Data
Data available

Library of Congress Cataloging in Publication Data
Data available

Typeset by SPI Publisher Services, Pondicherry, India
Printed in Great Britain
on acid-free paper by
MPG Books Group, Bodmin and King's Lynn

ISBN 978–0–19–959666–9

1 3 5 7 9 10 8 6 4 2

for Gordon

Acknowledgements

The chapters which follow started life as the Bampton Lectures, delivered in the University Church of St Mary the Virgin in Oxford in the Hilary Term, 2009. I am first of all delighted to thank the Bampton Electors and their Chairman, Professor Dame Averil Cameron, for giving me the opportunity to deliver them. I should also like to acknowledge the help given to me by Dr Gemma Simmonds, CJ, of Heythrop College, London, in preparing them; and by Dr Paul Joyce, Chairman of the Faculty of Theology, for his advice on many practical issues. Finally, it is my pleasure to thank the Master and Fellows of my own College, St Catherine's, for according me a term of study leave in which to prepare them for publication.

I have given all quotations from French originals in English and French, in that order. French spelling has been modernized throughout. Translations are my own, and seek to give the shape and sense of the original, rather than always aiming for a polished English style. A few words have caused a good deal of uncertainty on account of their polysemic nature, and have not always proved capable of a consistent translation. I have glossed these when it seemed necessary. Inevitably, a good many of the secondary references are to books written in French, but I have tried to offer English-language material as frequently as it is available, and of comparable authority. Biblical quotations in English will be given from the *New Jerusalem Bible (Study Edition)*, London, Dartman, Longman and Todd, 1994. Quotations from the liturgy are from the *Pope John Sunday Missal*, ed. Michael Buckley, Chawton, Redemptorist Publications, 1984.

Contents

Introduction

> No country offers us, concentrated in such a limited timescale, an equal intensity of religious thought; nowhere has the expression of this thought attained to an equivalent degree of artistic perfection. It is a unique achievement, an exceptional treasury.[1]

> What sense can we make of a sermon by Bossuet? – I mean for a Catholic; for someone who is not a Catholic, the distance is even greater.[2]

As I was writing this book, *The Times* religious affairs and Rome correspondents commented, on April 5, 2010, that the Easter sermons which had just been preached by Catholic bishops in various European countries, carrying as they had an appropriate emphasis on the Roman Church's response to the prevailing scandal of the time (that of child abuse by priests), had differed in their actuality and controversy from the "age-old and often anodyne messages about the Crucifixion and Resurrection of Christ".[3] Age-old, of course. But anodyne ("unlikely to cause offence or disagreement but somewhat dull" (*OED*))? That the creator of the only universe we know was killed as a criminal and returned to life? It seems as though the blunting combination of familiarity and scepticism with which we approach the dogmas of the Christian Incarnation has not changed since the seventeenth century in France; and the idea that they are "unlikely to cause offence or disagreement" bears little historical scrutiny.[4] As to how dull they are, I hope that the range of texts I shall introduce will go some way to challenge that assertion as well.

[1] "Aucun pays ne nous offre, rassemblée sur un si court espace, une telle intensité de pensée religieuse ; nulle part l'expression de cette pensée n'a atteint une pareille perfection d'art. C'est une réussite unique, une richesse originale" (Jean Calvet, *La Littérature religieuse de François de Sales à Fénelon*, Paris, del Duca, 1956, p. 434).

[2] "Que faire d'un sermon de Bossuet? – j'entends pour un catholique ; pour qui ne l'est pas, la distance est plus grande encore" (Bossuet, *Sermon sur la Mort*, ed. Jacques Truchet, Paris, Garnier-Flammarion, 1970, p. 16).

[3] Ruth Gledhill and Richard Owen, in *The Times*, April 5, 2010, p. 14.

[4] A straightforward introduction to earlier Christian history and teaching is provided by the first four volumes of the Penguin [formerly Pelican] *History of the Church*: Henry Chadwick, *The Early Christian Church*, 1967, 2nd edn 1993; Richard Southern, *Western Society and the Church*

The Bampton Lectures were founded in the eighteenth century by the will of John Bampton, Canon of Salisbury, who died in 1751. They were first delivered in 1780, and since 1895 have occurred biennially. The remit of the lecturer is to speak about any (or presumably all) of the following:

> To confirm and establish the Christian Faith, and to confute all heretics and schismatics – upon the divine authority of the Holy Scriptures – upon the authority of the writings of the Primitive Fathers, as to the Faith and practice of the Primitive Church – upon the Divinity of our Lord and Saviour Jesus Christ – upon the Divinity of the Holy Ghost – upon the Articles of the Christian Faith, as comprehended in the Apostles' and Nicene Creeds.[5]

The topics dictated by Bampton are clear, dogmatic, and circumscribed; and their applicability to the century in which the Catholic Reformation[6] found its most vigorous expression in France was, to me at least, obvious (however far some elements of it would probably have been from their founder's own confessional allegiance). But to many people the terms of reference of the lectures are now more likely to appear opaque, intransigent, and remote. Put another way, to use the two key terms from my title, they are both particular and strange.

The question which I am seeking to address is aggravated by a combination of historical circumstances. On the one hand, there is a widespread assumption that, whatever the current relationship between Church and State,[7] most societies which adhere nominally to the Christian (that is non-Jewish and non-Islamic) branch of the Abrahamic religions have assented over many generations to a tacit or explicit assimilation of Christian dogma into their mores; but that assimilation often seems to coexist with an unwillingness, or indeed incapacity, to confront the specifics, the particularity, of the belief system whose values have been adopted. The readiness to expect Christianity to be something that it is not, and to accuse it of not being something which it never claimed to be (to both of

in the later Middle Ages, 1970, 2nd edn 1988; Owen Chadwick, *The Reformation*, 1964, 2nd edn 1968; G. R. Cragg, *The Church and the Age of Reason, 1648–1789*, 1960, 2nd edn 1966. See also Diarmaid MacCulloch, *A History of Christianity*, Oxford, Oxford University Press, 2009.

[5] Very clear expositions of most of the technical terms I have used are available in the *Oxford Dictionary of the Christian Church*, 3rd edn, ed. F. Cross and E. Livingstone, Oxford, Oxford University Press, 1997 [hereafter *ODCC*]. For a fuller treatment of specifically Catholic dogmatic issues, there are the collaborative *Dictionnaire de théologie catholique*, Paris, Letouzey et Ané, 1909–46, 15 vols [hereafter *DTC*]; *Sacramentum Mundi*, London, Burns and Oates, 1968–70, 6 vols; and the *New Catholic Encyclopedia*, McGraw-Hill, New York, 1967, 15 vols.

[6] I have preferred to write of the Catholic Reformation, in order to emphasize the reform and renewal which took place within the Roman Church, in preference to the Counter-Reformation, which seems simply to indicate a movement of reaction.

[7] The kings of France in the seventeenth century were accorded the title of "Most Christian King" ["Roi Très Chrétien"]. The formal separation of the French Church and State took place in 1905. The status of the Catholic Church in England and Wales in the twenty-first century combines certain technical impediments (such as forbidding the marriage of a Catholic to the heir to the throne) with a de facto tolerance – thus Pope Benedict XVI was received by the monarch on a state visit in September 2010.

which phenomena I shall draw attention at some length in discussing Pascal), seems to be comparably in evidence both in France in the seventeenth century, and in much of Western Europe in the early twenty-first.

That parallel will not, I hope, translate into an attempt to "make relevant" the writing of a period in which the social circumstances that defined Christian, and more specifically Catholic, teaching and practice differed in so many respects from either the current French or English experience of religious belief in the same tradition. The Catholic faith was practised under an absolute monarchy, in a primarily agrarian society, at a time and in a place in which the roles of women and men were clearly delimited, and the authority of the episcopacy went largely unquestioned. But if, as nearly all of the writers with whom I shall deal will repeatedly claim, the core doctrines of Catholic Christianity are immutable and enduring, then it must by definition have become no less or more applicable to current circumstances, and indeed to eternal circumstances. The degree to which that is dogmatically and empirically the case will be for theologians and sociologists of religion to assess.

Nor am I writing a catechism. In the course of teaching a paper which involved some familiarity with the material I am looking at, one undergraduate responded to my mention of the *felix culpa* paradox[8] that he "was very sorry, but he could not accept it". My purpose, mistakenly interpreted, had simply been to explain that it existed. Readers will come to this material with any number of convictions and preconceptions (and I was delighted to see a good turnout of self-declared atheists and sceptics, alongside believers within various traditions, in my Bampton audiences). What I have rather tried to do is to bring to light, and to gain enlightenment from, a particularly fertile corpus of written works, which are united by their time and place of composition, and by their common confessional allegiance. No more than that.

The assertion which I have adopted as my subtitle, and as my governing hypothesis, was written by Blaise Pascal (1623–62), the figure whom posterity has identified as the most influential Christian thinker in seventeenth-century France (in any tradition); he wrote it at a particular historical moment; and, to judge from all his religious writing in whatever context, was primarily moved to do so by the prevalent ethos of his age. There is thus a kind of contradiction in what will follow, in that I will aim to bring into focus a whole range of perspectives on unchanging Christian dogma that are surprising, strange, and indeed, in some cases, period-specific. Yet I am not as a result proposing that Catholic Christianity was strange *in the French seventeenth century*, but rather that the enduring features of its strangeness might have been better

[8] This liturgical formula, describing the Fall as a "happy fault", on account of the sin of Adam leading to the coming of Christ, occurs in the *Exultet* proclaimed at the Easter Vigil. I will attend to it at length in Chapter 3.

understood, more aggressively re-asserted or more potently expressed than at other historical moments.

Chronologically, I have taken what academia would now call "the long seventeenth century" as my timescale, understood in very broad political terms as stretching from the accession to the throne of Henri IV (1589) to the death of Louis XIV (1715); and I have most frequently, though not exclusively, taken the date of publication of the texts I have used, rather than the life-span of their writer, as the criterion for inclusion (the major exceptions would be the posthumous publications of the autobiographical texts I shall consider; and the use of modern editions of Pascal's *Pensées*, rather than the truncated *Édition de Port-Royal* of 1670).[9]

More broadly again, we might observe that the French seventeenth century is situated between two historical moments of overwhelming national and international significance: the Reformation, and the Revolution. The sixteenth century in France had witnessed the Wars of Religion, whose cessation was sealed by the (as it transpired, temporary) freedom of conscience granted to Protestants by Henri IV in the Edict of Nantes in 1598. Just under 200 years later, in 1789, the French Revolution in some comparable sense ratified the ideals of the Enlightenment. The period in question is therefore historically strange in that it seems to represent a point of hiatus in a dynamic which begins with reform, and which apparently moves towards tolerance and secularism. But if we turn that statement around, we find that the *grand siècle* can also be understood as a high point of Catholic writing and spirituality, in a sequence which was initiated in the devotional writing of the later Middle Ages (most obviously by such influential works as the *Imitation of Christ*),[10] and which would be perpetuated in France in the corpus of writing of such (very different) later exponents as Chateaubriand, Verlaine, Claudel, or Mauriac. It is simply a matter, as Pascal will so elegantly illustrate, of perspective:

> When you want to argue fruitfully with another person and show that he is wrong, you have to see from what angle he is looking at the question, since it is usually true from that side, and accord to him that truth, but [also] point out to him the side from which it is false.[11]

[9] I shall refer to the two currently most respected versions of the *Pensées*: that of Louis Lafuma, in Pascal, *Œuvres complètes*, Paris, Éditions du Seuil (L'Intégrale), 1963, 493–641 and Philippe Sellier and Gérard Ferreyrolles, in Pascal, *Les Provinciales, Pensées et opuscules divers*, Paris, Livre de Poche / Classiques Garnier (Pochothèque), 2004, 755–1373. I shall use the conventional abbreviations of L and S to refer to them. Further bibliographical information on Pascal is given in Chapter 1, n. 3 and Chapter 6, n. 45.

[10] The *De Imitatio Christi* was frequently translated in the period, by Pierre Corneille among others.

[11] "Quand on veut reprendre avec utilité et montrer à un autre qu'il se trompe, il faut observer par quel côté il envisage la chose, car elle est vraie ordinairement de ce côté-là, et lui avouer cette vérité, mais lui découvrir le côté par où elle est fausse" (*Pensées* L 701, S 579).

What changed the Catholic landscape in the French seventeenth century was above all the impact of the Council of Trent (1545–63), and the working-out of the Catholic Reformation within the traditions of the French Church. The specifics of that renewal, in terms of its promotion of Christocentrism, its intensification of personal devotion, its emphasis on the Eucharist, its return to the teaching of the Fathers and its re-evaluation of the dignity and responsibility of the priesthood will all emerge more fully, and find their exemplification, in the course of my argument.[12] But if post-Tridentine Catholic Christianity was engaged in defining its beliefs and practices within the Roman tradition (in actual or implied contradistinction to Protestantism), there is also evidence in the period of a whole spectrum of divergent opinions, ranging from Cartesian rationalism, through philosophical scepticism, to secular indifference, against which an assertion or a re-assertion of fundamentals had equally to be undertaken. One way of doing so, hypothetically at least, might have been predicated on a sort of atavistic reassurance: Christianity is true because it is familiar, obvious, or rational. Yet what the whole gamut of writers to whom I shall attend propose, both implicitly and explicitly, is how, on any number of fronts, Christianity is unfamiliar, strange, and counter-intuitive. What is achieved thereby is a double-edged revalorization of all that is disconcerting and unexpected in what had unquestionably, and frequently unquestioningly, been the dominant belief system of Western Europe for over a millennium.[13]

[12] Alongside the expanded reprint of Henri Bremond's monumental *Histoire littéraire du sentiment religieux en France* (new expanded edn, Grenoble, Jérôme Millon, 2006), Jean Calvet's very readable single-volume *La Littérature religieuse de François de Sales à Fénelon* (Paris, del Duca, 1956), and Henri Busson, *La Religion des classiques* (Paris, Presses universitaires de France, 1948), two more recent studies may be recommended: René Taveneaux, *Le Catholicisme dans la France classique 1610–1715* (Paris, SEDES, 1980) is primarily historical; and Henry Phillips, *Church and Culture in Seventeenth-Century France* (Cambridge, Cambridge University Press, 1997), whose emphases are accurately reflected in the title. An excellent brief survey is provided by Jacques Le Brun in the collaborative *Histoire spirituelle de la France* (Paris, Beauchesne, 1964), p. 227–85; and a penetrating analysis of the French Church between 1590 and 1630 is afforded in the second chapter ('L'univers de Bérulle') of Yves Krumenacker, *L'École française de spiritualité*, Paris, Éditions du Cerf, 1998. A briefer account is given by Louis Cognet, *Les Origines de la spiritualité française au XVIIe siècle*, Paris, La Colombe, 1949. More recently, Michael Moriarty's two-volume work on early-modern French thought provides a wide-ranging analysis (*The Age of Suspicion*, Oxford, Oxford University Press, 2003; and *Fallen Nature, Fallen Selves*, Oxford, Oxford University Press, 2006). A third volume is in preparation. It is worth noting at this stage with pleasure that the amount of primary material available in clear modern editions is expanding rapidly, thanks in no small measure to the output of such publishing houses as Champion and Jérôme Millon in particular.

[13] Bossuet writes of France, in the *Funeral Oration of Henriette-Marie de France*, as "the only nation in the universe which, for the nigh on twelve centuries during which its kings have embraced Christianity, has only ever seen on its throne princes who are the children of the Church" ["[la] seule nation de l'univers qui, depuis douze siècles presque accomplis que ses rois ont embrassé le christianisme, n'a jamais vu sur le trône que des princes enfants de l'Église"] (*Oraison funèbre de Henriette-Marie de France* in *Œuvres*, ed. Abbé Velat and Yvonne Champailler, Paris, Gallimard (Pléiade), 1961, 57–81, p. 60).

One internal development which that renewal perhaps inevitably, and certainly undeliberately, achieved was to bring certain emphases to the surface which, when followed through to their logical or illogical conclusions, pushed within the Roman Church at the limits of Catholic orthodoxy, and indeed of Christian dogma *tout court*. The Catholic Reformation in France introduced teachings that, in their integrated form, initiated an unparalleled reinvigoration of the devotional, spiritual, penitential, and eschatological potential of Catholic doctrine. Yet in its separate emphases, on individual spirituality, on penitential and Eucharistic discipline and on theological enquiry, it also proved capable of promoting developments that were less easily assimilated and which, it was claimed by the voices of authority, would drive their adherents progressively further away from sound doctrine. I shall, in the areas of sustained polemic which occurred as a result, take professed allegiance to Rome and to papal authority by the perceived offending party (or parties) as the minimal, if unsatisfactory, criterion for consideration.

My subtitle comes from Pascal, and he will often feature in what follows. The experience of reading, or trying to read, the bewildering text that is the *Pensées* often, by virtue of its formal heterogeneity, throws at its readership a surprising phrase, juxtaposition, or aphorism which had not struck home before with the same force. On occasion, the isolation, proximity, or sententiousness is clearly just the result of the work's disorder and incompleteness, and can be modified, amplified, or indeed contradicted by cross-reference to other parts of the project. But nothing that follows immediately on from my title assertion invalidates its primary impact; nor does anything that we read elsewhere in the *Pensées*; and nor, I suggest, does a great deal of what we read in other writers of the period. Pascal himself develops his assertion, to the effect that Christianity confronts humankind with a vertiginous paradox, which will in turn be the subject of my first chapter. "Christianity is strange," he writes: "it orders man to recognize that he is vile and even abominable, and orders him to want to be like God. Without such a counter-balance this self-promotion would render him horribly vain, or this self-abasement would render him horribly abject."[14]

The word "strange" ["étrange"] is defined in the 1694 *Dictionnaire de l'Académie Française* by three possible meanings. These, broadly speaking, are spatial: "distant, far away, from outside" ["éloigné, lointain, de dehors"]; medical: "all that afflicts the body of the animal against its nature" ["tout ce qui survient au corps de l'animal contre sa nature"]; and, more consistently with our understanding of the term in Pascal, behavioural: "that which is contrary to common order or usage" ["qui n'est pas dans l'ordre et dans l'usage

[14] "Le christianisme est étrange : il ordonne à l'homme de reconnaître qu'il est vil et même abominable, et lui ordonne de vouloir être semblable à Dieu. Sans un tel contrepoids cette élévation le rendrait horriblement vain, ou cet abaissement le rendrait horriblement abject" (*Pensées*, L 351, S 383).

commun"].[15] The last of these definitions most obviously corresponds to the paradoxical formulations which figure in the remainder of the fragment, as to much that I shall subsequently propose. Indeed, it would have been possible, if I had limited myself to this last definition, to write a whole book on, for example, the extraordinary corpus of spiritual autobiographies that I shall principally consider in the course of two of the chapters which follow (4 and 5). But it is tempting to retain at least a memory of the other meanings, so that alongside "against the common order" (dangerous, deluded, subversive) and "against the common usage" (paradoxical, inexpressible, polemical), we might as well continue to encounter "foreign" (Jewish, Roman) and "external" (physiological, perceptible in the physical domain).

The second term to need a brief gloss is "particularity", by which I simply mean to indicate "that which is distinctive and other". It might have been tempting to risk an even more ambitious Gallicism such as "specificity" or even "alterity", at least the former of which is probably closer to my meaning, and which I shall sometimes prefer. I am simply trying, by means of whichever term is the most accessible, to bring into focus some of what defines Catholic Christianity in the writers I shall consider, both in terms of what it is and, just as crucially, of what it is not.

One way of starting to talk about what Christianity is and is not (and one which would have been common both to the Catholic laity of the French seventeenth century and to a modern Catholic readership) is afforded by the sequence of prayers offered on Good Friday (the "General Intercessions"), which stretch out from the intra-ecclesial to the non-believer, and which invite the faithful thereby to situate Catholic Christianity's distinctiveness within its broadest framework of reference. Thus they pray for the Church, for its earthly leader, the Pope, and for its bishops, priests, religious, and laity; they then pray for those about to be received into the Church by the sacrament of Baptism, and for fellow Christians who are not in communion with the Holy See; for the Jewish people, for those who do not believe in Christ, and for those who do not believe in God. The prayers then conclude with intercessions for those in need.[16] What the Roman Church also does as a result, on one of the three holiest days in its calendar, is progressively to establish its otherness from different traditions, from different beliefs, and from none.

If we begin by taking up the idea of what Catholic Christianity is not, it is first of all not Protestantism.[17] Despite the promulgation of the Edict of Nantes in 1598,

[15] The adjective "commun", although singular, can be taken in the usage of the period to qualify both nouns.

[16] It goes without saying that the exact formulations have changed since the Second Vatican Council, and that terms such as "pagans", "heretics", and "perfidious Jews" have been replaced by more accepting descriptions.

[17] I shall not devote any time to exploring the degree to which the mainstream French Church in turn marked its independence from the Roman centre by virtue of what has become known as

the attempt to sway members of the "Religion Prétendue Réformée" (RPR) back into communion with Rome was enduring, even before the persecutions and eventual Revocation of the Edict by Louis XIV in 1685,[18] provoking as it did a significant level of emigration.[19] Of the range of writing undertaken to this end, it is Bossuet's *Exposition of Catholic doctrine* [*Exposition de la doctrine catholique* (1671)] which most corresponds to the emphases of this study,[20] and to which I shall devote some further attention in a variety of contexts. The work is offered as a patient and irenic presentation of Catholic teaching on certain of the most controversial points of divergence. It contrasts thereby in its tone with Bossuet's later *History of the Variations of the Protestant Churches* [*Histoire des variations des Églises Protestantes* (1688)],[21] which proposes that the reformed tradition is structurally bound to promote both dogmatic and ecclesial fragmentation, in the absence of a single source of authority.

Moving to other religions, we find that the differentiation from Judaism and Islam occurs on a predictably unequal scale. There is, as I shall consider in the second chapter, a strong awareness in Pascal's apologetics of the fundamental continuity which unites Judaism to Christianity, and indeed an emphasis on the degree to which the historical credibility of the Christian faith is predicated on that of the Jewish tradition. A single fragment in the *Pensées* can be taken, as a preliminary guide, to give an accurate summary of the kind of argument that is typically put forward:

> It is an astonishing thing, and worthy of a particular kind of attention to see this Jewish people survive after so many years, and to see it always wretched, since it is

Gallicanism. More extreme forms of perceived dissent will be examined in Chapters 6 and 7, on Jansenism and Quietism respectively; but, at least in its doctrinal features, the Gallican church can be taken to be orthodox. It was principally in administrative terms that it sought to assert its autonomy, with respect to matters of regal versus papal authority in France, and in particular to the responsibility for episcopal appointments.

[18] See in particular the recent book by Didier Boisson, *Consciences en liberté? Itinéraires d'ecclésiastiques convertis au protestantisme (1631–1760)*, Paris, Champion, 2009.

[19] See Elisabeth Labrousse, *Conscience et conviction : études sur le XVIIe siècle*, Paris, Universitas and Oxford, Voltaire Foundation, 1996. Krumenacker remarks on the implications of religious pluralism for the French monarchy: "For [the *Assemblée du Clergé*], the edict of Nantes is injurious to the religious obligation of Catholics, and cannot in any respect be seen as the acceptance of true religious pluralism" ["Pour [l'Assemblée du Clergé], l'édit de Nantes est dérogatoire à l'obligation religieuse catholique, et ne peut en aucun cas apparaître comme l'acceptation d'un réel pluralisme religieux"] (*École française*, p. 98).

[20] *Exposition de la doctrine de l'église catholique* in *Œuvres complètes*, ed. F. Lachat, Paris, Louis Vivès, 1875, vol. XIII, 51–105. This text in many respects constitutes a reply to the writings of Jean Daillé (1594–1670), who was a Protestant theologian and polemicist, and pastor of the major *temple* [Protestant church] at Charenton, outside Paris, from 1626 until his death. He rejected the authority of the Fathers, and insisted on the sole validity of Scripture. His *Apology for the Reformed Churches* [*Apologie des Églises réformées*] dates from 1633, and *The Faith Founded on Holy Scripture* [*La Foi fondée sur les Saintes Écritures*] from the following year.

[21] *Histoire des variations des Églises protestantes* in *Œuvres complètes*, ed. F. Lachat, Paris, Louis Vivès, 1875, vol. XIV.

> necessary for the proof of Jesus Christ both for it to survive in order to prove him, and that it should be wretched because they crucified him.[22]

Islam receives a yet more limited and hostile treatment in the same text, predominantly in the *liasse*[23] entitled "Falsity of other religions",[24] of which one fragment simply consists of juxtapositions of the attributes of Muhammad and Christ, invariably to the detriment of the former.[25] Here, once again, the case can be summarized in Pascal's typically paradoxical (and typically counter-intuitive) claim that: "It is not by what is obscure in Muhammad and which can be proposed to carry a mysterious meaning that I want him to be judged, but by what is clear: by his paradise and all the rest of it."[26] And it is on those grounds, for reasons that will soon become clear, that he takes issue with Islam.

A far more intangible set of contrary opinions was to be found in the period in the growth of "free-thought"; and it is instructive in this respect to look at the two voices of scepticism (in a non-technical sense of that word) as they are sketched into the background of the *Pensées*: "There are [only] three sorts of people: those who serve God, because they have found him, others who make it their business to seek God because they have not found him, [and] others who live without seeking him and who have not found him."[27] It is therefore, we might extrapolate from this text, a period in which two types of secular departure from Christianity, deism and atheism, were apparent, and in which as a result two (or more) types of conversion or re-conversion were in play;[28] and it is largely in this perspective, first of all, that I will consider apologetics in the opening chapter. There is, in other words, a need for Christianity to be

[22] "C'est une chose étonnante et digne d'une étrange attention de voir ce peuple juif subsister depuis tant d'années et de le voir toujours misérable, étant nécessaire pour la preuve de Jésus-Christ et qu'il subsiste pour le prouver, et qu'il soit misérable puisqu'ils l'ont crucifié" (*Pensées* L 311, S 342). The fragment occurs in the *liasse* "Proofs of Jesus Christ" ["Preuves de Jésus-Christ"]. See also following note.

[23] This term *liasse* (literally "bundle") is given to each of the series of fragments in the *Pensées* grouped under a particular heading by Pascal.

[24] "Fausseté des autres religions" (*Pensées*, L XVI, S XVII).

[25] "Difference between Jesus Christ and Muhammad" ["Différence entre Jésus-Christ et Mahomet"] (*Pensées*, L 209, S 241).

[26] "Ce n'est pas par ce qu'il y a d'obscur dans Mahomet et qu'on peut faire passer pour un sens mystérieux que je veux qu'on en juge, mais par ce qu'il y a de clair : par son paradis, et par le reste" (*Pensées*, L 218, S 251). There is also passing evidence of an awareness of the claims of less familiar religions, such as in the fragment "History of China" ["Histoire de la Chine"] (*Pensées*, L 822, S 663), although the fuller development of such discoveries will more typically be introduced by Enlightenment writers, and deployed in opposition to the claims of Christianity.

[27] "Il n'y [a que] trois sortes de personnes: les uns qui servent Dieu l'ayant trouvé, les autres qui s'emploient à le chercher ne l'ayant pas trouvé, les autres qui vivent sans le chercher ni l'avoir trouvé" (*Pensées*, L 160, S 192).

[28] This is an inexact summary in one sense, as will become apparent from several fragments. Deists, for Pascal, are in error because they are essentially looking for God in the wrong place; those who genuinely seek truth in Scripture are accorded a far higher degree of tolerance by the apologist.

asserted and re-asserted, and this need once again takes the form of a clarification of what exactly it is and is not.[29] Deism and atheism are both terms that recur in the *Pensées*; but what is perhaps surprising is the degree of opprobrium which is reserved for the former. Writing against those who erroneously believe that the Christian religion "consists simply of the worship of a God who is considered to be great and powerful and eternal", the apologist concludes that such a belief is "strictly speaking deism, almost as far removed from the Christian religion as atheism, which is entirely contrary to it".[30]

A final group which needs to learn about the faith is, of course, the faithful. The essay by Pascal devoted to a *Comparison of Christians from Early Times with Those of Today*[31] gives to understand that he lives in a period in which Christian belief has grown tired through familiarity, and for which a reassertion of its *un*familiarity was of primary importance. Bringing this negative indifference together with the positive aims and ideals of the Catholic Reformation serves as some sort of vindication of the whole range of intra-Christian didactic texts with which I shall deal, from catechisms and homilies, at the most basic level, to manuals of spiritual devotion or Saints' lives on the higher plane.

In order to gauge the extent of such a requirement in the period, we might cite the third of Fénelon's posthumous *Dialogues on eloquence*,[32] in which one of his fictive interlocutors puts forward a statement and a question. The statement, by disputant A, is as follows:

> [Preachers] speak every day to the people about Scripture, the Church, the two Laws, sacrifices, Moses, Aaron, Melchizedech, the prophets, the apostles, yet they do not put themselves out to teach them what all these things signify, and what all these people did.

There follows a brief dialogue, initiated by B, with an intervention by the more objective figure C, and a telling summary:

> B. Do you think they don't understand the things you are speaking about?
> A. Personally, I have no doubt that that is the case. Few people understand them well enough to benefit from sermons.
> B. Yes, the common people are ignorant of them.

[29] See David Wetsel, *Pascal and Disbelief : Catechesis and Conversion in the 'Pensées'*, Washington, DC, Catholic University of America Press, 1994.

[30] "Ils s'imaginent que [la religion chrétienne] consiste simplement en l'adoration d'un Dieu considéré comme grand et puissant et éternel : ce qui est proprement le déisme, presque aussi éloigné de la religion chrétienne que l'athéisme, qui y est tout à fait contraire" (*Pensées*, L 449, S 690). The differentiation of Christianity from "pagan" philosophies will also be discussed in the first chapter.

[31] *Comparaison des chrétiens des premiers temps avec ceux d'aujourd'hui* in L, 360–2.

[32] The *Dialogues sur l'éloquence* were composed between 1681 and 1686, although not published until 1718. They involve two principal disputants ('A' and 'B'), and a catalyst figure ('C').

C. In that case, is it not precisely those people who need instruction?

A. Add to that the fact that the majority of *honnêtes gens* are people as well in this respect. There are always three-quarters of the congregation who are ignorant of these first principles of religion, of which the preacher supposes them to be aware.[33]

Whatever the status of the disputants, it seems that exactly what Christianity *is* was no more straightforwardly mastered by the faithful in a period, and in a country, which we are invited to consider with hindsight to represent one of the great epochs of Western Christendom, than in other times and places. We might as a result also disingenuously wonder, along with the most famous Christian mystic of her age, Madame Guyon (1648–1717), why indeed all these technical terms and strange historical figures are intrinsic to a belief system which claims more simply to lead each and every follower into a direct and personal relationship with God.[34] I shall return to that conundrum in due course.

This is not then a book about history, philosophy, or even academic theology. It is first and foremost a book about seventeenth-century French writing on Catholic Christianity (and my avoidance of the term "literature" is simply a way of circumventing the need to confront questions about what is, and is not, "literary"). I should therefore move on to explain my choice of

33

A. [Les prédicateurs parlent] tous les jours au peuple, de l'Écriture, de l'Église, des deux Lois, des sacrifices, de Moïse, d'Aaron, de Melchisédech, des prophètes, des apôtres, et on ne se met point en peine de leur apprendre ce que signifient toutes ces choses, et ce qu'ont fait ces personnes-là [. . .].

B. Croyez-vous qu'on ignore les choses dont vous parlez ?

A. Pour moi je n'en doute pas. Peu de gens les entendent assez pour profiter des sermons.

B. Oui, le peuple grossier les ignore.

C. Eh bien! le peuple, n'est-ce pas lui qu'il faut instruire?

A. Ajoutez que la plupart des honnêtes gens sont peuple à cet égard-là. Il y a toujours les trois quarts de l'auditoire qui ignorent ces premiers fondements de la religion, que le prédicateur suppose qu'on sait.

(*Dialogues sur l'éloquence en général, et sur celle de la chaire en particulier* in Œuvres, vol. I, 1–87, p. 58–9). The term *honnêtes gens* can best be understood contrastively in the context as all those who were *not* the common people, that is to say the nobility and emergent bourgeoisie. I am taking the disputants compositely to reflect an accurate, if stereotypical, summary of the issues raised by Catholic preaching in the period with regard to the religious education of the faithful.

34 At the same time, the need to educate the faithful is widely recognized and respected, and it is stressed in the *Canons and Decrees of the Council of Trent (1545–1563)* that "the bishop shall see to it that on Sundays and other festival days, the children in every parish be carefully taught the rudiments of the faith" (*Canons and Decrees of the Council of Trent (1545–1563)*, trans. and ed. H Schroeder, St Louis, B. Herder, 1941, p. 196). Among more recent commentators, Krumenacker notes that "one of the essential objectives of the [Counter-] Reformation is to educate the Christian people" ["[l'un] des objectifs essentiels de la [Contre-] Réforme est d'enseigner le peuple chrétien"] (*École française*, p. 83). Lawrence Brockliss provides a full account of the academic teaching of both Catholic and Protestant theology in *French Higher Education in the 17th and 18th Centuries: A Cultural History*, Oxford, Clarendon Press, 1987, III, 5, pp. 228–76.

texts. The scope of my remarks was to some extent dictated by the thematic and presentational constraints of the Bampton Lectures, but also by an attempt at focus rather than comprehensiveness. Some figures need little justification for inclusion: Pascal, Bossuet, Fénelon, St François de Sales and probably Madame Guyon fall into that league. These are all figures whose influence in a whole range of areas was immense, and each of them could individually have been the subject of eight lectures. I am also strongly aware of whole categories of published works which are absent from my remarks: the memoirs written by members of the communities of Port-Royal, for example; correspondence (real and fictive); works of historical and exegetical scholarship; a wide range of poetic output, in just as many formats, including in particular translations of the divine offices or of the *Imitation of Christ*; or the sub-genre of the biblical epic. The single most important absentee is probably Malebranche, and my omission in this case arises principally from the fact that he is taking Christian writing the furthest into an intellectual domain (philosophy) on which I am unqualified to write; and because he offers, to me at least, less scope for investigation purely as a writer.[35] The same is true, for different reasons, of the Cardinal de Bérulle.[36] Even the writers I consider have, in many cases, been very selectively represented. Thus in the domains of lyric poetry, autobiography, martyr tragedy, and polemic, I have tried to reflect some of the sheer quantity of material available in the period, and indeed to point to directions for further enquiry; but the corpus of writing which these brief indications conceal is in all cases very substantial.

St François de Sales writes at the beginning of the *Introduction to the Devout Life*:

> The Holy Spirit disposes and arranges with so much variety the teachings of devotion that he administers by the tongues and pens of his servants, that although the doctrine is always one and the same, nonetheless the discourses which emanate from it are very different according to the different ways in which they are composed.[37]

It is these "different ways" which will be acknowledged and explored as I introduce different forms of writing over the chapters, and indeed two of those chapters, 3 and 4, will deal explicitly with questions of belief and language. Sometimes a purely stylistic excursus would have been tempting, but I have limited myself for the most part to a consideration of how the form and

[35] Sustained attention is given to Malebranche by Moriarty, *Fallen Nature, Fallen Selves.*

[36] See, on Bérulle, Krumenacker, *L'École française.*

[37] "Le Saint-Esprit dispose et arrange avec tant de variété les enseignements de dévotion, qu'il donne par les langues et les plumes de ses serviteurs, que la doctrine étant toujours une même, les discours néanmoins qui s'en font sont bien différents selon les diverses façons desquelles ils sont composés" (*Introduction à la vie dévote*, in St François de Sales, *Œuvres*, ed. André Ravier and Roger Devos, Paris, Gallimard (Pléiade), 1969, 1–317, p. 23).

substance interact, while indicating to readers whose approach is more guided by questions of genre, rhetoric or poetics as to where to read further. It remains, as François asserts, that the form of writing is closely tied in to the exposition of the Christian dogma which it conveys and that, as a result, the impact of that correlation will frequently constitute a further matter for reflection.

It could also be argued that I have distorted the picture by dividing my material thematically rather than chronologically, and indeed in many cases I have juxtaposed writing from different decades of the century (although obviously in the case of an evolving polemic, for example, I have respected the progress of the argument); and there is little doubt that the picture would have looked different if I had painted it diachronically. Finally I have, as my title indicates, attended exclusively to writers in the Catholic tradition. There would be another, very different book to attempt about the printed word in the Reformed tradition in the period, whose own particularity (or particularities) would be fertile ground indeed. But that is for someone else to write.

1

Particularity and Apologetics

It is both obvious and unhelpful to begin this enquiry with Blaise Pascal (1623–62), a man who, in the words of one his greatest non-admirers, Voltaire (1694–1788), was a sublime misanthrope,[1] yet a man, in the same writer's argument, who alone was "left standing upright amidst the ruins of his century",[2] even if a man whose written legacy was itself also largely in ruins. His great apology for the Christian religion was left at his death in a state of incompleteness and fragmentation, and it was only in the twentieth century that any kind of reliable working editions were pieced together.[3] It is unhelpful as well, as I hope to show in later chapters, to start from here, because Pascal stands some way apart from the centre of the Catholic spectrum of his times;

[1] Voltaire, *Lettres philosophiques*, ed. Frédéric Deloffre, Paris, Gallimard (Folio classique), 1986, p. 156: "[Pascal] imputes to the essence of our nature something that only belongs to certain men; he eloquently insults all humankind. I shall dare to take the side of humanity against this sublime misanthrope" ["[Pascal] impute à l'essence de notre nature ce qui n'appartient qu'à certains hommes ; il dit éloquemment des injures au genre humain. J'ose prendre le parti de l'humanité contre ce misanthrope sublime"].

[2] "Il est encore debout sur les ruines de son siècle" (Voltaire/Condorcet, *Éloge et Pensées de Pascal*, ed. Richard Parish, *Œuvres complètes de Voltaire* (*OCV*), vol. 80A, Oxford, Voltaire Foundation, 2008, p. 69). This curious amalgamation of textual strands is constituted by Voltaire's 1778 additions to the Marquis de Condorcet's 1776 eulogy and annotated edition of Pascal's *Pensées*. It reflects many of the attitudes expressed in the earlier *Lettres philosophiques* (1734).

[3] The two editions currently in most widespread use (and considered to be as nearly authentic as the state of the texts allows) are those of Louis Lafuma, in Pascal, *Œuvres complètes*, Paris, Éditions du Seuil (L'Intégrale), 1963, 493–641 and Philippe Sellier and Gérard Ferreyrolles, in Pascal, *Les Provinciales, Pensées et opuscules divers*, Paris, Livre de Poche / Classiques Garnier (Pochothèque), 2004, 755–1373. These are based respectively on the first and second copies of the manuscript. I shall give references to both versions, conventionally identified as L and S, followed by the fragment number. Where there are editorial divergences, I shall give the version of Sellier. The projected *Œuvres complètes* edited by Jean Mesnard (Desclée de Brouwer) remains incomplete. There is a well respected translation of Lafuma by A. J. Krailsheimer, London, Penguin Classics, 1966; a translation of Sellier is currently being prepared by the Catholic University Press of America. For a general study of the *Pensées*, see Jean Mesnard, *Les 'Pensées' de Pascal*, Paris, SEDES, 1976. A brief but helpful English introduction is provided by Alban Krailsheimer in the Past Masters series (Oxford, Oxford University Press, 1980). A range of insightful essays is afforded in the *Cambridge Companion to Pascal*, ed. Nicholas Hammond, Cambridge, Cambridge University Press, 2003. For further studies, see the Bibliography.

his adherence to the tenets of Port-Royal, to Jansenism in other words, places him in a tradition that was itself scarcely to survive the century, condemned as it was soon to be by the Bull *Unigenitus* promulgated in 1713 by Clement XI.[4]

And yet in other respects Pascal is the ideal starting point, because of his unique capacity to stand outside his faith in order better to understand it and, as a believer convinced that true conviction lies beyond reason, to give a rational account of that belief. He is writing to bring people to the same intensity of personal faith which he had himself been given in a moment of enlightenment,[5] by forcing them to address the first principles; and it is that tension between epiphany and rationality that will allow us to begin the process of constructive defamiliarization, the recognition of the strangeness of Catholic Christianity as it is manifested in the French seventeenth century, that will largely be my business in the chapters which follow.

Let me continue with another obvious if surprising remark: Pascal never wrote anything called the *Pensées*. The manuscripts we have are constituted by a certain number of fragments that were destined to be transformed into the chapters of an apologia, but by far the majority are not classified in any particular order, and indeed a good many are unlikely to have been intended for incorporation at any subsequent stage in a putative completed work.[6] We have then both less and more than the intended defence of the Christian religion, and the idea that all we lack is some key to the ordering of the surviving material is as misguided as it is attractive. The *Pensées* are, in Pol Ernst's phrase, "an apology in the making" ["une apologie en devenir"][7] whose *telos* – that is, presumably, the conversion of the hypothetical unbeliever[8] – lies beyond the scope of the surviving fragments. But it would no doubt have also lain beyond the remit of the completed project, in what Sara Melzer has elegantly called the "atextuality of the heart".[9] Yet it is also this incomplete

[4] There are, of course, eighteenth-century continuations of the tendency, but these take on a progressively more political nature, as manifested in the notorious episode of the "Convulsionnaires de Saint-Médard". On this topic see Catherine Maire, *De la cause de Dieu à la cause de la nation : le jansénisme au XVIIIe siècle*, Paris, Gallimard, 1998. The date of 1715 can however be taken as a practical *terminus ad quem* of the specifically religious dimensions to the movement which so profoundly marked the later seventeenth century. See also Chapter 6, and Bibliography.

[5] The so-called second conversion of 1654, recorded in the *Mémorial* (*Pensées*, L 913, S 742).

[6] On the earliest editions of the text, see Marie Pérouse, *L'Invention des 'Pensées' de Pascal: les éditions de Port-Royal (1670–1678)*, Paris, Champion, 2009.

[7] Pol Ernst, *Les 'Pensées' de Pascal: géologie et stratigraphie*, Paris, Universitas and Oxford, Voltaire Foundation, 1996, p. 145 ff.

[8] This should probably be plural, since there are clearly different audiences proposed. I will nonetheless take it as a given that the project as we have it was conceived in order to persuade the sceptic or atheist of the tenets of Christian dogma, rather than simply to confirm the believer in his or her faith. The existence of the brief work (or *Opuscule*) entitled *De l'art de persuader* [*On the art of persuasion*] (L pp. 355–9, S pp. 131–45) affords further evidence to that end.

[9] Sara Melzer, *Discourses of the Fall*, Berkeley, Los Angeles, London, University of California Press, 1986, p. 108.

state that allows the reader to make his or her own sense of the multiple trajectories the *Pensées* contain, and to construct from the disparate elements of the whole their own arguments for – or indeed against – Christian belief.

So Pascal's *Pensées* are not some kind of conversion kit; and indeed, no straightforward progression towards belief would be possible to chart on the strength of the material we have. Or rather several would; for the apologist seems at different moments to be proposing different (and sometimes indeed incompatible) sequences of discovery according to the temperament of his fictive interlocutor. These are nonetheless all predicated on a tripartite division of human epistemology into body, mind, and heart, even though here again the terms are far from stable, or indeed watertight, across the fragments. The constituent elements of belief are constant; but their mode of interaction is flexible. As the apologist writes, citing the authority of Christ, Paul, and Augustine, "the order of charity [. . .] consists mainly in digressions on each point that relates to the end, so that it is always kept in sight".[10] The end is never in question therefore, but the modes of its attainment will be diverse and indirect. Most famously, or infamously, the apologist asks the interlocutor of the wager argument to adopt the externals of belief in order to begin his journey to faith: "Learn from those who have been bound like you and who now wager all that they have [. . .]. Follow the way by which they began: it was by behaving just as if they believed, by taking holy water, having masses said, etc.";[11] and yet elsewhere it seems as though the believer must be rationally convinced before turning to the conventions of practice: "There are three ways of believing: reason, custom, and inspiration. [. . .]. You must open up your mind to proofs, endorse your beliefs by custom, but offer yourself by humiliations to movements of inspiration, which alone can work the true and salvific effect."[12] But this is already to move to an assumed state of readiness for belief, and begs the question as to how the apologist delivers his reader at this point of departure in the first place. Certainly a hypothetically fideistic statement by the believer of a supernaturally accorded faith which defies reason will not convince the unbeliever, who can argue exactly the same thing for his unbelief.

[10] "Jésus-Christ, saint Paul ont l'ordre de la charité [. . .]. Saint Augustin de même. Cet ordre consiste principalement à la digression sur chaque point qui a rapport à la fin, pour la montrer toujours" (*Pensées*, L 298, S 329).

[11] "Apprenez de ceux qui ont été liés comme vous et qui parient maintenant tout leur bien [. . .]. Suivez la manière par où ils ont commencé : c'est en faisant tout comme s'ils croyaient, en prenant de l'eau bénite, faisant dire des messes, etc." I will return to this much-debated fragment (*Pensées*, L 418, S 680), more accurately described by Pascal's own heading of "Infinity Nothingness" ["Infini Rien"], in Chapter 3.

[12] "Il y a trois moyens de croire : la raison, la coutume, l'inspiration [. . .]. Il faut ouvrir son esprit aux preuves, s'y confirmer par la coutume, mais s'offrir par les humiliations aux inspirations, qui seules peuvent faire le vrai et salutaire effet" (*Pensées*, L 808, S 655).

Put another way, "I know in my heart that I am right" can legitimately be countered by "I know in my heart that you are wrong".[13]

The first part of Pascal's project is simply called: "The wretchedness of man without God".[14] He begins, therefore, by writing in terms that exclude God absolutely, albeit provisionally, from his picture. In the bleak portrayal of the human condition which ensues, summarized as "inconstancy, world-weariness, anxiety",[15] he is initially at pains to give no signals of any eventual release from the relentless pessimism that informs it, dominated as it is by metaphors of futility, sickness, and death. On the other hand, he draws the reader's attention by two of his most celebrated paradoxical images to man's greatness. First, by the image of the thinking reed ["le roseau pensant"], to the dignity of thought: man might be the weakest created thing, yet if he is destroyed by an insentient force of nature, the consciousness of his own annihilation accords to him superiority over his destroyer. He knows that he is being destroyed; the insentient force does not know that it is destroying him.[16] And secondly, by the image of the king deprived of his throne ["le roi dépossédé"], to convey the attendant paradox that humankind would only recognize itself as falling short of an ideal if it had a prevenient concept of that same ideal.[17] Putting

[13] This is cryptically endorsed in fragments such as *Pensées*, L 382, S 414: "I fully admit that one of these Christians who believe without proof will not perhaps have the wherewithal to convince an unbeliever, who can say the same for himself" ["J'avoue bien qu'un de ces chrétiens qui croient sans preuve n'aura peut-être pas de quoi convaincre un infidèle, qui en dira autant de soi"].

[14] The bipartite division is announced in the introductory fragment of the *Pensées*, L 6, S 40: "First part: Wretchedness of man without God. // Second part: Happiness of man with God". ["Première partie: Misère de l'homme sans Dieu. // Deuxième partie: Félicité de l'homme avec Dieu"]. The fragment continues by indicating that arguments for the corruption of human nature will be afforded by evidence drawn from human nature itself; and that arguments for a Redeemer will be provided from Scripture. Pascal principally, but not exclusively, uses the word "félicité" for a higher, transcendent form of happiness than that indicated by the more frequent and predominantly immanent term of "bonheur".

[15] "Inconstance, ennui, inquiétude" (*Pensées*, L 24, S 58).

[16] *Pensées*, L 200, S 231: "Man is only a reed, the weakest thing in nature, but he is a thinking reed. It is not necessary for the whole universe to go to war to crush him, a vapour, a drop of water is enough to kill him. But if the universe killed him, man would be nobler yet than what kills him, because he knows that he is dying and the advantage that the universe has over him. The universe knows nothing about it" ["L'homme n'est qu'un roseau, le plus faible de la nature, mais c'est un roseau pensant. Il ne faut pas que l'univers entier s'arme pour l'écraser, une vapeur, une goutte d'eau suffit pour le tuer. Mais quand l'univers l'écraserait, l'homme serait encore plus noble que ce qui le tue, puisqu'il sait qu'il meurt et l'avantage que l'univers a sur lui. L'univers n'en sait rien"]. The convention in translations has been to use "thinking" to convey "pensant", although "conscious" is closer to the semantic resonance of the cognate noun "pensée" in Pascal's usage.

[17] *Pensées*, L 117, S 149: "The greatness of man is so visible that it emerges even from his wretchedness [...]. For who considers himself unfortunate not to be a king, other than a dethroned king?" ["La grandeur de l'homme est si visible qu'elle se tire même de sa misère. [...]. Car qui se trouve malheureux de n'être pas roi, sinon un roi dépossédé ?"]. The rhetorical device, whereby an unavoidable answer is offered as the solution to a rhetorical question (*percontatio*), is frequently used by Pascal.

these two together, the apologist[18] concludes, first, that man is wretched because he is wretched, and yet great because he knows that he is wretched; and secondly, that his greatness lies in the very consciousness of that loss. "After all", he writes, "if man had never been corrupted, he would, in his innocence, enjoy both truth and happiness with assurance. And if man had only ever been corrupted, he would have no idea either of truth or of fulfilment."[19]

Pascal's starting point thus lies in the establishment of what he calls the "incompatibilities" ("contrariétés")[20] emanating from the binary coexistence of greatness and wretchedness in human nature, and in the provisional exclusion (as it will ultimately transpire to be) of a transcendent explanation for the desperate condition that both entraps and frustrates it. Of course Pascal realizes that he is not the first to embark on such an enterprise, and the efforts of other apologists to bring readers to belief are also introduced; but far from building on any such precursors, Pascal approaches them entirely in an adversarial spirit of combat. Ontological and cosmological proofs of God's existence will serve him rather as a source of oppositional evidence, and indeed of parody, than of ratification. Thus abstract arguments which lead to the existence of a supreme being (what Pascal pejoratively calls metaphysical proofs ["preuves métaphysiques"]) are for him as watertight as they are worthless: "If a man were to be convinced that numerical proportions are immaterial, eternal truths", he writes, "dependent on a primary truth, as a result of which they have their existence, and which we call God, I would not consider him much further ahead on his path to salvation."[21] Similarly, the unbeliever who contemplates his place in the created world is as likely to feel a vertiginous bewilderment at his anthropocentrism as he is to infer from it the

[18] I shall use the term "apologist" to speak of the persuasive persona within the fragments, and "Pascal" to refer to the historical figure.

[19] "Car enfin, si l'homme n'avait jamais été corrompu, il jouirait dans son innocence et de la vérité et de la félicité avec assurance. Et si l'homme n'avait jamais été que corrompu, il n'aurait aucune idée ni de la vérité ni de la béatitude" (*Pensées*, L 131, S 164).

[20] The term constitutes the title of one of the classified *liasses* in the first part of the project (L VII, S VIII), as well as occurring in a variety of fragments, such as *Pensées*, L 404, S 23: "[The acknowledgement of] all these incompatibilities which seemed most of all to draw me away from the knowledge of any religion is what most rapidly led me to the true one" ["Toutes ces contrariétés qui semblaient le plus m'éloigner de la connaissance d'une religion est ce qui m'a le plus tôt conduit à la véritable"]. My translation conceals the grammatical irregularity of the original, which has a plural subject and a singular main verb. It also, in so doing, removes the freedom that Pascal's anacoluthon allows.

[21] "Quand un homme serait persuadé que les proportions des nombres sont des vérités immatérielles, éternelles et dépendantes d'une première vérité en qui elles subsistent et qu'on appelle Dieu, je ne le trouverais pas beaucoup avancé pour son salut" (*Pensées*, L 449, S 690). On this question see Vincent Carraud, *Pascal et la philosophie*, Paris, Presses universitaires de France, 1992.

existence of a loving creator.[22] Discoveries in the scientific domain in Pascal's own times, both of the unimaginably great and the infinitesimally small, had in their turn accorded an empirical corrective to that assurance.[23] The believer will of course know differently, but, crucially, the believer has not yet come into the picture.

Thus, as he moves towards the promotion of Christian beliefs, the apologist is adamant that the deism which he sees as the end point of such evidence is little better than atheism; it is in this context that he writes of "the worship of a God who is considered to be great and powerful and eternal, which is strictly speaking deism, almost as far removed from the Christian religion as atheism, which is entirely contrary to it".[24] If he aims therefore to show that Christianity is worthy of belief, he is also at pains to stress that it is legitimately rejected if its often surprising, unwelcome and indeed contradictory tenets are misrepresented, either by its adversaries, or, worse still, by its adherents. It is his purpose therefore to underline those aspects of Christian belief and practice that function in contradistinction to erroneous expectations. Christianity is strange, first of all, in that it is unexpected; but if it is not strange, in that perspective, it is not true.

One of the major difficulties in deciphering Pascal's project, given its incompleteness, lies in the uncertainty as to its eventual shape, although it is equally clear from several of the fragments that an overriding design was intended, even if no single linear trajectory can be traced.[25] If we need some guidelines to make sense of his project, however, two contemporary intertexts throw some light on the apology. The most immediately helpful is the record of a series of conversations (known as the *Entretien*) which Pascal held with the hardline Jansenist, Isaac Le Maistre de Sacy (1613–84), of which we retain a written record.[26] The dialogue follows a broadly dialectical sequence, in which Christianity is shown by Pascal, in opposition to the more intolerant position of his interlocutor, both to subsume and to transcend the ancient philosophies of

[22] This is above all developed in the long fragment "Disproportion of man" ["Disproportion de l'homme"] (*Pensées*, L 199, S 230).

[23] This is all the more pertinent in the light of Pascal's own scientific credentials. See Dominique Descotes, *L'Argumentation chez Pascal*, Paris, Presses universitaires de France (Écrivains), 1993.

[24] "L'adoration d'un Dieu considéré comme grand et puissant et éternel : ce qui est proprement le déisme, presque aussi éloigné de la religion chrétienne que l'athéisme, qui y est tout à fait contraire" (*Pensées*, L 449, S 690).

[25] The existence of the title "Order" ("Ordre"), given to the first *liasse* (*Pensées*, L I, S II) as to several individual fragments, is indicative of such a purpose. The fragment on *dispositio* (the second part of rhetoric) affords further evidence: "Let it not be said that I have said nothing new: the ordering of the material is new" ["Qu'on ne dise pas que je n'ai rien dit de nouveau: la disposition des matières est nouvelle"] (*Pensées*, L 696, S 575).

[26] Sacy was Pascal's spiritual director at the time of the meeting(s). It is plausibly argued that the document represents a compilation of evidence, rather than simply constituting the transcript of a single conversation.

stoicism and pyrrhonism; and three points might be drawn from this brief work, in order to throw light on the unfinished project of the *Pensées*.[27]

First, that Pascal is taking on board two (in his terms) pagan philosophies, both of which have nonetheless become assimilated into Christian thought; but that he is, for the purposes of his argumentational strategy, stripping them of that degree of accommodation. It is, in the first place, by the de-christianization of what are generally referred to as neo-stoicism and neo-scepticism that Pascal channels them into his re-valorization of Christianity.[28] The unique claims of Christianity are better served, it follows from this exchange, by an emphasis on its points of divergence from ancient philosophy, than by any syncretic developments.

Secondly, that Pascal accords to the Christian Gospel the capacity to assimilate the (perceived) immanent contradictions of the two secular philosophies into a transcendent synthesis. "They cannot survive alone", he argues, "because of their defects, nor can they be united because of their oppositions, and so they destroy and annihilate each other in order to make room for the truth of the Gospel. It is [the Gospel]", he goes on, "which resolves these incompatibilities by an art that is altogether divine."[29] Put another way, the stoics and the pyrrhonists are the heretics, *avant la lettre*, of the ancient world. This synthesis emanates, as we see in the *Pensées*, from Christ's capacity to reconcile two apparently incompatible notions: "The knowledge of God without that of one's wretchedness makes for pride. // The knowledge of one's

[27] This *Opuscule*, dating from 1658 (although not published until 1728), is included in Lafuma at p. 291–7, and in Sellier at p. 697–739. Its compilation is commonly attributed to Nicolas Fontaine, who was Sacy's secretary at the time. The most substantial treatment of it is by Pierre Courcelle, *L'Entretien de Pascal et Sacy. Ses sources et ses énigmes*, Paris, Vrin, 1960. See also the "Notice" in Sellier, p. 699–716. There is a recent critical edition by Richard Scholar carrying the title *Entretien avec Sacy sur la philosophie* in the series Actes Sud (*Les Philosophiques*), Arles, 2003.

[28] A more syncretic view of the pagan philosophers Plato and Aristotle is evinced by St François de Sales, for example, in the *Treatise on the Love of God*, as inherently understanding both the concept of God and the need to love God, even if they failed in their practice. He considers Epictetus to be "the most decent man in all of paganism" ["le plus homme de bien de tout le paganisme"], even if he is subsequently patronised as "that poor fellow Epictetus" ["le pauvre bon homme Épictète"], who errs by mentioning "gods after the pagan fashion" ["les dieux à la païenne"] (*Traité de l'amour de Dieu*, in St François de Sales, *Œuvres*, ed. A Ravier and R. Devos, Paris, Gallimard (Pléiade), 1969, 319–972, p. 365 ; 402). Julien Eymard d'Angers notes how, for François, "pagan authors are therefore neither in a state of absolute error or absolute corruption" ["les auteurs païens ne sont donc ni dans l'erreur absolue, ni dans l'absolue corruption"] (*L'Humanisme chrétien au XVIIe siècle: François de Sales et Yves de Paris*, The Hague, Martinus Nijhoff, 1970, p. viii). Krumenacker goes further in suggesting that *humanisme dévot* was defined by "a great optimism towards creation and above all the idea that the virtues of the pagans emanate from Jesus Christ" ["un grand optimisme envers la création et notamment l'idée que les vertus des païens proviennent de Jésus-Christ"] (*École française*, p. 218).

[29] "De sorte qu'ils ne peuvent subsister seuls à cause de leurs défauts, ni s'unir à cause de leurs oppositions, et qu'ainsi ils se brisent et s'anéantissent pour faire place à la vérité de l'Évangile. C'est elle qui accorde les contrariétés par un art tout divin" (*Entretien*, L p. 296, S p. 736).

wretchedness without that of God makes for despair. // The knowledge of Jesus Christ makes the transition, because we find in him both God and our wretchedness",[30] so that, in a positive correlative: "Happiness is neither beyond us nor within us. It is in God, and both beyond us and within us."[31]

Finally, it is important to underline Pascal's role as the persuader of Sacy, his interlocutor in this text, of the virtue of a discursive approach to the assertion of dogmatic truth, a fact recognized finally by Sacy in the image of Pascal as being "like those clever doctors who, by the skilful manner in which they prepare the most deadly poisons, succeed in drawing from them the most effective remedies";[32] and by the anonymous recorder of the conversations, who sees Pascal as arriving at his affirmation of Christian doctrine "after so many twists and turns".[33] What Pascal is at pains to instil in his interlocutor is not the terminus of the search for belief, which they evidently hold in common, but the means by which to achieve it, the "twists and turns" of his apology. Sacy sees the end point as being some kind of revelation, "the clear sight of Christianity"[34] as he calls it, and Pascal would not demur. His own experience of conversion lay unambiguously in the line of Paul and Augustine,[35] as a *coup de foudre* that transcends rational conviction. Where, however, he differs from Sacy is in according to the provisionally tenable beliefs of two putative disputants – in this case a stoic and a sceptic – an equally provisional degree of assent,[36] in order to transcend the thesis and antithesis which they offer by the synthesis of the Gospel. The apologist, in other words, will only achieve his purpose by arguing dialectically

[30] "La connaissance de Dieu sans celle de sa misère fait l'orgueil. // La connaissance de sa misère sans celle de Dieu fait le désespoir. // La connaissance de Jésus-Christ fait le milieu parce que nous y trouvons, et Dieu, et notre misère" (*Pensées*, L 192, S 225).

[31] "Le bonheur n'est ni hors de nous ni dans nous. Il est en Dieu, et hors et dans nous" (*Pensées*, L 407, S 26).

[32] "Il lui dit qu'il ressemblait à ces médecins habiles qui, par la manière adroite de préparer les plus grands poisons, en savent tirer les plus grands remèdes" (*Entretien*, L p. 297, S p. 737).

[33] "[. . .] beaucoup de détours" (*Entretien*, L p. 297, S p. 739).

[34] "[. . .] la claire vue du christianisme" (*Entretien*, L p. 297, S p. 739).

[35] St Augustine of Hippo (354–430) was consecrated Bishop of Hippo in North Africa in AD 404, after a conversion to Christianity following a previous engagement with Manichaeism, as recounted in the *Confessions*, the first work of Christian autobiography (although the title also, and importantly, carries the sense of "profession of faith"). His other major work, in a vast corpus of writing, is the *City of God*, which establishes a dichotomous relationship between Christian and worldly ideals. Augustine's polemical writing against the overly free-will-based theology of Pelagius has above all contributed to his nickname of "the Doctor of Grace" ["Le Docteur de la Grâce"], and obviously his influence on writing such as Jansenius's *Augustinus* (1640) and on its exponents is of primary importance in the period (see Chapter 6). What is more striking again is the range of his authority, quoted as he is by virtually all our writers, and indeed appearing in a vision to one of them (Antoinette Bourignon). On his influence on Pascal, see Philippe Sellier, *Pascal et saint Augustin*, Paris, Armand Colin, 1970.

[36] Bossuet also acknowledges this in the *Panegyric of St Catherine*: "Although the [pagan] philosophers were the guardians of error, they nonetheless discovered some shafts of truth" ["Encore que les philosophes soient les protecteurs de l'erreur, toutefois ils ont découvert quelques rayons de vérité"] (*Panégyrique de sainte Catherine*, in *Œuvres*, 459–78, p. 471).

from the starting point of the man or woman whom he is aiming to convert, as encapsulated in the two philosophical positions he deploys; he is, like St Paul in 1 Corinthians 9: 22–3, making himself all things to all men in order to save a few (although just how few will be a matter for later conjecture).[37] It is this principle which Pascal furthermore succeeds in articulating by standing rhetorically outside the faith, by converting himself, in other words, to the perspective of the cultured man of the world, the *honnête homme* of his day;[38] and it is in this way first of all that he adopts, in order to bring his reader to belief, a mode of exteriority. The fragments of Pascal's apologetic project thus start from an assumed position of neutrality, whereby he seeks to write as an objective portrayer of the human condition in the first instance.[39] It is this status as well that is enhanced by the vicarious and provisional exclusion of the transcendent perspective in the first sections of the *Pensées*.

But if a tonality of despair is in evidence in these fragments, it is essential to interpret it first of all in relation to the ethos of the exercise in which the apologist is engaged, that of trying to bring the complacent non-believer – or perhaps the lapsed fellow believer, or most likely both – to faith. Rather than seeing the anguished first person of the apology as indicative of a biographical Pascal racked by doubt and despair, therefore, I would suggest that we see him first and foremost as the deliberate creation of a proselytising believer. Pascal's strength lies initially in a kind of rhetorical self-exteriorization, as a result of which the Christian faith is represented with a unique degree of acquired objectivity. Leszek Kolakowski, in *God Owes Us Nothing*, writes of Pascal's "talent in using dramatic rhetorical cuts that lent traditional doctrine a striking freshness".[40] His *métier* is that of persuader, be it as apologist or polemicist; and his enduring appeal will lie in his capacity for extra-Christian projection and intra-Christian conflict, rather than in any exposition of the inter-Christian common ground. He is, in the

[37] The Jerusalem Bible translation gives: "I accommodated myself to people in all kinds of different situations, so that by all possible means I might bring some to salvation. All this I do for the sake of the Gospel, that I may share its benefits with others". Bossuet develops the same text in the *Panegyric of St Bernard*, concluding that "[the apostles] took a thousand different forms, [but] the same charity always prevailed" ["[les apôtres] prenaient mille formes différentes, et toujours la même charité dominait"] (*Panégyrique de saint Bernard*, in *Œuvres*, p. 279). See also Chapters 4 and 6.

[38] This complex and shifting term might for our purposes be best understood in the *Pensées* as negatively defined by the apologist himself: "*Honnête homme*. You must not be able to say of him: he is a mathematician, or a preacher, or eloquent, but that he is an *honnête homme*. This universal quality alone appeals to me" ["*Honnête homme*. Il faut qu'on n'en puisse [dire] ni : il est mathématicien, ni prédicateur, ni éloquent, mais il est honnête homme. Cette qualité universelle me plaît seule"] (*Pensées*, L 647, S 532). We are dealing with an élitist concept, therefore, which combines a broad culture with a degree of sociability and self-awareness.

[39] The French term *moraliste* corresponds exactly to this function, whereby an observer of humankind in society invites his reader to engage in a process of self-examination in his turn.

[40] Leszek Kolakowski, *God Owes Us Nothing: A Brief Remark on Pascal's Religion and on the Spirit of Jansenism*, Chicago and London, University of Chicago Press, 1995, p. 182.

words of an American critic, both "adversary and advocate";[41] but his advocacy of the faith is as often as not the more effective for its adversarial mode of engagement. The voices which he adopts in the apologetic project serve variously to lead its often sketchy addressees to the end point of his argument. But it is the capacity of the authorial figure of Pascal to underscore the unexpected elements of Christianity, to which the nominal adherent has become blunted, which singles out his self-proclaimed appeal to readers of all social categories (in his polemics)[42] and of all times and beliefs (in his apologetics).[43]

The *Pensées* are thus a kind of catechism for the indifferent, in which the dogmas that are pedagogically asserted by any number of contemporary prelates in a whole range of media need to be justified by evidence both of their appropriateness and of their veracity. Put another way, the *Pensées*, in common with the traditional format of the catechism, are a work of questions; but one in which the answers are bound to return to the first principles of religious – or more exactly Christian – belief.[44] Thus Pascal in this writing returns to the ground that other contemporary writers take for granted, asking *why* to believe, as opposed to *what* to believe (the domain of the catechist) or *how* to believe (the domain of the spiritual director). His method of doing so will be to present his case in terms of a problem, a solution and a commitment (or in the medical terms of the *Entretien*, an illness, a diagnosis and a remedy). But he will also present it in the *Pensées*, in distinction to his tidily dialectical conversation with his co-partisan, Sacy, as a drama, indeed as nothing less than the drama of salvation. His putative reader will not be given a thesis and an antithesis, but will be confronted by an existential dilemma. If there is to be a remedy, therefore, that remedy is not to be reached as an intellectual solution, as a synthesis might be attained in an argument. As he writes of his putative interlocutor:

> If he flatters himself, I cut him down to size;
> If he humbles himself, I flatter him.
> And I contradict him at every opportunity,

[41] Robert J. Nelson, *Pascal Adversary and Advocate*, Cambridge, MA, Harvard University Press, 1981.

[42] Thus in a fictional reply to the second of the *Provincial Letters*: "Everyone sees them, everyone understands them, everyone believes them" ["Tout le monde les voit, tout le monde les entend, tout le monde les croit"] (*Lettres provinciales*, p. 294).

[43] Thus in the response attributed to the interlocutor of the wager argument: "Oh, this argument uplifts me, delights me, etc." ["Ô ce discours me transporte, me ravit, etc"] (*Pensées*, L 418, S 680).

[44] Evidence for such a proposal would also be offered by comparing Pascal's use of the Bible with that of his episcopal (and indeed lay) contemporaries. For his apologetic purposes, the Bible is cited as a point of departure, rather than as a point of reference. See Philippe Sellier, "La Bible de Pascal", in *Le Grand Siècle et la Bible*, ed. Jean-Robert Armogathe, Paris, Beauchesne, 1989, pp. 701–19.

Until he understands
That he is an incomprehensible monster.[45]

The outcome will thus be that, at the end of the unbeliever's search for truth, its discovery will be experienced less as an explanation than as a liberation: "It is good", he writes, "to be tired and wearied by the fruitless search for the ultimate good [*le souverain bien*], so as to stretch out your arms to your Liberator."[46]

A natural description of bewilderment, grounded in immanent human experience, thus anticipates the exposition of Christian doctrine in the *Pensées*; put anachronistically, Pascal exploits the point of junction between secular psychology and Christian dogma—or, his critics would say, he predicates his portrayal of the human condition on a tacit, or indeed, on a suppressed postlapsarianism. If philosophy and cosmology promote deism, then the true cause of the human condition must lie in human history, in other words in the doctrine of the Fall, in the explanation afforded by original sin for the historically coexistent states of greatness and wretchedness that is the starting point for their reconciliation. But if Pascal presents this doctrine as a diagnosis, or perhaps better an ætiology, he does so in terms which are yet again utterly distant from the neat Christian synthesis of his conversations with a fellow believer. This is because it is here, above all, that the apologist resonates with the objections of his reader, in presenting not just the superficially unlikely nature of the doctrine of the Fall, in a passage of quite exceptional rhetorical indignation, but indeed its seemingly grotesque injustice:

> For there is no doubt that nothing offends against our reason more than to say that the sin of the first man should have inculpated those who, being so far from this source, seem incapable of participating in it. This transmission does not only seem impossible to us. It seems indeed deeply unjust [. . .]. Certainly nothing jolts us more sharply than this doctrine.

So how is this offensiveness to be reconciled with the need to believe it? Because, as the apologist goes on, "without this mystery, the most incomprehensible of all, we are incomprehensible to ourselves".[47] If the human condition is indeed as it is

[45] "S'il se vante, je l'abaisse / S'il s'abaisse, je le vante / Et le contredis toujours / Jusques à ce qu'il comprenne / Qu'il est un monstre incompréhensible" (*Pensées*, L 130, S 163). The textual arrangement of this fragment as if it were a poem is common to both L and S, although not authorized by the manuscript.

[46] "Il est bon d'être lassé et fatigué par l'inutile recherche du souverain bien, afin de tendre les bras au Libérateur" (*Pensées*, L 631, S 524). The polyvalence of the term *souverain bien* [*summum bonum*] is parodically signalled by Pascal when he identifies "280 sorts of ultimate good in Montaigne" ["280 sortes de souverain bien dans Montaigne"] (*Pensées*, L 408, S 27). The term also serves as the title for a short *liasse* (*Pensées*, L X, S XI).

[47] "Car il est sans doute qu'il n'y a rien qui choque plus notre raison que de dire que le péché du premier homme ait rendu coupables ceux qui, étant si éloignés de cette source, semblent incapables d'y participer. Cet écoulement ne nous paraît pas seulement impossible, il nous

described by Pascal (and by his patristic precursor St Augustine), as Moriarty remarks, "God's injustice, God's helplessness, or punishment for Adam's sin are the surviving alternatives."[48] Or in Pascal's own formulation: "We are born so contrary to this love of God, and it is so necessary, that we must have been born guilty or God would be unjust."[49] According to this reading, the explanation of the human condition afforded by the doctrine of the Fall is only acceptable because it provides a lesser paradox than the mystery of human nature devoid of an explanation. "Man is more inconceivable without this mystery", the apologist concludes, "than this mystery is inconceivable to man."[50]

As a result of this unpalatable doctrine, therefore, and in addition to a purely informative role, the apologist has to undertake to counteract error, and to work to correct misapprehension. Two of the most important fragments in the text betray by their opening sentences, attributed to a mysteriously anonymous "they", what has to be seen as a crucial determining cause of unbelief: "They should at least learn what the religion is which they are combating before they set about combating it",[51] he writes; or: "They blaspheme the Christian religion, because they know so little about it."[52] These passages then go on to underscore a further justification for Pascal to stand outside his belief, which stems from what he presents as a campaign against Christian doctrine that is based on ignorance. Christianity, he argues, is construed as deism by its opponents, who then dismiss it for not being what it never claimed to be in the first place; and, as a consequence, Christians are challenged for a failure that is in fact intrinsic to their belief system. Pascal is, indeed, very good at saying what Christianity is not; and most of what it is not would be easier to grasp, or more reassuring, or more consistent with natural religion, than what it is. But

semble même très injuste [. . .]. Certainement rien ne nous heurte plus rudement que cette doctrine. Et cependant, sans ce mystère, le plus incompréhensible de tous, nous sommes incompréhensibles à nous-mêmes" (*Pensées*, L 131, S 164). In a further fragment, now offering a sequence of "incomprehensible" truths, Pascal writes that it is "incomprehensible [. . .] that original sin should be, and that it should not be" ["incompréhensible [. . .] que le péché originel soit, et qu'il ne soit pas"] (*Pensées*, L 809, S 656).

48 *Fallen Nature, Fallen Selves*, p. 104.

49 "Nous naissons si contraires à cet amour de Dieu et il est si nécessaire qu'il faut que nous naissions coupables, ou Dieu serait injuste" (*Pensées*, L 205, S 237).

50 "De sorte que l'homme est plus inconcevable sans ce mystère que ce mystère n'est inconcevable à l'homme" (*Pensées*, L 131, S 164). Voltaire drafts a hypothetical reply in the twenty-fifth *Lettre philosophique*, which concludes: "If man were perfect, he would be God, and these supposed inconsistencies, that you call *contradictions*, are the necessary ingredients which enter into the composition of man, who is as he should be" ["Si l'homme était parfait, il serait Dieu, et ces prétendues contrariétés, que vous appelez *contradictions*, sont les ingrédients nécessaires qui entrent dans le composé de l'homme, qui est ce qu'il doit être"] (*Lettres philosophiques*, p. 159, original emphasis).

51 "Qu'ils apprennent au moins quelle est la religion qu'ils combattent avant que de la combattre" (*Pensées*, L 427, S 681).

52 "Ils blasphèment la religion chrétienne parce qu'ils la connaissent mal" (*Pensées*, L 449, S 690). Cf. Jude 10: "But these people abuse anything they do not understand."

Christianity does not claim to have a perpetual revelation of its God, accessible to reason alone; and crucially, if it did, that revelation could not correspond to the empirical awareness of the duality of the human condition. It would not, in this defective hypothesis, offer a theology which was consonant with the anthropology to which it is supposed to reply.[53] Such a belief might well appeal to a kind of optimistic deism, but it would give no account of the weakness of man; and yet the absence of any such belief would lead to atheistic despair. Pascal throws his reader back once again into the dizzying sequence of affirmation and denial that is so frequently the paradigm of his apology.

I want at this stage to introduce a second intertext, or more correctly series of generic intertexts, which give us an insight into the shape of Pascal's argument that merits our attention; and they are due to a figure who will loom large in the following chapters, Jacques-Bénigne Bossuet (1627–1704),[54] Bishop, in the later years of his life, of Meaux, and preceptor to the king's son, the Dauphin. But out of a vast published corpus, I want to concentrate initially on just one of his sermons,[55] since it is here that the paradigmatic similarities with Pascal in particular are instructive; and I want to suggest in doing so that, by pushing humankind's inconsistencies ("contrariétés") to their limits as he does in the *Pensées*, the pattern which Pascal is structurally following is first and foremost homiletic.[56]

The form of the sermon in the period is to a large extent predetermined; and it consists, put at its simplest, of an exordium, which establishes the architecture and introduces the thematics; then of a *division* into two or three argumentational *points*; and finally of a peroration.[57] It thus also lends itself to what we

[53] The terms are borrowed from Michel and Marie-Rose Le Guern, *Les 'Pensées' de Pascal, de l'anthropologie à la théologie*, Paris, Larousse (Thèmes et textes), 1972.

[54] Bossuet was appointed Bishop of Condom in 1669 (he resigned in 1671), Preceptor of the Dauphin (the eldest son of Louis XIV) in 1670 and Bishop of Meaux in 1681. A brief survey of his life and writing is provided by Jean Calvet (revised by Jacques Truchet), *Bossuet*, in the series 'Connaissance des Lettres', Paris, Hatier, 1968; and a wide-ranging series of articles is brought together in Thérèse Goyet and Jean-Pierre Collinet, eds, *Bossuet: la prédication au XVIIe siècle*, Paris, Nizet, 1980.

[55] The *Sermon sur la mort* was preached at the Louvre during Lent 1662 (*Le Carême du Louvre*). For this sequence of pieces I shall refer to the recent edition by Constance Cagnat-Debœuf, Paris, Gallimard (Folio classique), 2001 (henceforth *Sermons*), where the *Sermon sur la mort* appears at p. 146–61. References to other homiletic works (including the *Panégyriques* and *Oraisons funèbres*) will be to the Pléiade edition of *Œuvres* by the Abbé Velat and Yvonne Champailler, Paris, Gallimard (Pléiade), 1961 (henceforth *Œuvres*). The Gospel text that directs the *Sermon sur la mort* is taken from the episode of the raising of Lazarus in John 11: 34: "*Domine, veni et vide.* Lord, come and see" ["Seigneur, venez et voyez"].

[56] The editors of the Pléiade volume offer certain hypotheses in this respect (*Œuvres*, p. 1534, n. 8), but without any hard historical evidence. It is sufficient to note the comparison. Whether or not Pascal had heard Bossuet preach, or Bossuet had read some drafts of the apology, the assumption that Pascal, as a practicing Catholic, was familiar with the traditional structure of the sermon can be taken to be uncontroversial.

[57] I have italicized *division* and *points* in order to indicate their technical (French) use in homiletics. I shall return to Bossuet's pulpit oratory at greater length in Chapter 4. See also the later chapter for a fuller bibliography.

could anachronistically call a dialectical model;[58] and it is in the 1662 *Sermon on Death* [*Sermon sur la mort*] that we find some of the most striking paradigmatic as well as thematic parallels between Bossuet and Pascal. In this piece, Bossuet's exordium concludes with a statement of duality in humankind, strongly redolent of Pascal's incompatibilities: "[Man] is worthless insofar as he is transitory, and infinitely worthy insofar as he attains to eternity."[59] The *premier point* then turns to a meditation on the nothingness of man alongside the greatness of God, illustrated above all by his mortality:[60] it begins with an amplification of Psalm 39: 5–6;[61] and it ends with a contemplation of the individual's apparently random place in the immensity of time, now supported by a brief quotation from 1 Corinthians 7: 31: "This world as we know it is passing away."

But where the similarities are most telling is in the whole dialectical argumentation conducted by means of empirical contradictions, their defective explanations and their ultimate resolution in the doctrine of the Fall, before the remedy is offered in the person of Jesus and the promise of eternal life; and then reinforced, in the peroration, with words of consolation, triumph, and certainty. If the *premier point* recalls features of the Pascalian thematics of human weakness,[62] however, it is in the *second point* that the shape of the argument itself brings out the structural relationship most strongly. Bossuet begins, in considering man's greatness, by acknowledging the achievements of "human learning" ["connaissances humaines"], and seeing in them the sign of "an immortal breath of the Spirit of God" ["un souffle immortel de l'Esprit de Dieu"] present in humankind. He then goes on to acknowledge humankind's sense of duty as in turn the sign of "the light

[58] The degree of appropriateness of this term is helpfully explored by Jean Mesnard, *Les 'Pensées' de Pascal*, deuxième partie, "La dialectique des *Pensées*", p. 173–270. I shall use it simply as a shorthand term to convey the transition from a thesis and antithesis to a synthesis. Pascal's own term of "continual overturning of the arguments for and against" ["renversement continuel du pour au contre"] (*Pensées*, L 93, S 127), while not identical, proposes a clearer paradigm, as well as giving to understand a terminus which is proposed when the perspective of the Christian revelation is attained.

[59] "[L'homme] est méprisable en tant qu'il passe, et infiniment estimable en tant qu'il aboutit à l'éternité" (*Sermons*, p. 149).

[60] Bossuet had previously preached a widely admired sermon entitled *Meditation on the Brevity of Life* [*Méditation sur la brièveté de la vie*] in September 1648. It is included in the *Œuvres* at p. 1035–8.

[61] This, typically, is quoted first in Latin and then in French. The verses are as follows: "Look, you have given me but a hand's breadth or two of life, the length of my life is as nothing to you. / Every human being [. . .] that walks is nothing but a shadow."

[62] It also stresses, in common with Pascal, man's refusal to contemplate his own condition: "The human mind [. . .] touches so lightly on what is of most immediate concern to it, that we spend all our lives unaware of what affects us" ["L'esprit [. . .] passe cependant si légèrement sur ce qui se présente à lui de plus près, que nous passons toute notre vie toujours ignorants de ce qui nous touche"] (*Sermons*, p. 147). Compare *Pensées*, L 806, S 653: "We work tirelessly at adorning and maintaining our imaginary being, and neglect the true one" ["Nous travaillons incessamment à embellir et conserver notre être imaginaire, et négligeons le véritable"].

of your [God's] face" ["un rayon de votre face"];[63] and to attain the climax of his sequence as he admires fallen humankind's capacity to transcend its limitations and (albeit imperfectly) to contemplate God.

But it is in the development of faulty hypotheses to explain this duality that in turn the lexical resonances with Pascal also begin to occur:

> Some will make of him a God, others will reduce him to nothing; some will say that nature cherishes him like a [loving] mother, who delights in him; others, that she exposes him like a [cruel] stepmother, who rejects him; and a third party, not knowing any longer what to think about the origin of this mixture, will reply that [nature] has played tricks by joining together two components that have nothing to do with each other and therefore that, by a kind of whim, she has formed this prodigy that is known as man.[64]

Having denied all these options, Bossuet then asks the rhetorical question: "So what is the origin of such a strange disproportion?",[65] and goes on to provide the kind of solution that we recognize in Pascal, again in familiar terms: "It is because man wanted to build in his own way on the work of his creator, and so separated himself from the [divine] plan" (by original sin, in other words), in such a way that "the spiritual and the carnal, the angel and the beast, in a word, found themselves suddenly united".[66] The same tone of relief that we find in Pascal once again closes this section, albeit in a somewhat compressed form, before Bossuet returns to his primary subject of death and resurrection: "Here is the clue to the enigma, here is the way out of all the confusion: faith has returned us to ourselves, and our shameful weakness is no longer able to conceal our natural dignity."[67] But if in Bossuet the homiletic shift into the transcendent register is immediately available, in Pascal it is for the time being rhetorically delayed. And in that deferral of course lies the difference between the Pascal of the *Entretien* and the Bossuet of the pulpit on the one hand, with their variously complicit (actual) hearers; and the apologist of the *Pensées* on the other, with his variously unbelieving (rhetorical) interlocutors.

[63] Psalm 4: 6.

[64] "[Les] uns en feront un dieu, les autres en feront un rien ; les uns diront que la nature le chérit comme une mère et qu'elle en fait ses délices ; les autres, qu'elle l'expose comme une marâtre et qu'elle en fait son rebut ; et un troisième parti, ne sachant plus que deviner touchant la cause de ce mélange, répondra qu'elle [=la nature] s'est jouée en unissant deux pièces qui n'ont nul rapport, et ainsi que, par une espèce de caprice, elle a formé ce prodige qu'on appelle l'homme" (*Sermons*, p. 157–8). A very similar structure is found in a simpler form in the early *Funeral Oration of Yolande de Monterby* [*Oraison funèbre de Yolande de Monterby*] (*Œuvres*, p. 9–22).

[65] "Mais d'où vient donc une si étrange disproportion ?" (*Sermons*, p. 158).

[66] "C'est que l'homme a voulu bâtir à sa mode sur l'ouvrage de son créateur, et il s'est éloigné du plan : ainsi [. . .] le spirituel et le charnel, l'ange et la bête, en un mot, se sont trouvés tout à coup unis" (*Sermons*, p. 159).

[67] "Voilà le mot de l'énigme, voilà le dégagement de tout l'embarras : la foi nous a rendus à nous-mêmes, et nos faiblesses honteuses ne peuvent plus cacher notre dignité naturelle" (*Sermons*, p. 159).

According to the model we have established so far, then, to sketch it in its starkest terms, a paradoxical set of assertions about humankind (the problem) leads to the establishment of a cause, a diagnosis in medical terms – or perhaps better, as I suggested, an ætiology. But if the whole framework of the anthropology is binary, then the theology, if it is to correspond to it, must share that feature. The counterpoint to the Fall – the transcendent correlative to that residue of prelapsarian greatness in man – must be provided; and that divine remedy takes the form of the Redemption. The binary structure of the apology is therefore once more in evidence in the polarized expression of the appropriateness of Christianity to the human condition, whereby "the Christian faith hardly does more than establish these two things: the corruption of [human] nature, and the Redemption of Jesus Christ".[68] And elsewhere, to return to the fragment from which I have taken my title, where the paradox is articulated in its most hyperbolic terms: "Christianity is strange: it orders man to recognize that he is vile and even abominable, and orders him to want to be like God. Without such a counter-balance this self-promotion would render him horribly vain, or this self-abasement would render him horribly abject."[69]

The paradoxical statement of revealed truth is thus couched in a pattern we begin to find familiar, and yet whose familiarity does nothing by this stage to reduce its strangeness and above all its differentness from optimistic deism: "You can indeed know God without knowing your wretchedness, or [you can] know your wretchedness without knowing God", the apologist writes, "but you cannot know Jesus Christ without knowing God and your wretchedness both at once."[70] This leads in turn to a paradoxical way of attaining fulfilment (the cure), as the implications for the believer are finally introduced into the equation: "There must be movements of lowliness, not born of nature but of penitence, not in order to remain lowly, but to aspire to greatness. There must be movements of greatness, not born of merit but of grace, and as a result of having passed through lowliness."[71] Or, more affirmatively in the seventh letter to Mlle de Roannez, now following a ternary pattern: "The blessed have their [heavenly] joy with no sadness; the worldly have their [earthly] sadness with no joy; but Christians have this earthly sadness mingled with

[68] "La foi chrétienne ne va presque qu'à établir ces deux choses : la corruption de la nature, et la Rédemption de Jésus-Christ" (*Pensées*, L 427, S 681).

[69] "Le christianisme est étrange : il ordonne à l'homme de reconnaître qu'il est vil et même abominable, et lui ordonne de vouloir être semblable à Dieu. Sans un tel contrepoids cette élévation le rendrait horriblement vain, ou cet abaissement le rendrait horriblement abject" (*Pensées*, L 351, S 383).

[70] "On peut donc bien connaître Dieu sans sa misère, et sa misère sans Dieu. Mais on ne peut connaître Jésus-Christ sans connaître tout ensemble et Dieu et sa misère" (*Pensées*, L 449, S 690).

[71] "Il faut des mouvements de bassesse, non de nature mais de pénitence, non pour y demeurer mais pour aller à la grandeur. Il faut des mouvements de grandeur, non de mérite mais de grâce et après avoir passé par la bassesse" (*Pensées*, L 398, S 17).

heavenly joy."[72] Such a paradox lies at the heart of all such symmetrical expositions of the faith, or perhaps indeed allows for their symmetry.

Fundamentally linked to this search is the doctrine of the hidden God, the *Deus absconditus* of Isaiah,[73] interplaying with the intimate and indeed Christic relationship between seeking and finding.[74] These concepts come together in Pascal in a statement of the nature of God's postlapsarian concealment, whereby he is "revealed to those who seek him with all their heart, and hidden to those who flee him with all their heart".[75] The grace to seek, in a sequence that I shall explore further in later chapters, is thus the first gift of God.

It is in the light of this divine concealment too that Pascal shows himself at his most subtle in the deployment of apparent impediments to belief as arguments in its favour. The first lies in his presentation of a multiplicity of religions as evidence for the truth of Christianity. "If God had only allowed one religion, it would have been too obvious", he writes. "But if you look closely you can perceive the true religion amidst this confusion. [. . .]. Therefore all the most visible weaknesses are strengths."[76] The second stage, formulated as a defective hypothesis that contains its own negation, takes us further into the mystery adumbrated in that paradox: "If nothing of God had ever appeared", he writes,

> this deprivation would be ambiguous and could equally well point to the absence of any divinity as to man's unworthiness to know him. But [. . .] if he appears once, he is always. And so we can do nothing other than conclude that there is a God, and that men are unworthy of him.[77]

But the third stage of the argument is even more extraordinary, because Pascal goes on pre-emptively to wipe out the objections of his adversaries. In its

[72] "Les bienheureux ont cette joie sans aucune tristesse; les gens du monde ont leur tristesse sans cette joie, et les Chrétiens ont cette joie mêlée de tristesse" (*Lettres aux Roannez*, in L, p. 269). This sequence of letters was written between August 1656 and March 1657 to Charlotte de Roannez, who had decided, following a visit to Port-Royal to visit the relic of the Holy Thorn (to which was attributed a miraculous healing of Pascal's niece, Marguerite Périer – see Chapter 5), to become a religious at the house. The letters written by Pascal are addressed both to her and to her brother, the Duc de Roannez, who had taken her away from Paris to his native Poitou in order to distract her from her vocation. Extracts were included in the 1670 Port-Royal edition of the *Pensées*. In modern editions, nine extracts are included in Lafuma at p. 265–70. Sellier is limited to one letter at p. 151–3. References will therefore be to Lafuma.

[73] Isaiah 45: 15: "Truly, you are a God who conceals himself, / God of Israel, Saviour!"

[74] Matthew 7: 7; Luke 11: 9.

[75] "[Dieu veut paraître] à découvert à ceux qui le cherchent de tout leur cœur, et caché à ceux qui le fuient de tout leur cœur" (*Pensées*, L 149, S 182).

[76] "Si Dieu n'eût permis qu'une seule religion, elle eût été trop reconnaissable. Mais qu'on y regarde de près, on discerne bien le vrai dans cette confusion [. . .]. Ainsi toutes les faiblesses très apparentes sont des forces" (*Pensées*, L 236, S 268).

[77] "S'il n'avait jamais rien paru de Dieu, cette privation serait équivoque et pourrait aussi bien se rapporter à l'absence de toute divinité ou à l'indignité où seraient les hommes de le connaître. Mais [. . .] s'il paraît une fois, il est toujours. Et ainsi on n'en peut conclure sinon qu'il y a un Dieu, et que les hommes en sont indignes" (*Pensées*, L 448, S 690).

simplest form, we find: "Not only the zeal of those who seek him proves God, but also the blindness of those who do not seek him"[78]; and then, taking the device to its magnificently ingenious limits, in the imperative: "Recognize, then, the truth of religion in the very obscurity of religion, in the little light that we possess, and in the indifference that we show towards knowing it."[79] If humankind basked confidently in a perpetual and uninterrupted view of God, in other words, that view would be a deception, quite simply because it would not offer a transcendent correlative to the immanent self-perception that the apologist has so persistently promoted. Furthermore, and as a result of this, the first impediment to belief – that of indifference – becomes, viewed in the apologetic perspective, the first proof of that same belief that is placed into question. The very tendency to disbelief is thereby transformed into an argument for the truth of Christianity.

It is not, in this scheme of things, the visible evidence within the created universe that proves God, according to the cosmological proof model, systematically opposed by Pascal – "it is not in this way that Scripture, which knows best about things to do with God, speaks of them"[80]; what the apparently inexhaustible dimensions of the visible and projected universe rather transmit is its mystery and hostility. Of course, the believer will see God in his (God's) creation, indeed Christian belief will allow him to possess the correct (fallen) understanding of the place of humankind in nature; but the non-believer will reject such evidence, and will do so legitimately.

Yet to say as much is not to propose that the Judeo-Christian revelation affords a contrastive clarity, since both Christ and the truth of his doctrine are similarly hidden: "As Jesus Christ remained unknown amongst men, so his truth remains amidst commonly held opinions."[81] It is this same principle that in turn will inform Pascal's theory and practice of biblical hermeneutics; and it is in this way too (as he goes on to assert in the same cryptic fragment) that the Eucharist itself will be understood to reflect the multiple forms of divine concealment. This is summarized in an exponential sequence in the fourth letter to Mlle de Roannez: "[God] stayed hidden by the veil of nature that concealed him from us until the Incarnation; but when it was time for him to appear, he was yet more hidden, concealed in his humanity. He was more

[78] "Ainsi non seulement le zèle de ceux qui le cherchent prouve Dieu, mais l'aveuglement de ceux qui ne le cherchent pas" (*Pensées*, L 163, S 195).

[79] "Reconnaissez donc la vérité de la religion dans l'obscurité même de la religion, dans le peu de lumière que nous en avons, dans l'indifférence que nous avons de la connaître" (*Pensées*, L 439, S 690).

[80] "Ce n'est pas de cette sorte que l'Écriture, qui connaît mieux les choses qui sont de Dieu, en parle" (*Pensées*, L 781, S 644). This remark occurs in the so-called *Preface to the Second Part* [*Préface de la seconde partie*] in the context of a sustained attack on the natural proofs of God's existence based on cosmological evidence.

[81] "Comme Jésus-Christ est demeuré inconnu parmi les hommes, ainsi sa vérité demeure parmi les opinions communes" (*Pensées*, L 225, S 258).

recognizable when he was invisible, than when he made himself visible. And finally when he wanted [. . .] to stay with mankind until his last coming, he chose to stay here in the strangest and deepest secrecy of all, which is the Eucharistic species".[82] The principle that underlies this is then resumed as he asserts more generally later in the same letter: "All things [for the Christian] conceal some mystery; [for] all things are veils that conceal God. Christians must recognize him in everything."[83] We are back with the privileged ontology of the believer, even if, in the Christian era, the hidden God is above all to be found in the Church. It is there alone, for Pascal, that "God has established tangible marks, [. . .] to make himself known to those who might sincerely seek him".[84]

What we see in this kind of pattern is the subtlety of Pascal's vision, combining as it does a superficially simple sequence of analogies with a total reversal of any conventional association between absence of evidence and absence of existence. It is the divine concealment therefore which signifies the Christian God's unique appropriateness for fallen man. And if it was a form of divine concealment that constituted the stumbling block that confounded the pagans and the Jewish people in history, the *scandalum* of 1 Corinthians,[85] it is the same phenomenon in its variant manifestations that will continue to deflect those of later ages from recognizing the Catholic faith.

The acknowledgement of the incompatibilities inherent to the human condition is thus fundamental to the recognition of the truth of Christian doctrine, several of whose apparently contradictory tenets are resumed in a paratactic fragment which begins "Origin of the incompatibilities": "A God humiliated, to the point of dying on a cross. Two natures in Jesus Christ. Two comings. Two states in the nature of man. A Messiah who triumphs over death

[82] "[Dieu] est demeuré caché sous le voile de la nature qui nous le couvre jusqu'à l'Incarnation; et quand il a fallu qu'il ait paru, il s'est encore plus caché en se couvrant de l'humanité. Il était bien plus reconnaissable quand il était invisible, que non pas quand il s'est rendu visible. Et enfin quand il a voulu [. . .] demeurer avec les hommes jusqu'à son dernier avènement, il a choisi d'y demeurer dans le plus étrange et le plus obscur secret de tous, qui sont les espèces de l'Eucharistie" (*Lettres aux Roannez*, L p. 267). Bossuet too writes in the *Funeral Oration of Henriette-Marie de France* of how, during his earthly life, "even Jesus Christ found himself constrained [. . .] to seek other veils and other shadows than the mystical veils and shadows with which he willingly conceals himself in the Eucharist" ["Jésus-Christ même se voyait contraint [. . .] de chercher d'autres voiles et d'autres ténèbres, que ces voiles et ces ténèbres mystiques dont il se couvre volontairement dans l'Eucharistie"] (*Oraison funèbre de Henriette-Marie de France*, in *Œuvres*, p. 62).

[83] "Toutes choses couvrent quelque mystère ; toutes choses sont des voiles qui couvrent Dieu. Les Chrétiens doivent le reconnaître en tout" (*Lettres aux Roannez*, L p. 267).

[84] "Dieu a établi des marques sensibles dans l'Église pour se faire reconnaître à ceux qui le chercheraient sincèrement" (*Pensées*, L 427, S 681).

[85] 1 Corinthians 1: 22–3: "While the Jews demand miracles and the Greeks look for wisdom, we are preaching a crucified Christ: to the Jews an obstacle they cannot get over [*scandalum*], to the gentiles foolishness."

by his death."[86] The three central dualities in this fragment, summarizing the binary oppositions of the *Pensées* as a whole, resume the primary coexistence of Christ's nature as God and man; Christ's coming in humility and glory; and humankind's greatness and wretchedness. These are enclosed by the two definitional sentences, isolating the paradoxical specifics of the first duality: "A God humiliated, to the point of dying on the Cross"; and: "A Messiah who triumphs over death by his death". In that way, to return to the cryptic fragment I quoted earlier: "[The acknowledgement of] all these inconsistencies which seemed most of all to draw me away from the knowledge of any religion is what most rapidly led me to the true one."[87]

It is furthermore the coexistence of such apparently contradictory truths in a dogmatic synthesis that defines orthodoxy, so that "at the end of each truth, you should add that you must recall the opposing truth".[88] This is illustrated in the major series of fragments on heresy, devoted to an examination of the nature of Christ and of the Eucharist, and supported in turn by the more general statement: "There are thus a great number of truths, of both faith and morals, that seem incompatible and yet all exist in an admirable order. The source of all heresies lies in the exclusion of certain of these truths." This leads on to the yet more fundamental deduction, whereby the origin of the plurality of conflicting truths within orthodoxy lies in the "union of the two natures within Jesus Christ".[89] Bringing together the two models that I have introduced – the homiletic model that we can anachronistically call dialectic, and the inclusive model of orthodoxy as against heresy – we may assert that orthodoxy resides in the transcending through synthesis of oppositional terms, and heresy in the suppression of either given. Orthodoxy and synthesis are thereby conjoined, as indeed are the compatible paradigms of homiletics and dialectics.

So how can we argue against Pascal? Or first, how does his writing aim to pre-empt such an argument?

It does so, from the outset, by assimilating and countering material that is superficially hostile to his end point. He does not just detoxify the poisons that Sacy identifies, he transforms them into the material for his own remedy. It is

[86] "Source des contrariétés. // Un Dieu humilié, et jusqu'à la mort de la croix. Deux natures en Jésus-Christ. Deux avènements. Deux états de la nature de l'homme. Un Messie triomphant de la mort par sa mort" (*Pensées*, L 241, S 273).

[87] "Toutes ces contrariétés qui semblaient le plus m'éloigner de la connaissance d'une religion est ce qui m'a le plus tôt conduit à la véritable" (*Pensées*, L 404, S 23).

[88] "[...] à la fin de chaque vérité, il faut ajouter qu'on se souvient de la vérité opposée" (Pensées, L 576, S 479).

[89] "Il y a donc un grand nombre de vérités, et de foi et de morale, qui semblent répugnantes et qui subsistent toutes dans un ordre admirable. // La source de toutes les hérésies est l'exclusion de quelques-unes de ces vérités [...]. La source en est l'union des deux natures en Jésus-Christ" (*Pensées*, L 733, S 614). The two parts of this fragment are divided in Sellier by a horizontal line.

by taking on board and conceding the partial validity of his adversary's argument that he both comes some way to meet him and yet neutralizes his opposition by assimilating his terms within the dialectical process.

Secondly, he enhances his strategy by making of the picture of the human condition without God a starting point that the reader is driven to concede in immanent terms, before the transcendent perspective in introduced. What Pascal, as a *moraliste*, is initially and essentially trying to compel his interlocutor to admit is the existence and nature of a problem, not of a solution. Once his fundamentally pessimistic data have been conceded, and once the interlocutor has acknowledged his aspiration to go beyond them, then he is, in the apologist's term, embarked[90] on a journey towards faith. If he is to challenge Pascal, it will either be, *a priori*, in negating the picture of the human condition that he has been offered, by virtue of the optimistic deism of a Voltaire; or, *a posteriori*, in denying the aspiration to transcend it. That would indeed, in the twentieth century, be the outcome of Camus's great essay on the absurd, the *Myth of Sisyphus*, at the end of which Sisyphus, endlessly rolling his stone up the hill, achieves contentment in his denial of submission to God, so that, in the last words of the narrator: "We must imagine Sisyphus to be happy" ["Il faut imaginer Sisyphe heureux"].[91]

But Pascal's cleverest strategy is of course to make the very objections to Christianity into the arguments for its credibility. He cannot be accused of not recognizing the strangeness of Christianity; on the contrary, Christianity will be bound to project itself as strange if it knows itself correctly. The strangeness of Christianity is the strangeness of the human condition; and the knowledge of Christ, whilst a knowledge of God, is also a mode of access to self-knowledge. Adherents to Christianity will recognize, therefore, in that *scandalum* over which its earliest opponents stumbled, the very justification for their assent. "Original sin is folly in the eyes of men", the apologist writes. "But it is offered as such. So do not reproach me with a lack of reason in this doctrine, because it is offered as being beyond reason."[92] At the same time such a paradox can only carry conviction if it is reason itself which reaches this conclusion, which accepts the particularity of strangeness since, as the apologist insists, "the last operation of reason is to recognize that there are an

[90] The term is used by the apologist in the wager fragment: "Yes, but you have to bet. There is no choice, you are already under way" ["Oui, mais il faut parier. Cela n'est pas volontaire, vous êtes embarqué"] (*Pensées*, L 418, S 680).

[91] Albert Camus, "Le mythe de Sisyphe" in *Œuvres complètes*, ed. Jacqueline Lévi-Valensi, Paris, Gallimard (Pléiade), vol. I (2006), 217–304, p. 304.

[92] "Le péché originel est folie devant les hommes, mais on le donne pour tel. Vous ne me devez donc pas reprocher le défaut de raison dans cette doctrine, puisque je la donne pour être sans raison" (*Pensées*, L 695, S 574).

infinite number of things that lie beyond its grasp. It must indeed be weak if it cannot reach that point."[93]

The argument against Pascal – and various aspects of this will emerge in later chapters – would, I suggest, tend to focus on the problem that, precisely by virtue of his status as an apologist and, in one sense at least, as a convert, he finds it difficult ever to find an accommodation between his faith and the world. It is not perhaps a coincidence in the *Pensées* that alongside "strange" ["étrange"], we regularly find the occurrence of such terms as "incomprehensible" ["incompréhensible"], "inconceivable" ["inconcevable"] and even "incredible" ["incroyable"].[94] There is a sense in which Pascal's *telos* is always just beyond reach and, even if there is a strong appeal made to the desirability of adopting Christian belief, there is very little concrete information about what to do next. That is where we have to turn to other writing, with much of which Pascal felt himself profoundly at odds. Writing about the certainty of death is easy; writing about the uncertainties of life is far harder. It is as if Pascal's rhetorically imposed objectivity holds him back from any more integrated praxis. To this degree, he is perhaps in his apologetics showing a feature that we will also encounter in his polemic, which is a tendency to write for the zealot and for the outsider, but to give little account of the day-to-day experience of the faithful, either in their common experience of fulfilment or, more controversially again, in their inevitable experience of failure.[95] In that lies his dramatic power; in that too, as Voltaire was neither the first nor the last to notice, lies his historical isolation.

[93] "La dernière démarche de la raison est de reconnaître qu'il y a une infinité de choses qui la surpassent. Elle n'est que faible si ne va jusqu'à connaître cela" (*Pensées*, L 188, S 220).

[94] The concordance drawn up by H. M. Davidson and P. H. Dubé and published in 1975 (*A Concordance to Pascal's 'Pensées'*, Ithaca, NY, and London, Cornell University Press) identifies all individual lexical items in the Lafuma text.

[95] I shall return to this question in Chapter 6.

2

Particularity and Physicality

> It is with [the mystery of the Incarnation] that the Church must be piously and divinely occupied, and the piety of even the most elevated souls [must be] ravished by astonishment and admiration, as they contemplate the object in which we discover and perceive, in an ineffable way, the majesty of the divine essence, the distinction between the divine persons, the depth of his counsels, and the eminence, rarity, and singularity that God has wanted to show in this unique work [. . .]. It is a divine mystery that is [at] the centre of created and uncreated being, and the single subject in which God wanted, and has wanted from all eternity, to contain and reduce to a smaller scale the world and himself, that is to say both his own infinity and the immensity of the universe.[1]

If, as Pascal argues, the paradoxical explanation of the human condition by the Judeo-Christian doctrine of the Fall is unexpected to the point of being offensive, then the central tenet of the Christian Redemption, whereby God became man, died as a criminal and returned to life, is a yet more extraordinary dogma, whose "excellence and singularity" find dramatic expression in this vertiginous summary by the Cardinal de Bérulle.[2] Yet it is one which, as centuries of credal tradition are built up, is inevitably encumbered by a

[1] "C'est en ce mystère que l'Église doit être saintement et divinement occupé et la piété des âmes les plus élevées ravies d'étonnement et d'admiration, contemplant l'objet auquel on découvre et on aperçoit, en une manière ineffable, la majesté de la divine essence, la distinction de ses personnages, la profondité de ses conseils et l'éminence, la rareté, la singularité que Dieu a voulu être en cet unique ouvrage [. . .]. Divin mystère qui est comme le centre de l'être créé et incréé, et l'unique sujet auquel Dieu a voulu, pour jamais, comprendre et réduire au petit pied le monde et soi-même, c'est-à-dire son infinité propre et la grandeur de l'univers ensemble" (Pierre de Bérulle, *Discours de l'état et des grandeurs de Jésus*, Premier discours, 'De l'excellence et singularité du sacré mystère de l'Incarnation', in *Œuvres complètes*, ed. M. Join-Lambert et R. Lescot, vol. VII, Paris, Éditions du Cerf, 1996, p. 69). Krumenacker comments: "Bérulle does not attain to an expression of what the Incarnation is by means of the different theological systems he has at his disposal [. . .]. Rather the mystery of the Incarnation for him is one of absolute singularity" ["Bérulle ne parvient pas à exprimer ce qu'est l'Incarnation avec les différents systèmes théologiques qu'il a à sa disposition [. . .]. En fait, le mystère de l'Incarnation est pour lui d'une singularité absolue" (*École française*, p. 168)].

[2] The Cardinal de Bérulle (1575–1629) was founder of the French Oratory. See Erik Varden, *Redeeming Freedom: The Principle of Servitude in Béulle*, Rome, Studia Anselmiana, 2011.

blunting familiarity. At the same time, the specificity of the Christian revelation – that it is both precise and situated in history, and yet distant and improbable – will combine to make its credibility particularly tenuous, and its interpretation frequently controversial. It will as a result be rejected, extra-ecclesially, by the growing if unfocused movement of "free-thought"[3] in the early-modern period; but it will also be subject to a whole range of conflicting hypotheses, both within post-Reformation Christendom and, more pertinently to this enquiry, within professed adherents to the Roman tradition.

The first obligation of the apologist is that of veracity, that is the obligation, to put it simply, to show that the historical Jesus was who he claimed to be; and it is in this domain that the conventional use of prophetic and typological material is deployed by Pascal in the *Pensées*. The exact fulfilment of what is promised in the Old Testament by what occurs in the New is thus fundamental, with the figure of Christ shared axially between the two. As the apologist writes, in a composite spatio-temporal metaphor: "The two *testaments* look to Jesus Christ, the *Old* in anticipation, the *New* as its model, both as their centre."[4] Furthermore, as Pascal stresses in his project, the manifestations of the Judeo-Christian God in different ages are interconnected, so that, as a corollary, belief in one entails assent to all: so, retrospectively, belief in the Redemption implies assent to the Fall, which in turn implies assent to the Creation.[5]

Christian particularity is therefore predicated, first of all, on an antecedent Jewish particularity, and Pascal is in several fragments at pains to draw out the uniqueness and distinctiveness of the tradition from which Christianity stems, and to present it, from his perspective, as the flawed channel of truth: "Jesus Christ came at the appointed time, but not in the expected splendour."[6] The

[3] The two most accessible studies of this loosely defined concept are J. S. Spink, *French Free-Thought from Gassendi to Voltaire*, London, Athlone Press, 1960, and René Pintard, *Le Libertinage érudit dans la première moitié du XVIIe siècle*, Paris, Boivin, 1943.

[4] "Jésus-Christ que les deux *Testaments* regardent, l'*Ancien* comme son attente, le *Nouveau* comme son modèle, tous deux comme leur centre" (*Pensées*, L 383, S 7, original emphases).

[5] "The [Christian] religion is proportionate to all kinds of intellect. The most basic are satisfied with its institution [Sellier offers the gloss "the way that it has spread" (*Pensées*, S p. 1071, n. 1)], and this religion is such that the manner of its institution is sufficient to prove its truth. Others refer back to the Apostles. The most erudite go back to the beginning of the world" ["La religion est proportionnée à toutes sortes d'esprits. Les premiers s'arrêtent au seul établissement, et cette religion est telle que son seul établissement est suffisant pour en prouver la vérité. Les autres vont jusqu'aux Apôtres. Les plus instruits vont jusqu'au commencement du monde"] (*Pensées*, L 895, S 448). There is then a final stage, in which "Angels see it even better and from further away" ["Les anges la voient encore mieux et de plus loin"]. This kind of accretive credibility of the Judeo-Christian revelation is fundamental to Pascal's presentation of the Incarnation; and the apparently gratuitous presence of angels in the ascending evidential hierarchy is nonetheless characteristic of the theology of heavenly proximity, to which I shall return in Chapter 8.

[6] "Jésus-Christ est venu dans le temps prédit, mais non pas dans l'éclat attendu" (*Pensées*, L 270, S 301).

hermeneutic potential of this material is also exploited, as the composite evidence afforded by the survival and distress of the Jewish people correlates with the greatness and wretchedness of humankind as a whole; and its unique qualities are in turn foregrounded in a fragment of the *Pensées* which posits the discovery of Judaism as the convincing terminus of a fruitless search among other pre-Christian beliefs: "In this enquiry", the apologist writes, "the Jewish people first of all attracted my attention by any number of astonishing and singular features which come to light."[7] Indeed a fundamental element that he introduces into his argument for the truth of Christianity is what we might inelegantly translate as its "enduringness" ["perpétuité"], whereby, taking the antiquity of the Jewish religion itself as a starting point, the apologist asserts that the sheer survival of the Christian faith is transformed into a kind of exponential evidence, against all the odds, of the credibility of its claims: "The only religion against nature, against common sense, against our pleasures, is the only one that has always existed."[8]

If a central tenet of any such argument lies in the continuity with the Jewish tradition, however, it is clear that many Christian writers of the period found it well nigh impossible to stand even imaginatively within a pre-Christian mentality.[9] The Jewish antecedents of Christianity are perceived as just that, and the particularity of the Jewish calling is entirely mediated through the prism of its Christian fulfilment. The most compelling dramatic expression accorded to this continuity is to be found in the period in Racine's two Old Testament tragedies, dealing respectively with the biblical stories of Esther [*Esther*] (1689) and Athalia [*Athalie*] (1691),[10] both of which underscore the bloody history, the pathos, and the tenuousness of the line which leads to the Redemption. *Esther* essentially tells an Old Testament story in order to promote a New Testament ethic, as its author claims the subject to be "full of great lessons about the love of God, and about detachment from the world in the midst of the world itself".[11] But it is the second of these pieces, *Athalie*, which poses the more interesting problems about the compatibility of such

[7] "Dans cette recherche, le peuple juif attire d'abord mon attention par quantité de choses admirables et singulières qui y paraissent" (*Pensées*, L 451, S 691). The fragment is headed "Advantages of the Jewish people" ["Avantages du peuple juif"].

[8] "La seule religion contre la nature, contre le sens commun, contre nos plaisirs, est la seule qui ait toujours été" (*Pensées*, L 284, S 316). The term "perpétuité" is also the title of a *liasse* (*Pensées*, L XXI, S XXII).

[9] The major exception would probably be represented by the biblical epic, and in particular the *Moyse sauvé* (1653) of the poet Saint-Amant (1594–1661). See on this subject R. A. Sayce, *The French Biblical Epic in the Seventeenth Century*, Oxford, Oxford University Press, 1955.

[10] Racine, *Esther* and *Athalie* are in the first volume of the *Œuvres complètes*, ed. George Forestier, Paris, Gallimard (Pléiade), 1999. The Old Testament source books are respectively: Esther 1–8; 2 Kings 11–12; and 2 Chronicles 22–4. See Jean Dubu, "Racine et la Bible", in *Le Grand Siècle et la Bible*, ed. Jean-Robert Armogathe, Paris, Beauchesne, 1989, pp. 721–34.

[11] "[Esther est] pleine de grandes leçons d'amour de Dieu, et de détachement du monde au milieu du monde même" (*Préface* to *Esther*, in *OC*, p. 946). Compare John 17: 15–16.

subject matter for the tragic genre, making the eponym, who is presented biblically as little more than an impediment to Jehovah's ultimate purpose, into a more complex dramatic protagonist, caught up in what she understands as a polytheistic struggle, and one in which any human notions of justice or omniscience are difficult to discern. Nonetheless, whereas her purely tragic potential within the play is enhanced by the moral ambiguity surrounding her entrapment and death, it is only by the prophecy of the ultimate salvation which is thereby foretold that her destruction is able to make any sense to a Christian audience.

In his fervent affirmation of Judeo-Christian monotheism, Pascal writes in the document known as the *Mémorial* (a mosaic of biblical verses written on a piece of parchment which, according to tradition, he sewed into his coat), of the "*God of Abraham, God of Isaac, God of Jacob,* not of philosophers and wise men"; and this same God, in the same document, is then identified as the "God of Jesus Christ".[12] So the God of both covenants is defined by the names of men; and the personhood of the Christian Incarnation is already anticipated in the flesh and blood of the prophets and prefigurative players of the Old Testament. It is therefore a fundamental part of the credibility of Pascal's argument that the enquirer should give appropriate attention to the Jewish religion. Thus, for example, he writes: "I find this continuity, this religion which is utterly divine in its authority, in its duration, in its perpetuity, in its morality, in its behaviour, in its doctrine, in its effects."[13] At the same time, in Pascal's words, and in both parts of the Bible, it is "incredible that God should unite himself with us".[14]

Yet if the Incarnation is astonishing in its uniqueness and in its theological significance, the formulaic accounts given in the period by Pascal, Bossuet or Fénelon[15] of Christ's life on earth are above all remarkable for their detached and prosaic narratives, which convey, at least by their format and tonality, the impression of being no more than the statements of unexceptional biographical data. Thus for the Archbishop of Cambrai, Fénelon (1651–1715),[16] for example,

[12] "*Dieu d'Abraham, Dieu d'Isaac, Dieu de Jacob,* non des philosophes et des savants [. . .]. Dieu de Jésus-Christ " (L 913, S 742, original emphases, to indicate biblical quotation). The Old Testament reference is to Exodus 3: 6.

[13] "Je trouve cet enchaînement, cette religion toute divine dans son autorité, dans sa durée, dans sa perpétuité, dans sa morale, dans sa conduite, dans sa doctrine, dans ses effets" (*Pensées,* L 703, S 646 – although there are in the case of this fragment substantial editorial differences between the two texts).

[14] "Incroyable que Dieu s'unisse à nous" (*Pensées,* L 149, S 182).

[15] These are respectively: Pascal's *Summary of the life of Jesus Christ* [*Abrégé de la vie de Jésus-Christ*] (1655–6; L p. 297–310); Bossuet's account in the *Second Catechism* [*Second Catéchisme*] (Part VII). The treatment in the *Discourse on Universal History* [*Discours de l'histoire universelle*] (*Œuvres,* 657–1027, p. 725–8) is equally prosaic, albeit more fully contextualized. See also following notes.

[16] François de Salignac de La Mothe-Fénelon was Archbishop of Cambrai from 1695 and preceptor of Louis XIV's grandson, the Duc de Bourgogne, for whom he wrote the didactic novel *Télémaque* (1699 [1717]). Fuller attention to his involvement in Quietism will be given in Chapter 7.

> Christ is born in a stable; he is forced to flee to Egypt; he spends thirty years of his life in an artisan's shop; he endures hunger, thirst and tiredness; he is poor, scorned and abject; he teaches heavenly doctrine and no-one listens to him; all the great and the wise pursue him, capture him, subject him to dreadful torture, treat him as a slave, and put him to death between two thieves having preferred to save a thief.[17]

Yet more understated (albeit more reassuring) is the opening of Bossuet's manual of *Prayers of the Church*, which begins with the *Angelus*, "the prayer that the Church recites at the sound of the bell, in the morning, at midday and in the evening, so as to thank God at all hours of the day for the great benefits of the Incarnation".[18] By virtue of a simple responsorial prayer placed at the outset of the whole collection, he identifies the *Angelus* as a codification and as a prayerful recollection of the humble and ordinary circumstances of the Christian Incarnation as they are reflected in the humble and ordinary lives of its adherents, and so proposes its recitation as a pious discipline that is both unsophisticated and utterly fundamental; but also utterly familiar.

The full strangeness of the Incarnation will be developed elsewhere, and will be marked first of all by an exploration of its physicality – and the use of such a tautology speaks of itself for the need for such a re-evaluation to take place. We have to move into other domains, in order to find the Christocentric emphasis of the post-Tridentine Church translated into a whole spectrum of more exuberant – and in some cases more exuberantly carnal – expressions and responses, both written and lived, towards Christ's birth, life, death and resurrection.

The physical beginnings of divine corporeality lie obviously with the Christ child, to whom several writers in the course of their spiritual autobiographies express their allegiance. Such a focus is already strikingly evident in an apostrophe that closes the preface of a highly controversial devotional classic to which we shall return. This is the *Moyen court* or *Brief method* [*of mental prayer*] by the Quietist writer Madame Guyon, in which we find a telling dedication, consistent with the work's intended appeal to the simple faithful, to "the Holy Child Jesus", in the following terms: "It is your work, O God Child! O uncreated Love, O silent and abbreviated word! to make you loved,

[17] "Jésus-Christ naît dans une étable ; il est contraint de fuir en Égypte ; il passe trente ans de sa vie dans la boutique d'un artisan ; il souffre la faim, la soif, la lassitude ; il est pauvre, méprisé et abject ; il enseigne la doctrine du Ciel et personne ne l'écoute : tous les grands et les sages le poursuivent, le prennent, lui font souffrir des tourments effroyables, le traitent comme un esclave, le font mourir entre deux voleurs après avoir préféré à lui un voleur" (*Lettres et opuscules spirituels*, XXX (*De l'humilité*), in *Œuvres*, I, p. 693). The subject of this brief text does of course influence the deliberate simplicity of the account.

[18] "La prière que l'Église récite au son de la cloche, au matin, à midi et au soir, pour remercier Dieu à toutes les heures du jour du grand bienfait de l'Incarnation" (*Prières ecclésiastiques*, in *Œuvres complètes*, ed. F. Lachat, Paris, Louis Vivès, 1875, vol. V, 206–354, p. 208).

savoured and heard."[19] Closely related to this is the devotion accorded in the period to Our Lady and St Joseph. Mary is universally accorded a status of complete exceptionality, nowhere more so than in the two symbiotic chapters which conclude the seventh book of the *Treatise on the Love of God*: "That the most holy Virgin, Mother of God, died of love for her Son"; and: "That the glorious Virgin died an extremely gentle and peaceful death",[20] in the first of which the following words are attributed to her: "I have no other life than the life of my Son, my life is entirely in his, and his life entirely in mine", and then glossed by the writer: "It was no longer a union, but a unity of heart, soul and life between this Mother and this Son."[21] The place of Joseph is more complicated again. Bossuet refers in the *Panegyric of St Joseph* to its subject as a threefold depository – of the "virginity of Mary, the person of [God's] only Son, [and] the secret of his whole mystery".[22] He then goes on to evoke "Jesus-Christ hidden with all his humble family, with Mary and Joseph, whom he associates with the obscurity of his own life, because they are very dear to him",[23] and offers it as an invitation to the Christian to embrace a life of retreat from the world. In a popular devotional manual, the *Lives of the Saints* by the Jesuit Amable Bonnefons (1600–53), Joseph is described as "the lieutenant of God the Father in the conduct of his holy family", and the writer goes on to imagine how "he relished the innocent caresses of this little Saviour".[24] He also draws attention to their physical beauty, citing the late-medieval French theologian Jean Gerson (1363–1429): "Since, according to the learned Gerson, the face of Jesus Christ was similar to that of St Joseph, and since that of Jesus

[19] "C'est votre ouvrage, ô Enfant Dieu ! ô Amour incréée, ô Parole muette et abrégée ! de vous faire aimer, goûter et entendre " (Jeanne-Marie Bouvier de La Mothe Guyon, *Moyen court et autres écrits spirituels*, ed. Marie-Louise Gondal, Grenoble, Jérôme Millon, 1995, p. 60). A fuller account of the Quietist controversy that surrounded this writer will be given in Chapter 7. J. H. Davies draws attention to the disparity between "the minimal place that [Guyon] accords the humanity of Christ and [. . .] her cult for childhood and her devotion to the Infant Jesus" (J. H. Davies, *Fénelon*, Boston, MA, Twayne Publishers, 1979).

[20] These are Book VII, chapters 13 and 14: "Que la très sacrée Vierge, Mère de Dieu mourut d'amour pour son Fils" ; and "Que la glorieuse Vierge mourut d'un amour extrêmement doux et tranquille" (*Traité de l'amour de Dieu*, pp. 702–9).

[21] "Je n'ai point d'autre vie que la vie de mon Fils, ma vie est toute en la sienne, et la sienne toute en la mienne ; car ce n'était plus union, ains unité de cœur, d'âme et de vie entre cette Mère et ce Fils" (*Traité de l'amour de Dieu*, p. 704).

[22] "[. . .] la virginité de Marie, la personne de son Fils unique, le secret de tout son mystère" (*Panégyrique de saint Joseph*, in *Œuvres*, 327–48, p. 330).

[23] "Jésus-Christ caché avec toute son humble famille, avec Marie et Joseph, qu'il associe à l'obscurité de sa vie, à cause qu'ils lui sont très chers" (*Panégyrique de saint Joseph*, in *Œuvres*, p. 347).

[24] In his *Vies des saints* (Paris, Sébastien Piquet, 1649–50), Bonnefons uses the phrases: "Lieutenant de Dieu le Père en la conduite de sa sainte famille"; and: "Il a joui des innocentes caresses de ce petit Sauveur" (I, 264). This work contains a hagiographic account of the saint to be honoured on each day of the year, often with a high degree of *pittoresque*, sometimes followed by extracts from their writings, and in all cases by three or four straightforwardly didactic moral reflections drawn from the saint's example.

was the most beautiful and the most perfect among men, it is possible to say that the face of St Joseph was delightful too."[25] But it is the Bishop-in-Exile of Geneva, St François de Sales (1567–1622),[26] who extrapolates imaginatively from the relationship, in an ecstatic apostrophe which forms part of the dedicatory prayer of his *Treatise on the Love of God*: "O great saint Joseph," he writes,

> well-loved Spouse of the Mother of the beloved, say, how many times did you carry the Love of Heaven and earth in your arms, while, consumed by the gentle embraces and kisses of this divine Child, your soul melted with delight when he gently spoke into your ears (O God, what bliss), that you were his great friend and his dearly beloved Father![27]

The sensual and indeed aesthetic implications of divine corporeality are thus starting to become explicit, and further parts of the physiology of the Incarnation are brought together in the terms of an oath of encouragement

[25] "Puisque selon le docte Gerson, la face de Jésus-Christ était semblable à saint Joseph, et comme celle de Jésus a été la plus belle et la plus parfaite qui a été parmi les hommes, on peut dire que celle de saint Joseph a été ravissante" (*Vies des saints*, I, p. 264). A counter-example, or at least a qualification, is afforded by the Père Surin who, when he believes himself to be damned, describes Christ in glory: "Here there is greatness and majesty, and authority beyond all measure, but no gentleness or touching and ravishing beauty, although there is always the beauty worthy of a God" ["Ici il y a grandeur et majesté, mais point de douceur ni beauté touchante et ravissante, combien qu'il y ait toujours beauté digne d'un Dieu"] (Jean-Joseph Surin, *Triomphe de l'amour divin sur les puissances de l'Enfer* et *Science expérimentale des choses de l'autre vie* (hereafter *Science expérimentale*), ed. Jacques Prunair, Grenoble, Jérôme Millon, 1990, p. 207). The second and third parts of *La Science expérimentale*, containing the core of the autobiography, were previously published in the *Lettres spirituelles*, ed. L. Michel and F. Cavallers, Toulouse, Éditions de la *Revue d'ascétique et de mystique*, 1928, vol. II, pp. 1–151. The first and fourth parts, as well as the *Triomphe de l'amour divin*, are devoted to the Loudun possessions and exorcisms. The title of the autobiography is probably best (if not most elegantly) translated, with due regard to the etymology of the key terms, as *The Empirical Understanding of the Things of the Life to Come*. I will look at it in more detail in Chapters 4 and 5.

[26] St François de Sales was Bishop-in-Exile of Geneva from 1602 until his death, and was notably active in attracting converts from Calvinism to Catholicism. The teaching of the Reformation had been officially adopted by the city-state of Geneva in 1536, and the Catholic diocese which bore its name was thereafter detached from it, with the bishop residing in Annecy. Further attention will be given to him at various points in the following chapters, but especially in Chapter 5. See the later chapter for a fuller bibliography.

[27] "Ô grand saint Joseph, Époux très aimé de la Mère du Bien-aimé, hé, combien de fois avez-vous porté l'Amour du Ciel et de la terre entre vos bras, tandis que, embrasé des doux embrassements et baisers de ce divin Enfant, votre âme fondait d'aise lorsqu'il prononçait tendrement à vos Oreilles (ô Dieu, quelle suavité!) que vous étiez son grand ami et son cher Père bien-aimé!" (*Traité de l'amour de Dieu*, in *Œuvres*, ed. Ravier and Devos, 320–972, p. 333). The translation of "suavité", a recurrent term in spiritual writings and especially in St François de Sales, is far from straightforward. The 1694 *Dictionnaire de l'Académie Française* gives the following definition (explicitly with respect to spiritual writing): "A certain sweetness that makes itself felt occasionally by the soul, when it is favoured by God" ["Une certaine douceur qui se fait quelquefois sentir à l'âme, quand Dieu la favorise"]. "Ecstasy" seems too strong. I have used "bliss" here, but I have not been consistent in so doing.

pronounced by François to his disciple in the last pages of the *Introduction to the Devout Life*:

> I urge you by everything that is sacred in Heaven and on earth, by the Baptism you have received, by the breasts that Jesus Christ suckled, by the charitable heart with which he loved you and by the entrails of his mercy in which you place your hope, to continue and persevere in this blessed undertaking.[28]

A less sentimental and more challenging view of Christ's childhood is offered by Fénelon, when he writes: "We would rather die with [Christ] in pain than see ourselves wrapped with him in the cradle. Infancy is more fearful than death, because death can be endured out of courage and fortitude";[29] and the same prelate is equally clinical about the Feast of the Circumcision:

> O Jesus, I worship you under the knife of the circumcision [. . .]. I see you covered in shame, placed in the ranks of sinners, subjected to a humiliating law, suffering acute pain and already shedding, from the early days of your childhood, the first drops of that blood which will be the price paid on the cross for the sake of the whole world.[30]

It is in the maturity of Christ, predictably, that we encounter the most overtly physical implications of the Redeemer's corporeality, often floating ambiguously between the metaphorical and the literal, the devotional and the erotic, not least since, as Pascal reminds his reader, Christianity is a religion which requires the shift from the intellectual to the affective domain: "How far it is from knowing God to loving God."[31]

By far the most common New Testament image used in the period in this respect is that of Christ's marriage to his Church, taken from Ephesians 5: 21–33. This is developed by Bossuet with respect to the reception of Holy Communion, in the *Prayers of the Church*, and then individualized into a relationship between the believer and the sacrament, as the communicant is exhorted to combine humility with ardour as he or she receives the host (and note the cognitive order of body, heart, and mind):

[28] "[Je] vous conjure par tout ce qui est sacré au Ciel et en la terre, par le Baptême que vous avez reçu, par les mamelles que Jésus-Christ suça, par le cœur charitable duquel il vous aima et par les entrailles de la miséricorde en laquelle vous espérez, continuez et persévérez en cette bienheureuse entreprise" (*Introduction à la vie dévote*, in *Œuvres*, ed. Ravier and Devos, 1-317, p. 317).

[29] "On aimerait mieux mourir avec lui dans les douleurs que de se voir avec lui emmailloté dans le berceau. La petitesse fait plus d'horreur que la mort, parce que la mort peut être soufferte par un principe de courage et de grandeur" (*Entretiens affectifs pour les principales fêtes de l'année*, III (*Pour le jour de Noël*), in *Œuvres* I, p. 933).

[30] "Ô Jésus, je vous adore sous le couteau de la circoncision [. . .]. Je vous vois tout couvert de honte, mis au rang des pécheurs, assujetti à une loi humiliante, souffrant de vives douleurs et répandant déjà, dès les premiers jours de votre enfance, les prémices de ce sang qui sera sur la croix le prix du monde entier" (*Entretiens affectifs pour les principales fêtes de l'année*, V (*Pour le jour de la circoncision*), in *Œuvres* I, p. 937).

[31] "Qu'il est loin de la connaissance de Dieu à l'aimer" (*Pensées*, L 377, S 409).

> This is the mystery of the union of the celestial spouse with his Church, his bride; it is here that he is united with her body to body, heart to heart, mind to mind, so as to become just a single thing with her; it is here [too] that he gives himself to the chaste souls who are his wives, to be possessed entirely by them, and here that he wants to possess them without reserve.[32]

The Blessed Sacrament in turn, in the same prelate's *Exposition of Catholic Doctrine*, is described, in a rare moment of zealous lyricism in an otherwise restrained text, as "this living and life-giving flesh, and this blood, still warm on account of its love, and full to the brim of the spirit and of grace".[33]

The exploitation of the metaphor of the Christic marriage is often conflated with the more explicitly erotic motif of the lover, as inaugurated in the opening verses of the Song of Songs, so introducing the exploitation of what Grace Jantzen calls "erotic mysticism" in the process.[34] This is once again glossed by St François de Sales in the *Treatise on the Love of God*, where he writes to its (male) dedicatee: "Have you not noticed, Théotime, that the holy Bride expresses her wish to be united with the Spouse by a kiss, and that the kiss represents the spiritual union which occurs by [means of] the reciprocal communication of [their] souls?"[35] The motif is then taken up in the same text at a point of spiritual climax, where the futility of speech between lovers is equated to mystical prayer: "The eyes speak to the eyes and the heart to the heart, and no-one hears what is said other than the holy lovers who are

[32] "C'est ici le mystère de l'union de l'Époux céleste avec son Église, son Épouse ; c'est ici qu'il s'unit à elle corps à corps, cœur à cœur, esprit à esprit, pour ne faire avec elle qu'une même chose ; où il se donne à posséder tout entier aux âmes chastes qui sont ses épouses, et où il veut les posséder sans réserve" (*Prières ecclésiastiques* (*L'Office de l'Église*), in *Œuvres complètes*, ed. Lachat, vol. V, 206–354, p. 336–7).

[33] "[. . .] cette chaire vivante et vivifiante, et ce sang encore chaud pour son amour et tout plein d'esprit et de grâce" (*Exposition de la doctrine catholique*, p. 78). The text is primarily addressed to Protestants, and is generally marked more by carefully calibrated exposition than by spiritual exuberance.

[34] "Let him kiss me with the kisses of his mouth, for your love-making is sweeter than wine; delicate is the fragrance of your perfume, your name is an oil poured out, and that is why girls love you" (Song of Songs 1: 1–3). Le Brun notes that "mystical writers explore a more interior reading, and find in the Bible, above all in the Song of Songs [. . .], the grounding for their experience" ["les spirituels poursuivent une lecture plus intérieure et trouvent dans la Bible, surtout dans le *Cantique des Cantiques* [. . .], le support de leur expérience"] (*Histoire*, p. 231). The editor of the *Jerusalem Bible* comments that "no book of the Old Testament has been subjected to more diverse interpretations" (p. 1027). Grace Jantzen (*Power, Gender and Christian Mysticism*, Cambridge, Cambridge University Press, 1995) writes: "The use of erotic language allows the language of passion and desire to become a part of Christian spirituality, and to see the longed-for vision with God in terms of ecstasy and even 'ravishing'" (p. 90).

[35] "N'avez-vous pas remarqué, Théotime, que l'Épouse sacrée exprime son souhait d'être unie avec l'Époux, par le baiser, et que le baiser représente l'union spirituelle qui se fait par la réciproque communication des âmes ?" (*Traité de l'amour de Dieu*, p. 380). This work repeatedly returns to a few salient quotations from the *Song of Songs*; and indeed provides a sustained analysis of the first verse in Book I, Chapter ix (p. 376–8).

speaking."[36] A similar composite analogy with physical love is taken up by Bossuet in his *Panegyric of St Teresa of Ávila* where, he writes, "the admirable Teresa, night and day, without any rest or respite, sighed for her divine Lover", leading to the apostrophe to Christ: "Chaste Lover, who have wounded her, why do you delay in taking her up to heaven, where she is carried by holy desires?"[37] As Jantzen writes: "One of the most influential themes in the history of Christian spirituality [is] the language and symbolism of erotic love as a way of speaking about the relationship of God and the soul [. . .], [which] allows the language of passion and desire to become a part of Christian spirituality."[38] A third focus, now once again from the New Testament, is afforded by the figure of St Mary of Magdala, of whom Fénelon in his reflection on her Feast Day writes of how he seeks, in a Johannine paraphrase, to follow Christ with her, "out of love, into the dust of the tomb".[39] But whereas such language might exist as a devotional focus for the Church at large, it was taken at a far more literal level by certain writers in the period; and the problems begin when it is in a sense de-universalized and applied exclusively to particular believers. The vexed question arises as to the degree to which this marriage is typological, metaphorical or individual, not least because the disciples of Christ in later ages also have bodies.[40]

What so far in St François de Sales, Bossuet and Fénelon is an imaginative development of imagic potential is often accorded a yet more intense intimacy, and at times literalness, in certain of François's disciples. In the autobiography of St Margaret Mary Alacoque (1647–90), visionary instigator of the Feast of the Sacred Heart of Jesus, the bridal image is first attributed to Christ in a prosopopœia which occurs at a vital juncture in her spiritual development:

[36] "Les yeux parlent aux yeux et le cœur au cœur, et nul n'entend ce qui se dit que les amants sacrés qui parlent" (*Traité de l'amour de Dieu*, p. 611).

[37] "[L'] admirable Thérèse, nuit et jour, sans aucun repos ni trêve, soupirait après son divin Époux [. . .]. Chaste Époux, qui l'avez blessée, que tardez-vous à la mettre au ciel, où elle s'élève par de saints désirs?" (*Panégyrique de sainte Thérèse*, in *Œuvres*, p. 404/6).

[38] *Power, Gender*, p. 90. Surin spells out the parallelism, writing (decorously as a priest) of how "I can easily see by conjecture that there is likely to be something of this delight between married people who, even by the regulated order of nature, and according to God's plan, enjoy such an intimate liaison and familiarity of heart, that nothing can better express those same links which exist between God and the soul" ["Je vois bien par conjecture qu'il y peut y avoir quelque chose de cette suavité entre les mariés, qui, par l'ordre de nature même réglée, et suivant le dessein de Dieu, ont une si intime liaison et familiarité de cœur, que rien ne peut mieux exprimer celle qui est entre Dieu et l'âme"] (*Science expérimentale*, p. 331).

[39] "Je voudrais, mon Sauveur, comme sainte Madeleine, vous suivre par amour jusques dans la poussière du tombeau" (*Entretiens affectifs pour les principales fêtes de l'année*, XVII (*Sur sainte Madeleine*), in *Œuvres*, I, p. 961).

[40] Thus Madame Guyon, defending herself against the accusation by Bossuet that she had abrogated to herself the title of the woman of the Apocalypse, asserts that "there is nothing in the Church in general that does not occur in part in particular souls" ["il n'y a rien dans l'Église générale qui ne se passe en partie dans l'âme particulière"] (Madame Guyon, *La Vie d'elle-même et autres écrits biographiques*, ed. Dominique Tronc, Paris, Champion, 2001, 9–879, p. 802–3).

"'I have chosen you as my bride'" she is told by him, with the conventional paradox that "'we promised to be faithful to each other, when you took your vow of chastity'";[41] and, shortly afterwards, Christ appears to her after Holy Communion, in accordance with a long tradition of women mystics, as "the most beautiful, the richest, the most powerful, the most perfect and the most accomplished of all lovers".[42] If she protests the disinterestedness of her love on a number of occasions thereafter, it is only to re-emphasize the intense physicality that defines it. One of the most powerful expressions of these two tendencies occurs at the end of the work, as she addresses Christ in response to his "abundance of caresses and spiritual pleasures" ["abondance de caresses et de plaisirs spirituels"] with the words: "O my only love, I sacrifice all these pleasures to you. Keep them for those holy souls who will glorify you better than I do, I who only want you alone, naked on the Cross, where I want to love you alone for the love of you alone. Take all the rest away from me, so that I can love you without contamination of self-interest or pleasure"[43] (and the maladroit expression is already present in the French). The imagined erotic potential is high, even if, as Jantzen writes, such passages illustrate how writers "used the language of passion, but forbade any actual physical [expression] in an effort to channel all desire away from the body and towards God".[44] She evokes in the same context – and this will find its echo in one possible interpretation of the Quietist dispute – "a highly charged erotic and bodily-based mysticism which males [. . .] often found disturbing and threatening".[45]

[41] "'Je t'ai choisie pour mon épouse et nous nous sommes promis la fidélité, lorsque tu m'as fait vœu de chasteté'" (*Vie de la bienheureuse Marguerite-Marie Alacoque écrite par elle-même*, in her *Vie et œuvres*, ed. François-Léon Gauthey, Paris, Ancienne Librairie Poussielgue, 1915, vol. II, 29–118, p. 45). The editor was Archbishop of Besançon.

[42] "[. . .] le plus beau, le plus riche, le plus puissant, le plus parfait et le plus accompli de tous les amants" (*Vie*, p. 46–7). As Caroline Walker Bynum points out, this is entirely in conformity with a long tradition of visions of Christ, usually by women, either in the chalice or in the host (*Holy Feast and Holy Fast: the Religious Significance of Food to Medieval Women*, Berkeley, University of California Press, 1987, p. 55. There also exists a French version, *Jeûnes et festins sacrés: les femmes et la nourriture dans la spiritualité médiévale*, Paris, Éditions du Cerf, 1994).

[43] "'Ô mon unique amour, je vous sacrifie tous ces plaisirs. Gardez-les pour ces âmes saintes qui vous en glorifieront plus que moi, qui ne veux que vous seul, tout nu sur la Croix, où je vous veux aimer vous seul pour l'amour de vous-même. Ôtez-moi donc tout le reste, afin que je vous aime sans mélange d'intérêt ni de plaisir'" (*Vie*, p. 116).

[44] *Power, Gender*, p. 90. Jeanne des Anges is also convinced that her devotion to Christ will free her from earthly temptations of carnality: "I implore you by your precious blood never to let me be attached to another than yourself, since it is to you alone that I am committed, and you alone who can satisfy me" ["Je vous conjure par votre précieux sang, de ne permettre jamais que je m'attache à autre qu'à vous, puisque vous êtes le seul à qui je me dois, et qui pouvez me contenter"] (Jeanne des Anges, *Relation* [*Autobiographie*], ed. G. Legué and G. de la Tourette, Grenoble, Jérôme Millon, 1990, p. 72). I shall look at the work in more detail in Chapter 5. See also that chapter for a more detailed account of the difficulties surrounding its editing and, as a result, its title.

[45] *Power, Gender*, p. 109.

Countering this, or potentially aggravating it, we might turn to the last stages of Christ's life on earth, where we find another privileged biblical episode that explores the physical reality of Christ's body in terms of the expression of human feelings in Bossuet's *Panegyric of St John the Apostle*. If this text is principally remarkable for its imaginative extrapolation from Scripture into a sustained meditation on the theology of love, it is also a powerful reminder of the physical relationship which occurs between men. In particular Bossuet dwells on the image of John being invited to embrace Christ at the Last Supper, again in accordance with a devotional *topos*, but accords it an intense and indeed homoerotic physicality. François, in the *Treatise on the love of God*, has already evoked John "on the chest of his Master [. . .], so that his head was inclined towards the breast of his dear Lover"[46] and, in the same text, its addressee Théotime is invited to say of Jesus: "I will live and die on his chest".[47] Fénelon too begins his meditation for the Feast of St John: "Oh Jesus, I want to rest with John on your chest and to feed myself with love by placing my heart against yours";[48] and the writer of the *Lives of the Saints* even extrapolates from the episode the likelihood that it is from the inspiration accorded to him on Christ's chest that John derived the material for his Gospel.[49]

Bossuet goes further again: "What shows [Christ's] love most strongly", he writes, "is the beautiful present that he gives [John] at the sacred banquet of the Eucharist, when [he] [. . .] takes him into his arms, draws him to his chest; and so [. . .] accords him possession [. . .] of his very heart, on which he orders him to take his repose, in a place that is his as of right".[50] And, shortly afterwards, John at the foot of the Cross is "seized by the sight of so much suffering and by the memory, still fresh, of so many recent caresses".[51] Less

[46] "[. . .] sur la poitrine de son Maître [. . .] en sorte que sa tête tendait vers le sein de son cher Amant" (*Traité de l'amour de Dieu*, p. 634). This immediately follows an evocation of Mary (of the Martha/Mary contrast in Luke 10: 41–2), whose part was to remain "in peace, in rest, in quietness beside her gentle Jesus" ["en paix, en repos, en quiétude auprès de son doux Jésus"].

[47] "Je vivrai et mourrai sur sa poitrine" (*Traité de l'amour de Dieu*, p. 690).

[48] "Ô Jésus, je désire me reposer avec Jean sur votre poitrine et me nourrir d'amour en mettant mon cœur sur le vôtre" (*Entretiens affectifs pour les principales fêtes de l'année* (*Pour le jour de saint Jean l'Évangéliste*), in *Œuvres*, I, p. 934).

[49] *Vies des saints*, II, p. 740.

[50] "[Ce] qui montre le plus son amour, c'est le beau présent qu'il lui fait au sacré banquet de l'Eucharistie, où il [. . .] le prend entre ses bras, il l'approche de sa poitrine ; et [. . .] il le met en possession de [. . .] son propre cœur, sur lequel il lui ordonne de se reposer comme sur une place qui lui est acquise" (*Panégyrique de saint Jean, apôtre*, in *Œuvres*, p. 415).

[51] "[. . .] saisi par la vue de tant de tourments et par la mémoire, encore toute fraîche, de tant de caresses récentes" (*Panégyrique de saint Jean, apôtre*, in *Œuvres*, p. 421). The Pléiade editor remarks in his notes, rather drily, that "neither St Matthew [. . .] nor St Mark [. . .] mentions this detail, probably imagined by the speaker" ["Ni saint Matthieu [. . .] ni saint Marc [. . .] ne font allusion à ce détail, imaginé probablement par l'orateur"] (*Œuvres*, p. 1389). More

erotically, but again expressing the physicality of Christ in the expression of a man, St François de Sales cites the example of the Blessed Elzéar de Sabran who, in reply to an enquiry from his wife as to his prolonged absence, gives her the reassurance: "'I am in very good health, my dear wife; and if you wish to see me, seek me in the wound in the side of our dear Jesus, for that is where I live and where you will find me; elsewhere your search will be fruitless'".[52] François comments, very simply: "This man was indeed a Christian knight!"[53]

The potential for erotic imagery is also present, *mutatis mutandis*, in Marian devotions, and its abuse is powerfully illustrated in turn in the parody of the *Salve Regina*[54] that, no doubt, was one of the fundamental reasons for the furore caused by Molière's iconoclastic comedy *Le Tartuffe* (1669). In the central seduction scene of this play, the religious impostor tries to seduce Elmire, the wife of his host, Orgon, by a variant on one of the most common prayers of Marian devotion. Having praised Elmire's superhuman charms and her spiritual conquest of the eponym, Tartuffe continues:

> And if you look with a little favour in your heart
> On the trials of your unworthy slave,
> If your goodness could bring me some consolation
> And deign to abase itself to my lowly state,
> Then I will always show you, O sweetest of paragons,
> A devotion that is without all precedent.[55]

That is shocking in itself; but what is of course even more shocking is the fact that the prayer could lend itself to this deformation, and that the miscreant could apply devotional language to seduction only because the Church had applied erotic language to devotion. What all these examples variously illustrate is the central dilemma, whereby Christianity grapples with the fact that

sympathetically, Le Brun suggests that Bossuet's attitude towards the crucified Christ is born of "a balance between physical tension, that is betrayed in the style, and theological reflection on the Passion" ["un équilibre entre la tension sensible, qui se traduit dans le style, et la réflexion théologique sur la Passion"] (*Spiritualité*, p. 153).

[52] "'Je me porte fort bien, ma chère femme ; que si vous me voulez voir, cherchez-moi en la plaie du côté de notre doux Jésus, car c'est là où j'habite et où vous me trouverez ; ailleurs, vous me chercherez pour néant'" (*Introduction à la vie dévote*, p. 98).

[53] "C'était un chevalier chrétien, celui-là !" (*Introduction à la vie dévote*, p. 98).

[54] Hail, holy Queen, Mother of mercy! Hail, our life, our sweetness and our hope. To thee do we cry, poor banished children of Eve; to thee do we send up our sighs, mourning and weeping in his vale of tears. Turn, then, most gracious advocate, thine eyes of mercy towards us; and after this our exile, show unto us the blessed fruit of thy womb, Jesus. O clement, O loving, O sweet Virgin Mary.

[55] "Que si vous contemplez d'une âme un peu bénigne / Les tribulations de votre esclave indigne, / S'il faut que vos bontés veuillent me consoler / Et jusqu'à mon néant daignent se ravaler, / J'aurai toujours pour vous, ô suave merveille, / Une dévotion à nulle autre pareille" (*Le Tartuffe*, III, 3, 973–4; 981–6). See the Introduction to my edition (Bristol Classical Press, 1994), p. xix–xx.

God, by becoming incarnate, had become as a result all that had first caused the experience of physical shame to afflict postlapsarian man and woman.

The last manifestations of Christ's physical presence on Earth serve more traditionally as a focus of devotion; and the manner of their actualization will lead us into a more explicitly imaginative, and more poetically structured domain. The mode of engagement is first of all spelt out in what is perhaps the most important devotional text of the period, the *Introduction to the Devout Life* (1609), in which St François de Sales advocates "proposing to one's imagination the body of the mystery on which one wants to meditate, as if it were really and actually happening in one's presence".[56] This is a direct paraphrase of the practice of the composition of mental places ["fabrication de lieux"] which serve to concentrate the faith of the believer on discrete aspects of the incarnational datum, as it was advocated by St Ignatius Loyola in the *Spiritual Exercises*.[57] It is predictably on the subject of the Passion and death of Jesus, in an exercise no doubt inspired by the same Ignatian practice, that the most powerful poetic expression occurs in the period,[58] albeit in a relatively little-known sonnet cycle: "Thus the Immortal one dies, and gives, by his death, death to death itself."[59]

The sonnets of the early seventeenth-century poet Jean de La Ceppède, *Les Théorèmes*, one of whose incipits I have just quoted, are centred on the account of the Passion, accompanied by a prose commentary, which succeeds in isolating, evoking, and engaging with precise moments in that event within an overall organizational framework.[60] The title of the work too, in accordance

[56] "[. . .] proposer à son imagination le corps du mystère que l'on veut méditer, comme s'il se passait réellement et de fait en notre présence" (*Introduction à la vie dévote*, p. 85).

[57] St Ignatius Loyola (1491–1556), founder of the Society of Jesus in 1540. His most important writing is the highly influential *Spiritual Exercises*, originally conceived of as a manual for retreat directors, which "provides for a structured, individually guided programme of mainly imaginative prayer" (*ODCC*). The description of the practice of composition of place occurs in the First Week, as the first preamble to the first exercise, in which "the 'composition' consists of seeing through the gaze of the imagination the material place where the object I want to contemplate is situated" (St Ignatius of Loyola, *Personal Writings*, trans. Joseph A. Munitiz and Philip Endean, London, Penguin Classics, 1996).

[58] Anne Mantero notes more generally that "for many poets, the Bible appears [. . .] as the corpus of writing which is above all capable of enlivening and renewing their art" ["à beaucoup de poètes, la Bible apparaît [. . .] comme le fonds capable par excellence de vivifier et renouveler leur art"] ("Récits bibliques et poésie religieuse", in *Le Grand Siècle et la Bible*, ed. Armogathe, 455–80, p. 455).

[59] This is more powerful again in French, because of the phonetic similarity, enhanced by repetition and alliteration, between the verb "mourir", the noun "mort", and the nominal adjective "Immortel": "Ainsi meurt l'Immortel, qui donne par sa mort / La mort à la mort même".

[60] Jean de La Ceppède (c. 1548–1623), *Les Théorèmes sur le sacré mystère de notre rédemption*, ed. Jacqueline Plantié, Paris, Champion, 1996. On the poetry of La Ceppède, see Terence C. Cave, *Devotional Poetry in France c. 1570–1613*, Cambridge, Cambridge University Press, 1969 and P. A. Chilton, *The Poetry of Jean de La Ceppède*, Oxford, Oxford University Press, 1977. The incipit is from *Les Théorèmes* I, 3, sonnet 86. The first three books, dealing with the Passion, date

with its purposes, recalls the Greek etymology of the verb *theorein*, to be a spectator of, to contemplate something. By means of his subject, therefore, La Ceppède deals with a broad range of Christian *topoi*, although each sonnet has a clear and relatively precise angle of focus, with the poet homing in on a detail, a text or a motif which concentrates his meditation. Terence Cave describes how "the richness of the *Théorèmes* is due in part to the ever-present physical plane of reference [. . .]; but it is inconceivable without the special function of the sonnet in concentrating attention on each point".[61] The whole is intensely Christocentric; but it is often a specific material feature that is isolated as a focusing device, to which La Ceppède accords a meditational capacity, thereby developing the incarnational dimension present within the natural context of the account. The *Ecce homo*, for example, is explicitly evoked in the opening of "BEHOLD THE MAN, O my eyes, what a pitiable object!",[62] a sonnet which pays detailed attention to the brutality of the Crucifixion, although what emerges in implicit contrast is once again a physically beautiful Christ, so that the hair is parenthetically described as "the ornament of his venerable head", the eyes more explicitly again as "formerly so beautiful" and the previous colour of the mouth "like coral" and skin "like roses and lilies". A further sonnet, beginning with the double exclamation: "O tragic Royalty! O despicable garment!"[63] again pulls strongly away from any kind of abstraction, but also from any kind of periphrasis or indeed decorum, as two of the liquids evoked in the Passion narratives, Christ's blood and the spittle of his persecutors, mingle in the climactic couplet:

> This pure blood, this nectar, is profanely mixed
> With your filthy spittle, whose bloody border
> Changes this beautiful face into that of a leper.

from 1613; in the next four, dating from 1622, the poet turns his attention to the descent into Hell, the Resurrection appearances, the Ascension and Pentecost. I will quote the French text in full of the small number of poems I use.

61 *Devotional Poetry in France*, p. 242.

62 "VOICI L'HOMME, ô mes yeux, quel objet déplorable: / La honte, le veiller, la faute d'aliment, / Les douleurs, et le sang perdu si largement / L'ont bien tant déformé qu'il n'est plus désirable. // Ces cheveux (ornement de son chef vénérable) / Sanglantés, hérissés, par ce couronnement, / Embrouillés dans ces joncs, servent indignement : / A son test ulcéré d'une haie exécrable. // Ces yeux (tantôt si beaux) rebattus, renfoncés, / Ressalis, sont, hélas ! deux Soleils éclipsés, / Le coral de sa bouche est ores jaune pâle. // Les roses, et les lis de son teint sont flétris. / Le reste de son Corps est la couleur d'Opale, / Tant de la tête aux pieds ses membres sont meurtris" (*Les Théorèmes* I, 2, sonnet 70).

63 "Ô Royauté tragique ! ô vêtement infâme ! / Ô poignant Diadème ! ô Sceptre rigoureux ! / Ô belle et chère tête ! ô l'amour de mon âme ! / Ô mon Christ seul fidèle, et parfait amoureux ! // On vous frappe, ô saint chef, et ces coups douloureux / Font que votre Couronne en cent lieux vous r'entame. / Bourreaux, assénez-le d'une tranchante lame, / Et versez tout à coup ce pourpre généreux. // Faut-il pour une mort qu'il en souffre dix mille ? / Hé ! voyez que le sang, qui de son chef distille / Ses prunelles détrempe, et rend leur jour affreux. // Ce pur sang, ce Nectar, profané se mélange / A vos sales crachats, dont la sanglante frange / Change ce beau visage en celui d'un lépreux" (*Les Théorèmes* I, 2, sonnet 67).

In certain pieces the persona of the poet is more closely integrated at an early stage, effecting thereby a devotional link with the moment of composition, such as in the sonnet which opens: "The red coat of armour worn by triumphant Kings".[64] The last tercet here is an apostrophe of Christ; but the two intermediate stanzas take the far more unexpected form of an apostrophe of the colour purple: "O purple, fill my head with your precious liquid", allowing in turn the now specifically evoked poet to weep blood over his own creation, "So that [. . .] / With blood flowing from my eyes I stain my sonnet red". This play of associations, with the two colours identifying the coat of Christ and the sin of the poet, is finally resolved in a climactic two-line conceit, whereby the poet appeals to Christ to "hide / All my scarlet sins, like sparks from hell / In the bloody folds of the cloak of your flesh". A sustained play on colour association thus further contrives to accord a violent and highly pictorial imaginative potential to a single feature of the Gospel narrative. This is enhanced by the implicit reference to the sense of sight made by an appeal to the liturgical colours of purple, the colour of repentance, and scarlet, the colour of martyrdom.[65] Yet, as Cave writes, "La Ceppède's main task is not to produce poetic effects; he is concerned with transposing into verse a meditation on the Passion."[66] What is thereby made explicit is the degree to which the physicality of the Incarnation demands an equivalent physicality in the response of the incarnate believer. The reader is invited to imagine the episode portrayed, but then as well, and once again in the Ignatian spirit, to adjust his life, conduct, and spirituality as a result of this imaginative visualization. As Bossuet explains in the *Panegyric of St Francis of Assisi*, describing such a transformation by means of a composite metaphor: "Thus the faithful soul experiences wonderful transports in contemplating our crucified Master. This precious blood, that streams out on all sides from his

[64] "Aux Monarques vainqueurs la rouge cotte d'armes / Appartient justement. Ce Roi victorieux / Est justement vêtu par ces moqueurs Gens d'armes / D'un manteau, qui le marque et Prince, et glorieux. // Ô pourpre, emplis mon test de ton jus précieux / Et lui fais distiller mille pourprines larmes, / A tant que méditant ton sens mystérieux, / Du sang trait de mes yeux j'ensanglante ces Carmes. // Ta sanglante couleur figure nos péchés / Au dos de cet Agneau par le Père attachés / Et ce Christ t'endossant se charge de nos crimes. // Ô Christ, ô saint Agneau, daigne-toi de cacher / Tous mes rouges péchés (brindilles des abîmes) / Dans les sanglants replis du manteau de ma chair" (*Les Théorèmes* I, 2, sonnet 63).

[65] The precise liturgical use of colour has changed in recent times. The Tridentine Missal specifies purple ["pourpre"] for Passion [Palm] Sunday and the *Missale Parisiense* of 1684 orders black throughout Holy Week. Red was used from the Vigil of Pentecost until Corpus Christi ["La Fête-Dieu"]. I am grateful to the Rev. John Hunwicke for pointing out this detail.

[66] *Devotional Poetry in France*, p. 297. Mantero considers La Ceppède to have created "a veritable *summa* of poetic writing on the Passion [. . .]. His plurality of religious points of view is combined with a range of aesthetic means, unified by the vigour of his language" ["une véritable somme de l'écriture poétique sur la Passion [. . .]. La pluralité des points de vue religieux se combine avec la variété des moyens esthétiques qu'unifie une langue vigoureuse"] ("Récits bibliques", in *Le Grand Siècle et la Bible*, ed. Armogathe, p. 471).

cruelly torn veins, becomes for it like a river of flame, which burns it with an invincible ardour to be consumed on [Christ's] behalf."[67]

It is St Margaret Mary, however, who once again drives the desire for a physical association with the Passion to disconcertingly literal limits, now in an appeal to the sense of taste, as she recounts Christ's wish for her, "[that] I would no longer taste any other sweetness than in the bitterness of Calvary".[68] "I was so squeamish", she goes on,

> that the least dirtiness gave me palpitations. He [Christ] reproached me so strongly with this that once, when I wanted to clean up the vomit of a sick woman, I could not prevent myself from doing so with my tongue, and from eating it, while saying to him: "If I had a thousand bodies, a thousand lovers, a thousand lives, I would give them all up in order to be subjugated to you."[69]

The link between this action and the devotion to the Sacred Heart then becomes apparent when Margaret Mary records how Christ "held me for about two or three hours with my mouth glued to the wound of his sacred Heart".[70] But such a physical understanding of devotion to the wounds of Christ, as Caroline Walker Bynum has convincingly demonstrated in *Holy Feast and Holy Fast*, lies entirely within a medieval tradition whereby "the flesh of Jesus – both flesh as body and flesh as food – is at the very centre of female piety".[71] In addition, Margaret Mary seeks to reproduce the experience of the scourging (without specifically identifying it as such) when she writes:

> I bound my miserable criminal body with knotted ropes, and drew them so tight that it could hardly breathe or eat, and I left the ropes so long in place that it was as if they were embedded in my flesh, so that when it started to grow over them, I could only tear them off with great violence and cruel pain.[72]

[67] "[C]'est ici où l'âme fidèle ressent de merveilleux transports dans la contemplation de notre Maître crucifié. Ce sang précieux, qui ruisselle de toutes parts de ses veines cruellement déchirées, devient pour elle comme un fleuve de flammes, qui l'embrase d'une ardeur invincible de se consumer pour lui" (*Panégyrique de saint François d'Assise*, in *Œuvres*, 235–58, p. 251).

[68] "'[que] je ne goûterais plus aucune douceur que dans les amertumes du Calvaire'" (*Vie*, p. 100).

[69] "J'étais si fort douillette que la moindre saleté me faisait bondir le cœur. Il [Christ] me reprit si fortement là-dessus qu'une fois, voulant nettoyer le vomissement d'une malade, je ne pus me défendre de le faire avec ma langue et de le manger, en lui disant : 'Si j'avais mille corps, mille amours, mille vies, je les immolerais pour vous être asservie'" (*Vie*, p. 82). Earlier editors tend to shy away from Margaret Mary's more extreme practices, thus the Bishop of Soissons (1853) admits to his distaste for "these pious excesses" ["ces pieux excès"], and to having suppressed certain details out of respect for "the readers' sensibilities" ["la délicatesse des lecteurs"]. There are however both more recent occurrences and more distant precedents.

[70] "Il me tint bien environ deux ou trois heures la bouche collée sur la plaie de son sacré Cœur" (*Vie*, p. 82).

[71] *Holy Feast and Holy Fast*, p. 245.

[72] "Je liais ce misérable corps criminel de cordes avec des nœuds, et le serrais si fort, qu'à peine pouvait-il respirer et manger, et laissais si longtemps les cordes, qu'elles étaient comme tout enfoncées dans la chair, laquelle venait à croître dessus, je ne pouvais les arracher qu'avec de grandes violences et cruelles douleurs" (*Vie*, p. 41).

The autobiographical accounts of other figures whose lives sought to emulate that of Christ *au pied de la lettre* equally, and predictably, contain extensive and detailed episodes of mortification. Thus Sœur Jeanne des Anges (1602–65) also engages in repeated scourging (which then heals miraculously, as is the case for Madame Guyon), wears a spiked belt and hair-shirt, throws herself naked onto embers or ice (in winter) or into beds of brambles or stinging-nettles (in summer), and sprinkles wormwood and gall on her food.

As if to offer some relief from this brutality, the post-resurrection appearances are portrayed with a typical combination of the commonplace and the transcendent by St François de Sales in an exquisite passage, once again tellingly introduced by the imperative: "Let us imagine" ["Représentons-nous"]: "After three days, on account of his most holy Resurrection, his soul was re-clothed in his glorious body, and the body in his immortal skin", he writes, "and it was covered in different garments, either in those of a pilgrim, or of a gardener, or of another kind again, as the salvation of mankind and the glory of his Father required."[73]

The next imaginative reaction to the Incarnation, seen diachronically, is attributed to those who came immediately in its wake, as it is expressed in other words in the Christians of the first centuries; and once more we move through a theological *topos* to its literary amplification. In the *Panegyric of St Francis of Assisi*, Bossuet examines and explores systematically four possible attitudes to the Incarnation in terms of four groups of reactions in the earliest Christian times, in an amplified periphrasis of 1 Corinthians: the Jews, who saw in it a "stumbling-block" (*scandalum*), and the Gentiles an example of "folly"; heretics, such as Manicheans, who only managed to "believe things by halves"; and finally "the faithful": "They took care not to believe things by halves, nor to blush at the ignominy of their Master. They were not afraid to make both the scandal and the folly of the Cross resonate throughout the world in all their extent: they predicted to the Gentiles that this folly would destroy their wisdom".[74]

It is to one particularly fertile dramatic genre in the period, the martyr tragedy, that I want next to turn, in order to see how one of the most famous examples underscores the specificity of the Christian Incarnation by exploiting the opportunity for its dramatic effect. In Jean Rotrou's play on the martyrdom of the actor St Genesius [*Le Véritable Saint-Genest*][75] we find the *topoi* of

[73] "[Trois] jours passés, par sa très sainte Résurrection, l'âme se revêtit de son corps glorieux, et le corps de sa peau immortelle, et s'habilla de vêtements différents, ou en pèlerin, ou en jardinier, ou d'autre sorte, selon que le salut des hommes et la gloire de son Père le requérait" (*Traité de l'amour de Dieu*, p. 804).

[74] "Ils se sont bien gardés de croire les choses à demi, ni de rougir de l'ignominie de leur Maître. Ils n'ont pas craint de faire éclater par toute la terre le scandale et la folie de la croix dans toute leur étendue : ils ont prédit aux Gentils que cette folie détruirait leur sagesse" (*Panégyrique de saint François d'Assise*, in *Œuvres*, 235–58, p. 236). The text is a paraphrase of 1 Corinthians 1 : 22–4.

[75] Jean Rotrou (1609–50), *Le Véritable Saint-Genest*, ed. José Sanchez, Le-Mont-du-Marsan, Éditions José Feijóo, 1991. For a general study, see J. Morel, *Rotrou, dramaturge de l'ambiguïté*,

the acts of human Redemption placed into a starkly fresh perspective in two ways. First, perhaps because of the greater freedom allowed by the double illusion of the actor coming to believe the part that he is playing, Genesius's lines resonate devotionally far more intensely than in some other dramatists of the period. Secondly, because of the attribution to both believers and non-believers of the early Christian centuries of statements respectively of neophyte wonder and outright insult, which achieve as a result a particular quality of objectivity and thereby of reinvigoration.

The play narrates the enactment of a martyrdom performed for the emperor Diocletian by Genesius [Genest] in the role of Adrian, during which simulation the actor progressively adopts the values of the persona he is playing. This allows first of all for a simply but sharply expressed metonymic reference to Christ by the actor himself, as he embarks within his role on a poignant extended metaphor of the Crucifixion:

> 'My blood is ill at ease in my veins;
> It burns to water this precious tree,
> From which the most cherished fruit of the heavens is hanging for us.'[76]

But it is by combining the two dimensions of the Incarnation and Redemption that the play affords on several occasions succinct expressions of discrete elements of Christian dogma, which are thereby accorded a maximum impact by virtue of their dramatically imposed brevity (and the economy of the alexandrine verse form once again has its part to play): thus we find Adrian describing the Nativity in terms of '"Christ, who, man and God, was born in a stable"'; or the Crucifixion, evoking "' [...] a glorious tree / That was less a cross than a ladder to heaven'"; the role of Mary, relative to Eve, whereby "This sex, that closed them, then re-opened the heavens"; or the messenger Flavie's incredulous evocation of the entombment, in the vertiginous: "'The author of the universe goes into a coffin'".[77] But it is above all in a major outburst (vitally, for its dramatic impact, attributed to the unbeliever Marcele), that the explicit awareness of the sheer strangeness of the Christian revelation occurs, as she mockingly enumerates the features of the improbability of a humbled God, in a magnificently spiteful sequence:

Paris, Colin, 1968. See also Paul Scott, "Rotrou et la comédie de dévotion", in *Littératures classiques*, 63 (2007), pp. 85–96.

[76] "' [...] Mon sang se déplaît dans mes veines; / Qu'il brûle d'arroser cet arbre précieux, / Où pend pour nous le fruit le plus chéri des cieux'" (*Le Véritable Saint-Genest*, II, 7, 520–2). I shall use double plus single quote marks to indicate the role-playing within the persona.

[77] "'Christ, qui homme et Dieu, naquit dans une étable'" (*Le Véritable Saint-Genest*, II, 8, 608); "' [...] un bois glorieux / Qui fut moins une croix qu'une échelle aux cieux'" (II, 8, 593–4); "'Ce sexe qui ferma, rouvrit depuis les cieux'" (an alexandrine that is particularly resistant to concise translation) (IV, 3, 1097); '"L'auteur de l'univers entre dans un cercueil'" (II, 8, 597).

O ridiculous error! to boast of the power
Of a God, who gives, to his own, death as their reward!
Of an impostor, a trickster, a crucified man!
Who put him in the heavens? Who deified him?
A bunch of ignorant and useless men[;]
Down-and-outs, the dregs and scum of the cities.[78]

Such passages constitute a virtual summary of Christian doctrine in its most compressed and shocking form, powerfully severe in their stylistic devices, and yet ironically capable in their uncomprehending economy of transmitting a high degree of dogmatic precision, as they dramatically identify the contrast between the intrinsic majesty and the actual indignity of the murdered incarnate Creator.

I want to turn in the remainder of this chapter to a less emotive and yet empirically far more enduring aspect of Christic physicality. One of the unique features of Catholic Christianity is the degree to which the Incarnation is perpetuated in the physical domain by the material, spatial, and temporal specifics of Christian practice: with reference to sacraments and sacramentals; with reference to relics and the cult of saints; and with reference to the Church's year. The fact that Christ was fully man, and that his contemporaries and disciples were, equally, identifiable individual human beings, accords to the material world a vital importance in the enactment of the faith in future generations, lived out as it will be by other individual human beings within their own bodies, and in their own places and times.

The sacraments are the most tangible signs of Christian dogma; and, in the spiritual experience of the majority, the most frequent manifestation of the physicality of the Incarnation lies in their reception. The three that dominate the lives of the Catholic faithful in the period are Baptism, Penance, and above all the Eucharist;[79] and these are accompanied by the more minor but equally physical dimensions of the Church's practice in the form of sacramentals.[80] More modestly again, even the place for gesture is acknowledged in Christian texts: thus, in this simple perspective, the physical object of the crucifix takes on a particular poignancy in the *Funeral Oration of Henriette d'Angleterre*, the gradual stages of whose demise are minutely recorded, and who dies after venerating

[78] "Ô ridicule erreur! de vanter la puissance / D'un Dieu, qui donne aux siens la mort pour récompense! / D'un imposteur, d'un fourbe, et d'un crucifié! / Qui l'a mis dans le ciel? qui l'a déifié? / Un nombre d'ignorants, et de gens inutiles? / De malheureux, la lie et l'opprobre des villes?" (*Le Véritable Saint-Genest*, V, 2, 1495–1500).

[79] The remaining four, in Catholic teaching, are Confirmation, Orders, Matrimony, and Extreme Unction.

[80] The term includes such material supports to the faithful as holy water, signs of the cross, and the blessing of physical objects.

the Cross, at which point Bossuet exclaims: "Is that not to die in the very arms and embrace of the Lord?"[81]

By far the most controversial sacrament in terms of intra-Christian disputes is, however, the Holy Eucharist;[82] and, within that confessional disagreement, arguments prevail over the exact nature of the sacramental transformation that occurs, and over the status of the Mass as sacrifice or commemoration. The text in which the issues are most clearly and patiently aired from a Catholic perspective in the period is the *Exposition of Catholic Doctrine*, written by Bossuet as a brief introduction for believers in the Reformed tradition.[83] What we initially notice in this work however, in accord with the emphases of this chapter, is how in his treatment of Jesus, Mary and the Saints we are made aware of the degree to which, far from being a distant abstraction, they are transformed, by the existence of sacraments, holy objects, and relics, into a literally tangible presence. Entirely consistent with this physicality, there is then a substantial defence of Catholic teaching on the Real Presence, opening with the superficially attractive debating point, whereby it is those who do not understand things literally who have a greater responsibility to account for their interpretations than those who do.[84] What follows is strongly grounded in Jewish law, both in terms of continuity and contrast, making of the Christic injunction ("Take this, all of you, and eat it: this is my body") a means to "accomplish ancient prefigurations".[85] This is reinforced first of all by the lack of any ensuing explanation by Christ, in distinction to his other (figurative) utterances; and by an acknowledgement of the freedom of God the creator to disrupt the accepted relationship between signifier and signified.

It is in the more specifically intra-Catholic *Meaux Catechism* that the strangeness of the transformation is best (because most succinctly) encapsulated, as the catechist explains how the bread and wine retain respectively their "whiteness,

[81] "N'est-ce pas mourir entre les bras et dans le baiser du Seigneur ?" (*Oraison funèbre de Henriette-Anne d'Angleterre*, in *Œuvres*, p. 104).

[82] The Eucharist was also the object of a new devotional zeal as a manifestation of the Catholic Reformation, thus for example the introduction of the *Quarant'Ore*, a forty-hour devotion during which the Blessed Sacrament is exposed on the altar, based on the period of time during which Christ's body remained in the tomb. It was promoted from 1593 by the Capuchins in honour of the Eucharist. See Krumenacker, *L'École française*, p. 48.

[83] The full title is *Exposition de la doctrine de l'Église catholique sur les matières de controverse*. It appeared in 1671, and is included in the *Œuvres complètes*, ed. Lachat, vol. XIII, pp. 51–105.

[84] Compare Arnauld and Nicole's *La Logique ou l'art de penser* (the so-called *Logique de Port-Royal*) of 1662, I, xv, which is largely concerned with "ideas that are stimulated and ideas that are precisely signified" ["les idées excitées et les idées précisément signifiées"]; and in which, it is claimed, it is the latter which are conveyed by the deictic pronoun *hoc* with regard to the erroneous, because non-literal, interpretation of Christ's words at the Last Supper. Pascal (or at least a first-person utterance in the *Pensées*) is more impatient: "How I hate these idiocies, of not believing the Eucharist, etc. / If the Gospel is true, if Jesus Christ is God, wherein lies the difficulty?" ["Que je hais ces sottises, de ne pas croire l'Eucharistie, etc. / Si l'Évangile est vrai, si Jésus-Christ est Dieu, quelle difficulté y a-t-il là?"] (*Pensées*, L 168, S 199).

[85] "[...] accomplir les figures anciennes" (*Exposition*, p. 75).

roundness, and taste" and "colour, wetness, and taste",[86] while containing in each crumb and drop "the entire person of Jesus Christ [. . .], that is to say a perfect God and a perfect man".[87] The extraordinary disparity which is thereby evoked between object and meaning, against any conventional understanding, is thus enhanced; and the stark simplicity of the equivalence serves paradoxically to underscore the immensity of the *sacramentum* or mystery. Appropriate instructions for behaviour at all points of the liturgy are then provided, with a climactic injunction at the elevation of the host: "While the adorable body and the chalice of the precious blood are elevated, it is better to look on in silence and with a profound humility and just say in one's heart: 'I believe, Lord, I believe: strengthen my faith, change my life: live in me, and I in you.'"[88] In a similar way, in the *Prayers of the Church*, Bossuet offers a series of reflections on the Eucharistic species, equating in a lyrical analogy the materiality of the bread and wine with the physicality of Christ's death:

> Just as it was necessary, in order to make the bread, that the wheat was crushed and ground; and, in order to make the wine, that the grapes were pressed so as to give up all their juice; so in order for Jesus Christ to be our food and our support, it was necessary that in his Passion he underwent the ultimate ordeal, and that he shed all his blood for us.[89]

The Jesuit priest at the centre of the Loudun possessions, Père Jean-Joseph Surin (1600–65), characteristically takes Eucharistic literalism to dangerous limits, even if, equally consistently, he reasserts orthodox teaching in what follows: "I think I can say without error", he writes, "that, although it is contrary to scholastics and philosophers, my tongue feels God and tastes God; as it tastes muscat, or apricot, or melon, so it tasted a being, who is evidently none other than God."[90] He then recovers somewhat and qualifies his experience: "I am not saying that the flesh feels this as flesh, but I am saying: by the taste of the flesh I arrive at the notion of a being who is the happiness of every being and who is my

[86] "[. . .] la blancheur, la rondeur et le goût"; "[. . .] la couleur, l'humidité et le goût" (*Catéchisme de Meaux*, in *Œuvres complètes*, ed. Lachat, vol. V, i–xvi and 1.138, p. 125). See on the whole activity of catechetics J.-C. Dhôtel, *Les Origines du catéchisme moderne*, Paris, P. Aubier, 1967.

[87] "[. . .] la personne entière de Jésus-Christ [. . .], c'est-à-dire un Dieu parfait et un homme parfait" (*Catéchisme de Meaux*, p. 125–6).

[88] "Pendant qu'on élève le corps adorable et le calice du sang précieux, c'est mieux fait de regarder en silence et avec une profonde humilité en disant seulement du cœur : 'Je crois, Seigneur, je crois : fortifiez ma foi, changez-moi : vivez en moi, et moi en vous'" (*Prières ecclésiastiques*, p. 229).

[89] "Comme il a fallu pour faire du pain que le blé fût broyé et froissé ; et pour faire du vin, que le raisin sous le pressoir rendît toute sa liqueur ; ainsi, afin que Jésus-Christ fût notre nourriture et notre soutien, il a fallu qu'il souffrît dans sa passion les dernières violences, et qu'il y répandît tout son sang" (*Prières ecclésiastiques*, p. 224).

[90] "[Je] crois le pouvoir dire sans erreur quoique cela soit fort contraire aux scolastiques et philosophes, que ma langue sent Dieu et goûte Dieu ; comme elle goûte le muscat, et l'abricot, et le melon, ainsi elle goûtait un être, qui évidemment n'est autre que Dieu" (*Science expérimentale*, p. 277).

God."[91] Complementarily, he attributes to diabolic possession his transitional shift to the Calvinist conviction whereby "one received him [Christ] really by faith, although his body was not in the host that one had in front of one's eyes".[92]

What Bossuet, or even Surin, write about the Eucharistic sacrament is on occasion striking, but is essentially conventional in both its teaching and its formulations. It is once again Pascal who imposes some distance on this familiarity as he resumes, with characteristic exclusiveness, the unique status of Christianity relative to the bodily actions of the believer: "Only the Christian religion", he writes, "is proportionate to all, being a mixture of the external and the internal";[93] and elsewhere he goes on to draw out the ironic potential of this teaching:

> The external has to be joined to the internal to find favour with God, in other words you must get down on your knees, pray with your lips etc., so that the proud man who was unwilling to submit to God must now submit to his creatureliness. It is superstitious to expect help from these externals. It is arrogant not to be willing to join them to the internal.[94]

And he then adds, in the devotional fragment known as the *Mystère de Jésus*: "External acts of penitence dispose you to internal penitence, just as humiliations dispose you to humility."[95]

This thinking is nowhere more powerfully expressed in the *Pensées* than in what is sometimes known as the "automaton fragment", which begins: "For we should not be deceived about ourselves, we are automata as much as we are minds."[96] In this most radical of statements, Pascal stresses how the Christian religion is uniquely endowed with the capacity to take all that is most unthinkingly mechanistic in humankind and to turn it to the service of God. But such terminology was not Pascal's. What it rather reflects is one of the

[91] "[Je] ne dis pas que la chair sente cela comme chair, mais je dis : par le goût de la chair je viens à une notion d'un être qui est le bonheur de tout être et qui est mon Dieu" (*Science expérimentale*, p. 277).

[92] "[on] le recevait réellement par foi, quoique son corps ne fût pas dans l'hostie que l'on avait devant les yeux" (*Science expérimentale*, p. 189).

[93] "La seule religion chrétienne est proportionnée à tous, étant mêlée d'extérieur et d'intérieur" (*Pensées*, L 219, S 252).

[94] "Il faut que l'extérieur soit joint à l'intérieur pour obtenir de Dieu, c'est-à-dire que l'on se mette à genoux, prie des lèvres, etc., afin que l'homme orgueilleux qui n'a voulu se soumettre à Dieu soit maintenant soumis à la créature. Attendre de cet extérieur le secours est être superstitieux. Ne vouloir pas le joindre à l'intérieur est être superbe" (*Pensées*, L 944, S 767).

[95] "Les pénitences extérieures disposent à l'intérieure, comme les humiliations à l'humilité" (*Pensées*, L 919, S 751). There is also a fragmentary distinction made between piety and superstition in L 181, S 212, which also cryptically relates to the question of disputes over transubstantiation.

[96] "Car il ne faut pas se méconnaître : nous sommes automate autant qu'esprit" (*Pensées*, L 821, S 661).

major legacies of Cartesian dualism to writers later in the century and beyond, in understanding the body as a machine, as an automaton in other words, entirely distinct from the mind as *res cogitans*.[97] Yet Pascal does not, as one might have expected, see this separation as a spiritual downgrading of human corporeality (in a potential adumbration of atheistic materialism); rather he shows, by an explicit appeal to the physicality of sacramental theology, how it must be acknowledged and harnessed in the process of acquiring and maintaining belief, and so play its part in the progress towards human sanctification. Pascal notoriously wrote that Descartes was "useless and uncertain"[98]; and yet it is in his own christianization of Cartesian dualism that he reaffirms how the physical materiality of the human body is enabled to draw spiritual nourishment from the physical materiality of the divine body of Christ. In so doing he unites, via the language of his age, the corporeal and the spiritual, allowing as it does for the initial assent, but not the reiterated engagement, of an intellectual dimension.

As I noted in the last chapter, Pascal controversially sees this in the wager fragment as a way for some unbelievers to move towards belief, suggesting that sacramentals, such as the taking of holy water, and objective spiritual benefits, such as Mass intentions, might initiate a process of conversion, and so enable the unbeliever to make a physical start on a spiritual journey.[99] But he is also proposing in his writing in the automaton fragment that these same sacramental mechanisms accord to Christian dogma a means of enacting a belief that has already been acquired, and of doing so without the need for perpetual intellectual re-evaluation (and this once again is in distinction to solely metaphysical proofs ["preuves métaphysiques"], as he dismissively calls the philosophical arguments for the existence of God). "We must acquire an easier conviction", the apologist writes,

> which is that born of habit, which without violence, without artifice, without argument makes us believe things and inclines all our powers to that belief, so that our soul naturally falls into it. If we only believe by the force of conviction, and the automaton is inclined to believe the opposite, then that is insufficient.[100]

[97] The *Discours de la méthode* (1637) is the intellectual autobiography of René Descartes (1596–1650). A fuller account of his philosophy is given a decade later in the *Metaphysical Meditations* [*Méditations métaphysiques*]. In both works, the essential distinction between mind and body, referred to by the shorthand of Cartesian dualism, is a fundamental symptom of his enquiry.

[98] "Descartes inutile et incertain" (*Pensées*, L 887, S 445). Various other fragments, of more or less dubious provenance, are equally disparaging.

[99] See Richard Parish, "Automate et sacrement: figures de l'Incarnation", in *Religion et politique: les avatars de l'augustinisme*, Saint-Étienne, Université de Saint-Étienne, 1998, pp. 333–9.

[100] "Il faut acquérir une créance plus facile, qui est celle de l'habitude, qui sans violence, sans art, sans argument, nous fait croire les choses et incline toutes nos puissances à cette croyance, en sorte que notre âme y tombe naturellement. Quand on ne croit que par la force de la conviction, et que l'automate est incliné à croire le contraire, ce n'est pas assez" (*Pensées*, L 821, S 661).

The objective efficacy of sacraments, on condition that the correct disposition prevails in the recipient, and of sacramentals, where the criterion is more objective again, is predictably a constant in the theory and practice of the faith in the period. At the same time, the awareness of their supernatural power, performed, in the Church's terminology, *ex opere operato*, as of the status of perseverance in devout activities, accords to both an objective efficacy in the achievement of that progress; and it is, paradoxically, the dualist metaphysics of Descartes, assimilated to his own purposes by Pascal in this exceptional fragment, which renews that understanding. If the Word is made flesh, then *ipso facto*, albeit with a change of terminology, the spirit can be channelled through the materiality of the newly described Cartesian automaton.

The physical also relates to space and time. It is in this light that the relics of Saints play a central role, notably in Bossuet's panegyrics; and the universality of the principle that lies behind them is first established in the *Panegyric of St Joseph*:

> It is a received opinion, and a common sentiment among all men, that the remains [of a Saint] have something that is holy, and that we should conserve it on behalf of those who entrust it to us, not only out of fidelity but also with a sort of religious devotion.[101]

More precisely, Pascal writes in the first letter to Mlle de Roannez: "It is true that the Holy Spirit rests invisibly in the remains of those who have died in the grace of God, until he appears visibly in the Resurrection."[102] In this way, therefore, relics effect a kind of transition or continuity between the scriptural evidence of the Incarnation, the physicality of its witnesses, the bodily existence of the living believer and the end of time. In Bossuet's *Panegyric of St Gorgon*, furthermore, the evocation is itself compared to the relic in a further internal metaphor, so that the holy recollections of the Saint by the orator have themselves to be cherished, with the injunction to: "Keep them in your hearts, as in a holy reliquary",[103] and thus, by extension, to root the whole area of homiletics itself more firmly in the physicality of the Incarnation.

Within the autobiographies of the possessed souls of Loudun, as well, we notice the priority given to the tomb of the (then) Blessed François de Sales in the business of exorcism, indeed to the point at which a kind of demonic

[101] "C'est une opinion reçue et un sentiment commun parmi tous les hommes, que le dépôt a quelque chose de saint, et que nous le devons conserver à celui qui nous le confie, non seulement par fidélité, mais encore par une espèce de religion" (*Panégyrique de saint Joseph*, in *Œuvres*, 327–48, p. 327).

[102] "C'est une vérité que le Saint-Esprit repose invisiblement dans les reliques de ceux qui sont morts dans la grâce de Dieu, jusqu'à ce qu'il y paraisse visiblement en la résurrection" (*Lettres aux Roannez* I, in L p. 266).

[103] "Conservez-les dans vos cœurs comme dans un saint reliquaire" (*Premier panégyrique de saint Gorgon*, in *Œuvres*, 223–33, p. 224).

negotiation occurs in order for the exorcism to take place. Thus Béhémoth is adamant that, despite the difficulty and expense of Sœur Jeanne des Anges's displacement to Savoy, "he would leave me on the tomb of the bishop of Geneva and nowhere else".[104]

It is in the closing lines of another martyr tragedy that the greater significance of relics is spelt out. Pierre Corneille's *Polyeucte martyr* (1642) deals with an episode in early Christian history (the third century AD)[105], during which the recently baptized Polyeucte, filled with neophyte zeal, embarks on a campaign of iconoclasm against the pagan gods, and is martyred as a result, before the tragedy concludes with the *coup de foudre* conversion of his wife Pauline and father-in-law Félix. As the living witnesses of Polyeucte's martyrdom close the play, it is with the following theologically resonant quatrain:

> Let those of us who remain bless our fortunate destiny:
> Let us now give burial to our martyrs,
> Kiss their sacred bodies, install them in a worthy place[,]
> And have the name of God resound throughout the world.[106]

First of all, these lines reiterate the *topos* of the martyrs' bodies being revered, and thus of the holiness of the physical, of which the Incarnation itself is the archetype; second, and alongside this, they provide for the placing of the relics in a specified place of honour, for the sanctification of place, in other words, by the founding of a church over the bodies of the martyrs; but third, and most fundamentally, they evoke the capacity for both of these actions to extend the boundaries of Christendom in the proselytizing activities of the early Church.

Finally, Bossuet, in the *Catechism of Feasts*, which deals with the Church's year, explains the relationship between Catholic dogma and its temporal representation: "The Christian year," he writes, "like the ordinary year, is divided into seasons; and [...] its solemnities are spread over different

[104] "[il] sortirait au tombeau de l'évêque de Genève, et non ailleurs" (*Relation*, p. 175).

[105] The source text, according to Corneille's own *Abrégé*, is by the tenth-century Byzantine historian Simeon Metaphrastes, mediated by the French Renaissance martyrologists Baronius and above all Surius, in turn amplified by Mosander (*De probatis sanctorum historiis*, 1579).

[106] "Nous autres, bénissons notre heureuse aventure: / Allons à nos martyrs donner la sépulture, / Baiser leurs corps sacrés, les mettre en digne lieu, / Et faire retentir partout le nom de Dieu" (*Polyeucte martyr*, V, 6, 1811–14). Reference to Corneille is made to the Seuil (L'Intégrale) edition of the *Œuvres complètes*, ed. André Stegmann, Paris, 1963. There is a very helpful general introduction to the whole area of early-modern sacred drama in J. S. Street, *French Sacred Drama from Bèze to Corneille*, Cambridge, Cambridge University Press, 1983, esp. 161–214. Particular attention is given to *Polyecute martyr* in the perspective of this book by Michel Prigent, *Le Héros et l'État dans les tragédies de Pierre Corneille*, Paris, Quadrige / Presses universitaires de France, 1986, who also gives a full treatment of Corneille's other martyr tragedy, *Théodore*. For Prigent, "Christianity is the apotheosis of heroism" ["le christianisme est l'apothéose de l'héroïsme"] (*Le Héros et l'État*, p. 111), so that "at the dénouement of *Polyeucte*, the Cornelian universe is perfect" ["au dénouement de *Polyeucte*, l'univers cornélien est parfait"] (*Le Héros et l'État*, p. 174).

times, in order to instruct us by this means of all that God has been gracious enough to do for our salvation, and of what is necessary for its accomplishment."[107] Thus the faithful observance of Sundays, of Feasts, and of certain other periods specifically designated as sacred, such as Lent and Holy Week, fulfils both a didactic and a salvific purpose; and on Saints' days the anniversary of the death of the Saint in question is celebrated, in accordance with the Christian paradox, in order to mark his or her entry into eternal life. The purpose is also explained as being to profit from their examples and to gain help from their prayers, so that a cyclical interaction between heaven and earth is foregrounded, and so that further spiritual advantages may in turn be accorded to humankind. It is in these ways too that we begin to see how an accretive sanctification of the created world is implicitly proposed by the different modes of physical reverberation of the divine.

Many of these elements will recur in the autobiographies which I shall examine in more detail later, not least because many of the supernatural experiences recorded are directly linked to Feasts in the Church's year. This is nowhere more fundamentally the case than in the devotion of St Margaret Mary to the Sacred Heart of Jesus, which brings together the two emphases of this chapter: the personally incarnate and the sacramentally enduring. She is given specific instructions by Christ for the establishment of the Feast,[108] even though her own earthly persecutions are increased when her devotions are disallowed on the grounds of novelty (and indeed the Feast was not declared until 1765). The links with the Church's year, and thus the relationship to established doctrine, are however both obvious and significant. Initially, the recurrence of the revelation of the Sacred Heart is accorded to her on the first Friday of each month, when the Blessed Sacrament was exposed in her community (the Visitandines, founded by St François de Sales), giving rise in due course to the widespread Catholic convention of associating Communion on the First Friday with particular spiritual privileges. Another powerful vision then takes place on the eve of the Feast of the Presentation (February 2); and thereafter the climactic episode of the exchange of hearts between Christ and Margaret Mary gives physical expression to the exceptional nature of the saint's vocation.[109] Most importantly of all, and uniting the two focuses in

[107] "L'année chrétienne, comme l'année ordinaire, est comme distribuée en ses saisons ; et [. . .] les solennités sont répandues en divers temps, afin de nous instruire par ce moyen de ce que Dieu a daigné faire pour notre salut, et de ce qu'il y a de nécessaire pour y parvenir" (*Catéchisme des fêtes*, in *Œuvres complètes*, ed. Lachat, vol. V, 139–205, p. 140).

[108] The devotion itself has its origins in earlier devotions to the wounds in the side of Christ, themselves instituted through the efforts of a medieval French mystic, Juliana of Cornillon, in 1264. See Walker Bynum, *Holy Feast and Holy Fast*, p. 55.

[109] This kind of devotion is also expressed by Fénelon in a letter to a penitent, albeit more spiritually and less physiologically – and as a father rather than a lover: "[May the Lord] open to you the infinite extent of his paternal heart so that your heart may be cast into his [. . .] and so that your heart and his might become as one" ["[Que le Seigneur] vous ouvre toute l'étendue

terms of the temporal codification of the Church's doctrine, is the institution of the Feast of the Sacred Heart on the Friday following the Feast of Corpus Christi. This is initiated by the most significant of all the revelations, and by Christ's words to her that, to those who make their Communion on that day, "'my Heart will dilate in order to pour out in abundance the influences of its divine love on those who will honour it in this way, and who will ensure that it is so honoured'".[110] These words stress most obviously and powerfully the Feast's threefold relationship to the physical, but they also illustrate in so doing three fundamental ways in which this particular devotion is symptomatic of the intense Christocentrism of the French Catholic Reformation: by the individual's devotion to the body of the incarnate Saviour, first of all, in the tradition of what Jantzen calls erotic mysticism; by the transformed materiality of the sacramental presence, as ingested in Pascal's Cartesian perspective by the body-automaton of the believer; and, finally, in the didactic and sanctifying purposes of the Church's year. In so doing, they also accord a status of synecdoche to that life-giving detail of the Christic body and, thereby, to a devotional focus which was to become, in the Western Church in later centuries, an icon of the improbable physiological particularity of the Incarnation itself. "The Word was made flesh", as St John writes at the beginning of his Gospel, "[and] he lived among us".

infinie de son cœur paternel pour y plonger le vôtre [. . .] et pour ne faire plus qu'un même cœur du sien et du vôtre"] (*Lettres et opuscules spirituels*, V (*Sur les fautes volontaires*), in *Œuvres*, I, p. 573).

[110] "Mon Cœur se dilatera pour répandre avec abondance les influences de son divin amour sur ceux qui lui rendront cet honneur, et qui procureront qu'il lui soit rendu" (*Vie*, p. 102–3).

3

Particularity and Language (i): Talking *about* God

Talking about God, as will probably have become apparent from some of what has preceded, is both possible and impossible. It is possible for the Christian to the degree that the Incarnation has accorded some knowledge of the divine to humankind; it is impossible in that certain transcendent concepts do not allow of immanent expression, and lead very quickly to the limits of language. If the Word became flesh, "incomprehensibly" for Pascal, the ways in which that divine flesh became words are equally mysterious, marked as they are by all kinds of linguistic strangeness.

I argued in my opening chapter that orthodoxy, in one possible definition, resides in the synthesis of apparent oppositions. It follows from this that one of the ways in which the mystery of the Incarnation is most susceptible to verbal expression is through the linguistic equivalents of that assimilation. This is above all exemplified by the exploitation of paradox, globally, and by figures such as oxymoron and chiasmus, more locally,[1] uniting as they do a range of superficially incompatible semantic elements in a greater or lesser relationship of proximity. As the primary illustration of this, two governing paradoxes, both Pauline in origin, inform much of the writing in the period, and it is with the first of these that I shall begin the examination of the relationship between language and Christian dogma. The second will be explored in the later parts of the next chapter.

St Paul writes in Romans 5: 14–15: "[Adam] prefigured the One who was to come [. . . But] there is no comparison between the free gift and the offence". This is amplified by Pascal in the first of his *Writings on Grace*,[2] where he evokes the mystery of God's justice with regard to the enormity of Adam's sin, and illustrates the disproportion by the fact that "it was necessary, for it to be expiated, that a God should become incarnate, and that he should have

[1] Formal stylistic analysis would probably prefer the terms "macrostructural" and "microstructural".

[2] These will be treated in more detail in Chapter 6. They are reproduced by Lafuma at p. 310–48. They are not included in Sellier.

suffered even death, in order to convey the greatness of the evil by the greatness of the remedy".[3] This equivalence accords to the primal fault [*culpa*] the status of catalyst for the greatest imaginable good, and so the most unexpected retrospective modifier [*felix*] is appended to it. This is proclaimed in the astonishing compression of redemptive dogma that is the *Exultet*, sung across the Western Church at the beginning of the Easter Vigil:

> Father, how wonderful your care for us!
> How boundless your merciful love!
> To ransom a slave
> you gave away your Son.
>
> O happy fault [*O felix culpa*], O necessary sin of Adam,
> which gained for us so great a Redeemer!

This is in turn paraphrased in our period by St François de Sales in the *Treatise on the Love of God*, before he goes on to elucidate the paradox: "Our loss has been beneficial, because human nature has in fact received more graces by the redemption of its Saviour, than it would ever have received by the innocence of Adam."[4] It is first of all therefore in this extraordinary dogmatic conundrum, whereby what is intrinsically bad is made actually good (and, in the liturgical context of its proclamation, made thereby the cause not just of gratitude but of rejoicing), that paradox and orthodoxy are most succinctly conjoined. Put another way, and playing on the etymologies of the two terms, what is contrary to accepted teaching is true.

If we first turn, for the purposes of these two chapters, to the basic linguistic and stylistic (rather than theological) features of this doctrine, we find that it represents the nexus of a whole gamut of similar figures, in which a pejorative or negative part of speech or concept is qualified, directly or indirectly, by an affirmative or positive contrast. The original contradiction is resolved and resumed in humankind's response to the mortal divinity of Christ, whereby, now in Fénelon's binary formulation, "nothingness believes itself to be something, while the All-Powerful annihilates himself".[5] This fertile chiasmus is then both illustrated and compressed in the teaching and example of Christ's followers: thus in Bossuet's *Panegyrics of the Saints*, for example, we find references to Christianity's "victorious weakness" ["faiblesse victorieuse"],[6]

[3] "Il a fallu, pour l'expier, qu'un Dieu se soit incarné et qu'il ait souffert jusqu'à la mort pour faire entendre la grandeur du mal à la grandeur du remède" (*Écrits sur la grâce* I in L, p. 314).

[4] "[Notre] perte nous a été à profit, puisqu'en effet la nature humaine a reçu plus de grâces par la rédemption de son Sauveur, qu'elle n'en eût jamais reçu par l'innocence d'Adam" (*Traité de l'amour de Dieu*, p. 424–5).

[5] The chiasmus is clearer in French: "Le *néant* se croit quelque chose, et le Tout-Puissant s'*anéantit*" (*Lettres et opuscules spirituels*, XXX (*De l'humilité*), in *Œuvres*, I, p. 693, my emphasis). The French also obviates the need to distinguish between an impersonal and a personal pronoun.

[6] *Panégyrique de l'apôtre saint Paul*, p. 353.

and to the Gospel of Christ itself, characterized as it is by a "glorious infamy" ["glorieuse infamie"].[7] Among his subjects' ordeals, Bossuet evokes the "blessed prisons"[8] of the martyrs, St Thomas of Canterbury wears an infested hair-shirt, full of "precious filth",[9] and St Teresa is afflicted by "[the] divine sickness of love" ["[la] divine maladie d'amour"],[10] causing her, in a further extension of the conceit, "to die each day, because she cannot die once and for all".[11] Oxymoron opens up slightly (by the introduction of a single verb) into a sequence of semantic inversions, so that the lives of the apostles, for St François de Sales, are lived in such a way that their "sadness is joyful, their poverty is rich, their deaths are vital and their dishonour is honourable".[12] Amplifying this model, causes give way to antithetical effects, so that in the context of the *Treatise on the love of God*, François's addressee is invited to consider with wonder how, in the context of divine love, "*tribulation* produces *glory*, lightness gives *weight* and movements operate eternity".[13] Introducing now a tone of sententiousness, the last book of the same work contains an extended amplification of the Gospel injunction to lose one's life in this world, affording a culminating binary sequence, whereby "our [free will] has never as much life as when it dies to itself, and it never has as much death as when it lives for itself",[14] so that "[the] Death and Passion of Our Lord is the gentlest and most violent motive that can enliven our hearts in this mortal life".[15] Pascal in the seventh letter to Mlle de Roannez writes: "We would never leave

[7] *Panégyrique de sainte Catherine*, p. 466.

[8] The "prisons bienheureuses" of the martyrs are compared with the "true prison" ["prison véritable"] of the world (*Panégyrique de saint Victor*, p. 382).

[9] Bossuet writes of "a fearful hair-shirt crawling with vermin" ["un cilice affreux tout plein de vermine"], before the disconcerting injunction: "Ah ! but do not let us scorn such a depiction, and do not let us be fearful to disturb such precious filth" ["Ha ! ne méprisons point cette peinture, et ne craignons point de remuer ces ordures si précieuses"] (*Panégyrique de saint Thomas de Cantorbéry*, p. 588).

[10] *Panégyrique de sainte Thérèse*, p. 406.

[11] We note too how in Bossuet's account this is approvingly witnessed by the Holy Spirit: "[Le Saint Esprit] se plaît à regarder du plus haut des cieux que Thérèse meurt tous les jours, parce qu'elle ne peut pas mourir une fois" (*Panégyrique de sainte Thérèse*, p. 405–6). A celebrated poem by the Spanish mystic begins: "Muero porque no muero". See Alphonse Vermeylen, *Sainte Thérèse en France au XVIIe siècle (1600–1660)*, Leuven, Bibliothèque de l'Université, 1958, p. 241. As Alain Michel remarks, "[Bossuet] is always paradoxical because he transfigures and converts values" ["[Bossuet] est toujours paradoxal parce qu'il transfigure et convertit les valeurs"] ("La grandeur et l'humilité", in *Le Grand Siècle et la Bible*, ed. Armogathe, 425–54, p. 442).

[12] "[. . .] leur tristesse est joyeuse, leur pauvreté est riche, leurs morts sont vitales et leurs déshonneurs honorables" (*Traité de l'amour de Dieu*, p. 771).

[13] "Voyez, de grâce, ces merveilles: la *tribulation* produit la *gloire*, la légèreté donne le *poids*, et les mouvements opèrent l'éternité" (*Traité de l'amour de Dieu*, p. 887, original emphases, to indicate terms borrowed from Scripture).

[14] "[Jamais notre franc arbitre] n'a tant de vie que quand il meurt à soi, et jamais il n'a tant de mort que quand il vit à soi" (*Traité de l'amour de Dieu*, p. 967).

[15] "La Mort et la Passion de Notre-Seigneur est le motif le plus doux et le plus violent qui puisse animer nos cœurs en cette vie mortelle" (*Traité de l'amour de Dieu*, p. 970).

the pleasures of the world to embrace the cross of Jesus Christ if we did not find more pleasure in scorn, poverty, deprivation, and the rejection of men, than in the delights of sin"[16]; and Fénelon summarizes the economy of immanent and transcendent suffering in two further chiastic assertions, now combining the linguistic and the admonitory: "How fine it is to endure one's purgatory in the place where others seek out their paradise [. . .]. In visible prosperity, the only good is to be found in hidden crosses."[17] Finally, in the *Introduction to the Devout Life*, St François de Sales apostrophizes the *modus vivendi* that is its subject with an enumeration of the results of this change of perspective: "O devout life, how beautiful, gentle, agreeable and sweet you are: you make tribulations bearable and consolations delightful; without you good is evil, and pleasures are filled with anxiety, uncertainty and shortcomings."[18]

It is this kind of paradox as well that takes Christian dogma in a direction ripe for dramatic exploitation, as adumbrated by François in the same work: "Fire, flames, the wheel, and the sword seemed like flowers and perfumes for the martyrs."[19] This is expanded in Corneille's martyr tragedy *Polyeucte martyr*, as the unbelieving Pauline characterizes the zeal of the new converts:

> Death for them is neither shameful nor fearful;
> They seek glory from despising [pagan] gods;
> Blind to the earth, they aspire to the heavens;
> And, believing that death opens up their doors,
> Tormented, ripped to pieces, killed, it does not matter,
> *Since torture for them is what pleasures are for us,*
> And leads them to the goal of all their desires:
> The most ignoble death, they call it martyrdom.[20]

More perversely still, zeal is intensified by persecution, so that a strongly dramatic sense is conveyed of the invulnerability of the Christian position,

[16] "On ne quitterait jamais les plaisirs du monde pour embrasser la croix de Jésus-Christ, si on ne trouvait plus de plaisir dans le mépris, dans la pauvreté, dans le dénuement et dans le rebut des hommes, que dans les délices du péché" (*Lettres aux Roannez*, VII, in L, p. 269). The three synoptic Gospels carry this text: Matthew 10: 38–9; Mark 8: 34–5; Luke 9: 23–4.

[17] "Qu'il est beau de faire son purgatoire dans le lieu où les autres cherchent leur paradis [. . .]. Dans la prospérité apparente, il n'y a rien de bon que la croix cachée" (*Lettres et opuscules spirituels*, V (*Des croix qu'il y a dans l'état de prospérité, de faveur, de grandeur*) in *Œuvres*, I, 566–9, p. 568–9).

[18] "Ô vie dévote, que vous êtes belle, douce, agréable et suave: vous adoucissez les tribulations, et rendez suaves les consolations; sans vous le bien est mal, et les plaisirs pleins d'inquiétude, troubles et défaillances" (*Introduction à la vie dévote*, p. 308).

[19] "Les feux, les flammes, les roues et les épées semblaient des fleurs et des parfums aux Martyrs" (*Introduction à la vie dévote*, p. 34).

[20] "Le trépas n'est pour eux ni honteux ni funeste ; / Ils cherchent de la gloire à mépriser nos dieux ; / Aveugles pour la terre, ils aspirent aux cieux ; / Et croyant que la mort leur en ouvre la porte, / Tourmentés, déchirés, assassinés, qu'importe, / *Les supplices leur sont ce qu'à nous les plaisirs*, / Et les mènent au but où tendent leur désirs : / La mort la plus infâme, ils l'appellent martyre" (*Polyeucte martyr*, III, 3, 946–53, my emphasis).

and thus of the strategic dilemma of the persecutor. Indeed such a tendency is compressed in this play into a one-line summary of the martyr's zeal as the hero goes to his death pronouncing a memorable line – and giving a memorable example of catachresis in the process: "I consent, or rather I aspire to my destruction".[21]

These features predictably find consistent and often disconcerting expression in most of the spiritual autobiographies of the period. Thus the question of suffering and salvation is expressed through the metaphor of food and drink in the autobiography of St Margaret Mary Alacoque when, early in the work, she evokes her life as being sustained by the "nourishment of the Cross, which would be my delicious meal",[22] some of whose more unpleasantly literal implications we saw in the last chapter. It is precisely as she strives to overcome her natural repugnance by indulging in repellent mortifications that the development of paradox reaches its limit, and she writes of how, "in so doing, I found such delight in the action, that I should have wanted to come across similar ones every day, to teach me to overcome myself and to have only God as my witness".[23] In a related area, Madame Guyon, the principal exponent of Quietism (and whose preferred mortification is spittle rather than vomit), recalls how she is afflicted by the "delicious and loving wound"[24] of God's love. This experience is stylistically identified by her elsewhere in the rhetorical device of self-correction [*correctio*], strongly (if, in the historical circumstances, ironically) redolent of Bossuet, when she recounts the death of her eldest daughter: "She died from an ill-advised bleeding: but what am I saying? She died at the hands of love, which wanted to take everything away from me."[25] In a further variant, amplifying another Pauline substitution into a chiasmus, she exclaims: "At present my poverty is my wealth, and I have found my strength in my extreme weakness".[26]

[21] "Je consens, ou plutôt j'aspire à ma ruine" (*Polyeucte martyr*, IV, 2, 1139).

[22] "[l']aliment de la Croix, laquelle serait mon mets délicieux" (*Vie*, p. 32).

[23] "Et lors je trouvai tant de délices dans cette action, que j'aurais voulu en rencontrer tous les jours de pareilles, pour apprendre à me vaincre et n'avoir que Dieu pour témoin" (*Vie*, p. 82). Walker Bynum's account of similar tendencies in medieval women writers is eloquent, seeing as she does both fasting and communion as a means of control and of renunciation (*Holy Feast and Holy Fast*, p. 5).

[24] "[...] plaie [...] délicieuse et amoureuse" (*Vie*, p. 208). St François de Sales devotes a chapter of the *Treatise on the Love of God* to "the wound of love" ["De la blessure d'amour"] (*Traité de l'amour de Dieu*, VI, 13). Gondal comments that "in the Bible itself, it is the figure of the quest for love between the lover and the beloved which suggests itself irresistibly to her as a means of expressing the spiritual search of God and humankind" ["dans la Bible même, c'est la figure de la quête d'amour entre l'aimé et l'aimée qui s'impose à elle pour exprimer la recherche spirituelle de Dieu et l'humanité" (*Moyen court*, p. 21).

[25] "Elle mourut d'une saignée à contre-temps; mais que dis-je? Elle mourut par la main de l'amour, qui me voulut dépouiller de tout" (*Vie*, p. 300).

[26] "À présent mes pauvretés sont mes richesses, et j'ai trouvé ma force dans mon extrême faiblesse" (*Vie*, p. 117).

Developing this further, she opens the Bible at random during a period of particular awareness of her own sinfulness; she reads from the same passage in 2 Corinthians the divine words: "Strength is perfected in infirmity: my grace is enough for you"[27] (a binary phrase which she then tellingly inverts); and so she interprets her own weakness as precisely constituting the means of her salvation. This brings us full circle as she is led, solipsistically one might argue, to apply the *topos* of the *felix culpa* to her own circumstances, and so to construct the syllogism, whereby: "I rejoice only in my weaknesses, since it is they which have earned me such a Saviour".[28] These claims are then justified by a further paraphrase of the same Pauline text, whereby "that which is weak in God is stronger than the greatest strength", again amplified and individualized by her when she writes of how "our very weaknesses, our wretchedness, and our imperfection, indeed our sins themselves [. . .] often become in the hands of God a source of life through the humiliation which they cause".[29]

So far, what Guyon writes is coherently if uncomfortably contained within the paradoxical specifics of Christian dogma, insofar as it is bound into the doctrine of the Fall; but such paradox is then taken further, and moves in so doing out of the realm of linguistic tropes and into the domain of theological contention. She is happy to die, she writes, and her director shares her feelings: "He [said he would] manifest [. . .] much happiness to see me die, and we laughed together over the moment that [would give] me such pleasure."[30] (And even here, although the cosiness and jolly complicity of the scene as it is recounted reads as somewhat caricatural, it is still not fundamentally distinct from the world-denying ethos which is present in many more mainstream writers.) The dangerous potential of such passivity is shown when it reaches an absurd reversal of any conventional understanding, such as when she writes, given her love of God's will, of how "even in hell I would be content with the disposition in which I find myself".[31] It is in this kind of context that the apparently logical extension of dogmatic paradox leaves the realm of what even a flexible application of doctrine can accommodate and which, sure

[27] "'*La vertu se perfectionne dans l'infirmité: ma grâce te suffit*'" (*Vie*, p. 366). The text is 2 Corinthians 12: 9–10. As Le Brun comments, "for [Guyon] as for Fénelon [. . .], the Bible is not a book of history or morality, but depicts the adventure of the soul, with its progress and its trials" ["pour [Guyon] comme pour Fénelon [. . .], la Bible n'est pas un livre d'histoire ou de morale, mais peint l'aventure de l'âme, sa marche et ses épreuves"] (*Histoire*, p. 231).

[28] "Je ne me glorifie que dans mes faiblesses, puisqu'elles m'ont mérité un tel Sauveur" (*Vie*, p. 369).

[29] "Nos faiblesses mêmes, nos misères et défauts; je dis plus, nos péchés, [. . .] deviennent souvent en la main de Dieu une source de vie par l'humiliation qu'ils nous causent" (*Vie*, p. 317).

[30] "Il témoignait [. . .] beaucoup de contentement de me voir mourir, et nous riions ensemble du moment qui faisait tout mon plaisir" (*Vie*, p. 547).

[31] "[. . .] dans l'enfer même je serais contente de la disposition où je suis" (*Vie*, p. 714). The scriptural precedent for such formulas is found in Romans 9: 3, where Paul writes: "I could pray that I might myself be accursed, if this could benefit my brothers, who are my own flesh and blood."

enough, met its condemnation by the ecclesiastical authorities, to which we shall return at length.

For the time being, however, the issues remain linguistic. As Bossuet comments in the anti-Quietist *Instruction on the States of Mental Prayer*: "The mystics of our day, not content to take such expressions as they stand, have driven them to an excess that was no longer bearable, and have added things that no-one had thought of before them."[32] This, he crucially explains, is as a result of understanding what he calls "impossible suppositions" ["suppositions par impossible"][33] as literal, rather than as an attempt at the expression of the inexpressible by means of a conditional hyperbole, to which he gives the Scholastic term of "imperfect volitions" ["volontés imparfaites"] or "velleities" ["velléités"].[34] Such utterances, which Bossuet admits have had currency among mystics, in particular in the Spanish tradition, are more correctly understood as "strong figures of speech, where the possible is mixed with the impossible, to show that one gives no limits to one's submission".[35] But it is interestingly enough Fénelon, in the context of the Quietist dispute, who shows the most acute awareness of the risk involved in such an over-development of paradox, of which the potential outcome is "to renew the impiety of the false Gnostics, who sought to purify themselves by the practice of impurity itself".[36]

One way of talking both of God and of religious experience is, of course, through imagery; and the primary text available to the writer in search of imagery is, once again, the Bible. The access of the laity to the Bible was, as Bernard Chédozeau has shown, of itself a point of intra-Catholic polemic in

[32] "Les mystiques de nos jours, non contents de prendre à la lettre ces expressions, les ont poussées jusqu'à un excès qu'il n'y avait pas moyen de supporter, et y ont ajouté des choses que personne n'avait pensées avant eux" (*Ordonnance et instruction sur les états d'oraison*, in *Œuvres complètes*, ed. Lachat, vol. XVII, 353–673, p. 389).

[33] Fénelon also uses the term in the *Lettres et opuscules spirituels*, XXIII (*Du pur amour*), in *Œuvres* I, p. 659.

[34] These terms both occur in the ninth book of the *Instruction sur les états d'oraison*, on p. 581 and 586. The medieval Latin term is "velleitas", indicating a wish that is not strong enough to lead to action. François de Sales describes the term as indicating "the beginning of a wish that has no sequence" ["un commencement de vouloir lequel n'a point de suite"] (*Traité de l'amour de Dieu*, p. 372).

[35] "[. . .] [de] fortes manières de parler, où l'on mêle le possible avec l'impossible, pour montrer qu'on ne donne point de bornes à sa soumission" (*Instruction sur les états d'oraison*, p. 584).

[36] "[. . .] renouveler l'impiété des faux gnostiques, qui voulaient se purifier par la pratique de l'impureté même" (*Explication des maximes des saints sur la vie intérieure*, in Fénelon, *Œuvres* I, ed. J. Le Brun, Paris, Gallimard (Pleiade), 1983, 999–1095, p. 1052). Christian Gnosticism was prevalent in the second century, and was constituted by a range of sects, whose common feature was a syncretic mixture of pagan mysteries and Christian doctrine. In particular it denied the physical reality of the Incarnation. It had many points of resemblance with Manichaeism. Fénelon's warning points in turn towards the heresy of antinomianism, according to which "Christians are by grace set free from the need of observing any moral law" (*ODCC*, art. Antinomianism).

the period; but its apostolic use both in a range of devotional writing and above all in pulpit oratory is at once extensive and effective.[37] St François de Sales writes of biblical quotations, in the "Note to the Reader" ["Avis au lecteur"] of the third edition of the *Introduction to the Devout Life*, that he includes them in a prescriptive spirit "[not] always in order to explain them, but to explain myself through them";[38] and the mode of their integration throughout his corpus of writing indeed reinforces the impression that they are coming to the aid of his own search for clarity of understanding and pertinence of expression. Bossuet too writes at the opening of the *Funeral Oration of the Princess Palatine*: "How good it is to meditate on Holy Scripture! And how well God is able to speak through it not just to the whole Church, but to each believer according to his needs!",[39] even if it is inevitably the Church which directs that applicability.[40] And Pascal, perhaps more predictably given the tendency of Port-Royal to promote the lay reading of sacred texts, writes that "Scripture has provided passages to console all conditions and to intimidate all conditions."[41]

[37] "Les grandes étapes de la publication de la Bible catholique en français du Concile de Trente au XVIIe siècle", in *Le Grand Siècle et la Bible*, ed. Armogathe, 341–60. No complete French Catholic translation of the Bible was available for the greater part of the century. The so-called *Nouveau Testament de Mons*, translated by Jansenist Isaac Le Maître de Sacy, was published in 1667; and his translation of the Old Testament appeared between 1672 and 1696. Chédozeau identifies three tendencies: the "ultra-restrictive" ["ultra-restrictif"] (and ultramontane) position; the somewhat less restrictive French Catholic tradition, associated with "a moderate Gallicanism" ["un gallicanisme modéré"], informed by the Wars of Religion and by the need to address newly converted Protestants; and the "innovators" ["novateurs"], identified in particular with Port-Royal.

[38] "Quand j'use des paroles de l'Écriture, ce n'est pas toujours pour les expliquer, mais pour m'expliquer par icelles" (*Introduction à la vie dévote*, p. 22). Ravier notes that "Holy Scripture is familiar to him, and the most succulent of sacred texts pour out of his pen while he is writing" ["La Sainte Écriture lui est familière, et les plus savoureux des textes sacrés affluent sous sa plume, tandis qu'il écrit"] (*Œuvres*, p. 326). Some further attention is given to François's biblical sources by the same author in "Saint François de Sales et la Bible", in *Le Grand Siècle et la Bible*, ed. Armogathe, pp. 617–26. And Alain Michel notes that "François de Sales always uses and quotes the Bible [. . .] in an anagogic sense, culminating in the hyperbole of love" ["François de Sales utilise et cite la Bible [. . .] toujours en un sens anagogique qui aboutit à l'hyperbole de l'amour"] ("La grandeur et l'humilité", in *Le Grand Siècle et la Bible*, ed. Armogathe, p. 432).

[39] "Qu'il est beau de méditer l'Écriture sainte! et que Dieu y sait bien parler non seulement à toute l'Église, mais encore à chaque fidèle selon ses besoins !" (*Oraison funèbre d'Anne de Gonzague de Clèves*, in *Œuvres*, 135–61, p. 135–6).

[40] The contrary position is described in the anti-Protestant writing in the *Funeral Oration of Henriette de France*: "[Since] each believer would become the interpreter [of Scripture], and would believe that the Holy Spirit was dictating the explanation to him, there was no individual who did not see himself as authorized by this doctrine to worship his inventions, to consecrate his errors, to call anything he liked by the name of God" ["[Comme] chaque fidèle en deviendrait l'interprète, et croirait que le Saint-Esprit lui en dicte l'explication, il n'y a point de particulier qui ne se voie autorisé par cette doctrine à adorer ses inventions, à consacrer ses erreurs, à appeler Dieu tout ce qu'il pense"] (*Oraison funèbre de Henriette-Marie de France*, in *Œuvres*, p. 68).

[41] "L'Écriture a pourvu de passages pour consoler toutes les conditions, et pour intimider toutes les conditions" (*Pensées*, L 800, S 652).

We saw in the last chapter how marital, indeed sexual imagery was drawn from the Bible in the evocation of the relationship to the divine; and a related metaphorical field is that of the family, which develops all kinds of more tenuous ramifications. In a rather bleak exploitation of the paternal image, first of all, Fénelon writes, quoting an unidentified patristic source, that

> [God] is more of a father [. . .] than all fathers together. He has loved us with an eternal love; yet what has he loved in us? [. . .] What has he found in us that is worthy of his love? Nothing, when we did not exist, and sinfulness when we did.[42]

Bossuet, in the *Panegyric of St Bernard* develops the same image more comfortingly with respect to the figures of the apostles relative to their converts, for whom they were "fathers on account of their conduct, and mothers on account of their tenderness, and nursemaids on account of their gentleness";[43] and in the Preface of the *Introduction to the Devout Life*, St François de Sales comments on the First Letter of John, to the effect that these men called their disciples "not only their children, but indeed more tenderly still their *little children*".[44]

Surin, in the course of his recovery from diabolic possession, develops an excessively literal childlikeness towards God, although in his case the imagery becomes rather chaotic, in common stylistically with many other features of his account; but initially he too stresses how God's love can be understood as being like that of a spouse or father, before developing the second analogy: he calls God "papa",[45] quoting St Paul in support; but then later again evokes his "childlike disposition" ["disposition enfantine"] towards Christ and Mary, whom he now addresses in turn as "papa" and "maman".[46] Madame Guyon blurs the picture again, conflating—in common with many medieval women mystics—her devotion to the Spouse with a fervent attachment to the Christ child. These two images then come somewhat incoherently together as she writes a contract "to take as my Spouse Our Lord as Child, and give myself to him as his bride, however unworthy",[47] before yet further confusion is

[42] "Il est plus père [. . .] que tous les pères ensemble. Il nous a aimés d'un amour éternel ; et qu'a-t-il aimé en nous ? [. . .] [Qu'a-t-il] donc trouvé en nous digne de son amour ? Le néant, quand nous n'étions pas, et le péché, quand nous avons été" (*Lettres et opuscules spirituels*, XVI (*Conférences sur l'amour de Dieu*), in *Œuvres*, I, 631–5, p. 632).

[43] "Ils étaient pères pour la conduite, et mères pour la tendresse, et nourrices pour la douceur" (*Panégyrique de saint Bernard*, in *Œuvres*, p. 278). This is taken in part from St Bernard, *Sermon XXIII*. Bossuet concludes that all these qualities were shared by St Paul.

[44] "[. . .] non seulement leurs enfants, mais encore plus tendrement leurs *petits enfants*" (*Introduction à la vie dévote*, p. 27, original emphases, to indicate scriptural borrowing). The reference is to 1 John 2: *passim*.

[45] "I can only call God *papa*, and I have often thought that this is what St Paul tells us" ["Je ne puis appeler Dieu que *papa*, et souvent j'ai pensé que c'est ce que dit saint Paul"] (*Science expérimentale*, p. 286). The reference is Galatians 4: 6.

[46] *Science expérimentale*, p. 301.

[47] "'Je promets de prendre pour mon Époux Notre-Seigneur Enfant, et me donne à lui pour épouse, quoiqu'indigne'" (*Vie*, p. 300).

introduced when she goes on to write of her imprisonment: "I am experiencing at present two states simultaneously: I am carrying Christ crucified and the Christ child".[48] It is only possible to disentangle all this by recognizing how the interweaving of such familial images (kept separate in other writers) expresses coexistent aspects of the believer's relationship with the first two persons of the Holy Trinity, and indeed with the Holy Family, without, it seems, being possible to establish a coherent composite familial metaphor. The potential for such confusion is in turn afforded by the fact that the Father, the Son, and the Spirit are both one and distinct;[49] but that, unlike the Father and the Spirit, the Son, in his earthly life, was subject to the same developmental sequence as the rest of humankind.[50]

Underlying all such difficulties, and identifying the major attendant complication which biblical language affords, is the distinction between figurative and literal interpretation; and Pascal addresses this dilemma with respect to the Judeo-Christian tradition in a sequence of fragments in the *liasse*: "That the law was figurative" ["Que la loi était figurative"] of the *Pensées*.[51] But far from clarifying or even simplifying the hermeneutic issues, the whole section is often particularly opaque, above all in those fragments where detached references to Scripture, St Augustine or the liturgy in both French and Latin are either juxtaposed with longer passages of discourse, or else simply placed in a paratactic relationship. One sequence brings all these elements together in what amounts to a referentially complex enigma:

> Figures.
>
> Jesus Christ opened their minds to understand the Scriptures.
>
> These are two great openings: 1. *Everything happened to them in figures. Vere Israelita, Vere liberi, True bread of heaven.*
>
> 2. A God humiliated even to the Cross. Christ had to suffer to enter into his glory. That he would conquer death by his death. Two comings.[52]

[48] "J'éprouve deux états à présent tout ensemble : je porte Jésus-Christ crucifié et Enfant" (*Vie*, p. 733). She also considers that, predestined to be born of the Sacred Heart on Calvary, she is "associated with that divine maternity in Jesus Christ" ["associée à cette maternité divine en Jésus-Christ"] (*Vie*, p. 579).

[49] See my cover illustration, and remarks later in this chapter.

[50] François de Sales expresses this as follows: "He was perfectly glorious from the moment of his conception [. . .], and yet at the same time he was subject to sadness, regrets and afflictions of the heart" ["[Il] fut parfaitement glorieux dès l'instant de sa conception [. . .] et néanmoins il fut à même temps sujet aux tristesses, regrets et afflictions de cœur"] (*Traité de l'amour de Dieu*, p. 388).

[51] L 246–76, S 278–307. See in particular on this issue Pierre Force, *Le Problème herméneutique chez Pascal*, Paris, Vrin, 1989 and David Wetsel, *L'Écriture et le reste: the 'Pensées' of Pascal in the exegetical tradition of Port-Royal*, Columbus, Ohio State University Press, 1981.

[52] "Figures. / Jésus Christ leur ouvrit l'esprit pour entendre les Écritures. / Deux grandes ouvertures sont celles-là : 1. *Toutes choses leur arrivaient en figures. Vere Israelita, Vere liberi, Vrai pain du ciel.* / 2. Un Dieu humilié jusqu'à la croix. Il a fallu que le Christ ait souffert pour entrer en sa gloire. Qu'il vaincrait la mort par sa mort. Deux avènements." The fragment is *Pensées* L 253, S 285. The biblical references are to: Luke 24: 27, 32; 1 Corinthians 10: 11; John 1:

The accumulation of references and resonances in such a text opens up by its very obscurity the density of Pascal's allusiveness and, as a result, the complexity of the evidence that he adduces. The subtitle ("Figures"), first of all, places what follows it within the ordering of his project; the elliptical reference to Scripture in French and Latin affords the security of the biblical texts, albeit without any identification or amplification; and the paraphrase in a more vernacular style completes the evocation. Such fragments also serve to demonstrate how disembodied phrases can have a near-poetic as well as a demonstrative quality and, however far it may have been from the exegetical purposes of Pascal, may affect the reader subliminally for that reason.[53]

More simply, other fragments deal with the alleged Jewish misinterpretation of Scripture, whereby "Jesus Christ came at the predicted time, but not in the expected splendour";[54] and yet show, in the same way, how Judaic teaching played a fundamental role in the establishment of Christ's dual nature, since "in testing whether he was God, [they] established that he was man".[55] Pascal then goes beyond the demonstration of the fulfilment of prefigurative texts by the Incarnation, and explores the whole semantic principle in the major fragment entitled "Reason for figures",[56] summarized in the (deleted) opening sentence: "They had to engage a carnal people and make it the depository of the spiritual legacy."[57] Such a need to achieve a spiritual understanding of the carnal was not limited to the Jewish people, however, as we have seen from much of what has preceded; and other fragments then broaden out the question, so as to deal with the whole theory (and to some degree practice) of hermeneutics. Thus, in a fragment entitled "Contradictions" we find: "To understand the meaning of a writer, you have to reconcile all the contrary passages",[58] leading to such sententiously expressed principles as: "When the word of God, which is trustworthy, is literally false, it is spiritually true."[59]

47; John 8: 26; John 6: 32; Philippians 2: 8; Luke 24: 26. The last line quotes from the Easter Preface of the Mass.

[53] If ever Valéry's notorious description of Pascal's writing, accidentally or deliberately, as consistent with the achievements of a poet was justified, it would be in such extracts (Paul Valéry, "Variation sur une pensée", in *Œuvres*, I, ed. Jean Hytier, Paris, Gallimard (Pléiade), 1957, 458–73).

[54] "Jésus-Christ est venu dans le temps prédit, mais non pas dans l'éclat attendu" (*Pensées*, L 270, S 301).

[55] "[. . .] en éprouvant s'il était Dieu, [ils] ont montré qu'il était homme" (*Pensées*, L 306, S 337).

[56] "Raison pourquoi figures" (*Pensées*, L 502, S 738).

[57] "Ils avaient à entretenir un peuple charnel et à le rendre dépositaire du testament spirituel" (*Pensées*, L 502, S 738).

[58] "Pour entendre le sens d'un auteur, il faut accorder tous les passages contraires" (*Pensées*, L 257, S 289).

[59] "Quand la parole de Dieu, qui est véritable, est fausse littéralement, elle est vraie spirituellement" (*Pensées*, L 272, S 303). This is not entirely convincingly illustrated by the need to ascertain the divergent meanings for the Latin *omnes* in the context of communion under both kinds. I have used "trustworthy" as a translation of "véritable" to distinguish the epithet from "vrai", which Pascal uses in the same fragment.

Here again we come, now semantically, onto the related questions of inclusivity as against heresy, and of the coexistence of apparently contrary truths in a dogmatic synthesis.

Moving down to more earthly analogies, we find that imagery from the natural world is also common, above all in St François de Sales's *Introduction to the Devout Life*, affording almost without exception in this case a refreshing contrast by its appropriateness and concreteness.[60] André Ravier remarks of François's sources: "All those who have penetrated into the hearts of man in his natural and supernatural life are welcomed [. . .]. But he assimilates all these readings, he makes them his own."[61] Many of his images are adapted from Pliny's *Historia naturalis*, and show in particular a predilection for the allegorical potential of bees and honey. This arises from the capacity of the bee to transform, within itself, the often poisonous raw material which it ingests, into the honey-like qualities of "softness" ["douceur"] and "sweetness" ["suavité"], which above all characterize the devout life. But his bestiary is far more wide-ranging, and in a typical example, in the chapter on confession, François writes to his penitent: "[Never] allow your heart to remain infected for long by sin, Philothée, since you have such an easily available remedy. The lioness who has been accosted by a leopard goes quickly to wash herself to take away the stench that this frequentation has left on her, so that when the lion arrives, he will not be offended and irritated by her".[62] Another natural image, memorable by its simplicity and visual immediacy, is used to convey the need to maintain a firm hold on the faith while living in the world: "Do as small children do", François advises, "who, [when they go for a walk], with one hand hold on to the hand of their father, while with the other they pick the strawberries and blackberries along the hedgerows."[63]

[60] See H. Lemaire, *Les Images chez François de Sales*, Paris, Nizet, 1962, and Philippe Legros, *François de Sales: une poétique de l'imaginaire*, Tübingen, Narr (Biblio 17), 2004.

[61] "Tous ceux qui ont sondé le cœur de l'homme en sa vie naturelle comme en sa vie surnaturelle sont les bienvenus [. . .]. Mais toutes ces lectures, il les assume, il les fait siennes" (*Œuvres*, p. 326).

[62] "Ne permettez donc jamais, Philothée, que votre cœur demeure longtemps infecté de péché, puisque vous avez un remède si présent et facile. La lionne qui a été accostée du léopard va vitement se laver pour ôter la puanteur que cette accointance lui a laissée, afin que le lion venant n'en soit point offensé et irrité" (*Introduction à la vie dévote*, p. 112–13).

[63] "Faites comme les petits enfants qui de l'une des mains se tiennent à leur père, et de l'autre cueillent des fraises ou des mûres le long des haies" (*Introduction à la vie dévote*, p. 160). Surin attempts a similar, but less immediately compelling comparison, thereby throwing François's imagic facility into relief: "[This] comparison occurs to me with certain people of whom it is said that, when going down to the seabed to search for pearls, they have a tube that reaches to the surface, supported by cork from one end to the other, through which they can breathe even though they are in effect at the bottom of the ocean" ["[Cette] comparaison me vient de certaines gens que l'on m'a dit qui, pêchant des perles en allant jusqu'au fond de la mer pour les prendre, ont un tuyau qui va jusqu'au haut, et qui est soutenu par un liège, au bout d'en haut, et par là ils respirent et sont effectivement au fond de la mer"] (*Science expérimentale*, p. 338).

Natural images may on the other hand appear charmingly comic by their frivolity or disproportion, such as in the extended simile of false penitents, who "abstain from sin as sick people do from melons"[64]; and the antics of the animal world are notably susceptible to what even François must have seen as potentially bathetic effects. Thus the progress of the devout soul is compared to the flying capacity of various birds, starting with ostriches (not at all), chickens (rarely, with difficulty, and close to the ground) and swallows and eagles (frequently, effortlessly and high in the sky),[65] to which degree of elevation the work's dedicatee should of course aspire. Back to earth, the Bishop of Geneva expresses his admiration for the virtue of fidelity among elephants: "The bull elephant is just a very large beast", he writes; "but it is also the most worthy among those that live on the earth, and the one with the most common sense. I will tell you one thing about its honourable nature: it never changes its cow elephant, and loves tenderly the one that it has chosen."[66] Moving even nearer the ground, the introspective act of spiritual recollection is likened to the reclusive instincts of a tortoise or a hedgehog. As Peter Bayley comments: "Each part of the universe, if examined closely, will be seen to represent in some way one of God's attributes or an element of his plan for the world"[67]; and even Pascal admits that "those men honour nature who teach it that it can talk about everything, and even about theology".[68] Just as La Ceppède sanctified the physical in his sonnets on the Passion so too, in François, the supernatural realm is enlivened and explained by the natural world, and in particular by the animal kingdom, for the benefit of the human race that lies somewhere between the two.[69] If, in Pascal's memorable formulation, humankind is "neither angel nor beast",[70] it can nonetheless, in François's hands, find in the beasts a sure means of talking about the angels.

[64] "Ainsi il y a des pénitents [. . .] qui s'abstiennent du péché comme les malades font des melons" (*Introduction à la vie dévote*, p. 44).

[65] "Les autruches ne volent jamais ; les poules volent, pesamment toutefois, bassement et rarement ; mais les aigles, les colombes et les arondelles volent souvent, vitement et hautement" (*Introduction à la vie dévote*, p. 32).

[66] "L'éléphant n'est qu'une grosse bête, mais la plus digne qui vive sur la terre et qui a le plus de sens ; je vous veux dire un trait de son honnêteté : il ne change jamais de femelle et aime tendrement celle qu'il a choisie" (*Introduction à la vie dévote*, p. 243).

[67] Peter Bayley, *French Pulpit Oratory 1598–1650*, Cambridge, Cambridge University Press, 1980, p. 150. This is given poetic expression in the period in, for example, the Psalm paraphrases of Martial de Brive. See his *Œuvres poétiques et saintes*, ed. Anne Mantero, Jérôme Millon, Grenoble, 2000.

[68] "Ceux-là honorent bien la nature qui lui apprennent qu'elle peut parler de tout, et même de théologie" (*Pensées*, L 675, S 554). I admit that this is a reductive interpretation of Pascal's fragment.

[69] Krumenacker remarks: "For [François] it is not just a matter of simple analogies. The use of examples introduces the whole relationship between the spiritual and the material" ["Pour [François], il ne s'agit pas de simples analogies. L'exemplarisme met en jeu le rapport entre le spirituel et le matériel"] (*École française*, p. 93).

[70] "L'homme n'est ni ange ni bête, et le malheur veut que qui veut faire l'ange fait la bête" (*Pensées*, L 678, S 557).

In a more ambitious domain, we find in François the extended metaphor, stretching on occasion across several related chapters, developing the potential of an anecdotal visualization in the analysis of a spiritual state or course of action. Images may illustrate images, such as when the soul in its spiritual progress is likened successively to angels on Jacob's ladder (I, 2) and to sunlight at dawn (I, 5), so that "the soul which rises from sin to devotion can be compared to the dawn, which does not as it lifts banish all darkness in an instant, but little by little".[71] Even heaven and hell are compared to physical realities, together with a description of the heavenly company and activities, although here even François takes his image beyond the limits of its visual potential, and borders on the surreal in his evocation of paradise: "Consider a beautiful, serene night, and think of how good it is to see the sky with its multitude and variety of stars. Now join that beauty to that of a fine day, in such a way that the brightness of the sun does not prevent the clear view of the stars or of the moon",[72] he writes, before stressing in conclusion that such a vision is incomparably less fine than the reality.

The greater spiritual ambition of the subject matter of the *Treatise on the Love of God* necessitates in turn a greater imagic range, although the natural world remains central to it. The sheer voluptuousness of the imagery in the Preface conveys of itself something of the incandescent nature of François's subject matter, and the very acts of writing are compared (through an extended play on the word "plume") to the feathers of a dove in the sunlight.[73] The metaphor of the sun retains a central importance, such as in the comparison, which opens the second book, between man's defective (because subjective and anthropocentric) perception of it at different times of day, and the flawed human perception of the perfection of God. Later in the same book, François deals with the reception of the knowledge of divine love by faith ["Du sentiment de l'amour divin qui se reçoit par la foi"], but the precision of the explanation, despite the interplay of abstractions, combined with a physically beautiful and entirely apposite image of the sun now seen though a fog, make the clinching *chiaroscuro* of "this dark brightness of faith" ["cette obscure clarté de la foi"] seem revelatory rather than contrived.[74] Alongside the

[71] "[L'âme] qui monte du péché à la dévotion est comparée à l'aube, laquelle s'élevant ne chasse pas les ténèbres en un instant, mais petit à petit" (*Introduction à la vie dévote*, p. 41).

[72] "Considérez une belle nuit sereine, et pensez combien il fait bon voir le ciel avec cette multitude et variété d'étoiles. Or, joignez maintenant cette beauté avec celle d'un beau jour, en sorte que la clarté du soleil n'empêche point la claire vue des étoiles ni de la lune" (*Introduction à la vie dévote*, p. 61).

[73] *Traité de l'amour de Dieu*, p. 335.

[74] *Traité de l'amour de Dieu*, p. 451. More simply, dramatizing the opening of St John's Gospel, Fénelon writes of how "Jesus Christ scatters the dazzling truths of his Gospel into the dark night of the world" ["Jésus-Christ répand les vérités éclatantes de son Évangile dans la profonde nuit du siècle"], *Lettres et opuscules spirituels*, XXXIX (*Jésus-Christ est la lumière de tout homme qui vient en ce monde*), in *Œuvres*, I, 735.

elemental image of the sun, and almost as recurrent, is that of water, such as in the soul's desire for "the cool waters of immortal life and the most holy divinity",[75] a psalmic image which is soon paralleled by the Pauline metaphor of a mother's milk, as "this gentle fountain of sweet and longed-for liquor".[76] This combination of biblical images then gives way to an explicit scriptural quotation in the form of a paraphrase of Psalm 35: 10:

> In God lies the fountain
> Of supreme life and pleasure;
> His brilliance will appear to us
> In the rays of his living light,
> And our fullness of joy
> Will come to birth only from his daylight.[77]

In addition to such motivic features, new images are also introduced at significant points in the text, so that an interwoven and at times kaleidoscopic network is gradually built up to convey, however inadequately, the desire for and reality of the love of God. As Krumenacker writes, "[for François], earthly realities have no real consistency, they are only interesting as signs of a reality of a different order, which causes them to exist".[78]

Elsewhere in François, it is the complex interplay of parts of speech which serves to point to the limitations of language. Even the implicit reference in the Preface of the *Treatise on the Love of God* to the doxology, whereby: "Everything is of love, in love, for love, and from love in the holy Church",[79] implies an inexpressible reality by its amplification of the more familiar ternary formula. But it is in the mystical climax of the third book, evoking the "union of the blessed spirits with God" ["De l'union des esprits bienheureux avec Dieu"], that the writing comes close to stasis in its abstract passages, as variously capitalized absolutes and superlatives interact with and complement each other, coming finally to rest on "the divinity of this infinite Beauty, or the beauty of this infinite Divinity".[80] Again, understanding God may be attempted contrastively, leading in turn to a play of adjectives and nouns or adverbs and adjectives, suggesting implicitly that neither formulation may

[75] "[...] les fraîches eaux de la vie immortelle et la très sainte Divinité" (*Traité de l'amour de Dieu*, p. 511). Compare Psalm 42 : 1.

[76] "[...] cette douce fontaine de suave et désirée liqueur" (*Traité de l'amour de Dieu*, p. 512). Compare 1 Corinthians 3: 2.

[77] "En Dieu gît la fontaine même, / De vie et de plaisir suprême; / Sa clarté nous apparaîtra / Aux rais de sa vive lumière, / Et notre liesse plénière / De son jour seulement naîtra" (*Traité de l'amour de Dieu*, p. 521).

[78] "[...] les réalités terrestres n'ont pas vraiment de consistance, elles n'intéressent que comme signes de la réalité d'un autre ordre qui les fonde" (*École française*, p. 94).

[79] "Tout est à l'amour, en l'amour, pour l'amour et d'amour en la sainte Église" (*Traité de l'amour de Dieu*, p. 336).

[80] "[...] la divinité de cette Beauté infinie, ou la beauté de cette infinie Divinité" (*Traité de l'amour de Dieu*, p. 524).

suffice alone, thus in evoking the need for "a single very purely simple and very simply pure act"[81]; or of faith and the believer, who is brought to "love the beauty of its truth and believe the truth of its beauty".[82] The effect of this frequent device is much more than ludic or lyrical, since it crucially establishes the coexistence and equivalence of spiritual states by the disruption of the semantic stability within given parts of speech or syntactic relationships. Yet the sense is much stronger here of language reaching its limits, even though François clearly believes it to be capable of the highest approximations to the spiritual states and concepts to which it attends.

Turning to another area of vertiginous coexistence in the *Panegyric of St Bernard*, Bossuet aims to understand the relationship between Father and Son, struggling similarly to François with concepts which are necessarily semantically distinct yet theologically inseparable, and quotes in conclusion a technical neologism from the Church Fathers:

> Thus is was that the early Fathers, speaking of the actions of this Man-God, called them theandric operations, that is to say operations which combine the divine and the human, operations that are divine and human at the same time; human by their nature, divine by their origin; so that the God-Word, having made his own the sacred humanity of Jesus, considers the Son's actions to be his own.[83]

St François de Sales, in the *Treatise on the Love of God*, is no less mysterious: "He who was living eternally in his divine life lived temporally in his human life, and he who for all eternity had only ever been God will now for all eternity still be man."[84]

At the other extreme we find the exploitation of a kind of literalism, a verbalization of the physicality of the Christic body, rather than an attempt to marshal words to describe it. Thus in the opening words of the *Sermon on the Passion*, preached on Good Friday 1662, Bossuet takes the most literal meaning of "testament" (in the sense of a written will) and develops its potential in a kind of inverted metaphor. What inevitably strikes us here is the assimilation of word and image, as the very words of the will of Christ are presented in terms of his crucified body: "The will of Jesus Christ was sealed with wax

[81] "[. . .] un seul acte très purement simple et très simplement pur" (*Traité de l'amour de Dieu*, p. 412).

[82] "[. . .] aimer la beauté de sa vérité et croire la vérité de sa beauté" (*Traité de l'amour de Dieu*, p. 452).

[83] "De là vient que les anciens Pères, parlant des actions de cet Homme-Dieu, les ont appelées actions théandriques, c'est-à-dire actions mêlées du divin et de l'humain, opérations divines et humaines tout ensemble; humaines par leur nature, divines par leur principe : d'autant que le Dieu-Verbe s'étant rendu propre la sainte humanité de Jésus, il en considère les actions comme siennes" (*Panégyrique de saint Bernard*, in *Œuvres*, p. 262).

[84] "Celui qui vivait éternellement de sa vie divine vécut temporellement de la vie humaine, et Celui qui jamais éternellement n'avait été que Dieu sera éternellement à jamais encore homme" (*Traité de l'amour de Dieu*, p. 866).

throughout his life. It is opened today publicly on Calvary, while Jesus is stretched out on the cross. This is where we see this will engraved in bloody letters on his unjustly torn flesh; so many wounds, so many letters; so many drops of blood that flow from this innocent victim, so many features which carry the marks of the last wishes of this divine testator"[85] (and the impact of its delivery must have been all the more potent in that, on this day alone, the Cross is publicly and solemnly venerated). It is therefore, by implication, the capacity to decipher this writing of the will, as encrypted in the wounds of Christ, which distinguishes the true believer; or, put another way, that the gift of faith is presented as the gift to decipher the Crucifixion. In this extraordinary abandonment of the capacity of language to describe the Passion, the crucifix itself is accorded a semantic status, and endowed with the bloody alphabet with which to transmit its meaning. The Passion, literally, dictates its significance, and Bossuet can identify his subject as *stricto sensu* prescriptive, in that it precedes writing. It is the Cross itself that will determine the mode of its own deciphering.

This leads us to the most linguistically intractable of all mysteries, that of the Holy Trinity, described by Bossuet in the *Catechism of Feasts* as "altogether beyond our senses and our human intelligence"[86]; and it is perhaps not surprising that we turn to another poet to deepen our understanding of this supremely inaccessible dogma. The early seventeenth-century poet Claude Hopil may justly be seen in the period as the poet of the mystery of the Holy Trinity, expressed in a cycle of 100 canticles, entitled *The Divine Outpourings of Love*.[87] As Jean Rousset writes: "Every mystic experiences a paradox, because he seeks to grasp that which escapes from all attempts to grasp it, to think what is unthinkable, to see the one who is Invisible."[88]

Certain features are consistent across the sequence. First and most obviously is the mystery of the Trinity itself, manifested in the ternary lexis and patterns which seek to represent it mimetically. God is the "unfathomable ternary" ["ternaire incompris"], and neologisms once again help the poet to express the

[85] "Le testament de Jésus-Christ a été scellé et cacheté durant tout le cours de sa vie. Il est ouvert aujourd'hui publiquement sur le Calvaire pendant que l'on y étend Jésus à la croix. C'est là qu'on voit ce testament gravé en caractères sanglants sur sa chair indignement déchirée ; autant de plaies, autant de lettres ; autant de gouttes de sang qui coulent de cette victime innocente, autant de traits qui portent empreintes les dernières volontés de ce divin testateur" (*Sermon sur la Passion de Notre-Seigneur*, in *Sermons*, p. 249). Cf. Hebrews 9: 15–18.

[86] "[. . .] qui est tout à fait au-dessus des sens et de l'intelligence humaine" (*Catéchisme des fêtes*, p. 140).

[87] Claude Hopil (c. 1585–c. 1633), *Les Divins Élancements d'amour exprimés en cent cantiques faits en l'honneur de la Très-Sainte-Trinité*, ed. Jacqueline Plantié, Paris, Champion, 1999. Peter France notes in the *OCLF* that "in strikingly negative images he attempts to express the inexpressible".

[88] "Tout mystique vit un paradoxe, puisqu'il prétend saisir ce qui échappe à toute saisie, penser ce qui ne se pense pas, voir celui qui est l'Invisible" (*Anthologie*, II, 301–2).

inexpressible, thus: "Trin'un(e)", "trin'unique", or "Trin'unité". Simple tripartite structures also intrude into the verse: thus an ensuing statement of unity contrasts abruptly with the ternary repetition: "I see it [Trinity], I see it, I see it, it is one"[89]; or an amplification extends through enjambment across a couplet:

> This angelic choir containing more than a thousand
> And a thousand and a thousand voices.[90]

More soberly, God "is one in essence, and in mystery three",[91] where the contrast is heightened by the chiasmus across the alexandrine; and a tripartite human epistemology, of memory, spirit, and heart, responds in several of the canticles by its threefold attempt to penetrate the divine mystery.

Second, Hopil makes appeal to more enlightened intermediaries to convey the dogma, thus the angels, archangels, and seraphim, "to whom [God] reveals his essence", but who in turn may not communicate it directly. The poet is aware that it is only the angels and saints who see God face to face, and thus himself asks only (in repeated verbal play of a similar kind) to "glimpse" ["entrevoir"], or to "see without seeing" ["voir sans voir"].

Finally, and predictably, imagery is central in understanding the Holy Trinity, above all in images of cloud, dawn, shadow, mist, and the mirror, all variants on the imperfect clarity or directness of vision which dominate the writing. The poet explores the most extreme elements of *chiaroscuro*, reaching finally the dizzying evocation in which, vitally, the metaphorical eclipses the literal:

> My Sun who makes a cloud of the sun
> And a night of its day.[92]

Elsewhere, the optical illusion of the sun reflected in cloud is evoked in an address to the reader: "Have you never seen in a dark cloud, / In which the sun is reflected / Three similar suns appear to the naked eye? / That is the imperfect figure of the Trinity [. . .]",[93] before coming to rest on a more straightforward appeal to the eyes of faith:

> Close the eyes of the body and the intellect,
> And aspiring ceaselessly to the heavenly resting place,
> Opening the eyes of your heart, look lovingly on
> This perfect essence.[94]

[89] "Je la [Trinité] vois, je la vois, je la vois, elle est une" (Cantique 13).

[90] "[. . .] ce chœur angélique contenant plus de mille / Et mille et mille voix" (Cantique 67).

[91] "Il est un par essence, et par mystère trois" (Cantique 23).

[92] "[. . .] mon Soleil qui fait du soleil une nue, / Une nuit de son jour" (Cantique 67). The alliteration and assonance resist translation.

[93] "N'avez-vous jamais vu dans une épaisse nue / Se mirant le soleil, apparaître à la vue / Trois semblables soleils ? / C'est de la Trinité l'imparfaite figure" (Cantique 67).

[94] "Ferme les yeux du corps et de l'intelligence, / En aspirant sans cesse au céleste séjour, / Ouvrant l'œil de ton cœur regarde par amour / Cette parfaite essence" (Cantique 46).

Yet even at his most exuberant, Hopil synthesizes his various images, so that a combination of control and awe is achieved; and even (or especially) at the highest moments of inspiration, a self-awareness ensues, thus of the belief that the divine vision is accorded to the poet by means of an angelic mirror: "This mirror is dark, but a heavenly Angel / Manifests in a more beautiful mirror this object / Of the Trin'unity"; and yet (completing the same stanza): "I blaspheme in saying that I see its image, / I simply glimpse the ravishing shadow / Of the Divinity".[95] In this way the approximations of language repeatedly face the temptation of believing that they are approaching the reality, before the equally consistent recoil. The movement is thus made forwards and backwards towards the attempt at understanding and the need humbly and silently to adore the ineffable. Ignorance, combined with adoration, remains the state of the poet and of humankind.

What is most remarkable in the context is the degree of control which Hopil achieves, only rarely giving any impression of pointless linguistic conundrums. Indeed the whole series can be summarized in the simple line (proleptically overturning Wittgenstein): "How full of mystery is the number three! / I cannot speak of it, and yet I may not be silent",[96] so that the conceit of verbal speechlessness is the *telos* of the writing. The ultimate paradox nonetheless occurs in its most compressed form, as the believer's final vision is contemplated, and the Christic specifics re-introduced: "He will see in heaven this great God of life, / Who is called LIVING, / Through the eyes of the dead God, who has taken his own death away".[97] Since death denies itself, so from that reversal ensues the double potential for the language of earthly suffering to be transcended and that of earthly fulfilment to be negated. What these pieces nonetheless show is the degree to which the poetic treatment accords new insights into the unchanging Christian dogmas, the degree to which, in other words, the doctrine of the Trinity is always the same, and yet always surprising, and always strange.

In the narrative domain too, the writers and subjects of spiritual autobiographies draw particular attention to the uniqueness and inexpressibility of their experiences. Thus Madame Guyon and her director emphasize the discovery of a previously unknown and incommunicable state, "a union unknown to all those who do not experience it".[98] When she finally reaches what she terms "the way of faith" ["la voie de foi"], she finds herself unable

[95] "Ce miroir est obscur, mais un Ange céleste / Dans un plus beau miroir cet objet manifeste / De la Trin'unité ; / Je blasphème en disant que je vois son image, / J'entrevois seulement le ravissant ombrage / De la Divinité" (Cantique 11).

[96] "Que le nombre trois est rempli de mystère ! / Je ne puis en parler, et si ne m'en peux taire" (Cantique 51).

[97] "Il verra dans le Ciel ce grand Dieu de la vie / Appelé le VIVANT, / Par les yeux de Dieu mort, qui sa mort a ravie" (Cantique 75).

[98] "[une] union inconnue à tout autre qu'à ceux qui l'éprouvent" (*Vie*, p. 242).

adequately to account for her disposition, exclaiming rather: "O if only I could express what I conceive in this state. But I can only stammer"[99]; and Christ's acts of mercy to her are "of a nature which can only be described in terms of their purity and their depth".[100] The intense indwelling of Christ as experienced by Surin on the eve of the Feast of the Ascension is approximated by a simile, before it too defies description: "I was penetrated by something as a sponge might be, by a liquid that had come down from heaven; which infiltrated me entirely and gave me an inexplicable liveliness and blissfulness [again the problematic term 'suavité']".[101] Exclusiveness is equally stressed as Jeanne des Anges, in common with many other writers in a more exuberant vein, explicitly struggles with the difficulty of recording her release from evil spirits: "It would be quite impossible to describe all that happened in these struggles", she writes, "and the particular help which I received from God, and few people can conceive of what I would say, if they did not themselves share the experience."[102] Bossuet too, in the *Panegyric of St Teresa of Ávila*, vicariously deploys the *topos* of inexpressibility:

> What shall I say? [...] Who will give me the words to express adequately the divine ardour which drives her? And even if I can represent it as strongly and as fervently as it is in the heart of Teresa, who will understand what I am saying? And how will our earthbound minds grasp these heavenly transports?[103]

As Krumenacker says of Bérulle (but his remark is more widely applicable): "The use of a great profusion of words and of multiple repetitions [...] paradoxically gives birth to the silence that is propitious to mystical contemplation."[104] Or Jantzen: "Human words should be used as aids to think about

[99] "Ô si je pouvais exprimer ce que je conçois en cet état. Mais je ne puis que bégayer" (*Vie*, p. 301).

[100] "[...] d'une nature à ne pouvoir être décrites à cause de leur pureté et de leur profondeur" (*Vie*, p. 347).

[101] "[Je] fus pénétré comme une éponge la [*sic*] serait, par une liqueur descendue du ciel ; qui s'insinua par tout, et me donna une allégresse et suavité inexplicable" (*Science expérimentale*, p. 329).

[102] "Il me serait tout à fait impossible de décrire tout ce qui s'est passé dans ces combats, et les assistances particulières que j'ai reçues de Dieu, et peu de personnes peuvent concevoir ce que j'en dirais, à moins d'en avoir fait l'expérience" (*Relation*, p. 145).

[103] "Que dirai-je ? [...] Qui me donnera des paroles, pour vous exprimer dignement la divine ardeur qui la presse ? Mais quand je pourrais la représenter aussi forte et aussi fervente qu'elle est dans le cœur de Thérèse, qui comprendra ce que j'ai à dire ? et nos esprits attachés à la terre, entendront-ils ces transports célestes ?" (*Panégyrique de sainte Thérèse*, in *Œuvres* 393–412, p. 404).

[104] "[L]'usage d'une grande profusion de mots, de nombreuses répétitions [...] fait paradoxalement naître le silence propice à la contemplation mystique" (*École française*, p. 159). Bérulle proposes a more active solution to inarticulacy: "We [...] who are touched by such a rare subject that is capable of silencing eloquence itself, should have recourse to the eloquence of works and service, praising, admiring and worshipping Jesus Christ our Lord with all our power" ["Nous donc, [...] touchés d'un si rare sujet capable de rendre l'éloquence même muette, devrions avoir recours à l'éloquence des œuvres et des services, louant, admirant et adorant Jésus-Christ notre Seigneur de toute notre puissance"] (*Grandeurs de Jésus* in *OC*, VII, 71).

the transcendent understanding of God; but they should not be taken as a substitute for that understanding."[105]

It is however Bossuet who, in dealing with death in his *Funeral Orations*, moves towards the limits of language that he will both extend and transcend. Thus, in the *Funeral Oration of Henriette d'Angleterre*, the horror of death is famously encapsulated in the failure of language to account for it:

> Our body takes on another name; even that of corpse, Tertullian says, because it still indicates a human form, does not stay with it for long: it becomes a *je ne sais quoi*, something which has no name in any language; such is it true that everything dies in it, even to these funereal terms with which we once expressed its sad remains.[106]

Specific words in this perspective are not just accorded an inversion of meaning, but a negation of meaning: "Health is just a name, life is just a dream, fame is just an appearance, pleasures and delights are no more than a dangerous amusement."[107] This extends even to the name and titles of an individual; thus of the Princess Palatine: "There is no more Princess, nor Palatine; these great names which dazzle us do not endure."[108] All that is human fails; and it is in the last of his *Funeral Orations*, that of the Prince de Condé, that Bossuet reaches the most grandiose expression of this nothingness. The dramatic cadence which follows itself reinforces the negation of all the splendour that has preceded it, as Bossuet invites his hearers to survey their surroundings:

> Look all around you: this is everything that magnificence and piety could invent to honour a hero; titles, inscriptions, the vain signs of all that is no longer; figures that seem to weep around a tomb, and fragile images of a sorrow which time will carry away with all the rest; columns, that seem to want to bear to heaven itself the magnificent witness of our annihilation.[109]

[105] *Power, Gender*, p. 104.

[106] "Notre corps prend un autre nom ; même celui de cadavre, dit Tertullian, parce qu'il nous montre encore quelque forme humaine, ne lui demeure pas longtemps : il devient un je ne sais quoi, qui n'a plus de nom en aucune langue ; tant il est vrai que tout meurt en lui, jusqu'à ces termes funèbres par lesquels on exprimait ses malheureux restes" (*Oraison funèbre de Henriette-Anne d'Angleterre*, in *Œuvres* 83–105, p. 93). And cf. *Sermon sur la mort* in *Sermons*, p. 151. In Fénelon's *Dialogues on Eloquence*, reference is made to Tertullian's diction as "extraordinary and full of splendour" ["extraordinaire et pleine de faste"] (*Dialogues sur l'éloquence*, p. 78).

[107] "La santé n'est qu'un nom, la vie n'est qu'un songe, la gloire n'est qu'une apparence, les grâces et les plaisirs ne sont qu'un dangereux amusement" (*Oraison funèbre de Henriette-Anne d'Angleterre*, p. 84).

[108] "Il n'y a plus de princesse, ni Palatine ; ces grands noms dont on s'étourdit ne subsistent plus" (*Oraison funèbre d'Anne de Gonzague de Clèves*, in *Œuvres* 135–61, p. 159).

[109] "Jetez les yeux de toutes parts : voilà tout ce qu'a pu faire la magnificence et la piété pour honorer un héros ; des titres, des inscriptions, vaines marques de ce qui n'est plus ; des figures qui semblent pleurer autour d'un tombeau, et de fragiles images d'une douleur que le temps emporte avec tout le reste ; des colonnes qui semblent vouloir porter jusqu'au ciel le magnifique témoignage de notre néant" (*Oraison funèbre de Louis de Bourbon*, in *Œuvres* 191–218, p. 216).

This whole range of features that we have explored – oxymoron, semantic inversion, velleity, neologism, and imagic ingeniousness or over-extension, leading ultimately to stasis and aphasia – is then finally identified and resolved by Bossuet through the metaphor of translation. There is a duality in all his writing, a double perspective, the human and the divine ways of seeing things, immanence and transcendence, and the one will quite simply demonstrate the obverse of the other. Thus, biblically, the negativity of the first quotation of Ecclesiastes: "Vanitas vanitatum", which stands at the head of the *Funeral Oration of Henriette d'Angleterre* is balanced by the perspective of the last: "Deum time, et mandata eius observa: hoc est enim omnis homo" ["Fear God and keep his commandments, since this is the whole duty of man"]. In this way, in Bossuet's words, to which Pascal would equally subscribe: "Let us ponder [. . .] the first and last words of Ecclesiastes, the one showing the nothingness of man, the other establishing his greatness."[110] The nothingness/greatness opposition is once again exploited, but now in an eschatological perspective, and the view of humankind as seen through the eyes of God, *quasi oculo Dei*, will again restore meaning to those terms which have been deprived of it. His hearers must see with new eyes or, in his own governing image, speak a new language, as he explicitly urges in the same piece:

> Let us now change our language; let us no longer say that death has suddenly interrupted the course of the most beautiful life on earth, and the story which had such noble beginnings; let us say that it has put an end to the greatest perils that can assail a Christian soul.[111]

As Bayley remarks: "What would otherwise remain a tragic lament over man's estate is transformed by the revelation of an alternative reality and the prospect of an ultimate triumph."[112]

Such an image equally makes sense of the phrases that play on the word "name": "Health is only a name"; "these great names [. . .] do not survive". Such names, constrained by earthly usage, have no role in heavenly terms, because they correspond to no enduring post-semantic reality (at least, that is, until they become that new name, evoked in the *Funeral Oration of Marie-Thérèse*, which is inscribed on the column of the Apocalypse, alongside those of God and of the new Jerusalem).[113] But whereas the earthly manifestation of death is simply a meaningless experience of annihilation, the heavenly

[110] "Méditons [. . .] la première et la dernière parole de l'Ecclésiaste, l'une qui montre le néant de l'homme, l'autre qui établit sa grandeur" (*Oraison funèbre de Henriette-Anne d'Angleterre*, p. 85).

[111] "Changeons maintenant de langage ; ne disons plus que la mort a tout d'un coup arrêté le cours de la plus belle vie du monde, et de l'histoire qui se commençait le plus noblement ; disons qu'elle a mis fin aux plus grands périls dont une âme chrétienne peut être assaillie" (*Oraison funèbre de Henriette-Anne d'Angleterre*, p. 102).

[112] *French Pulpit Oratory*, p. 123.

[113] *Oraison funèbre de Marie-Thérèse d'Autriche*, p. 118. Cf. Revelation 3: 5; 12.

counterpoint is eternally meaningful, albeit in a world that lies beyond human language. A new view of death will emerge once the signifying standpoint has been changed: for the non-believer it will be a source of fear, anger, and resentment; yet seen through the eyes of faith, it will become a moment of triumph, so that "however cruel death seems to us, it can only serve to [. . .] complete the workings of grace".[114] The *Funeral Orations* effect the transition from the life of the earthbound believer aspiring to redemption, and signal the ultimate purpose of that life as understood *sub specie æternitatis*. So far, whatever the reality of the transcendent order, we have been looking up to heaven from earth; what Bossuet uniquely effects is the transition to the heavenly perspective, to which the omnipresent theme of death is, by definition in the *Funeral Orations*, the most commonly privileged mode of access.

Dramatically, the most powerful expression of this divergence of perspective occurs once again in Corneille's martyr tragedy, *Polyeucte martyr*, in the great fourth-act confrontation between the neophyte zealot Polyeucte and his former lover Pauline. It is the utter polarization of perspectives and their terminology that leads directly to the frequent occurrences of symmetrical antithesis in the play; and this culminates in a rapid exchange in which the unbeliever's cry of "Fantasies!" is answered by the martyr's "Heavenly truths", and her "Strange blindness" is met with his "Eternal enlightenment".[115] In this way, the precise impression is given of a translation from one language into another, as the transcendent and immanent perspectives compete within the alexandrines for priority, in a dialogue of the deaf which has already been identified as such by Polyeucte:

> But what point is there in talking about hidden treasures
> To minds that God has not yet touched?[116]

As Pascal writes in the fifth letter to Mlle Roannez: "Jesus Christ in the Gospels gave this sign by which to recognize those who have faith, which is that they will speak a new language, and indeed the renewal of their thoughts and desires brings about that of their speech."[117]

The single term with which we might finally explore this linguistic transition is that of madness, "folie", in Pascal, Fénelon, and Bossuet. For Pascal, first of all, the concept of folly is a particularly polysemic one, starting with a

[114] "[. . .] quelque cruelle que la mort nous paraisse, elle ne doit servir [. . .] que pour accomplir l'œuvre de la grâce" (*Oraison funèbre de Henriette-Anne d'Angleterre*, p. 99). Cf. Pascal's letter on the death of his father (*Lettre à M. et Mme. Périer* in L 275–9).

[115] "PAULINE : Imaginations ! POLYEUCTE : Célestes vérités ! / PAULINE : Étrange aveuglement ! POLYEUCTE : Éternelles clartés !" (*Polyeucte martyr*, IV, 3, 1285–6).

[116] "Mais que sert de parler de ces trésors cachés / A des esprits que Dieu n'a pas encore touchés ?" (*Polyeucte martyr*, IV, 3, 1233–4).

[117] "Jésus-Christ a donné dans l'Évangile cette marque pour reconnaître ceux qui ont la foi, qui est qu'ils parleront un langage nouveau, et en effet le renouvellement des pensées et des désirs cause celui des discours" (*Lettres aux Roannez*, V, in L p. 268). The biblical reference is Mark 15: 17.

simple play on the immanent term: "Men are so necessarily mad", he writes, "that it would be another sort of madness not to be mad",[118] before moving to the pragmatic statement that "true Christians obey follies nonetheless, not because they respect them, but because they respect the order of God which, for the punishment of mankind, has tied it to these follies".[119] It is in a cognate sense, therefore, that "original sin is a folly in the eyes of men, but it is acknowledged as such".[120] Secondly, now translating the most natural immanent meaning into its transcendent correlative, he asserts that, whereas the immanent "folly" of Christian doctrine is so undeniable in human terms, it becomes, viewed now in the transcendent perspective, in a paraphrase of 1 Corinthians 1: 25, "wiser than all the wisdom of men".[121] But Pascal then affords a final twist, since it is paradoxically from this perspective that the original immanent meaning is re-applied to non-believers, of whom, in an elegant semantic conceit, "all the charity of the religion they despise is required so as not to despise them to such a point as to abandon them to their folly".[122] Fénelon, in an inverse development of the same potential for ambiguity, is also content to "let the crazy world say whatever it likes about [the Crucifixion], let it make it a cause of scandal [. . .]. It is the opprobrium and the folly of the Saviour that I love"[123]; so that in his reflection on Good Friday, "the true worship of Jesus Christ crucified consists of being sacrificed with him, of losing one's reason in the folly of the Cross, [. . .] of consenting to pass for a madman like Jesus Christ".[124] It is ultimately, then, because the Incarnation is itself the expression of one thing by its opposite (omnipotence by fragility, glory by weakness, and so on) that words in the Christian context may acquire the meaning *sub specie æternitatis* that directly contradicts their immanent sense. Christianity is only a divine folly in a perspective that is itself governed by human folly.

[118] "Les hommes sont si nécessairement fous que ce serait être fou par un autre tour de folie de n'être pas fou" (*Pensées*, L 412, S 31).

[119] "Les vrais chrétiens obéissent aux folies néanmoins, non pas qu'ils respectent les folies, mais l'ordre de Dieu qui pour la punition des hommes les a asservis à ces folies" (L 14, S 48). Sellier glosses the term as indicating here "the randomness of the social and political order" ["l'arbitraire de l'ordre social et politique"].

[120] "Le péché originel est folie devant les hommes, mais on le donne pour tel" (*Pensées*, L 695, S 574).

[121] "Mais cette folie est plus sage que toute la sagesse des hommes, *sapientius est hominibus*" (*Pensées*, L 695, S 574).

[122] "[. . .] il faut avoir toute la charité de la religion qu'ils méprisent pour ne les pas mépriser jusqu'à les abandonner dans leur folie" (L 427, S 681).

[123] "Que le monde insensé en dise tout ce qu'il voudra, qu'il s'en scandalise même [. . .]. C'est l'opprobre et la folie du Sauveur que j'aime" (*Entretiens affectifs pour les principales fêtes de l'année* (*Pour le jour des Rois*), in *Œuvres*, I, p. 940).

[124] "La véritable adoration de Jésus-Christ crucifié consiste à se sacrifier avec lui, à perdre la raison dans la folie de la croix [. . .], à consentir de passer pour insensé comme Jésus-Christ" (*Entretiens affectifs pour les principales fêtes de l'année* (*Pour le vendredi saint*), in *Œuvres*, I, p. 952). Compare Surin in Chapter 5.

It is in Bossuet's *Panegyrics* that we return to the event that lies at the theological centre of this substitution. We first see in the *First Panegyric of St Francis of Paola* the coexistence of the presence of a "God most high", with the injunction that "one can only approach him by lowering oneself",[125] coming in turn from the seminal oxymoron that is Pascal's "religion of a humiliated God".[126] Then, in the *Panegyric of St Francis of Assisi*, based again on 1 Corinthians, we find the attitude of the early believers described as being one of fearlessness "to bring out for all the world to see the scandal and the folly of the Cross in all their extent"[127]; and this is in turn endorsed by the words of St Paul himself, "'that he should be foolish in order to be wise: *stultus fiat ut sit sapiens*'".[128] This, he goes on, is that "illustrious, noble, wise and triumphant folly of Christianity".[129] But it is in this *Panegyric* too that we attain to the linguistic crux of the phenomenon as here, once again, the contradictory givens of the crucified God are reduced further and most potently to their core, and indeed bilingual statement, that "the first and greatest folly, that is to say the highest and most divine wisdom that the Gospel preaches, is the Incarnation of the Saviour".[130]

[125] "Or, encore que Dieu soit très haut, [. . .], on ne l'approche qu'en s'abaissant" (*Premier panégyrique de saint François de Paule*, in *Œuvres*, 303–26, p. 303).

[126] *Pensées*, L 220, S 253. And developing the same conceit: "Jesus Christ is a God whom one approaches without pride, and beneath whom one lowers oneself without despair" ["Jésus-Christ est un Dieu dont on s'approche sans orgueil, et sous lequel on s'abaisse sans désespoir"] (*Pensées*, L 212, S 245).

[127] "[. . .] de faire éclater par toute la terre le scandale et la folie de la croix dans toute leur étendue" (*Panégyrique de saint François d'Assise*, in *Œuvres*, 235–58, p. 236).

[128] "'Qu'il soit fou afin d'être sage' *stultus fiat ut sit sapiens*" (*Panégyrique de saint François d'Assise*, p. 239). The Pauline text (1 Corinthians 3: 18) serves as the epigraph for the whole panegyric.

[129] "[. . .] cette illustre, cette généreuse, cette sage et triomphante folie du christianisme" (*Panégyrique de saint François d'Assise*, p. 239).

[130] "[. . .] la première et la plus grande folie, c'est-à-dire la plus haute et la plus divine sagesse que l'Évangile nous prêche, c'est l'Incarnation du Sauveur" (*Panégyrique de saint François d'Assise*, p. 237).

4

Particularity and Language (ii): Talking *for* God

In a fragment of the *Pensées* which tellingly occurs in the *liasse* devoted to the proofs of Christ's divinity ["Preuves de Jésus-Christ"], Pascal writes: "Jesus Christ said great things so simply that it seems as if he has not thought about them, and yet so clearly that there is no doubt about what he meant. This clarity joined to this naturalness is remarkable."[1] Such an impression correlates with the words of the guards in John 7: 46: "No-one has ever spoken like this man"; and the theology behind the phenomenon is developed by Fénelon in a play on the French words *Verbe* and *parole*: "This speech [*cette parole*] issued from the mouth of the Saviour during his mortal life only had such power and produced such fruit on earth because they were animated by this word of life which is the Word [*le Verbe*] itself."[2] The qualities accorded to the language of the mature Christ are also, by general consent, shared by his immediate disciples, and by those who record his life in the Gospels. Thus, in the third of Fénelon's *Dialogues on Eloquence*, the question of Christ's style is taken somewhat further, and the issues are nuanced in so doing, with the concession that "although simple and informal, it is sublime and figurative in several places".[3] It nonetheless remains that "all these splendours which astonish us are natural to him; he is born to them, and he only speaks as he sees, as he himself assures us".[4] In the writing of the apostles too, however

[1] "Jésus-Christ a dit les choses grandes si simplement qu'il semble qu'il ne les a pas pensées, et si nettement néanmoins qu'on voit bien ce qu'il en pensait. Cette clarté jointe à cette naïveté est admirable" (L 309, S 340). The word *naïveté* in the period keeps its etymological resonances of innateness (Latin *nativitas*). The *liasse* is *Pensées*, L XXIII, S XXIV.

[2] "Cette parole, sortie de la bouche du Sauveur pendant les jours de sa vie mortelle, n'a eu tant de vertu, et n'a produit tant de fruits sur la terre, qu'à cause qu'elle était animée par cette parole de vie qui est le Verbe même" (*Lettres et opuscules spirituels*, X (*De la parole intérieure*) in *Œuvres*, I, p. 591). The Latin formulation of the same contrast is achieved by the singular ("verbum") and the plural ("verba") forms of the same word.

[3] "[. . .] quoique simple et familier, il est sublime et figuré en bien des endroits" (*Dialogues sur l'éloquence*, p. 68).

[4] "Toutes ces grandeurs qui nous étonnent lui sont naturelles ; il y est né, et il ne dit que ce qu'il voit, comme il nous l'assure lui-même" (*Dialogues sur l'éloquence*, p. 68).

much they lack the authority of Christ, and "notwithstanding all [their] minor irregularities of diction, everything is noble, lively and affecting".[5]

The paradox inherent in this with respect to the Incarnation is developed by the same prelate, as he writes in his reflection for Christmas Day of how, as the Word is made flesh, so "the omnipotent speech of the Father is reduced to silence, stammering, crying and making childish noises",[6] and it is indeed, as we have seen and shall see in some of the more extreme cases of mystical experience, to that same state that certain of his later disciples are in turn reduced. For the majority of those who come in later ages, however, the more pragmatic question arises as to what devices to use in order to speak and write in order most effectively to promote Christian belief, dogma, and spirituality; and this conscious artifice is in turn necessary because, as Sara Melzer has memorably remarked, the Fall is the Fall into rhetoric.[7]

I finished the last chapter by suggesting that a phrase by Bossuet was bilingual, in other words that it held in tension the immanent and transcendent connotations of a given word. This is often the case too in Pascal's writing, where the polysemic nature of many of his key terms might well lead a reader to understand one thing when another meaning is implied, and indeed to feel semantically disoriented as a result. Thus, when the apologist promises the hesitant unbeliever that "no-one is happy like a true Christian, nor reasonable, nor virtuous, nor likeable",[8] these epithets will be understood quite differently by the addressee before and after he or she has moved to the position of faith. This kind of semantic flexibility is in one sense necessitated for Pascal in the *Pensées* by the duality of status within the apologist, whereby he is both external (by design) and internal (by conviction) to the end point of his argument. This is nowhere more apparent than in the notorious wager argument, probably the best known, but also one of the most questionable, of Pascal's strategic ploys, proposing as it does that the unbeliever has nothing to

[5] "[. . .] nonobstant tous ces petits désordres pour la diction, tout y est noble, vif et touchant" (*Dialogues sur l'éloquence*, p. 69).

[6] "Le Verbe fait chair, la parole toute-puissante du Père se tait, bégaie, pleure, pousse des cris enfantins" (*Entretiens affectifs pour les principales fêtes de l'année (Pour le jour de Noël*) in *Œuvres*, I, p. 932).

[7] "Although rhetoric may wreak havoc with logic, it shows that language can express meaning indirectly. In this way, rhetoric opens itself up to a Christian discourse that, in this fallen world, can communicate only indirectly" (*Discourses of the Fall*, p. 40). On Pascal's language see also Patricia Topliss, *The Rhetoric of Pascal*, Leicester, Leicester University Press, 1966 and Michel Le Guern, *L'Image dans l'œuvre de Pascal*, Paris, Colin, 1969. Although rhetoric is primarily understood in the period as the art of speaking well ("l'art de bien dire" according to the 1694 *Dictionnaire de l'Académie Française*), it retains its original meaning of the art of persuasion, as evidenced in the second part of the title of Pascal's *Opuscule*, "De l'esprit géométrique et de l'art de persuader".

[8] "Nul n'est heureux comme un vrai chrétien, ni raisonnable, ni vertueux, ni aimable" (*Pensées*, L 357, S 389).

lose and everything to gain by betting on the existence of God.[9] One of the many difficulties here with the apologist's role is that he seems to be assuming on the part of his interlocutor that a transition to the transcendent perspective has been made in the course of an argument for making it. Indeed, several briefer and less well known fragments afford a more straightforward, because more immanently focused expression of the same question, and they do so entirely because of their conceded element of unknowable risk: thus (in an unidentified first-person utterance) the complementary strategy, now predicated on fear rather than on hope: "I would be much more frightened of being wrong and of discovering that the Christian religion is true, than of being mistaken in believing it to be true";[10] or, in the un-loaded presentation of alternatives: "You have to live differently in the world according to these different suppositions."[11] Such statements contain both a psychological and a pragmatic dimension, as indeed does the apologist's insistence in the wager argument on the fact that a non-choice is a choice against belief.

What in a sense he adds to these stakes, and one of the reasons for the wager fragment's highly contested problematics, is the element of a unilaterally conceded afterlife. As Sellier remarks, "the mathematical developments of the Wager indeed presuppose, in order to be valid, that the interlocutor perceives the total insignificance of the type of life that he is being invited to renounce"[12]; he is thereby presumed to have made a qualitative shift which, by definition, he cannot have made, and thus can accept neither that there is nothing to lose, and even less that there is, in Pascal's exuberant phrase, "an infinity of infinitely happy life to gain".[13] The unbeliever's here-and-now, as

[9] Voltaire was to comment: "Your reasoning would only serve to create atheists, if the voice of all nature did not cry out to us that there is a God, with as much strength as these subtleties have weakness" ["Votre raisonnement ne servirait qu'à faire des athées, si la voix de toute la nature ne nous criait qu'il y a un dieu, avec autant de force que ces subtilités ont de faiblesse"] (*Lettres philosophiques*, p. 161). This kind of cosmological optimism was to be fatally vitiated by the Lisbon earthquake of 1755, to which Voltaire reacted in the "Poem on the Lisbon Disaster" ["Poème sur le désastre de Lisbonne"] the following year. There is a substantial amount of attention devoted to the reception of this fragment, starting with its immediate critics, and analysed by Antony McKenna, *De Pascal à Voltaire: le rôle des 'Pensées' de Pascal dans l'histoire des idées entre 1670 et 1734*, Oxford, Voltaire Foundation, 1990 and Arnoux Straudo, *La Fortune de Pascal en France au XVIIIe siècle*, Oxford, Voltaire Foundation, 1997. A succinct bibliography of more recent critical responses is provided by Sellier in *Pensées*, p. 1208, n. 2.

[10] "J'aurais bien plus de peur de me tromper et de trouver que la religion chrétienne soit vraie que non pas de me tromper en la croyant vraie" (*Pensées*, L 387, S 6).

[11] "Il faut vivre autrement dans le monde selon ces diverses suppositions" (*Pensées*, L 154, S 187).

[12] "Les développements mathématiques du Pari supposent en effet, pour être valides, que l'interlocuteur entrevoie le néant du type de vie auquel il est proposé de renoncer" (*Pensées*, S, p. 789).

[13] "Une infinité de vie infiniment heureuse à gagner" (*Pensées*, L 418, S 680). The same idea is given dramatic expression by Rotrou, as Genest is encouraged by Natalie: "Fight, suffer and win for yourself, by dying as a Christian / For one moment of ill, an eternity of goodness" ["Combats,

Fontenelle was to insist in the next century, at least has the virtue of being real[14]; and it is only if that reality is endowed with the pessimistic opprobrium which Pascal so persistently accords to it, that it becomes vilified to such a degree that a hypothetical better life becomes a potentially more attractive punt. The wager has been described as bad theology and even worse mathematics. Both might be true; but the real problem is that it is bad psychology and even worse semantics. And that is simply because, in order to understand the implications of a bilingual statement, both speaker and hearer must have a command of both languages. Pascal's unbelieving interlocutor, for the time being at least, is a monoglot.

The rhetorical principle behind this flawed example is undeniably more sound, however, since Pascal is not for the most part playing some disingenuous game with language. Rather, his conscious deployment of a whole range of persuasive techniques lies in the recognition that, in the business of engaging with fallen humankind through a fallen medium, the clarity and naivety of Christ or the authority of the apostles will not usually be enough.[15] What replaces it is a maieutic process whereby, as Pascal spells out in his essay *On the Art of Persuasion*, the apologist begins by moving imaginatively towards the starting point of his interlocutor: "Whatever you want to persuade someone of, you have to pay attention to the person you are trying to persuade. You must know his mind and his heart, what principles he holds to, what things he likes."[16] And this is because "the art of persuasion consists as much in the art of enticing as in that of convincing, to such a degree are men moved more

souffre et t'acquiers, en mourant en Chrétien / Par un moment de mal, l'éternité d'un bien" (*Le Véritable Saint Genest*, IV, 4, 1193–4).

14 The text is the *Réflexions* attributed to Fontenelle in Condorcet/Voltaire's *Éloge et 'Pensées' de Pascal*, in which a fictive Chinese philosopher objects that, "[in] a word, you advise me to renounce, for the love of this [hoped-for life], everything in which all my happiness has so far consisted" ["En un mot, vous m'insinuez de renoncer, pour l'amour de cette espérance, à tout ce en quoi j'ai fait consister jusqu'ici tout mon bonheur" (*Éloge et 'Pensées' de Pascal*, p. 176). In the dramatic medium, we equally notice the description of eternal life by the (for the time being) non-believing Pauline in Corneille's *Polyeucte martyr* as "the idiotic dreams of your Christians" ["de vos chrétiens les ridicules songes"] (*Polyeucte martyr*, IV, 3, 1199).

15 I would therefore find it difficult fully to endorse Sellier's remark that "in Pascal, we see the imitation of Christ taken—to an exceptional degree in the Christian tradition—as far as the *rhetorical* imitation of Jesus-Christ" ["Chez Pascal, l'imitation de Jésus-Christ se trouve [. . .] poussée – à un degré exceptionnel dans la tradition chrétienne – jusqu'à l'imitation *rhétorique* de Jésus-Christ"] ("La Bible de Pascal", in *Le Grand Siècle et la Bible*, ed. Armogathe, p. 713, original emphasis).

16 "[Quoi] que ce soit qu'on veuille persuader, il faut avoir égard à la personne à qui on en veut, dont il faut connaître l'esprit et le cœur, quels principes il accorde, quelles choses il aime" (L p. 356, S p. 135). The bipartite *Opuscule* entitled *On the Geometric Mind and on the Art of Persuasion* [*De l'esprit géométrique et de l'art de persuader*] is reproduced in Lafuma at 348–59 and in Sellier at 109–45, preceded by a brief "Notice" and bibliography (103–8). It is tentatively dated at 1657–8, but was not published in its entirety until the nineteenth century.

easily by whim than by reason".[17] Rhetoric, in this definition, involves the provisional transition of the persuader to the perspective of the addressee, which will in turn allow him to create the illusion in his hearer that "we are more effectively persuaded, usually, by reasons we have thought of ourselves, than by ones that have occurred in the minds of other people".[18] For Pascal to speak convincingly for God, therefore, he must adopt the whole panoply of fallen devices—including the appeal to self-interest and immanent common sense (psychologically), images drawn from the court, the salon, or the hunt (socially), or the potentials of ambiguity and polysemy (linguistically)—in order to bring his interlocutor to transcend them.[19]

Pascal will thus use a diversity of means to attain the same goal; and, to return to the image used by Le Maistre de Sacy in the *Entretien*, the poison of rhetoric—of the art of persuasion, in other words—will be put to a homeopathic end in order for the remedy to ensue. The incompleteness of the *Pensées* is of course always a complicating factor, but it is clear that even the fragments as we have them incorporate a polyvocal apparatus, and that there are embryonic dialogues in place between a whole range of speakers, each adopting a different, or perhaps an evolving position, in the process of the discovery of faith.[20] It is not a coincidence therefore that in the later *Provincial Letters*,[21] as in the second part of the *Pensées*,[22] the authority of Scripture takes over when the secular strategies of rhetoric have run their course. The contingent

[17] "[L'art] de persuader consiste autant en celui d'agréer qu'en celui de convaincre, tant les hommes se gouvernent plus par caprice que par raison" (*De l'esprit géométrique et de l'art de persuader* in L, p. 356, S p. 135). Relatedly, in defence of homiletic ornament, in the first of Fénelon's *Dialogues on Eloquence*, a disputant draws attention to the fact that "*honnêtes gens* have more delicate ears, and it is necessary to adapt to their taste" ["les honnêtes gens ont les oreilles plus délicates, et il est nécessaire de s'accommoder à leur goût"] (*Dialogues sur l'éloquence*, p. 6).

[18] "On se persuade mieux, pour l'ordinaire, par les raisons qu'on a soi-même trouvées, que par celles qui sont venues dans l'esprit des autres" (*De l'esprit géométrique et de l'art de persuader*, in L 737, S 617).

[19] As Hugh Davidson observes: "Pascal's terminology shows its rigor when it is needed, but it seems to thrive on a certain imprecision; the key words refer less to objects than to areas with shifting boundaries" (H. Davidson, *The Origins of Certainty: Means and Meanings in Pascal's 'Pensées'*, Chicago, University of Chicago Press, 1979, p. 73). See also Nicholas Hammond, *Playing with Truth: Language and the Human Condition in Pascal's 'Pensées'*, Oxford, Clarendon Press, 1994.

[20] See Louis Marin, "'Pascal': text, author, discourse . . . ", in *Yale French Studies*, 52 (1975), 129–51; Richard Parish, "Mais qui parle?: voice and persona in the *Pensées*", in *Seventeenth-Century French Studies*, 8 (1986), 23–40. It is at the same time clear that the eventual ordering of the material preoccupied Pascal, and that, even if we accept the likelihood of a putative non-linear and polyvocal apologia, we cannot assume that a fragmentary format was intentional. As Sellier's edition makes explicit, the fragment that was advanced to this end in certain critical approaches (*Pensées*, L 532, S 457) is devoted to Pyrrhonism, and not to the human condition.

[21] That is to say from the eleventh letter onwards, after the fiction of ingenuousness has been abandoned by Montalte.

[22] Understood in Pascal's bipartite division, according to which it will be shown in the second part that there is a Redeemer, by drawing evidence from Scripture: "Second part: That there is a

deployment of fallen language, in such a model, makes way in the end for the transition to a simpler, more direct and so more authoritative register. (As a more extreme illustration of the same phenomenon, we could cite the diabolically possessed Surin, who is afflicted on Good Friday by a kind of physical and mental paralysis until such time as he enters the pulpit and makes the sign of the Cross, whereupon he is enabled to preach eloquently for three hours, before relapsing immediately afterwards into his previous aphasic condition.)[23]

Moving to the intra-Christian domain, it is predictably true that by far the most extensive examples of didactic utterance in the period are to be found in the tradition of pulpit oratory. The three sub-genres concerned are: the sermon, preached both in the context of the Mass and at certain points of the year (especially Lent) as an autonomous series; the panegyric, pronounced in honour of a Saint; and the funeral oration. And the figure who will dominate my remarks will, also predictably enough, be Bossuet.[24] The form of the different sub-genres is furthermore clearly structured. All three share a strict plan, appropriate to the spoken word, and it is usually easy to see at a glance the architecture of the whole, whose detail is invariably held in a tight and indeed explicitly drawn framework of delivery.[25]

The sermon and panegyric both begin with the exordium. This essentially serves to introduce the thematics and structure of the homily, but is itself broken into two by a curious feature called the *Ave Maria* cadence ["la chute à l'*Ave*"]. This is explained by Bossuet in the *Panegyric of St Bernard*, where he makes the following equation:

> The Church has come easily to believe, O most fortunate Mary, blessed among all women, [that] you [who] were predestined from all eternity to engender in the

Redeemer, by Scripture" ["Deuxième partie: Qu'il y a un Réparateur, par l'Écriture"] (*Pensées*, L 6, S 40).

23 "After he had made the sign of the cross, he felt such a fire in his spirit, and such strength in his chest, that he continued [to preach] for three hours as vigorously as it is possible" ["Après avoir fait le signe de la croix il sentit un tel feu dans l'esprit, et une telle vigueur dans la poitrine, qu'il continua trois heures aussi vigoureusement qu'il fut possible"] (*Science expérimentale*, p. 169). As is the case of many of Surin's ordeals, this is but one of a recurrent sequence of similar manifestations.

24 On Bossuet's pulpit oratory see in particular Jacques Truchet, *La Prédication de Bossuet, étude des themes*, Paris, Éditions du Cerf, 1960; and the chapter on Bossuet in Peter France, *Rhetoric and Truth in France*, Oxford, Clarendon Press, 1972, 113–48. On the substance of his arguments, see Jacques Le Brun, *La Spiritualité de Bossuet*, Paris, Klincksieck, 1972 and Thérèse Goyet, *L'Humanisme de Bossuet*, Paris, Klincksieck, 1965. Peter Bayley, *French Pulpit Oratory*, is an invaluable guide to the period immediately preceding the activity of Bossuet, as to the conventions of the genre.

25 This practice is criticized by one of Fénelon's disputants in the *Dialogues on Eloquence* as "a very modern invention that comes to us from scholasticism" ["une invention très moderne qui nous vient de la scolastique"] (*Dialogues sur l'éloquence*, p. 50). As is often the case in this text, the status of the remark remains open-ended.

flesh the Son of the Most High, would willingly help with your pious intercessions those who must engender him in spirit in the hearts of all the faithful.[26]

The *Hail Mary* is thus interposed at the moment of transition from the exordium into the central sections [*divisions*] of the argument. There then follow the two (or occasionally three) *points* that make up the exposition[27]; and finally the peroration. The form of the panegyric imitates it closely.[28] These pieces were typically delivered at Masses in honour of the Saint in question, often in the presence of their relics or in a Church dedicated to them, and the readings are taken from the Proper (that is, the readings particular to the Feast Day) of the Saint. This recalls in turn the parallelism between the relic and the panegyric as, in a sense, two modes of recollection of the holy men and women whom they commemorate. In this way too they afford a compendium of exemplary Christian virtues,[29] to say nothing of the frequent opportunity for gory narratives: thus, for example, St Victor who, having exhausted his flagellants, was dragged by a wild horse through the streets of Marseille, before being ground to death on a millstone, as resumed by Bossuet in a prefatory summary: "Against him alone were carefully assembled all the strength possessed by men, by animals, by the most violent of machines"[30]; or St Gorgon, who "was lying on a bed of burning coals, melting on all sides by the force of the fire, and feeding by his own entrails the pale, dark flame that was devouring him".[31] The structure, as with the sermon, is clearly divided and sub-divided, thus in the *Panegyric of St John the Apostle*, a tripartite *division* is announced in the opening apostrophe:

[26] "[. . .] l'Église s'est persuadée aisément que vous, ô très heureuse Marie, bénite entre toutes les femmes ; vous qui avez été prédestinée dès l'éternité pour engendrer selon la chair le Fils du Très-Haut, vous aideriez volontiers de vos pieuses intercessions ceux qui le doivent engendrer en esprit dans les cœurs de tous les fidèles" (*Panégyrique de saint Bernard*, in *Œuvres*, 259–83, p. 260).

[27] See Jacques Truchet, "La division en points dans les sermons de Bossuet", in *Revue d'histoire littéraire de la France*, 52 (1952), 316–29.

[28] See on this subject Jacques Truchet, *Bossuet panégyriste*, Paris, Éditions du Cerf, 1962. Truchet's study is particularly strong on the question of sources, and he notes in particular: "Bossuet took his inspiration from neither art, literature, or the discourses of his predecessors. He returned, when necessary, to martyrologies and to breviaries, to be certain of the traditions of the Church" ["Bossuet ne s'inspirait ni de l'art, ni de la littérature, ni même des discours de ses prédécesseurs. Il recourait, si nécessaire, aux martyrologues et aux bréviaires, pour s'assurer des traditions de l'Église"] (*Bossuet panégyriste*, p. 92).

[29] Truchet comments that "each Saint appears specialized, if one can put it like that, in the practice of one or of several virtues" ["chaque saint apparaît comme spécialisé, si l'on ose dire, dans la pratique d'une ou de plusieurs vertus"] (*Bossuet panégyriste*, p. 119).

[30] "On a soigneusement ramassé contre lui seul tout ce qu'il y a de force dans les hommes, dans les animaux, dans les machines les plus violentes" (*Panégyrique de saint Victor*, in *Œuvres*, 371–91, p. 387).

[31] "Gorgon gisait sur un lit de charbons ardents, fondant de tous côtés par la force du feu, et nourrissant de ses entrailles une flamme pâle et obscure qui le dévorait " (*Premier panégyrique de saint Gorgon*, in *Œuvres*, 223–33, p. 230).

> O truly fortunate disciple, to whom Jesus Christ gave his cross, to associate him with his life of suffering; to whom Jesus Christ gave his mother, to live eternally in his memory; [and] to whom Jesus Christ gave his heart, so as to become one and the same thing with him.[32]

What the panegyric also shows is how Bossuet, by starting from a biblical quotation, illustrating it from saintly examples, and applying it to the faithful of his day, situates the Saints as intermediaries between the imperative of the scriptural injunction and the vacillating faith of his congregation.[33]

The funeral oration differs in certain respects from the sermon and panegyric, quite apart from the sheer scope and overpowering impact of Bossuet's later examples, which are quite simply in a different league from any other Christian oratory in the period. Its form, still strictly ordered, consists of the grieving (*déploration*) over the death of the subject, and of their eulogy; but this is invariably followed both by the religious and on occasion political lessons that may be learnt from the material. In this way, individual subjects are often accorded a quasi-allegorical status[34]; and indeed the skilful discovery of the appropriate biblical epigram text in French and in Latin contributes a vital *entrée en matière*, as well as an opening for later didactic potential.[35]

What powerfully punctuates the delivery of all these pieces is the use of biblical quotation in a motivic way, so as, on the one hand, to allow the Latin of the Vulgate to resonate in all its potency, and at the same time to provide a didactic commentary in the vernacular. The sheer flexibility of the Bible in

[32] "Ô disciple vraiment heureux, à qui Jésus-Christ a donné sa croix, pour l'associer à sa vie souffrante ; à qui Jésus-Christ a donné sa mère, pour vivre éternellement dans son souvenir; à qui Jésus-Christ a donné son cœur, pour n'être plus avec lui qu'une même chose" (*Panégyrique de saint Jean, Apôtre*, in *Œuvres*, 413–29, p. 415).

[33] Truchet notes: " Holiness plays two roles in the economy of salvation: one with respect to God, the other with respect to future generations" ["La sainteté joue deux rôles dans l'économie du salut: l'un à l'égard de Dieu, l'autre à l'égard des générations futures"] (*Bossuet panégyriste*, p. 19). He also considers that "of all the forms of sacred eloquence, the panegyric is the one that is the most closely intergrated into the framework of liturgical celebration" ["de toutes les formes de l'éloquence sacrée, le panégyrique est celle qui s'intègre le plus étroitement dans les cadres de la célébration liturgique "] (*Bossuet panégyriste*, p. 13). It is noticeable too, in the contemporary *Vies des saints*, that the saints of the calendar are immediately identified in terms of a biblical text at the outset, so once again serving to effect the vital link between Scripture and the present day, and to function as intermediaries both by intercession and example.

[34] Truchet comments on how the sub-genre provides new exemplary material for the orator, in distinction to the established paradigms of the saints (*Bossuet panégyriste*, p. 149). The four parts of the oration are thus summarized as "the grieving over the subject's death; their eulogy; some more strictly religious lessons that may be drawn; the adoption of positions, often political in nature, concerning contemporary issues" ["la déploration de la mort du défunt; son éloge; des leçons proprement religieuses; des prises de position, souvent de nature politique, sur les questions d'actualité"] (*Bossuet panégyriste*, p. 158).

[35] In addition to the Pléiade version, attention should be drawn to the edition of the *Oraison funèbres* by Jacques Truchet in the "Classiques Garnier" series (Paris, Garnier Frères, 1961), not least on account of its excellent illustrations. As Peter France comments, "the verbal splendour [. . .] [matches] the pomp of the decorations" (*Rhetoric and Truth*, p. 123).

producing appropriate texts for the widely divergent circumstances of its subjects is impressive in all these pieces,[36] and this diverse and integrated use of Scripture is a major feature of Bossuet's mature preaching. Far from the Bible being underplayed by the Church, its omnipresent influence, at least in its Gallican prelates, is felt across the whole spectrum of pulpit oratory,[37] even if certain books are the most recurrent with, alongside the Gospels and the Psalms, Job, Ecclesiastes, the Song of Songs, Wisdom, Isaiah, Jeremiah, St Paul, and the Revelation taking pride of place. Often the French translation will be followed immediately by its Latin original, so that, as Laurent Thirouin has pointed out (albeit in a different context), "the phrase is heard twice, [in such a way that] [...] its importance and dignity are underscored"[38]; and it is thereby enabled to convey through the text of the Vulgate some sense of the mystery and authority of which the vernacular paraphrase is deprived. Thus the chiastic text from Psalm 2: 10: "Et nunc, Reges, intelligite; erudimini, qui judicatis terram" ["So now, you kings, come to your senses, learn your lesson, you earthly rulers!"] is taken up as Bossuet's own in the *Funeral Oration of Henriette de France*; but it is also made to serve a structuring, didactic, and indeed mnemonic function, chiming like a motif through the duration of the delivery, and reiterated climactically as the preacher concludes, now endowed with the full weight of exposition which it has enjoyed in the interim. It serves as a *fil conducteur* in the sense that, however far the argument seems to be straying into personal or political specifics, it eventually returns to the

[36] Le Brun notes that "Bossuet [follows] with adaptations the laws of those sermon-givers who reserve such and such a biblical text for such and such a circumstance" ["Bossuet [suit] en les adaptant les lois des sermonnaires qui réservent toujours à telle circonstance tel texte biblique"] (*Histoire*, p. 229). And Velat remarks of the *Oraisons funèbres* on how he uses the biblical lead text as "both theme and structuring principle" ["thème et ligne directrice"] for the oration, so that "[the] biblical passage will form its structure and will receive a substantial commentary" ["[le] passage biblique en formera la trame et sera largement commenté"] (*Œuvres*, p. 5). The acontextual use of biblical verses is however criticised by implication in Fénelon's *Dialogues on Eloquence*: "Should not [the preacher] have begun by understanding the true meaning of the text, before applying it to his subject?" ["Ne devait-il [le prédicateur] pas commencer par entendre le vrai sens de son texte, avant de l'appliquer au sujet ?"] (*Dialogues sur l'éloquence*, p. 5).

[37] Armogathe, in the introduction to *Le Grand Siècle et la Bible*, evokes "the thirst for the Scriptures" ["la soif des Écritures"] and notes how "from the pulpit to the stage, Scripture illustates every trope, and each literary genre, traditional as well as new, owes a debt to the sacred books" ["de la chair à la scène, l'Écriture illustre tous les lieux, et chaque genre littéraire, traditionnel aussi bien que nouveau, est débiteur envers les livres sacrés"] (p. 15). A particularly important overview is provided in the same volume by the contribution of Alain Michel, "La grandeur et l'humilité. La Bible dans l'esthétique littéraire en France", 425–54. See also the still excellent study of René de La Broise, *Bossuet et la Bible*, Paris, Retaux-Bray, 1890.

[38] "[...] la [phrase] [se fait] entendre deux fois, [afin de] [...] signifier son importance, sa dignité" ("La figure de saint Augustin dans les *Provinciales*", in *La campagne des 'Provinciales'*, Paris, Chroniques de Port-Royal, 2008, 225–41, p. 229). Thirouin's more immediate point concerns the need to render credible the superficially improbable teaching that is attributed to the Society of Jesus.

quotation, which serves thereby as a point of reference, rather than simply being taken as a point of departure.

Additional biblical texts may also be introduced to effect a climax of their own, or to serve as a summary. Thus in the *Funeral Oration of the Princess Palatine*, the faithful are invited to admire a phrase from 1 John 4: 16:

> We believe, he said, and we profess the love that God has for us: *Et nos credimus charitati quam habet Deus in nobis*. This is the whole of the Christian faith; this is the cause and the summary of the entire creed. It is here that the Princess Palatine found the resolution to her previous doubts.[39]

Elsewhere, the three names inscribed on the column of the Apocalypse ("*I will write the name of God,* he said, *the name of the city of my God, the new Jerusalem, and my new name*")[40] serve as a subsidiary patterning device for the *Funeral Oration of Marie-Thérèse*, after a text itself taken from the same book (Revelation 14: 5): "*Sine macula enim sunt ante thronum Dei.* They are spotless before the throne of God."[41] And the holy death of Condé points the way forwards through the attribution to the *agonisant* of another biblical *topos* (in fact conflating two verses from 1 Corinthians 13: 12 and 1 John 3: 2):

> *Yes*, he said, *we shall see God as he is, face to face*. He repeated in Latin with a faultless taste these great words: *Sicuti est, facie ad faciem*; and we did not tire of seeing him in this gentle transport. What was going on in this soul? What new illumination was appearing? What sudden ray of light pierced through the cloud, and reduced to a shadow at that moment, with all the ignorance of the senses, the darkness itself and, so to speak, the holy obscurity of faith?[42]

Literary parallels come easily to mind[43]: we could argue that this flexibility within a formal structure is not dissimilar in the period to a neo-classical tragedy; or we could note how the powerfully didactic and admonitory peroration of the *Funeral Oration of the Princess Palatine* is reached through

[39] "'Nous croyons, dit-il, et nous confessons l'amour que Dieu a pour nous' : *Et nos credidimus charitati quam habet Deus in nobis*. C'est là toute la foi des chrétiens ; c'est la cause et l'abrégé de tout le symbole. C'est là que la princesse Palatine a trouvé la résolution de ses anciens doutes" (*Oraison funèbre d'Anne de Gonzague de Clèves*, in *Œuvres*, 135–61, p. 157).

[40] "*J'y écrirai*, dit-il, *le nom de mon Dieu, et le nom de la cité de mon Dieu, la nouvelle Jérusalem, et mon nouveau nom*" (*Oraison funèbre de Marie-Thérèse d'Autriche*, in *Œuvres*, 107–33, p. 118).

[41] "*Sine macula enim sunt ante thronum Dei*. Ils sont sans tâche devant le trône de Dieu" (*Oraison funèbre de Marie-Thérèse d'Autriche*, in *Œuvres*, 107–33, p. 107).

[42] "*Oui*, dit-il, *nous verrons Dieu comme il est, face à face*. Il répétait en latin avec un goût merveilleux ces grands mots : *Sicuti est, facie ad faciem* ; et on ne se lassait pas de le voir dans ce doux transport. Que se faisait-il dans cette âme ? quelle nouvelle lumière lui apparaissait ? quel soudain rayon perçait la nue, et faisait comme évanouir en ce moment, avec toutes les ignorances des sens, les ténèbres mêmes, si je l'ose dire, et les saintes obscurités de la foi ?" (*Oraison funèbre de Louis de Bourbon*, in *Œuvres*, 191–218, p. 216).

[43] Peter France remarks that "for all [Bossuet's] protestations, his sermons afford many of the traditional pleasures of literature" (*Rhetoric and Truth*, p. 137).

something like the turn of a sonnet, effecting the link between the grandiosely universalized paradigm and the intensely individual experience of death. Yet the most pertinent analogy of this defined yet flexible form is with the liturgy of the Mass itself, which has its Ordinary and its Proper, alongside or within which the homily stands as a kind of freer microcosm. Indeed liturgy and homiletics are complementary, and the variety within the office as within the genre shows that dynamic relationship. The canon of the Mass is unchanging, but the Ordinary is complemented from day to day by the Proper: in the readings, of course, but also in the Preface, which focuses on that element of divine Providence which leads the faithful into the *Sanctus*; and then more individually again in the two *mementos*, in which the faithful in turn pray for the living and the dead within the framework of the universal prayer of the Church. The eulogy of the dead, by definition personal, is thus by analogy both universalized, and inserted into the timeless didactic framework of Christian fundamentals.[44]

It is plain as a result to see how Bossuet's oratory is characterized by the balance between the formal sections, the absolute mastery of the more grandiose figures and images, the interdependence and interweaving of the didactic and eulogistic with the historical and liturgical, and the explicit and implicit biblical and patristic references. All these are supported in turn by infallible prose rhythms, climaxes, moments of calm, cadences, and symmetries, maintained over long periods of delivery,[45] as by the adept transition from literal to metaphorical, negative to positive, and immanent to transcendent. In the last of these pieces, the *Funeral Oration of the Prince de Condé*, the final intrusion of the orator as he contemplates his own death affords the *coup de grâce* of pathos, although even here the force and indeed universality of the utterance prevents it from any superficial theatricality:

> Instead of grieving over the death of others, great Prince, henceforth I want to learn from you how to make my own death holy, content if, alerted by these white hairs of the account I must give of my administration, I reserve, for the flock that I must feed with the words of life, what remains of a voice that is failing and an ardour that is growing dim.[46]

[44] Writing of the Mass, Jacques Le Brun comments of Bossuet: "This unique reality which remains present in its essence is so to speak renewed in each liturgical festival in a particular aspect" ["Cette réalité unique qui demeure présente dans sa vertu est pour ainsi dire renouvelée à chaque fête liturgique sous un aspect particulier"] (*Spiritualité de Bossuet*, p. 141).

[45] For a more detailed study of these features, see J. Fayard, "Les structures de la phrase oratoire et la résolution des tensions chez Bossuet", in *Bossuet: la prédication au XVIIe siècle*, ed. Goyet and Collinet, 291–310.

[46] "Au lieu de déplorer la mort des autres, grand Prince, dorénavant je veux apprendre de vous à rendre la mienne sainte : heureux si, averti par ces cheveux blancs du compte que je dois rendre de mon administration, je réserve au troupeau que je dois nourrir de la parole de vie les restes d'une voix qui tombe, et d'une ardeur qui s'éteint" (*Oraison funèbre de Louis de Bourbon*, in *Œuvres*, 191–218, p. 217–18).

Bossuet has achieved his own mastery in the genre: his style is now that of an orator entirely in command of his material; and in this final piece, in a sense, he signs his work. Homiletic *auctoritas* is now his, and the motivic reinforcements from Scripture, the Fathers, and the Saints have given way to another kind of authoritative voice.

In one sense, therefore, Bossuet's negations of stylistic effect, modesty *topoi* and preterition all ring untrue.[47] In the *Sermon on Death*, for example, he appeals: "But let us leave this long and scrupulous enumeration to rhetoric",[48] a denial that recurs in the *Panegyrics*, ironically and memorably in a particularly inflated passage in the *Panegyric of St Francis of Assisi*: "Let us leave, please, let us leave to the orators of this world the pomp and majesty of the panegyric style; they do not put themselves out to be understood so long as they recognize that they are admired",[49] leading to the claim once again that all that is being sought is the simplicity of the Gospels. (And the contemporary *moraliste* La Bruyère was to comment sourly in *Les Caractères* that the preachers of his day were so adept at evoking human disorders from the pulpit that he needed "some apostle with a more Christian style to deter [him] from the vices of which such an agreeable picture had been painted".)[50]

The definition of rhetoric is what is at issue, since in one respect Bossuet seems to use the term in a debased (indeed modern) sense, as he occasionally makes explicit by appending the epithet "worldly". In this sense Bossuet does not eschew rhetoric (indeed to do so would itself be a rhetorical act), rather its "false colours" and "strange ornaments".[51] The difference between such

[47] Peter France also explores this paradox (*Rhetoric and Truth*, p. 129 ff.), and comes to the conclusion that "the splendour of Bossuet's style may [. . .] be seen in part as a concession to his audiences" (p. 136), and reminds the reader that "many funeral orations were designed for posterity and published almost as soon as they were spoken" (*Rhetoric and truth*, p. 143). Voltaire reports in *Le Siècle de Louis XIV* that Bossuet was forced to interrupt his orations as "his hearers burst into sobs" ["l'auditoire éclata en sanglots"] (quoted in *Oraisons funèbres*, p. 1227, n. 3).

[48] "Mais laissons à la rhétorique cette longue et scrupuleuse énumération" (*Sermon sur la mort*, in *Sermons*, p. 154).

[49] "Laissons, laissons, s'il vous plaît, aux orateurs du monde la pompe et majesté du style panégyrique ; ils ne se mettent pas en peine qu'on les entende, pourvu qu'ils reconnaissent que l'on les admire" (*Panégyrique de saint François d'Assise*, in *Œuvres*, 235–58, p. 244).

[50] "J'ai besoin du moins que quelque apôtre avec un style plus chrétien me dégoûte des vices dont l'on m'avait fait une peinture si agréable" (*Les Caractères*, ed. Marc Escola, Paris, Champion, 1999, "De la Chaire", 9). On the Christian engagement of La Bruyère see more broadly: Robert Garapon, *Les 'Caractères' de La Bruyère*, Paris, SEDES, 1978; and, in particular, François-Xavier Cuche, *Une pensée sociale catholique*, Paris, Éditions du Cerf, 1991. See also, on his anti-Quietist writing, Chapter 6. Fénelon's *Dialogues on Eloquence* begin with a more constructive desideratum: "I am looking for a man who gives me such a taste and such respect for the word of God that I am more inclined to listen to it whenever possible" ["Je cherche un homme qui me donne un tel goût et une telle estime pour la parole de Dieu, que j'en sois plus disposé à l'écouter partout ailleurs"] (*Dialogues sur l'éloquence*, p. 3).

[51] The terms ("fausses couleurs et ornements étranges") occur in the early *Oraison funèbre du Père Bourgoing*, in *Œuvres*, p. 24.

worldly rhetoric and true Christian rhetoric appears to lie therefore in the balance accorded to the different parts, in the establishment of what is primary, and in the acknowledgement that language, which has failed and which will fail again, may not be. Bossuet's *ars rhetorica* lies in stressing that the substance will inspire the style (or, in formal rhetorical terms,[52] that the *inventio* will take priority), and indeed will fulfil the requirements of persuasion if the style (that is the right structure and words—the *dispositio* and *elocutio*) fails. As he writes in the immanent domain in the *Funeral Oration of Henriette-Marie de France*: "If the words fail us, if the expressions do not do justice to a subject that is so vast and so elevated, then the things will speak for themselves",[53] of which we saw the paramount Christic exemplification in his evocation of the eloquence of the Cross.

It is therefore the power of the content as against the presentation that will prevail since, as Bossuet insists in the *Panegyric of St Bernard*, "the true sacerdotal sign, the true ornament of the great priest is doctrine and truth".[54] Further, given the recognized difficulty of expressing the transcendent, the reader or hearer may infer that, whereas no amount of oratorical skill will convey the fullness of the Christian mystery, a perfectly chosen simple phrase—what others in more secular contexts will identify as the sublime—might paradoxically do so, just as a glass of water offered in Christ's name will open the gates of the kingdom of heaven.[55] Like Pascal and Fénelon, Bossuet, in the anti-Quietist tract known as the *Instruction on the States of Mental Prayer*, once again recalls the language of Christ and the apostles, "who, having to expound impenetrable mysteries, hidden to all the centuries, proposed them in simple and vulgar terms", and contrasts them with "those of a lower station who [. . .] only seem to think of flying beyond the clouds and being lost from sight by their readers".[56]

[52] For a general introduction to rhetoric, with a particular emphasis on writing in French, see Michael Hawcroft, *Rhetoric: Readings in French Literature*, Oxford, Oxford University Press, 1999.

[53] "Si les paroles nous manquent, si les expressions ne répondent point à un sujet si vaste et si relevé, les choses parleront assez d'elles-mêmes" (*Oraison funèbre de Henriette-Marie de France* in *Œuvres* p. 58).

[54] " [. . .] la vraie marque sacerdotale, le vrai ornement du grand prêtre, c'est la doctrine et la vérité" (*Panégyrique de saint Bernard*, in *Œuvres*, 259–83, p. 260).

[55] Matthew 10: 42. The text is used by Bossuet in the *Oraison funèbre de Louis de Bourbon*, albeit in a different context; and by St François de Sales in the *Treatise on the Love of God* in a chapter advocating "[that] we should use all available opportunities in the practice of divine love" ["Qu'il faut employer toutes les occasions présentes en la pratique du divin amour"] (*Traité de l'amour de Dieu*, p. 957).

[56] "[. . .] qui ayant à développer des mystères impénétrables et cachés à tous les siècles, les ont proposés en termes simples et vulgaires [. . .] au lieu [. . .] que ceux-ci dans une moindre élévation semblent ne songer qu'à percer les nues et à se faire perdre de vue par leurs lecteurs" (*Instruction sur les états d'oraison*, in *Œuvres complètes*, ed. Lachat, vol. XVII, 353–673, p.385). A similar distinction is made in Fénelon's *Dialogues on Eloquence*, where it is made clear that, unlike the apostles, who were miraculously inspired by the Spirit, their successors must work to

It is one of Bossuet's most powerful panegyrics that places this contradiction in some sort of a context. In the first part of the *Panegyric of St Paul the Apostle* we find the core of his theology of writing and speaking, introduced in a sort of *mise en abyme* by a compressed epigraph from a favourite verse from 2 Corinthians 12: 10: "'I only take pleasure in my weaknesses: for when I feel weak, it is then that I am powerful'";[57] and it is the strangeness and indeed human unacceptability of the Christian message which has to be transmitted that makes of it a superficial source of weakness in the messenger. The principal contrast is again established therefore between "human eloquence" and "the venerable simplicity of the Gospel of Jesus Christ", as evidence of which Bossuet predictably writes of St Paul that "he puts the force of persuasion in the simplicity of his discourse".[58] He then goes on to sub-divide the conventional means of achieving efficacy in speech (to present a paraphrase of the rules of formal rhetoric, in other words), with the importance accorded to the speaker and the material over and against the language and presentation chiming entirely with the emphases elsewhere.

But Bossuet then goes further in his subversion of rhetoric by proposing that the example of St Paul is especially potent by virtue of the absence of *any* such advantages: physical attractiveness and an acceptable message are both notably lacking, and neither is compensated for by "the flowers of rhetoric" ["les fleurs de la rhétorique"]; rather, in a further dialectical sequence, all three are transcended by "a hidden wisdom" ["une sagesse cachée"]. In order to explain this substitution, Bossuet goes on to develop a central metaphor between the Incarnation as flesh (Christ) and as word (Scripture), in such a way that Scripture shares both the lowliness ["bassesse"] and greatness ["grandeur"] of the Incarnation. It is, in Bossuet's words, because "the discourse of the Apostle is simple, but his thoughts are utterly divine"[59] that he may persuade against the rules; and, resuming the whole argument, because "this marvellous weakness that accompanies his preaching is a consequence of the abasement by which my Saviour himself was annihilated".[60] As one of

become impregnated with the doctrine and spirit of the Scriptures ["la doctrine et l'esprit des Écritures"], in order to preach effectively, with the two tendencies of "evangelical simplicity" ["simplicité évangélique"] and eloquence, and their degree of compatibility, introduced at an early stage. The debates as a whole come to rest on two equally valid types of preaching, both founded on ancient models, which could be summarized as exemplary textual explication on the one hand, and scripturally inspired eloquence on the other (*Dialogues sur l'éloquence*, p. 85–6).

[57] "Je ne me plais que dans mes faiblesses: car lorsque je me sens faible, c'est alors que je suis puissant" (*Panégyrique de l'apôtre saint Paul*, in *Œuvres* 347–369, p. 349).

[58] "Il met la force de persuader dans la simplicité de son discours" (*Panégyrique de l'apôtre saint Paul*, p. 353).

[59] "Le discours de l'Apôtre est simple, mais ses pensées sont toutes divines" (*Panégyrique de l'apôtre saint Paul*, p. 357).

[60] "Cette merveilleuse faiblesse qui accompagne la prédication, est une suite de l'abaissement par lequel mon Sauveur s'est anéanti" (*Panégyrique de l'apôtre saint Paul*, p. 357).

Fénelon's disputants explains: "St Paul argued, St Paul persuaded, so that he was, essentially, an excellent philosopher and orator. But his preaching [. . .] was not founded on argument or on human persuasion. It was a ministry whose whole force came from on high."[61]

It is in the light of these remarks that we may perhaps handle the apparent contradiction in terms of Bossuet's own achievement, always remembering that the disciple of St Paul is bound to lack the "hidden wisdom" of the master. First, by stressing that he is all the time putting language at the service of a higher ideal than itself; it might of itself be impressive, and often is, but that may never be the end point. Rhetoric, the "discourse of the Fall" in Melzer's phrase, is a provisional, pragmatic, and, essentially, a transcendable medium. Second, by noting that the force of pulpit oratory is born of the subject matter, which is itself weak, yet is only weak in the perspective of humankind. It thus carries the potential for its divine strength to be revealed as the reader or hearer "changes his language", and adopts the transcendent perspective. The idea of the weakness of the preacher being equated to his power is thus a further linguistic development of the whole *topos* of the folly of the Cross. Third, and paradoxically, we may also address the apparent contradiction by emphasizing that Bossuet's rhetoric is universally open about its own functioning, and visible in its forms. It is in this way a simple and not a subtle rhetoric, wherein art does not conceal artifice, and thus, far from eliciting praise, should in fact be seen as a failure of simplicity.

Finally, and most importantly, it is a part of Christian incarnational theology itself to eschew eloquence. Alongside St Paul, therefore, Bossuet has recourse, as he brings his metaphors together, to the authority of Origen, for whom "the word of the Gospel is a kind of second body which the Saviour has assumed for our salvation".[62] It is from this that he derives the logical consequence whereby, since Christ's body in its first incarnation is humble, so, therefore, should it be in its verbal equivalent: "After this fine doctrine", he writes,

> it is indeed easy to understand that the preaching of the apostles, whether it issues in living form from the mouths of these great men, or whether it flows in their writings so as to be carried across to the following ages, should have nothing showy. For, my brothers, do you not understand that, according to the thinking of

[61] "Saint Paul a raisonné, saint Paul a persuadé; ainsi il était, dans le fond, excellent philosophe et orateur. Mais sa prédication [. . .] n'a été fondée ni sur le raisonnement ni sur la persuasion humaine. C'était un ministère dont toute la force venait d'en haut" (*Dialogues sur l'éloquence*, p. 64).

[62] "La parole de l'Évangile est une espèce de second corps que le Sauveur a pris pour notre salut" (*Panégyrique de l'apôtre saint Paul*, p. 355). The text of Origen is the *Commentary on Matthew*.

> St Paul, this Jesus, who must appear to us in his flesh and in his word, wishes to be humble in the one as in the other?[63]

Just as the often contorted tropes of the language used to talk about God may reflect the contradictory specifics of the Christian revelation, and just as the privileged interlocutors of God may give birth to the word in silence, so too, in Bossuet's governing paradox, the rhetorical splendour of his Christian oratory, defective by its very potency, affords *a contrario*: a verbal image of the Incarnation.

I want to return in the second part of this chapter to some of the spiritual autobiographers, the "secretaries of God", in the title of Diane Watt's book,[64] who often carry their witness to extremes, but who are nonetheless representative of their age insofar as they hyperbolically exemplify, within the experience of exceptional individuals, certain of the major spiritual tendencies and dilemmas which define it. They also, by the reiterated conviction of Christic indwelling, exemplify the second of the Pauline *topoi* which I shall explore, and which dominates so much of their writing. This is the verse taken from Galatians 2: 20, which unites an emphasis on individual devotion and self-abnegation with an intense Christocentrism: "I am alive; yet it is no longer I, but Christ living in me."[65] It is Pascal who, in the third of the *Writings on Grace*, draws out the theological implications thus:

> [St Paul] says, then, *I live*, and [he] adds *I do not live*. Such it is true that life is in him and yet does not come from him [. . .]. Therein lies the origin of all these apparent contradictions [concerning grace and free will], which the Incarnation of the Word, who joined God to man and power to infirmity, has placed in the works of his grace.[66]

[63] "Après cette belle doctrine, il est bien aisé de comprendre que la prédication des apôtres, soit qu'elle sorte toute vivante de la bouche de ces grands hommes, soit qu'elle coule dans leurs écrits pour y être portée aux âges suivants, ne doit rien avoir qui éclate. Car, mes Frères, n'entendez-vous pas, selon la pensée de saint Paul, que ce Jésus, qui nous doit paraître et dans sa chair et dans sa parole, veut être humble dans l'une et dans l'autre" (*Panégyrique de l'apôtre saint Paul*, p. 356). Fénelon too in the *Dialogues on Eloquence* asks: "Did not God want to test our faith, not just by the obscurity, but also by the lowliness of style of Scripture, as by the poverty of Jesus Christ?" ["Dieu n'a-t-il pas voulu éprouver notre foi non seulement par l'obscurité, mais encore par la bassesse de style de l'Écriture, comme par la pauvreté de Jésus-Christ?"] (*Dialogues sur l'éloquence*, p. 60). France writes: "It is the preacher's duty to imitate the Incarnation; just as Christ manifested himself to men, so he, however imperfectly, must manifest Christ to other people" (*Rhetoric and Truth*, p. 127).

[64] Diane Watt, *Secretaries of God: Women Prophets in Late Medieval and Early-Modern England*, Cambridge, Cambridge University Press, 1997. Although her specific examples are drawn from English accounts, Watt is at pains to stress "the continuity in certain aspects of female revelatory experience" (p. 4).

[65] "Vivo ego iam non ego, vivit vero in me Christus." The range of French translations in the period is surprisingly diverse. The Jerusalem Bible translation is more expansive: "I am alive; yet it is no longer I, but Christ living in me".

[66] "[Saint Paul] dit donc *je vis*, et il ajoute *je ne vis pas*. Tant il est vrai que la vie est de lui et qu'elle n'est pas de lui [. . .]. Voilà l'origine de toutes ces contrariétés apparentes, que

But it is the autobiographers who explore these contradictions experientially, and who do so to the limits (and sometimes beyond) of both sanity and orthodoxy.

The sub-genre in which they record their lives, that of the spiritual autobiography, is a central one to Christian literature. The *Confessions* of St Augustine represent the earliest model, and the *Life* of St Teresa of Ávila, written in Spain in the sixteenth century, constitutes a more recent, but equally influential, example. The trajectories of their subjects are perhaps best described by Surin, who writes of the spiritual life in a sustained, albeit conventional, image of a sea journey: "On such a difficult sea as the spiritual life, on the extraordinary journeys on which there are so many reefs, so many sandbanks, so many winds, and so many storms", it is necessary to "follow a sure and tried course, so as to arrive finally and safely in the harbour."[67] The sense of being spiritually privileged, which is common to them all, tends in addition to promote the need for unremitting self-examination, so as to make the first-person narrative a particularly appropriate medium, akin to a kind of examination of conscience delegated to posterity. As Frank Bowman writes of Madame Guyon, but more universally applicable, such figures write "[as] a means of self-justification, of proving that [their] mission is divine and orthodox".[68] The parallel with auricular confession is telling too, since all of the examples we shall consider are addressed both to God and to a (usually) posthumous readership. They are thus typically interrupted by apostrophic prayer; but they also accord to their readership, by extension, the conjoined if discrete functions of interpreter and absolver.

Most commonly, the writers insist that they record their lives by virtue of a kind of divine authorization, in both the common and etymological meanings of that word: their writing is undertaken both with the permission, but also in many cases at the dictation, of God. Thus it is interpreted as a sign of God's pleasure that St Margaret Mary is enabled to recall her past at all: "I thought it would be impossible for me to write about these things that happened so long ago, but [Christ] showed me that the opposite was true. [And], to make it easier for me, he made me feel on each occasion the same disposition of which I speak."[69] She is told by Christ that she writes, in his words, "'to show that you are my plaything, by making useless all the precautions that I have allowed you

l'Incarnation du Verbe qui a joint Dieu à l'homme et la puissance à l'infirmité, a mises dans les ouvrages de la grâce" (*Écrits sur la grâce*, III, L p. 324).

[67] "Dans cette mer si difficile de la vie spirituelle, dans les voies extraordinaires dans lesquelles il y a tant d'écueils, tant de bancs, tant de vents et tant de tempêtes, [il faut] tenir une bonne route et assurée, pour surgir enfin à bon port" (*Science expérimentale*, p. 312–3).

[68] "Suffering, madness and literary creation" in *French Forum*, I, 1, 1976, 24–48, p. 38.

[69] "Je croyais m'être impossible de pouvoir parler de ces choses passées depuis tant de temps; mais il m'a bien fait voir le contraire. Car, pour me donner facilité, il me fait ressentir sur chaque article la même disposition dont je parle" (*Vie*, p. 91).

to take, in order to conceal the profusion of graces with which I have been pleased to endow such a poor feeble creature as you are'".[70] Relatedly, Madame Guyon, on the questionable activity of recording her dreams, justifies herself on two accounts: first, that she does so (in what we would now call a veracity *topos*) "out of fidelity, having promised to omit nothing which might come into my mind"; but, second, "because it is the way which God uses in order to communicate with faithful souls", in defence of which she typically, if controversially, cites scriptural precedent.[71]

What increasingly becomes obvious as well is the belief, shared by certain of her fellow autobiographers, that she writes entirely under inspiration. Thus she professes that: "I say things as they come to me, without knowing if I speak well or badly. When I speak or write, these things seem to me as clear as the day; but, after that, I perceive them as things that I have never known about, let alone written down".[72] In a later parenthesis too, she protests, again emphasizing the uniqueness of her experience (albeit, curiously enough, a uniqueness that is common to all the other writers in the sub-genre): "I would willingly suppress [the rest of my story] if I was in control of anything that I did, as much because of the difficulty I have in explaining myself, as because there are few souls capable of conduct that is so little known, and so little understood, that I have never read anything similar".[73] Thus when she composes the meditation entitled *Les Torrents* in 1683, it is described as "a whole treatise about the internal way in comparison with streams and rivers, [which] flowed as if from their origin and did not even travel through my head".[74] Where this subsequently became a matter of intractable polemic was in her various

[70] "'[. . .] pour te faire voir que je me joue, en rendant inutiles toutes les précautions que je t'ai laissée prendre pour cacher la profusion de grâces dont j'ai pris plaisir d'enrichir une aussi pauvre et chétive créature que toi'" (*Vie*, p. 35).

[71] "[. . .] par fidélité, ayant promis de ne rien omettre de ce qui me viendrait dans l'esprit, [. . .] [et] parce que c'est la manière dont Dieu se sert et se communique aux âmes de foi" (*Vie*, p. 399). Gondal writes of Madame Guyon's autobiography: "We can often [. . .] recognize a brave attempt to reinterpret and transform by faith episodes [in her life] that were often painful and obscure" ["On peut [. . .] y reconnaître une entreprise courageuse pour relire et transfigurer par la foi des épisodes souvent douloureux et obscurs"] (*Moyen court*, p. 28–9). The notion of the autobiographical pact ("le pacte autobiographique"), whereby the autobiographer undertakes to be truthful and comprehensive in return for the reader's good faith and indeed indulgence, is initiated by Philippe Lejeune in *L'Autobiographie en France*, Paris, Colin, 1971, and developed in *Le Pacte autobiographique*, Paris, Seuil, 1975.

[72] "[Je] dis les choses comme elles me viennent, sans savoir si je dis bien ou mal. Lorsque je les dis ou écris, elles me paraissent claires comme le jour ; après cela je les vois comme des choses que je n'ai jamais sues, loin de les avoir écrites" (*Vie*, p. 800).

[73] "Je le supprimerais volontiers si j'avais quelque chose qui me fût propre, tant à cause de la difficulté de m'en expliquer, que parce qu'il y a peu d'âmes capables d'une conduite si peu connue, et si peu comprise, que je n'ai jamais rien lu de semblable" (*Vie*, p. 442).

[74] "[un] traité entier de toute la voie intérieure sous la comparaison des rivières et des fleuves [et qui] coulait comme du fond et ne passait point par ma tête" (*Vie*, p. 518). Cognet describes the work rather quaintly as "a prolix and disorganised book, which nonetheless contains a very elevated doctrine and in which there are numerous admirable things to be found" ["un livre

attempts at biblical exegesis. Thus in the second book of *Les Torrents*, she writes of how God inspires her not only to read biblical texts, but also to write an exposition of them; yet, "before writing, I did not know what I was going to write; [and] as I wrote, I saw that I was writing things that I had never known [. . .]. In this way, Our Lord had me explain all of Holy Scripture".[75] As we shall see, the result (and disadvantage) of this immediacy in her conflictual dealings with authority, always assuming her description to be accurate, is that "it is very difficult for me, not to say impossible, to account for [my interpretations] in a dogmatic manner".[76]

Expressing herself more simply, Antoinette Bourignon[77] claims to write as an intermediary: "I have written all this for no other purpose than to make known what God tells me, for the benefit of those who are inclined to follow his teaching."[78] Surin's professed motive in publishing, as well, is presented as didactic and altruistic, so that he, like St Paul, might "establish [his readers] in the faith that you have in the words of the prophets, to whom you do well to be attentive, as to a torch which lightens our darkness", in order to "affirm the faith in which the profession of the Catholic religion engages us".[79] In addition, the recurrent motif is immediately introduced of God's permission for the possession to which he is subjected to happen, with the accompanying providential assurance of his [God's] ultimate design for good. Despite the wildly improbable nature of some of what follows, Surin is still able to conclude on a fragile note of acceptance of the common lot, from which the less afflicted reader might learn. The surface structure of the account is chaotic, however, above all in its pronominal insecurity, as it swerves between the first and the third person, sometimes within the same grammatical unit.[80]

bavard et désordonné, mais d'une doctrine très élevée et où abondent des trouvailles admirables"] (*Crépuscule*, p. 79).

[75] "Avant que d'écrire je ne savais pas ce que j'allais écrire ; [et] en écrivant, je voyais que j'écrivais des choses que je n'avais jamais sues. [. . .] De cette sorte, Notre Seigneur me fit expliquer toute la Sainte Écriture" (*Vie*, p. 603).

[76] "[Il] m'est très difficile, pour ne pas dire impossible, d'en rendre raison d'une manière dogmatique" (*Vie*, p. 801).

[77] The autobiography of Antionette Bourignon is the most obscure, and the most unorthodox, of the accounts we shall consider. There is no recent edition, and references are made to the first two volumes of the *Œuvres*, Amsterdam, R. and G. Wetstein, 1717.

[78] "Je n'ai point écrit tout ceci à autre fin sinon que pour déclarer ce que Dieu m'apprend, à ceux qui sont disposés à suivre ses enseignements" (*La Parole de Dieu*, p. 129).

[79] "[. . .] pour vous établir en la foi que vous avez à la parole des prophètes à qui vous faites bien de vous rendre attentifs, comme à un flambeau qui éclaire nos ténèbres [. . .] pour affermir la foi dans laquelle la profession de la religion catholique nous engage" (*Science expérimentale*, p. 128). How much of his writing was undertaken with these purposes is however ambiguous, since the third part of the *Science expérimentale* contains the explicit subtitle "(Which is secret, and should be communicated to no-one)" ["(Ce qui est secret et ne se doit communiquer à personne)"] (*Science expérimentale*, p. 255).

[80] Thus he writes: "I have said that during all this time the Father was reduced to such a state, that there was nobody that did not believe he was completely out of his mind" ["J'ai dit que

In the end, though, a loose general pattern does emerge, whereby the individual chapters (in which the reported episode occurs) tend to begin informatively in the third person, which thus takes on the function of a narrative voice, before moving into the first for more intimate revelations. It is as if the writer can impose some distance from his biographical past, but not from his spiritual ordeal.[81]

Apostrophe is predictably a major stylistic feature of many of the autobiographies, of which God is the omnipresent if largely implicit addressee (and the recurrent shift to the vocative is a feature that is also present in a wide range of less extreme devotional writing). Thus apostrophic prayer punctuates St Margaret Mary's account, as if to underline the need perpetually to refer to the transcendent as an authorizing force. In Madame Guyon again, the specific if unidentified human addressee is of minor importance alongside the repeated and universally exclamatory apostrophes to God; and in Antoinette Bourignon too, the autobiography is punctuated by direct appeals to Christ for guidance, in the form of the recurrent question taken from the Pauline model in Acts 9: 6: "Lord, what do you want me to do?"[82] An additional and more intrusive readerly function is thereby conveyed, whereby the reader becomes an observer, and perhaps even a voyeur, in an intimate exchange with the divine.

More disconcerting again, and entirely in conformity with such an impression, is the common claim that God communicates directly in reply. As a result, the question arises as to how the autobiographer accounts for the experience of individuated divine communication and, more problematically again, as to the epistemological status we can accord to such utterance. As Thomas Szasz memorably wrote: "If you talk to God, you are praying. If God talks to you, you have schizophrenia."[83] It is furthermore clear from what is claimed that we are not dealing with a phenomenon of the much-cited variety of an inner voice of conscience, eloquently evoked by Fénelon, in a paraphrase

pendant tout ce temps le Père fut réduit en un état, qu'il n'y avait personne qui ne crût qu'il était tout à fait hors de sens"] (*Science expérimentale*, p. 200).

[81] Bowman remarks on how "his syntax is stretched to breaking point" ("Suffering, madness", p. 47). Surin acknowledges these shifts, but gives no explanation for them, simply writing along the lines of: "I am speaking now sometimes in the first person, sometimes in the third, and I have, for whatever reason, swerved away from my path, without knowing either how I write with such freedom, as if it was only for my own purposes" ["Je parle ici tantôt à la première personne, tantôt en la troisième, et je suis, je ne sais comment, détourné de ma route, sans aussi savoir comment j'écris avec liberté, comme si je n'étais que pour moi-même"] (*Science expérimentale*, p. 204). I have only rendered the French approximately, in an attempt to make some greater sense of it than it superficially offers.

[82] "Seigneur, que voulez-vous que je fasse?" (*La Parole de Dieu*, p. 1 and *passim*). The same text is used by Fénelon in his reflection for the Feast of the Conversion of St Paul (*Entretiens affectifs pour les principales fêtes de l'année*, VII (*Sur la conversion de saint Paul*) in *Œuvres* I, 940–2).

[83] Thomas Szasz, *The Second Sin*, New York, Doubleday, 1973.

of Jeremiah 16: 9: "We must have every creature silenced, we must even have ourselves silenced, so as to listen in this deep silence of the entire soul to this ineffable voice of the bridegroom."[84] Nor is it understood in the more orthodox literary form of prosopopœia (the attributing of utterance to a third party who is either absent or imaginary), even less of a biblical or patristic quotation or paraphrase, but as an audible individual privilege.

One set of definitions occurs in the near-contemporary commentary on Bourignon's autobiography, tellingly entitled *The Word of God* [*La parole de Dieu*], in which her anonymous editor borrows terms from the (then) Blessed John of the Cross.[85] The editor asserts that the title phrase ("la parole de Dieu") is capable of three kinds of understanding: as the written word, primarily the Scriptures, and so far so straightforward; as "vocal words" ["paroles vocales"], tantamount to phenomena such as signs and visions; but finally as the "internal word of God" ["parole de Dieu intérieure"], whereby the chosen disciple achieves a direct communion, "by means that approximate closely to the most divine and to those that will prevail in eternal life".[86] These "internal words of God" are then again subdivided, once more in terms borrowed from St John of the Cross: into "discursive", whereby "the Holy Spirit speaks to the soul and the soul to the spirit"; "formal", "as if a third person spoke them within the soul"; and "substantial", "which [. . .] operate within the soul the living substance of the good which they signify or which they command".[87]

If we first take the simplest form of this (what Bourignon's editor would call "formal words"), we find that verbal communication with Christ is also a regular feature of the experience of St Margaret Mary, with the phenomenon most commonly described along the lines of "these words were spoken internally to me".[88] Such interventions are recorded as simple statements, however, not necessarily in need of deciphering, and usually reflect the writer's own style in a simplified form. (This is symptomatic as well of the recurrent tendency for both divine and diabolic utterance to be transmitted in the

[84] "Il faut faire taire toute créature, il faut se faire taire soi-même, pour écouter dans ce profond silence de toute l'âme cette voix ineffable de l'époux" (*Lettres et opuscules spirituels*, X (*De la parole intérieure*), in *Œuvres*, I, p. 590).

[85] The *Préface apologétique* is included in the first volume of the complete works. Although the claims for Bourignon which it contains are generally unconvincing, the material derived directly from St John of the Cross (who was canonized shortly after its publication, in 1726) is independently more persuasive.

[86] "[. . .] par des manières très approchantes des plus divines et de celles qu'on aura dans la vie éternelle" (*Préface apologétique*, p. 186–7).

[87] "discursives [. . .] le Saint Esprit parle à l'âme et l'âme à lui" ; "formelles, comme si une tierce personne les prononçait dans l'âme" ; "substantielles, qui [. . .] opèrent dans l'âme la vive substance du bien qu'elles signifient ou qu'elles commandent" (*Préface apologétique*, p. 193–4).

[88] Thus: "il me fut dit intérieurement ces paroles" (*Vie*, p. 54). Variants include: "j'entendis intérieurement ces paroles" (*Vie*, p. 92); the more tentative "il me semble que [j']entendis ces paroles" (*Vie*, p. 86); or the more explicit "il me fut dit intelligiblement" (*Vie*, p. 76).

language and idiom of the writer.) Dialogue with Christ too is recorded by her in a matter-of-fact way, and indeed on occasion is itself also relatively demotic. But it is more particularly the first revelation of the Sacred Heart that is recorded as an extended individual address: "'My divine Heart is so consumed with love for men'", Christ tells her,

> 'and for you in particular, that not being able to contain within itself the flames of its ardent charity, I have to use you as a means to disseminate them [. . .]; and I have chosen you as an abyss of unworthiness and ignorance for the accomplishment of this great project, so that everything will be done by me'.[89]

The stylistic questions which arise from such communications also drive us back to the fundamentals of language and doctrine. Do they imply, in a fallen world, that God simply adapts his instructions to the language and idiom of the believer?[90] Or that, in a redeemed world, such speech is accorded the stylistic privilege of simplicity and naivety that is consistent with the spiritual privilege which is accorded to the speaker? And, if so, does it thereby allow the exceptional believer to aspire to that redeemed language which will be the vernacular of the kingdom? Given the quality of some of St Margaret Mary's prose, it is certainly to be hoped that this is not invariably the case.

Moving to "substantial words", Bourignon herself writes, concerning the nature of her revelations, that her "words of God" "are not verbal [. . .], but rather a debate between God and the soul, which takes place by understanding, but cannot be explained to others without similar vocal words, in order to be understood".[91] Such divine intelligences are however only infallible "when the soul is free of all images", but are "doubtful when it is driven by imagination", which lead rather to "visions, spoken words, ecstasies or other sensations".[92] Both the liminary text and the autobiography itself are enlightening

[89] "'Mon divin Cœur est si passionné d'amour pour les hommes, et pour toi en particulier, que ne pouvant contenir en lui-même les flammes de son ardente charité, il faut qu'il les répande par ton moyen [...] ; et je t'ai choisie comme un abîme d'indignité et d'ignorance pour l'accomplissement de ce grand dessein, afin que tout soit fait par moi'" (*Vie*, p. 69).

[90] A further complicating factor lies in claims made that the linguistic idiom is unfamiliar to the recipient, most commonly because it is in Latin.

[91] "Les paroles de Dieu [...] ne sont point paroles verbales, [...] ains un raisonnement de Dieu avec l'âme, qui se fait dans l'entendement, lequel ne se peut expliquer aux autres sans semblables paroles vocales, pour être entendu" (*La parole de Dieu*, p. 130). Surin, who himself frequently quotes St John of the Cross, affords a compatible definition: "Then I heard in my heart a word, which was like those living words that Our Lord can pronounce, and that he alone can say, which are words of life that carry their effects with them, and which are called substantial words" ["Alors j'entendis dans mon cœur une parole, qui était comme ces paroles vitales que Notre-Seigneur sait prononcer, et qu'il n'y a que lui qui puisse dire, qui sont paroles de vie qui portent leurs effets avec elles, et que l'on nomme paroles substantielles"] (*Science expérimentale*, p. 227).

[92] "Les intelligences de Dieu [sont] infaillibles lorsque l'âme est libre de toute image, [mais] douteuses lorsqu'elle agit par imaginations, [qui produisent] visions, paroles de voix, extases ou autres sensibilités" (*La parole de Dieu*, p. 133).

here, and the mode of operation, if not the substance of what is communicated, correlates closely with certain more orthodox figures; yet the legitimacy of her own experience is mitigated by the apparently blasphemous parallels with the life of Christ, all the more so that these are presented (again in modern autobiographical terms) as a kind of self-defeating veracity pact with the reader: "Consider what I tell you on God's behalf with suspicion only if you observe that my life, my behaviour and my actions are not fully in conformity with those of Jesus Christ, and that my doctrine is not entirely similar to Holy Scripture."[93]

Finally Madame Guyon, in one of the most important of the parenthetical digressions which punctuate her life story, deals with the precise nature of divine communication. In her case, the difference is stressed between "distinct internal words" ["les paroles intérieures distinctes"], which she will later define as "mediate words" ["parole médiate"], transmitted by an angel, and therefore subject to illusion; and again "substantial words" ["parole substantielle"]. This mode of communication, she significantly asserts, is no less than the ineffable commerce of the Holy Trinity itself, communicated in turn to the blessed spirits and then finally to humankind. Such commerce notably occurred at certain great moments of Scripture, such as between Christ and St John at the Last Supper, between the Christ Child and the Kings and Shepherds or between Mary and Elizabeth—and indeed occurs, closer to home, between Madame Guyon and her spiritual director, with whom she spends hours on end, "always communicative, without being able to say a word".[94] It is, as a result, the delegated responsibility of those privileged to receive it to convey its purport to others through more conventional linguistic means. Furthermore, the efficacy of such "substantial words", whereby "it is the Word who speaks and operates what it says",[95] lies in the immediate impact of the word spoken as if by God, in distinction, say, to a miracle granted in answer to a prayer. Thus, in common with Surin, she defines this experience by a quotation from Psalm 33: 9 as "dixit et facta sunt" ["he spoke, it was so"], and proposes as the archetype for her carrying of this word the carrying by Mary of the Word in her womb. In a scene entirely reminiscent of Christ's actions (and indeed style), Guyon therefore orders a disciple to "'Get up, and be cured of your illness', [whereupon] she got up, and was cured."[96] From this, she makes the more profound if, to say the least, hubristic theological point, that such an operation affords in microcosm "the secret of the operation of the Word and

[93] "Tenez pour suspect ce que je vous dis de la part de Dieu en cas que remarquerez que ma vie, mes mœurs et mes actions ne soient toutes conformes à celles de Jésus-Christ, et que ma doctrine ne soit entièrement semblable à la Sainte Écriture" (*La parole de Dieu*, p. 134).

[94] "[. . .] toujours communicatif, sans pouvoir dire une parole" (*Vie*, p. 536).

[95] "[. . .] c'est le Verbe qui parle et opère ce qu'il dit" (*Vie*, p. 525).

[96] "'Levez-vous et ne soyez plus malade'. Elle se leva et ne fut plus malade" (*Vie*, p. 524).

the free will of mankind".[97] We are back to *parole* and *Verbe*; but we are once again, and for reasons that I shall soon develop further, pushing as a result at the limits of the degree to which it is possible to accommodate individual inspiration with orthodoxy.

I have treated the autobiographical texts I have cited in this chapter, together with their commentaries, with some sort of equivalence. But we have next to move from a linguistic enquiry to a theological and indeed a psychological one, since their authors range from a woman who was eventually canonized to one who was probably deluded, passing through an imprisoned mystic and two victims of diabolic possession. As Watt concludes, "the public character of the prophet was fluid; hailed as a Saint or Christian witness one moment [. . .], [he or] she might gain the notoriety of a reprobate, lunatic, devil or witch the next".[98] The question therefore inevitably arises as to who decides on which is which, and how; the question, in other words, of discernment or, as it was brilliantly encapsulated in the title of a recent article by D. Z. Phillips: "Mysticism and epistemology; one devil of a problem".[99]

[97] "[. . .] le secret de l'opération du Verbe et de la liberté de l'homme"(*Vie*, p. 526).
[98] *Secretaries of God*, p. 155
[99] D. Z. Phillips, in *Faith and philosophy*, 12 (2), 1995, 167–88.

5

Particularity and Discernment

"The particular manifestation of the Spirit granted to each one is to be used for the general good. [. . .] To [one is given] the working of miracles; to another, prophecy; [and] to another the power of distinguishing spirits: *alii discretio spirituum*" writes St Paul in 1 Corinthians 1: 6; 10.[1] I finished my last chapter with some accounts of exceptional Christian experience, but I want to return initially to a figure who has often been in the background of my remarks, and who might in some respects have been the more logical starting point for them, a writer and prelate who more than any other resonates with what we might now most comfortably identify as a common, and enduring, understanding of post-Tridentine Catholic spirituality. His tradition is often accorded the label of Christian humanism; and his writing and teaching were to mark the remainder of the century, albeit, as we shall see, in frequently conflicting ways. This is St François de Sales, Bishop-in-Exile of Geneva in the early years of the century, canonized – exceptionally rapidly – in 1665; and the author of the spiritual bestseller of his age, the *Introduction to the Devout Life*.[2] This work was written as a guide for the woman of the world (one Philothée, or lover of God), to encourage her to lead a life that was compatible both with her spiritual aspirations and with her social duties, a life that was, in his phrase, "ordinary, as far as appearances were concerned".[3]

[1] The Old Testament anticipation of this attitude is found in 1 Kings 3: 7–12, as Solomon asks for the gift of discernment, and is rewarded for so doing.

[2] *Introduction à la vie dévote*, in St François de Sales, *Œuvres*, ed. Ravier and Devos, 1–317. An attractive introduction to the spiritual ethos of François is afforded by Ruth Murphy, *Saint François de Sales et la civilité chrétienne*, Paris, Nizet, 1964. She particularly stresses "the interpenetration of the temporal and the spiritual" ["l'interpénétration du temporel et du spirituel"] (p.xiii) in his work. See also Angers, *L'Humanisme chrétien au XVIIe siècle*. Krumenacker (*École française*, p. 72) considers the four seminal figures of the Catholic Reformation to be St Ignatius Loyola, St Teresa of Ávila, St Charles Borromeo, and St François de Sales.

[3] "[une] vie commune, quant à l'extérieur" (*Introduction à la vie dévote*, p. 23). Angers comments: "The most remarkable thing about this gradation is its flexibility [. . .]. It is lived out; the ascent towards God is an imperceptible ascent" ["Le plus remarquable de cette gradation c'est sa souplesse [. . .]. C'est du vécu ; la montée vers Dieu est une montée qui ne se perçoit pas"] (*Humanisme chrétien*, p. 32). Although the addressee is named within the text, it is at the same

As François reminds his addressee in this work, the battle of the devout soul in the world might appear to be a lonely struggle, but it is not one which is, or indeed should be, attempted alone. The support of the spiritual director and behind him the presence and authority of the whole Church, militant on earth and triumphant in heaven, all sustain and guide the addressee in her efforts. The delegated authority of the priest is thus central to any spiritual progress; and the presence of some objective, ratifying dimension reminds us of the element of Christian experience which is common as opposed to individual, as of the need for the path of spiritual progress to be monitored. Not only are there recognized methods and exercises which may be followed, there are also identified areas and particular experiences which demand counsel and teaching (and all this, once again, is very much in the spirit of St Ignatius Loyola). The man or woman who is seeking to lead the devout life is not doing something new or untried; rather he or she is doing what the Saints have done, whose presence and encouragement take on an additional significance in this context. The accumulated wisdom of spiritual authority must therefore be transmitted to those who require it; but the Church must in turn be their constant point of reference, as it is for the spiritual director. It affords the common channel of sanctification for all its individual members, and it constitutes the perpetuation in history of the Incarnation through the acts of its adherents: François is a son of the Church in the same way that his disciple must be a daughter, and in that spiritual co-operation lies the touchstone of authority and authenticity.

What we find in this writing first of all, therefore, is an expression of all that is anti-inspirational, in the most affirmative sense of that negative term, even if it is ironically enough the advice of such exceptional Christian figures as Sts Teresa of Ávila and Catherine of Siena which is cited by François in order to draw his disciple's attention to the practices of "many good souls [who], after and before her [. . .], in order the better to subject themselves to God, have submitted their will to that of his servants".[4] It is also worth stressing the emphasis which is accorded to the role of the priest in the period following the Council of Trent. Thus, for François, bishops and priests, "by a sacramental consecration and by a spiritual character which cannot be effaced, devote themselves [. . .] to the perpetual service of God".[5] And Le Brun remarks that "the exaltation of the dignity of the ecclesiastical state from the beginning of the century in writers of all tendencies [. . .] is both the cause and the

time evident that her status is largely that of a focusing device, and that the work's applicability is far more extensive.

[4] "[. . .] après et devant elle, plusieurs bonnes âmes, [. . .] pour se mieux assujettir à Dieu, ont soumis leur volonté à celle de ses serviteurs" (*Introduction à la vie dévote*, p. 38).

[5] "[. . .] par une consécration sacramentelle et par un caractère spirituel qui ne peut être effacé, se vouent [. . .] au perpétuel service de Dieu" (*Traité de l'amour de Dieu*, p. 960).

consequence of a whole corpus of priestly literature [. . .]. This literature contributes to the formation of a whole generation of holy priests."[6]

One substantial aspect of François's writing concerns what we might call the creation of an attitude of discernment in the reader. The question first arises from the simple need to discern, in a variety of empirical moral contexts, what is good and what is evil, what is desirable and what should be avoided. One entirely commonplace area which requires attention, for example, given the implied social standing of his addressee, is that of wealth and poverty. Here we are confronted with the likelihood that she enjoys more than adequate means by which to live; and yet she is not exhorted to take the rigorist line and give it all away. So, the question inevitably arises, will she never enter the kingdom of heaven? Yet François does not see such a problem as an impasse, but instead foregrounds the attitude towards riches, rather than their existence, as the central criterion: "To be rich in fact and yet poor in spirit is the great happiness of the Christian; for by this means there are the commodities of wealth for this world, and the merit of poverty for the world to come",[7] one of which commodities is, reassuringly enough, the means to give alms. What such a routine problematics more generically brings to light, however, is the vast middle ground of moral complexity that will correspond to the experience of the majority. It would not be difficult to imagine an answer to simple moral questions which offered a rationalization for committing such and such an action, or indeed an interdiction from doing so, but François refrains from either. It is the attitude of mind that will regulate the quality of the action; and the whole tenor of the work serves to promote the acceptance and sanctification of the given. The social *status quo* is morally neutral, in other words, even if certain conditions have within them a greater potential for holiness than others; and it is the act of discernment in making nuanced distinctions between different attitudes towards the same material disposition that will mark out the devout soul in the world. It is in this understanding too, we might argue, that the empirical givenness of the penitent is progressively adjusted to the historical givenness of the Incarnation, by the exercise of the kind of judgement which François so perfectly exemplifies.

[6] "L'exaltation de la dignité de l'état ecclésiastique à partir du début du siècle chez les auteurs de toute mouvance [. . .] est à la fois la cause et la conséquence de toute une littérature sacerdotale. [. . .] Cette littérature contribue à former toute une génération de saints prêtres" (*Histoire*, p. 244–5). Extensive attention is also given to the question by Krumenacker, including a brief section on the Père Bourgoing, whose *Funeral Oration* is pronounced by Bossuet (*École française*, 227–33).

[7] "Être riche en effet et pauvre d'affection c'est le grand bonheur du Chrétien, car il a par ce moyen les commodités des richesses pour ce monde et le mérite de la pauvreté pour l'autre" (*Introduction à la vie dévote*, p. 170). Angers remarks: "Salesian psychology has nothing absolute about it, [. . .] but takes circumstances into account" ["la psychologie salésienne n'a rien d'absolu, mais [. . .] tient compte des circonstances"] (*Humanisme chrétien*, p. 29).

Two further considerations will inform the question of François's attitude towards discernment (and the French word in the period carries both the sense of differentiation and of good judgement).[8] First of all, in his attitude towards sin, where it is confirmed that sinfulness principally lies in the consciousness of wrongdoing, or in the will to sin, as defined in three stages—of temptation, delectation, and consent. Temptation is therefore not wrong in itself, and indeed the opportunity to resist it can be the source of great grace; rather, he considers, "dishonourable behaviour lies to such a degree in the application of the heart, that without it the application of the body cannot be sinful".[9] The whole issue of the abuse of casuistry, to which I shall turn in the next chapter, is perhaps above all an abuse of discernment.

More fundamentally again, this same need for discernment is applied to matters of inspiration.[10] Thus François is careful to advise his penitent to exercise discretion, for example, in her experience of what he calls "sensory consolations" ["consolations sensibles"], and so to distinguish carefully between "sentimental tendencies" ["tendances sentimentales"] and those impulses which are good and truly come from God.[11] Equally, and complementarily, the origins of "spiritual droughts and sterilities"[12] have to be objectively examined, notably in discerning whether they might in fact be nothing more than physical in origin. All in all, the exposition of the means of discernment which lie within the human psyche are so typical of François, both in his attitude and in his style, imagery, and biblical grounding, that I can do no better than to quote him, writing to his addressee, *in extenso*:

> It is a general doctrine [. . .], for the affections and passions of our souls, that we must *know them by their fruits*. Our hearts are trees, affections and passions are their branches, and their works or actions are the fruits. The heart is good when it has good affections, and affections and passions are good when they bring about in us good effects and holy actions. If the feelings of gentleness, tenderness, and consolation [we enjoy] make us more humble, patient, accommodating, charitable, and sympathetic towards our neighbour, more fervent in mortifying our lustful drives and bad inclinations, more constant in our [spiritual] exercises, more docile and flexible towards those whom we should obey, more simple in our

[8] The *Dictionnaire de l'Académie Française* (1694) defines the verb "discerner" as meaning "to distinguish one thing from another, or to make a judgement on the basis of the comparison" ["distinguer une chose d'une autre, ou en juger par comparaison"].

[9] "[La] déshonnêteté consiste tellement à l'application du cœur, que sans icelle l'application du corps ne peut être péché" (*Introduction à la vie dévote*, p. 264).

[10] See also Chapter 7.

[11] The chapter devoted to these distinctions, Chapter XIII of the Fourth Part, is entitled: "Spiritual and sensory consolations and how to behave when these occur" ["Des consolations spirituelles et sensibles et comme il faut se comporter en icelles"] (*Introduction à la vie dévote*, 276–83).

[12] The following chapter, Chapter XIV of the Fourth Part, is then entitled: "Des sécheresses et stérilités spirituelles" (*Introduction à la vie dévote*, 283–8).

> lives, then surely [. . .] they come from God; but if [they] [. . .] make us curious, bitter, touchy, impatient, stubborn, proud, presumptuous, hard towards our neighbour, and if, believing ourselves already to be little Saints, we no longer wish to be subject to direction or correction, undoubtedly they are false and pernicious consolations. *A good tree* only *produces good fruits.*[13]

Much of François is resumed in this passage.[14] His pragmatism, his clarity, and precision in exemplification, his teaching of an attitude of mind, his insistence on obedience, and his impeccable and interwoven use of biblical quotation and related imagery in the application of Christian theology, moving as he does from the bookish specifics of the Gospels to the lived-out specifics of the believer. It is hard not to be impressed by his common sense and by the broad terms in which he couches his advice, basing his morality as he does on practice and example. In his more ambitious *Treatise on the Love of God* as well, destined now for the male religious rather than for the laywoman (one Théotime, or "chosen by God"), we find that the higher spiritual aspirations are subject to the same kind of discernment; and this requirement, which is present as we have seen in the humdrum and the compromised, is accentuated rather than reduced in the higher aspirations of those who believe their vocations to be less worldly. Where it is above all emphasized is in the context of inspiration, one of whose defining marks, the desire for a "holy obedience to the Church and to one's superiors",[15] lies stubbornly at the origin of the dilemmas that we shall see exemplified in much that follows.

[13] "C'est une générale doctrine [. . .], pour les affections et passions de nos âmes, que nous les devons *connaître par leurs fruits.* Nos cœurs sont des arbres, les affections et passions sont leurs branches, et les œuvres et actions sont les fruits. Le cœur est bon qui a de bonnes affections, et les affections et passions sont bonnes qui produisent en nous de bons effets et de saintes actions. Si les douceurs, tendretés et consolations nous rendent plus humbles, patients, traitables, charitables et compatissants à l'endroit du prochain, plus fervents à mortifier nos concupiscences et mauvaises inclinations, plus constants en nos exercices, plus maniables et souples à ceux que nous devons obéir, plus simples en notre vie, sans doute [. . .] qu'elles sont de Dieu ; mais si elles [. . .] nous rendent curieux, aigres, pointilleux, impatients, opiniâtres, fiers, présomptueux, durs à l'endroit du prochain, et que pensant déjà être des petits saints, nous ne voulons plus être sujets à la direction ni à la correction, indubitablement ce sont des consolations fausses et pernicieuses : *Un bon arbre* ne *produit* que *des bons fruits*" (*Introduction à la vie dévote*, p. 281) (original emphases to denote biblical quotation).

[14] This in turn affords an extended paraphrase of what a more recent theologian, Nelson Pike, will describe as the "spiritual-effects test" of the authenticity of supernatural experience (Nelson Pike, "On mystic visions as sources of knowledge", in *Mysticism and Philosophical Analysis*, ed. Steven T. Katz, New York, Oxford University Press, 1978, 214–34, p. 219).

[15] "La sainte obéissance à l'Église et aux supérieurs" is identified as the third sign of authentic inspiration in the title of Book VIII, Chapter xiii of the *Traité de l'amour de Dieu*. It follows on from perseverance in vocation and peace of mind ["cœur"]. At the same time in this text, François compares speculative and mystical theology to the detriment of the former: "Who loved God more, I wonder, the theologian [William of] Occam, whom certain have called the most subtle of mortals, or St Catherine of Genoa, a stupid woman? The former knew him better by learning, the latter by experience, and her experience led her far forwards in the realm of seraphic love" ["Qui aima plus Dieu, je vous prie, ou le théologien Occam, que quelques-uns ont nommé

This is all the more striking in contrast to many of those who will appear to deform his integrated spirituality, as of those who will in turn parody that deformation. Some such developments will base their arguments on caricatural examples of casuistry in the ethical domain, proposed in order to discredit the practice of case ethics, as we shall see from the Jansenist polemic; others will embark on a critique of the extreme implications of unmediated inspiration in the spiritual realm, as will be illustrated by the Quietist dispute. But neither tendency will be true to the spirit of Christian humanism from which they stem.

The question of individual inspiration is therefore a centrally important issue in Catholic spirituality in the period. St François de Sales sees a place for inspiration, but surrounds it with ecclesially mediated caveats.[16] Pascal sees it as a condition *sine qua non* of authentic belief, yet says little about the precise nature of its symptoms or its reception even if, in a coda to the *Mémorial*, we note that his undertaking of obedience chimes with a major preoccupation of those privileged by such exceptional spiritual experiences as the one to which this text bears witness: "Total submission to Jesus-Christ *and to my director*."[17] A more complete epistemology is then provided by a fragment of Christic prosopopœia in the *Pensées*: "'I am present with you in my word through the Scriptures, in my Spirit through the Church and through inspirations [note the cognitive order], in my power through the priesthood, and in my prayer through the faithful.'"[18] Bossuet too, in the *Funeral Orations*, shows on occasion how God works in a very precise way through the Scriptures and spiritual counsel; but equally shows how such an operation has always to be understood through the intermediary of the Church and her ministers. He insists as well in the Preface to his *Instruction on the States of Mental Prayer* above all on the need to "ask God for his spirit of discernment and of understanding to differentiate between the true and the false",[19] for which the rule must once again be Scripture and tradition, rather than experience; and he does so, as he ironically and empirically asserts, because it is "experience

le plus subtil des mortels, ou sainte Catherine de Gênes, femme idiote? Celui-là le connut mieux par science, celle-ci par expérience, et l'expérience de celle-ci la conduisit bien avant dans l'amour séraphique"] (*Traité de l'amour de Dieu*, p. 620).

[16] This is developed in a sequence of chapters in the *Treatise on the Love of God* (*Traité de l'amour de Dieu*, VIII, 10–13).

[17] "Soumission totale à Jésus-Christ *et à mon directeur*" (*Pensées*, L 913, S 742, my emphasis). This line only exists in one of the texts which together constitute the so-called *Mémorial*. See Sellier's annotation in S, p. 1301, nn. 2 and 13.

[18] "Je te suis présent par ma parole dans l'Écriture, par mon esprit dans l'Église et par les inspirations, par ma puissance dans les prêtres, par ma prière dans les fidèles" (*Pensées*, L 919, S 751).

[19] "[. . .] demander à Dieu son esprit de discernement et d'intelligence pour démêler le vrai d'avec le faux" (*Instruction sur les états d'oraison*, p. 368).

itself which prevents you from attributing everything to experience".[20] So, to put it simply, and at least on this evidence consensually: that the salvation of the individual soul is of primary importance is of little doubt; what is questionable is the degree to which the individual participates *qua* individual in receiving directly the dictates of the Holy Spirit to that end.

The issue of exceptional witness must therefore come into the debate. The early Church was seen, as we are told in Bossuet's *Panegyrics*, as rich in such witness, as the semantically cognate "martyr"[21] itself betokens. Pascal charts its features in the *Pensées* in a fragment entitled "Holiness" ["Sainteté"]: "Princes leave their splendour behind, young girls suffer martyrdom. Where does this power come from? It is because the Messiah had arrived. These are the effects and the signs of his coming."[22] This in turn is given dramatic expression in Corneille's *Polyeucte martyr*, where the conflict between Polyeucte and Néarque personifies the tension between neophyte zeal and tarnished belief, and where we find an allegorical reflection of the contrast between the lively faith of the young Church and the established, and thus potentially complacent, belief of early-modern Christendom. Thus, in two couplets which resume the whole scene in which they occur:

NÉARQUE This zeal is too ardent; you should try to moderate it.
POLYEUCTE You cannot have too much zeal towards the God whom you revere.[23]

And later:

NÉARQUE But within that temple, in the end, your death is assured.
POLYEUCTE But in Heaven, the martyr's palm is already prepared.[24]

Yet although great feats of Christian witness or endurance frequently feature in Bossuet's *Panegyrics* and even in his *Funeral orations*, it is the ordinary Christian requirements that concern him in a more pastoral capacity, and the excesses of the saintly examples he narrates are never proposed as a pattern. They serve paradoxically as models for Christian moderation, and the extraordinary achievements of the Saints encourage the more modest Christian soul,

[20] "[. . .] c'est l'expérience elle-même qui empêche de tout donner à l'expérience" (*Instruction sur les états d'oraison*, p. 372). Compare Madame Guyon, accounting for her experience of carrying the crucified Christ: "Only experience can convey what I am trying to say" ["Il n'y a que l'expérience qui puisse faire comprendre ce que je veux dire"] (*Vie*, p. 447).

[21] The Greek word *martur* means "witness".

[22] "Les princes quittent leurs grandeurs, les filles souffrent le martyre. D'où vient cette force ? C'est que le Messie est arrivé. Voilà l'effet et les marques de sa venue" (*Pensées*, L 772, S 332).

[23] NÉARQUE : "Ce zèle est trop ardent, souffrez qu'il se modère" / POLYEUCTE : "On n'en peut avoir trop pour le Dieu qu'on révère" (*Polyeucte martyr*, II, 6, 653–4). The original is given additional emphasis by the rhyme words.

[24] "NÉARQUE : Mais dans ce temple enfin la mort est assurée. / POLYEUCTE : Mais dans le Ciel déjà la palme est assurée" (*Polyeucte martyr*, II, 6, 661–2). This time it is the use of anaphora that enhances the symmetrical contrast.

living in less turbulent times, to lesser if related efforts. It is the basics that Bossuet seeks to promote—innocence, piety, charity, justice—and nothing can take the place of these fundamentals: "It is these common practices of the Christian religion", he writes in the *Funeral oration of the Prince de Condé*, "that Jesus Christ will praise on the last day before his holy angels and his heavenly Father"[25]; and, far from being a form of compromise, such practices will take on a privileged identity precisely because of their conformity with the central demands of the faith. Christian aims should not, on the one hand, be softened, he writes in an earlier piece; but nor, on the other, should they be augmented out of whatever motive, so as to make "virtue [seem] too burdensome, the Gospel excessive, [and] Christianity impossible".[26] What is promoted in distinction is the quality of Christian moderation, of *médiocrité*, in the non-pejorative sense of that word which was current at the time, expressed by Bossuet through a simple but strong image. This is in the 1662 *Sermon on Ambition*: "A river, in order to do good," he writes, "has no need to burst its banks or to flood the countryside; just by flowing peacefully in its bed, it does not fail to irrigate the land, or to give water to the people, for the common good."[27] Fénelon is similarly clear, at least in his theoretical writing:

> Our works of supererogation often inspire a reckless confidence in us. When we do more than we are required to do, we pass without noticing to a state of believing ourselves dispensed from ordinary rules concerning matters of obligation [. . .]. Let us [rather] do what is good, according to the rule of the situation in which God has placed us, with discernment, courage and perseverance.[28]

We are back therefore, and entirely in the spirit of St François de Sales, with the sanctification of the given.

So far in this chapter I have looked predominantly at the writings of three bishops, whose job it was to exercise that discernment with which their apostolic consecration endowed them. All three prelates concur that what was a necessary criterion for witness in the early centuries of the Church needed to be viewed with much greater circumspection in later times. It is as if the exceptional impetus required for the establishment of the faith is better

[25] "Ce sont ces communes pratiques de la vie chrétienne que Jésus-Christ louera au dernier jour devant ses saints anges et devant son Père céleste" (*Oraison funèbre de Louis de Bourbon*, in *Œuvres*, p. 210).

[26] "[. . .] faire paraître la vertu trop pesante, l'Évangile excessif, le christianisme impossible" (*Oraison funèbre de Nicolas Cornet*, in *Œuvres*, 41–55, p. 45).

[27] "Un fleuve, pour faire du bien, n'a que faire de passer ses bords ni d'inonder la campagne ; en coulant paisiblement dans son lit, il ne laisse pas d'arroser la terre et de présenter ses eaux aux peuples pour la commodité publique" (*Sermon sur l'ambition*, in *Sermons*, 131–45, p. 141).

[28] "[. . .] nos œuvres de surérogation nous inspirent une confiance téméraire. Quand on fait plus qu'on n'est obligé de faire, insensiblement on passe jusqu'à se croire dispensé des règles communes pour les choses d'obligation. [. . .] Faisons donc le bien selon les règles de l'état où Dieu nous a mis, avec discernement, avec courage, avec persévérance" (*Exhortations, entretiens, sermons*, II (*De la véritable et solide piété*), in *Œuvres*, I, p. 862/8).

sustained in later ages by a more even-tempered continuity. The whole question takes on a different tenor, however, when we consider the lives of individuals who believe they have a privileged relationship with God. Indeed it is superficially surprising that the devotion to St François de Sales is in many cases matched in the period only by the degree of dissimilarity to the ethos which he appears to promote.[29] We might wonder as a result how such experiences fit into the whole post-Tridentine Catholic tradition, to which one answer is: not very well.[30] The context which François provides for the assessment of such experiences in the *Introduction to the Devout Life* is itself telling, making as it does no difference between physical and spiritual excesses: "Do not desire things that are dangerous to the soul," he advises, "such as dancing, gambling, and other such pastimes; nor honours and responsibilities, *nor visions and ecstasies*, for there is much danger, vanity and deceit in such things."[31] He goes on to write in the *Treatise on the Love of God*, incorporating a statement of the obvious that is as universally self-evident as it is individually overlooked, that the only legitimate "extraordinary inspirations" ["inspirations extraordinaires"] are those which "incite us to practice with extraordinary fervour and perfection the ordinary exercises of the Christian".[32] Those on the other hand which "carry [the soul] to actions contrary to the laws, rules and customs of the most holy Church [are] therefore more to be wondered at than imitated".[33] Bossuet, in the *Panegyrics*, discourages Christians in later ages from according undue significance to apparently supernatural experiences; and Fénelon too is clear that, whereas we are all ceaselessly inspired, "this inspiration should not persuade us that we are similar to the prophets".[34] Thus, "[individual inspiration] is not a divine movement [which is intended] to predict, to change the laws of nature, [or] to give orders to men on God's behalf" (which will indeed be the claim made by Antoinette Bourignon);

[29] The Pléiade editor summarizes the tension well: "Love is not demonstrated by mental prayer, which can turn into quietism, or by apostolic action, which can turn into activism, but by the life of charity" ["L'amour ne se prouve ni dans l'oraison, qui peut tourner au quiétisme, ni par l'action apostolique, qui peut tourner à l'activisme, mais par la vie de charité"] (*Œuvres*, p. cii).

[30] Fénelon writes: "This life of enlightenment and of perceptible tastes, if it you become so attached to it that nothing else is taken into account, is a most dangerous trap" ["Cette vie de lumières et de goûts sensibles, quand on s'y attache jusqu'à s'y borner, est un piège très dangereux"] (*Lettres et opuscules spirituels*, XXV (*Que la voie de la foi nue et de la pure charité est meilleure et plus sûre que celle des lumières et des goûts*), in *Œuvres*, I, p. 672).

[31] "Ne désirez point les choses qui sont dangereuses à l'âme, comme sont les bals, les jeux et tels autres passe-temps ; ni les honneurs et charges, *ni les visions et extases*, car il y a beaucoup de péril, de vanité et de tromperie en telles choses" (*Introduction à la vie dévote*, p. 231, my emphasis).

[32] "[. . .] nous incitent à pratiquer avec une extraordinaire ferveur et perfection les exercices ordinaires du Chrétien" (*Traité de l'amour de Dieu*, p. 747).

[33] "[. . .] portent [l'âme] à des actions contraires aux lois, règles et coutumes de la très sainte Église [. . .] partant [sont] plus admirables qu'imitables" (*Traité de l'amour de Dieu*, p. 747).

[34] "Cette inspiration ne doit point nous persuader que nous soyons semblables aux prophètes" (*Lettres et opuscules spirituels*, X (*De la parole intérieure*), in *Œuvres*, I, p. 591).

rather, he goes on, if "understood simply and within its own limits, [it] should contain nothing other [. . .] than the common doctrine of the Church".[35]

I want to turn in the light of these remarks to three areas of Catholic experience where discernment is perceived as most vitally important, and as most divisively controversial: to the interlinked questions of visions; of possessions; and of miracles.

Visions and miracles, first of all, are understood as essentially neutral or indeed ambiguous supernatural phenomena, and have thus to be both validated and interpreted; more problematic again is the status of diabolic possessions, and of the physical signs of their evacuation. At all these points, furthermore, Christian teaching comes into proximity with the multiple alternative explanations for disconcerting behaviour in the individual, whether they be diabolic, in the terms of the period, or psychogenic, in the language of later interpreters. In all these cases, however (and, for the purposes of this book, first and foremost within a seventeenth-century French perspective), we arrive at the point at which questions of authority and discernment most critically come into play. And, unsurprisingly, it is in these three areas that the strangeness of Christianity manifests itself in some of its most disturbing forms.

Many of the events recorded occur in the quintet of spiritual autobiographies which I have been mentioning in other contexts over the last few chapters. Yet the judgements formed of their writers, both by the contemporary and later Church and by subsequent critical scrutiny, are widely divergent: one, St Margaret Mary Alacoque, was canonized, albeit not until the twentieth century (1920); one, Madame Guyon, considered at least in recent years to have made a major contribution to the understanding of individual spirituality, nonetheless ended her life in involuntary confinement; and three (one a man, the other two women – so this is not simply a gender issue)[36] are variously considered to have been possessed, inspired, or deluded. And yet it might not always be obvious from a more disinterested appraisal – from a purely secular angle of discernment in other words – as to which exactly was which.

If we first of all amplify the definition of visions, we find that a contemporary dictionary (the 1694 *Dictionnaire de l'Académie Française*) affords a helpful distinction. For some, visions are "those things which God or some

[35] "[L'inspiration] n'est point un mouvement divin pour prédire, pour changer les lois de la nature, et pour commander aux hommes de la part de Dieu [. . .]. Cette inspiration, prise [. . .] dans ses bornes et dans sa simplicité, ne renferme [. . .] que la doctrine commune de toute l'Église" (*Lettres et opuscules spirituels*, X (*De la parole intérieure*), in *Œuvres*, I, p. 592).

[36] Indeed, writing of the experience of Christic indwelling, Surin is critical of those "speculative and learned men" ["hommes spéculatifs et savants"] who "are scornful of it, and compare it to the tears and emotional outbursts of certain women" ["font mépris de cela, et le comparent aux larmes et tendretés de certaines femmes"] (*Science expérimentale*, p. 325).

intelligence makes you see in your mind *or by the eyes of your body*", and this is illustrated initially by such obviously Judeo-Christian usages as "the visions of the Prophets, this Saint had such-and-such a vision".[37] But the term might also be deemed to apply, according to the same dictionary, to "a false, mad and deluded imagination" ["une imagination fausse, folle, extravagante"]; and it is in this loose and exclusively pejorative sense that the word will be used, for example, by Bossuet of Madame Guyon, when he writes of her "empty visions about the pregnant woman";[38] or by those who hostilely labelled St Margaret Mary or Antoinette Bourignon, at the two ends of the spectrum of orthodox acceptance, as *visionnaires*. In their authentic form, however, visions are held to be a visible symptom of an indwelling and invisible spirit: they are similar in this respect to sacraments, albeit crucially lacking both in their materiality, and in the objective means of assessment of their validity.

The Catholic encyclopædia, *Sacramentum Mundi*, adds three significant points: first, that "the genuineness of such experiences cannot be established simply on the grounds of the piety or sincerity of the subject, [since] these are no proofs against error with regard to visions". Second, that "the psychic process cannot be adequately scrutinized and it thus remains ambiguous, [so that] one must be satisfied with a greater or lesser probability in distinguishing genuine from psychogenic visions". And thirdly that "[although] in their content they [can] only correspond to that which is known already in faith and theology, nevertheless they can express an imperative demand of the will of God for the actions of the Church in a given historical situation".[39]

If visions are understood as an experience which, it is claimed, appeals directly to the external sensory perception of sight, however, such occurrences only rarely happen in isolation, and indeed it is symptomatic of the phenomenon that the other senses are also frequently involved, of which the most obvious is hearing. Thus all of our subjects are equally the beneficiaries, if that is the right word, of divine utterance, taking a whole diversity of manifestations, as we saw in the last chapter. There are also tactile encounters: so, caresses and embraces typically occur, as do sensory experiences which

[37] "Les choses que Dieu ou quelque intelligence fait voir en esprit, *ou par les yeux du corps*. Les visions des Prophètes, ce Saint eut une telle vision" (my emphasis). Consistent with this, and fairly typically, Surin writes of his visions of Christ that "several times, [he] appeared to my soul so manifestly, that I have never seen anything more clearly" ["diverses fois, [il] a paru à l'âme si manifestement, que jamais je n'ai rien vu plus clairement"] (*Science expérimentale*, p. 204).

[38] "[...] creuses visions sur la femme enceinte" (*Relation*, p. 1111). These references, at an advanced stage of the Quietist dispute, are to Madame Guyon's *Exposition of the Book of the Apocalypse* [*Explication sur l'Apocalypse*].

[39] *Sacramentum Mundi*, article "Visions". It is however notable in our examples that, with the exception of Antoinette Bourignon, the majority of supernatural revelations concern individual or doctrinal issues, and do not reflect the range of concerns evoked by Watt, who enumerates their substance as being potentially "doctrinal, soteriological, apocalyptic, millenarian [...], orthodox or heretical, entirely religious or also political" (*Secretaries of God*, p. 2).

directly reflect the life and attributes of Christ; and, albeit less frequently, smelling and even tasting are involved. Visions therefore most commonly contribute to a composite ordeal,[40] and indeed unite on occasion in a kind of synesthetic epiphany. Thus, to start with a dramatic example, the Père Surin, writing of himself at this point in the third person, records a composite verbal, visual, and sensory experience: "It was as if he was carried away in his spirit, and saw before him some writing in fine big letters: PURE LOVE, and beside it, also written in the air: TERESA OF JESUS."[41] He then sits down and, shifting to the first person, writes: "I had the impression of Jesus Christ suffering, and I was internally bound to my chair, and found myself as if I was being crucified."[42] He goes on, equating his experience to the scriptural duration of the Crucifixion, to say that he remained in this position for three hours; a brother then brings him wine to drink, which turns out to be sour; he is insulted; and he finds for years afterwards, when he sleeps, that his feet involuntarily assume the position of Christ's feet on the Cross. This scene is then followed by a sequence of messages and warnings, allegedly transmitted by his guardian angel.

St Margaret Mary is perhaps the most important, and certainly the most ecclesially respected figure with whom we shall deal.[43] The different forms of vision of Christ which she experiences are manifold, and persist from childhood. Christ's promise that "'I will teach you to know me and will make myself known to you'"[44] is apparently respected and, at least in the early stages of her development, the form in which he manifests himself corresponds

[40] I use the term in both current senses: "a prolonged painful [...] experience"; and "a [...] test of guilt or innocence" (*OED*). "Guilt" or "innocence" might also be expressed as "delusion" or "enlightenment" in the cases under consideration.

[41] "Il fut comme enlevé en esprit, et vit devant soi une écriture faite en beau et grand caractère : AMOUR PUR, et à côté aussi écrit en l'air : THÉRÈSE DE JÉSUS" (*Science expérimentale*, p. 271).

[42] "[Il] me vint une impression de Jésus-Christ souffrant, et je fus lié sur mon siège intérieurement, et me trouvai comme si j'eusse été en croix" (*Science expérimentale*, p. 271). In common with other supernatural experiences, such accounts are recurrent in the autobiography. There also seems likely to be an Ignatian dimension to this, since in the *Spiritual Exercises*, it is recommended in the Second Week, Fifth Contemplation, that "it is helpful to pass the five senses of the imagination over the First and Second Contemplations" (*Spiritual Exercises*, p. 307).

[43] We learn that she reads from an early age the *Vies des Saints*, and the examples of St Catherine of Siena (I, 394–6) and St Claire of Montefalco (II, 206–7) seem likely to have influenced her. Catherine is described in that work as a faithful spouse of the crucified Christ. She has a vision of Christ as a child, and becomes a nun in her early teens. She then accepts from Christ a crown of thorns, and engages in a sequence of mortifications, in reward for which Christ gives her liquid from his side to drink. Finally, there is an exchange of hearts, and the infliction of his five wounds (the stigmata). St Claire shows equally precocious zeal, and equivalent ordeals with matters of obedience (thus when forbidden by her Superior from making her communion, she appeals to Christ, who gives her the host with his own hand). Thereafter Christ appears to her and plants his cross in her heart where, at the dissection of her body after her death at the age of 33, the marks of the Crucifixion are found. See Jantzen, *Power, gender* p. 216–23.

[44] "[...] je t'apprendrai à me connaître et me manifesterai à toi" (*Vie*, p. 47).

didactically to the aspect of his life and Passion which it is appropriate for her to consider. Accordingly, he appears to her as depicted in specific scriptural episodes: thus, for example, at the Flagellation, in order to reproach her for dressing to please the world, and to remind her "that it was my vanities that had reduced him to this state".[45] More frequently, however, there is a freer interpretation of Gospel evidence, such as when Christ's wounds are particularly vividly described: "Jesus Christ, my gentle master, appeared to me, blazing with glory, his five wounds glowing like five suns, and flames leaping out from all parts of this sacred humanity, but above all from his adorable chest, which looked like a furnace".[46]

Certain of St Margaret Mary's most persistent visions of Christ are associated with his attributes as spouse or lover, in conformity with the imagery that we have looked at: thus on one occasion she is shown a great cross, "of which I could not see the end, but it was entirely covered in flowers",[47] whereupon she is told by Christ that he is offering her the bed reserved for his "chaste spouses", in a particularly disconcerting sequence, moving as it does from pleasure to pain in its erotic transformation of a botanical metaphor: "Here is the bed of my chaste spouses, where I will have you consummate the joys of my pure love: little by little these flowers will fall and only the thorns will remain, which they conceal because of your weakness; but they will make their thorns felt so sharply that you will need all the force of my love to endure the pain".[48]

Most importantly of all, it is when the Blessed Sacrament is exposed that Christ appears to her, revealing his Sacred Heart. It is the circumstances of this appearance, furthermore, which are fundamental to the debate surrounding discernment and orthodoxy, since they enable the particular sign with which the individual is favoured to be interpreted as the ratification of a received doctrine with which the whole Church is entrusted, in this case that of the Real Presence. The episode therefore affords a central example of personal inspiration endorsing, or arguably indeed reviving, orthodox teaching, and is therefore in due course admitted as authentic. As a result, and in recognition of her obedience, St Margaret Mary is granted a vision during the elevation of the host at Mass, with Christ at its centre, who gives her a crown of thorns, with the words: "'Receive, my daughter, this crown as a sign of the one that will

[45] "que c'étaient mes vanités qui l'avaient réduit en cet état" (*Vie*, p. 41).

[46] "Jésus-Christ, mon doux Maître, se présenta à moi, tout éclatant de gloire, avec ses cinq plaies, brillantes comme cinq soleils, et de cette sacrée humanité sortaient des flammes de toutes parts, mais surtout de son adorable poitrine, qui ressemblait une fournaise" (*Vie*, p. 71).

[47] "[dont] je ne pouvais voir le bout, mais elle était toute couverte de fleurs" (*Vie*, p. 65).

[48] "'Voilà le lit de mes chastes épouses où je te ferai consommer les délices de mon pur amour: peu à peu ces fleurs tomberont et il ne te restera que les épines qu'elles cachent à cause de ta faiblesse; mais elles te feront sentir si vivement leurs piqûres, que tu auras besoin de toute la force de mon amour pour en supporter la douleur'" (*Vie*, p. 65).

soon be given to you in conformity with me.'"[49] This experience once again seems to conflate paradigmatically within the individual the doctrine of Eucharistic sacrifice, the Gospel account of the Crucifixion, and the apocalyptic figure of the woman crowned with stars (Revelation 12: 1), most commonly encountered in the fifth glorious mystery of the Rosary as the Coronation of the Virgin. Such an account seems on the one hand, once again, to run the risk of individuating an ecclesial model, and yet at the same time to fall into conformity with the liturgy, with Scripture, and with a received focus of popular devotion.[50] In this respect too it passes what Nelson Pike refers to as the "Scripture-dogma test", whereby the supernatural revelation is deemed to accord with the revealed truth.[51]

But what exactly does Margaret Mary claim to experience? There is in fact more precision in her account about hearing and feeling than about seeing, although a broader synesthetic impression is once again conveyed when she writes: "I saw him, I felt him close to me, and heard him, better than if I had done so by my physical senses"[52] (although this picture is again blurred by the occasional veracity *topos*, such as "yet [I] am always wary of being deceived in everything which I say happened within me").[53] What is even more unclear is the status of physical objects. Thus we might wonder what happens when she is offered by Christ the choice between two paintings, one of which shows a life of consolation, and the other a life of crucifixion, "a poor, abject life, always crucified by all kinds of humiliations, scorn and confusion",[54] the latter of which she unsurprisingly chooses. Do the "paintings" simply represent allegorical mental pictures? Apparently not, since Margaret Mary considers them to be concrete objects, and indeed goes on to write of how her chosen painting is "[pressed] against my bosom".[55]

[49] "'Reçois, ma fille, cette couronne en signe de celle qui te sera bientôt donnée par conformité avec moi'" (*Vie*, p. 114).

[50] Le Brun writes as follows: "The psychology of the Saint, the characteristics of a sensibility that is alternatively exalted and broken begin to appear familiar [. . .]. [But] the metaphors she uses, the insistence on a heart of flesh, on the sufferings which it both reveals and inflicts, the dread of the stains of sin and the concern for reparation give her [account], if not a new significance, then at least a new emphasis" ["La psychologie de la sainte, les caractères d'une sensibilité alternativement exaltée et brisée commencent à être connus [. . .]. [Mais] les métaphores qu'elle emploie, l'insistance sur le cœur de chair, sur les souffrances qu'il révèle et qu'il impose, la hantise des taches du péché et le souci de réparation lui donnent sinon une signification du moins un accent nouveau"] (*Histoire*, p. 269).

[51] Pike, "On mystic visions as sources of knowledge", p. 220.

[52] "[Je] le voyais, je le sentais proche de moi, et l'entendais beaucoup mieux que comme si ce fut [*sic*] été des sens corporels" (*Vie*, p. 62).

[53] "[je] crains pourtant toujours de me tromper en tout ce que je dis se passer en moi" (*Vie*, p. 69).

[54] "[une] vie pauvre et abjecte, toujours crucifiée par toutes sortes d'humiliations, mépris et contradictions" (*Vie*, p. 78).

[55] "[serré] sur ma poitrine" (*Vie*, p. 79).

All such favours and signs are thus a frequent and defining part of her life; yet she is continually attacked on account of them, as she sees it, by the orthodox forces of authority. Thus, after what she describes as an experience of pure love, she writes: "I was attacked once again, and was told that it was clear that I was not an appropriate person to adopt the spirit of the Visitation [her order], which feared all these channels which were subject to deception and illusion."[56] Nonetheless, when the intervention of an earthly mediator breaks down for her, it is to a direct engagement with Christ that she returns; and it is clear, from the (singularly uninspired) verses that she composes, that she believes herself to have an entirely individual channel of approach to the Redeemer, and that she is being persecuted by attempts to distract her from it:

The more my love is constrained
The more this unique goodness enflames me.
If I am afflicted night and day,
It cannot be taken away from my soul,
The greater the pain I endure,
The more closely he will unite me to his Heart.[57]

After receiving the enflamed heart, the power of the transcendent is once more so overwhelming as to impede mediation, so that "I felt within myself such a plenitude of the divine presence, that I could not give any account of it to my Superior as I had wished."[58]

Indeed, this unresolved conflict between obedience and inspiration encapsulates the whole dilemma of her unmediated responsibility to Christ, as of the role of her order and of the Church as a whole in the process. It is not that Christ in any way exempts her from obedience to earthly authorities; on the contrary, there is a kind of pact established between him and her Superior, whereby she should be made "'useful to [our] holy religion by the exact practice of all its observances'".[59] This is in turn a formulation of the hierarchical anomaly whereby it is the Superior who must instruct her to obey all of Christ's demands. Christ indeed promises her in return that "'from now on I will adjust my graces to the spirit of the rule [by which you live], and I want you to give it priority over everything else"',[60] and he goes on to explain the

[56] "L'on m'attaqua encore, me disant que l'on voyait bien que je n'étais pas propre à prendre l'esprit de la Visitation, qui craignait toutes ces sortes de voies sujettes à la tromperie et illusion" (*Vie*, p. 60).

[57] "Plus l'on contraint mon amour, / Plus cet unique bien m'enflamme. / Que l'on m'afflige nuit et jour, / On ne peut l'ôter de mon âme, / Plus je souffrirai de douleur / Plus il m'unira à son Cœur" (*Vie*, p. 58).

[58] "Je me sentais une si grande plénitude de Dieu, que je ne pouvais m'exprimer à ma supérieure comme je l'avais souhaité" (*Vie*, p. 70–1).

[59] "'[utile] à la sainte religion par la pratique exacte de toutes ses observances'" (*Vie*, p. 61).

[60] "'[. . .] désormais j'ajusterai mes grâces à l'esprit de la règle, laquelle je veux que tu préfères à tout le reste'" (*Vie*, p. 61).

apparent contradiction in this injunction by a complementary paradox: "'I shall be well able to find the means to bring my plans to fruition, even if these means seem opposed and contrary to their fulfilment.'"[61] Put another way, Christ's advice to her amounts to indicating that his work through the specially favoured individual must at the same time still function through the channels of orthodox authority in the Church, in order for the divine plan to be fulfilled; and that, as a result, the duty of obedience prevails in the lived circumstances of the individual's ordeal over the perceived privilege of inspiration.

This is most clearly illustrated in a simple form in the practice of exceeding a given, and objectively pious, religious duty. Fénelon makes the general point as follows: "When we do more than our obligation requires, we move unconsciously to a state in which we believe ourselves to be dispensed from the common rules concerning matters of obligation."[62] Elsewhere, he gives a balanced and sober expression of this tension, when he writes: "There is even for fervent souls a very pure mortification that lies in not mortifying oneself in one's own way, but in letting oneself be mortified moment by moment according to God's will."[63] This is then given a characteristically intense and individualized exemplification in St Margaret Mary's account of how, when reciting the *Ave Maris Stella* in obedience to a discipline imposed, she exceeds the requirements: "[As I finished, Christ] said to me 'That is my share'; but as I continued: 'That is the devil's share that you have now started', which made me stop immediately."[64]

There is thus a total assurance of God's will prevailing in the fullness of time; and yet such a conviction coexists within the person of St Margaret Mary with an immense confusion as to how, why and when it will prevail in the body, mind, and soul of the individual. She seems at times to be a battleground for the interplay of various forces; and, because of her ecstatic tendencies, is treated with deep suspicion and mistrust by her order and by her superiors: "I was just considered", she writes, "to be a *visionnaire* [in the pejorative definition of that word], stubbornly convinced of her illusions and imaginings",[65] a phrase which recurs later in almost exactly the same form after the final

[61] "'[Je] saurai bien trouver le moyen de faire réussir mes desseins, même par des moyens qui y semblent opposés et contraires"' (*Vie*, p. 61).

[62] "Quand on fait plus qu'on est obligé de faire, insensiblement on passe jusqu'à se croire dispensé des règles communes de l'obligation" (*Entretiens spirituels*, II (*De la véritable et solide piété*), in *Œuvres*, I, p. 862).

[63] "Il y a même pour les âmes ferventes une mortification très pure à ne se pas mortifier à sa mode et à se laisser mortifier de moment en moment suivant que Dieu le veut" (*Lettres et opuscules spirituels*, XLVI (*Sur la mortification*), in *Œuvres*, I, p.762).

[64] "Il me dit : 'Voici ma part' ; et comme je poursuivais : 'Voici celle du démon que tu fais maintenant', ce qui me fit cesser bien vite" (*Vie*, p. 68).

[65] "[L'on] ne me regardait que comme une visionnaire, entêtée et de ses illusions et imaginations" (*Vie*, p. 96).

revelation of the Sacred Heart. She thus resumes much of her experience, on the last page of her short autobiography, in the following paradox:

> I never received any particular grace from the divine bounty that was not preceded by this kind of torment; and when I had received it, I felt degraded and cast into a purgatory of humiliation and confusion, where my suffering exceeded everything that I can express; but I was [nonetheless] in a state of unalterable tranquillity, feeling that nothing could trouble the peace within my heart.[66]

As the negative correlative to the canonized Margaret Mary, we have the sad story of Antoinette Bourignon (1616–84).[67] Her early vocation to separate herself, not just from the world but from, as she saw it, the corrupted ideals of the religious orders to which she might have become affiliated, is expressed in terms of her wish to "return into the womb of [her] mother [. . .] that is to say into the spirit of the early Church".[68] To this end she is accorded a vision of St Augustine, together with the injunction to "'[re-establish] my evangelical spirit among male and female congregations, who will live like the first Christians, away from all human frequentation'".[69] Her often animated account then records a series of attempts to achieve her ideal, alternating, with monotonous consistency, between some modest degree of spiritual fulfilment and various kinds of impediment or persecution. Both of her autobiographical narratives conclude with perhaps the most memorable episode, in which she is persuaded by a man whom she meets, named Jean de Saint-Saulieu, to found and run an orphanage, only to discover both that he is a hypocrite, determined to seduce her, and that the entire household of apparently virtuous girls is in fact consecrated to the devil, and active in the pursuits of witchcraft. Overall the writing is remarkable more for its hubristic claims (thus she compares her arrest on suspicion of witchcraft to Christ's arrest in the garden of Olives),[70]

[66] "[Jamais] je ne recevais aucune grâce particulière de sa bonté, qu'elle ne fût précédée de ces sortes de tourments; et après les avoir reçues, je me sentais jetée et abîmée dans un purgatoire d'humiliation et de confusion, où je souffrais plus que je ne peux l'exprimer; mais toujours dans une paix inaltérable, ne me semblant pas que rien pût troubler la paix de mon cœur" (*Vie*, p. 117).

[67] The very substantial published works include in their first volume two autobiographies, entitled *La Parole de Dieu, ou sa vie intérieure à elle-même* and *La Vie extérieure*, preceded by a long *Préface apologétique touchant la personne et la doctrine de Mlle Bourignon*. There is then a third document, filling the whole of the second volume, *La Vie continuée de Mlle Bourignon*, in which a third-person account is given of her life, covering the period from the conclusion of the autobiographies up to her death.

[68] "[. . .] rentrer dans le ventre de sa mère, c'est-à-dire [. . .] dans l'esprit de l'Église naissante" (*La Parole de Dieu*, p. 128).

[69] "'Vous rétablirez mon esprit évangélique entre les congrégations d'hommes et de femmes, qui vivront comme les premiers Chrétiens, hors de toute conversation humaine'" (*La Parole de Dieu*, p. 20). Bowman remarks: "hers is a highly egotistical text, in the grammatical and the moral sense" ("Suffering, madness", p. 42).

[70] "Il semblait la prise de Notre Seigneur au jardin d'olivier" (*La Parole de Dieu*, p. 90).

and millenarian delusions, than for any ecclesial reforms, believing as she does (and as she believes she is told by God) that the reign of the Antichrist had arrived, and that it was her job to warn the world of his powers. To take up St François de Sales's original criterion, no part of Antoinette Bourignon's mission was blessed with results, and the growing sense in the reader is one of a quest which is not just fruitless, but which records its subject's slide into unlucidity, obsession, and solipsism.

It might be helpful here briefly to re-introduce a further figure—indeed the best known of the five—Madame Guyon, although it is perhaps superficially surprising to discover that she alone is situated on the relatively sceptical wing insofar as visions are concerned. But on closer reflection we realize that this is entirely in accordance with her theological emphases, since for her the state of mental prayer to which she aspired, and which she promotes in most of her writing, is "way above ecstasies, [. . .] raptures [and] visions [. . .], because all such graces are far less pure".[71] She then takes her distinction further, and specifies of her own such experiences: "[My] Vision is never of God himself, and almost never of Jesus Christ [. . .]; it is an angel of light, that [. . .] is represented to the soul"[72]; and, in distinction to any such "intellective visions, which are the most perfect",[73] she contrasts the dangers of ecstasies, coming as they do, in her opinion, from mere "spiritual sentimentality" ["sentimentalité spirituelle"]. Guyon's questionable relationship with the specifics of the Incarnation will be developed later; but it is nonetheless she who most succinctly identifies the underlying problem: "These graces are highly subject to illusions, because everything which has form, image and distinctness, can be counterfeited by the devil."[74] Indeed in the account of her life, as in all of our

[71] "[. . .] bien au-dessus des extases, [. . .] des ravissements, des visions, [. . .] parce que toutes ces grâces sont bien moins pures" (*Vie*, p. 200).

[72] "La vision n'est jamais de Dieu même, ni de Jésus-Christ [. . .] ; c'est un ange de lumière, qui [. . .] fait voir à l'âme sa représentation" (*Vie*, p. 201). Surin too writes expansively of a sequence of visions based on light and flames, which he interprets as a foretaste of paradise: "Once when I was in this state I went into our garden at the Bordeaux college; this light was so great, that I seemed to be walking in paradise, and the leaves of the trees seemed to me like those of the nut-trees that are in this garden. It seemed to me as though they were all brilliant and alight, and of almost the same colour as that which bright clouds display, but with a light that is incomparably more beautiful and with colours that are livelier and more natural" ["Une fois étant dans cet état j'entrai dans notre jardin du collège de Bordeaux; cette lumière fut si grande, qu'il me semblait marcher dans un paradis, et les feuilles des arbres me paraissaient comme celles des noisilliers qui sont dans ce jardin. Il me semblait que tous étaient brillants et lumineux, et de couleur comme quasi celle que des nuées bien claires représentent, mais d'une lumière sans comparaison plus belle et de couleurs plus vives et plus naturelles"] (*Science expérimentale*, p. 334).

[73] "[. . .] visions intellectuelles, qui sont les plus parfaites" (*Vie*, p. 201).

[74] "Ces grâces sont fort sujettes à l'illusion, parce que ce qui a forme, image et distinction, le démon le peut contrefaire" (*Vie*, p. 201). There are strong resonances here of St John of the Cross. Henri Sanson considers that "[Madame Guyon] had certainly read, and probably annotated St John of the Cross" ["[Madame Guyon] avait certainement lu et peut-être annoté saint

autobiographers, the experiential reality of visions of Christ, Mary, and the Saints and angels is matched only by the equally compelling presence of the diabolic.[75] The features of Christian particularity, therefore, understood by her as the manifestations of its "form, image, [and] distinctness", is often deceptive, as we shall see, precisely because its characteristics are so easily counterfeited by the diabolic; and it is their physicality which lies at the origin of this potential.

The presence of the devil is a very powerful one for St Margaret Mary too, as well as her fear of hell, "these gaping jaws of hell that I saw open, ready to engulf me"[76]; and indeed, as she says at the end of the work, the continual awareness that she is granted of the inevitability of God's judgement is an almost unbearable ordeal for the sinner. She is therefore unsure on occasion of the nature of her indwelling spirit, which it is necessary to identify as not being satanic; and it is precisely at this vitally important point that earthly authority must intervene and identify, or distinguish between, the different possible causes of the same manifestation. It is to this end therefore that a series of tests is established: thus, after her first major vision, during a particularly protracted illness, St Margaret Mary is asked by her Superior to validate the nature of her experience: "As my infirmities were so constant that they did not leave me for four successive days without my becoming ill, our Mother [Superior] [. . .] needed to be assured that what was happening in me came from the Spirit of God."[77] If it did, she would recover; if it did not, she would not. God might, it is thereby understood, work through the infliction of physical suffering, but so might the devil, and the subjection of what in the end transpires to be divine indwelling to the scrutiny of ecclesial analysis, according to the appropriate hierarchy of judgement, is understood as a delegated safeguard against both the deluded and the demonic.

It is to the autobiographies that record the Loudun possessions[78] that we next turn, and move into yet stranger and more disquieting realms as we do so.

Jean de la Croix"] (*Saint Jean de la Croix entre Bossuet et Fénelon*, Paris, Presses universitaires de France, 1953, p. 36).

[75] Frank Bowman is particularly enlightening on this range of phenomena. He notes of the whole corpus of texts he treats: "The world, the flesh and the devil take new forms which create a veritable anguish in the author not only about sanctity but about sanity" ("Suffering, madness", p. 25).

[76] "[. . .] cette gueule béante de l'enfer que je voyais ouverte, prête à m'engloutir" (*Vie*, p. 85).

[77] "Comme mes infirmités étaient si continuelles qu'elles ne me laissaient pas quatre jours de suite sans que je fusse malade, notre Mère [. . .] avait besoin de s'assurer si tout ce qui se passait en moi était de l'Esprit de Dieu" (*Vie*, p. 111).

[78] On the whole episode, see Michel de Certeau, *La Possession de Loudun*, Paris, Gallimard, 1990. A readable if tendentious account is given by Aldous Huxley, *The Devils of Loudun*, London, Chatto and Windus, 1952, on the basis of which Ken Russell made the film *The Devils* in 1971.

The two accounts of Sœur Jeanne des Anges (1602–65)[79] and of Père Jean-Joseph Surin (1600–65) offer two narratives that are substantially interconnected, on account of the vital link whereby Surin, in his capacity as exorcist of Jeanne des Anges, himself becomes the target of the same kind of phenomena to which she had been subjected. These two texts take us to the limits of discernment, the limits of orthodoxy, and, indeed, the limits of the strangeness of Christianity.

St Paul writes in 2 Corinthians 2: 11: "Whatever I have forgiven [. . .], I have done it for your sake in Christ's presence, to avoid being outwitted by Satan, whose scheming we know only too well." In 1634, Jean-Joseph Surin, a Jesuit from Bordeaux, was sent as part of a team to Loudun, to exorcise the members of the order of nuns who were resident there and who, it is claimed, were possessed by the devil. The exorcisms themselves are recounted both in the autobiography of Jeanne des Anges, and in the *Triumph of Divine Love over the Forces of Hell* [*Triomphe de l'amour divin sur les puissances de l'Enfer*] by Surin.[80] To complicate matters, the issue of the reader's critical interpretation of professed supernatural experiences is guided in modern editions by two contrasting liminary essays by Michel de Certeau.[81] In these pieces, Jeanne des Anges emerges as having been alternatively "a holy exhibitionist" ["une exhibitionniste sacrée"] or "an actress taken in by her own role" ["une actrice prise à son propre rôle"],[82] so that what she writes "is impossible to situate on either side of the frontier that separates sincerity from simulation".[83] He nonetheless reminds the reader that "[we must] take account of the fact, impressive in itself, that so many people, astute ecclesiastics, holy nuns or tradesmen felt able to venerate her, and to find enlightenment in her

[79] The full title of the text is in fact *Relation de ce qui s'est passé dans la possession des Religieuses Ursulines de Loudun, tirée d'un manuscrit de la mère Jeanne des Anges, supérieure de ladite communauté.* It was however published under a value-judgemental nineteenth-century title, given to the text as it appeared in 1886 in the review *Progrès médical* as part of the *Autobiographie d'une hystérique possédée*, ed. G. Legué and G. de la Tourette, reprinted in 1985 (Montbonnot-St-Martin, Éditions Jérôme Million). It is prefaced in this edition by a long, anonymous and ferociously hostile historical and biographical sketch (1–51), in which the editors explain that "we have been guided by the firm belief [. . .] that all the phenomena presented by Mme de Belcier [Jeanne des Anges] were entirely explicable [. . .] by medical knowledge alone" ["Nous avons été guidés par la ferme croyance [. . .] que tous les phénomènes que présente Mme de Belcier [Jeanne des Anges] étaient parfaitement explicables [. . .] par les seules connaissances médicales"] (p. 189, n. 2). It is followed by interpretative studies by F. Cavallera (323–332) and Michel de Certeau (337–379). There is now a second edition (1990 –"revue et corrigée") that tones down the editorial denigration, and I shall make reference to it.

[80] The *Triomphe de l'amour divin sur les puissances de l'Enfer* occupies p. 7–123 of the Jérôme Millon edition of the *Science expérimentale.*

[81] These are respectively on p. 301–44 of the Jeanne des Anges text and 421–37 of the Surin text.

[82] The phrases occur in *Relation*, p. 318–19.

[83] "[. . .] impossible à situer au-delà ou en-deçà de la frontière qui sépare la sincérité de la simulation" (*Relation*, p. 319).

frequentation".[84] Of Surin, on the other hand, Certeau is much more tolerant, seeing him, on the evidence of his vast if fragmentary corpus of spiritual writing, as well as his personal testimony, as someone whose lucid awareness of his ordeal is marked by his "understanding of experience, [an understanding which] discerns in it, more and more acutely, the true from the false".[85] His role, for Certeau, was thus "to help the believer to recognize, in the situation in which he finds himself, the form which his commitment to God must take".[86] Our natural response (and that of many of his contemporaries), is probably one of scepticism, and yet the last pages of his account are strangely moving, in the humble way in which his exceptional intensity of knowledge of Christ is resumed, more as a perilous risk than as an unambiguous gift, as a result of which he was more often than not thought to be mad. "It is still a great good", he concludes, "to pass for a deluded man, and, if God so wishes, to die in that opprobrium, as his own Son did."[87]

What, in both of the Loudun accounts, most immediately strikes the reader, however, is the orderly way in which the names and characteristics of each devil are enumerated with a high degree of precision. Thus Jeanne des Anges specifies: Asmodée (lust), the chief demon; Léviathan (pride); Béhémoth, who by opposing the service of God is a personification of temptation, as well as giving rise to spontaneous blasphemy; Isacaaron (impurity), both more brutal and more direct than Asmodée; Balaam, who works on the imagination; and Aman, whose roles are less distinctly delimited. They combine in her case in their attempts to effect her total detachment from God, by virtue of a dereliction of all forms of prayer as of the sacraments; and their *modus operandi* is specified as depending on a knowledge of and sympathy with their host, so gaining "a tacit consent to operate on the mind of the creature which they possess".[88] By stressing thereby the compatibility of the possessions with the innermost desires of the victim, it is made clear that human nature is inherently corrupt, and that the victim is considered thereby in some way responsible for the diabolic activities which it endures. Thus when, in response to a priest of whom she disapproves, Jeanne des Anges spits out the host at

[84] "[il faut] rendre compte du fait lui aussi impressionnant, que tant de gens, ecclésiastiques avertis, saintes religieuses ou hommes d'affaires, ont pu la vénérer et trouver lumière dans sa fréquentation" (*Relation*, p. 362).

[85] "[une] intelligence de l'expérience ; elle y discerne, d'une façon de plus en plus aiguë, le vrai du faux" (*Science expérimentale*, p. 435–6).

[86] "[d'aider] le fidèle à reconnaître, dans la situation où il se trouve, la forme que doit prendre l'adhésion à Dieu" (*Science expérimentale*, p. 437).

[87] "Ceci est pourtant un grand bien de passer pour un homme d'illusion, et si Dieu le veut, mourir dans l'opprobre comme son Fils" (*Science expérimentale*, p. 341). Bowman comments: "For [Surin], autobiography is a means of communicating to others [. . .] his own dark night of the soul which by that communication becomes an act of charity" ("Suffering, madness", p. 39).

[88] "[. . .] un tacite consentement pour opérer dans l'esprit de la créature qu'ils possèdent" (*Relation*, p. 83).

Communion, she concedes "that I gave the demon room to commit [this act], and that he would not have had this power if I had not been bound to him".[89]

It is the symptoms of the first exorcism, which is conducted by the Bishop of Poitiers and which rids her of three demons, that place the whole phenomenon in some kind of ecclesial context. Jeanne des Anges records them as follows: "As a sign of their departure, they left three wounds below my heart, in the sight of everyone present. It was by the intercession of the Blessed Virgin and the good angels that this marvel occurred."[90] First, then, we note what will become a central feature of her experience, whereby the demons mark their departure by a physical sign, in this case by one which affects the parts of her body that are near the heart. Secondly, that the demons mark their departure by a sign that is indicative of a divine manifestation. And thirdly, that they do so by the intervention of a figure who is of a higher rank in the corresponding divine hierarchy (Mary) as well as those of an equivalent rank (angels) to the diabolic forces. The Saints, of whom Mary is the highest, have achieved their status by doing God's will in their earthly lives; the angels are of a higher order of creation, and are thus perceived to constitute the positive correlative to the demons. All such features are furthermore consistent with Surin's accounts of the exorcisms.

We then embark on the extraordinary sequence of episodes which manifest the demonic presence, all of which occur after the arrival of Surin. On one occasion, for example, Jeanne des Anges is made to believe that she is pregnant, complete with the attendant physical symptoms, whereupon she contemplates both immediate suicide and a longer process involving abortion, following which she would baptize the child before killing it and herself (and she is only prevented from so acting by the knife being thrown supernaturally from her hand). The sense is once again conveyed thereby of a human battleground, on which God's intentions are perpetually countered by the diabolic and vice versa. This sequence nonetheless leads to the moment of her conversion, as a voice addresses her from the crucifix to which she has had recourse: "'Desist from your evil scheme'", she is told, "'turn back to your Saviour and be converted to him, for he is ready and waiting to receive you'",[91] whereupon the arm of the crucifix holds out a hand, and further encouraging words are spoken. The features of her long recovery, guided by Surin, from the belief in her own damnation and from the external diagnosis of her as afflicted by madness, begin appropriately with the practice of mental prayer

[89] "[...] que je donnai lieu au démon de la [cette action] faire, et qu'il n'eût point eu ce pouvoir si je ne me fusse point liée à lui" (*Relation*, p. 85).

[90] "Pour marque de leur sortie, ils me firent trois plaies au-dessous du cœur à la vue de tous les assistants. Ce fut par l'intercession de la sainte Vierge et des bons anges que cette merveille s'opéra" (*Relation*, p. 81–2).

[91] "'Désiste de ton mauvais dessein, aie recours à ton Sauveur et te convertis à lui, car il est tout près de te recevoir'" (*Relation*, p. 95).

["oraison"]. Such a transition is manifestly perceived as a benchmark in the achievement of spiritual progress and, in common with St François de Sales, St Margaret Mary and Madame Guyon, understood as a transformative pious exercise. This is then accompanied by the physical application of the Blessed Sacrament to her heart and head, in a further powerfully carnal understanding of its efficacy, and by the recitation of Psalms. In this most extreme and disputed expression of Christian belief and practice, we nonetheless find the central trio of prayer, sacraments, and Scripture being presented as the fundamental mechanisms of spiritual healing and progress.

What is yet more dramatic in this account is the counterpoint provided by visions of beasts (a lion, a black dog, a dragon, a mastiff, and so on), which reflect the binary opposition between what she terms her "higher part" ["partie supérieure"] and her "lower part" ["partie inférieure"].[92] Most confusingly of all, Léviathan appears to her in the protean form of a man "whose countenance changed from one moment to the next"[93]; and, worse still, he deploys on occasion this flexibility to the most diametrically confusing effect by impersonating her spiritual director, Surin. In the same spirit, Surin himself writes of how, in his enduring temptation to kill himself, for example by hanging himself behind the tabernacle, "the devil had so obscured my reason that it always seemed as though it was God and reason that were ordering me to kill myself".[94] And, in the deluded narrative of Antoinette Bourignon, the devil's disciples are recorded as enacting the major features of Christian practice, such as prayer, fasting, and the reception of the sacraments, as a parody of their authentic counterparts,[95] as well as infecting the minds of her more sceptical readership.[96] What these desperate illustrations have in common is that they show an exact parallelism of symptoms between divine and diabolic manifestations, and thereby accord to discernment a vital if at times seemingly impossible function. The arbitrator, whether he takes the form of the contemporary exorcist or the posthumous reader, is thus confronted with a kind of aporia, in which the methods and procedures for diagnosis are themselves subject to the same degree of ambiguity as the symptoms.

But for Jeanne des Anges, as for Surin, it is finally consolation that becomes the dominant tonality, with a vision of a particularly beautiful guardian angel accorded to the (as it was believed) dying sister, holding "a white candle, very

[92] The distinction is frequently made in the period, and is extensively amplified by François de Sales in the first book of the *Traité de l'amour de Dieu*. It is Augustinian in origin.

[93] "[...] qui changeait à tout moment de contenance" (*Relation*, p. 152).

[94] "Le diable avait tellement obscurci ma raison qu'il me semblait toujours que c'était Dieu et la raison qui me commandait de me tuer" (*Science expérimentale*, p. 17).

[95] These are narrated in the closing pages of the *Vie extérieure*.

[96] "This is why the devil puts doubts and scruples into the minds of those who read my writings" ["C'est pourquoi le diable jette des doutes et des scrupules dans les esprits de ceux qui lisent mes écrits"] (*Vie extérieure*, p. 142).

tall and very big and very bright".[97] In particular, when she receives the sacrament of Extreme Unction, she is accorded a vision of St Joseph; and five drops of the holy balm fall on her shirt, from which they become miraculously irremovable, as well as retaining their sweet odour. Thereafter, as she goes on to relate, "God operated several miracles by virtue of this relic, the account of which would be enough to fill a book".[98] Whatever their epistemological status, such an attribution of miracles to individuals remained predictably a crowd-puller, as is betokened by the triumphal tour of France which she then undertook, and which is recounted in the last pages of her narrative.[99]

Miracles,[100] finally, find common ground with much of what I have treated so far, by virtue essentially of their secondary relationship to orthodox doctrine. As C. S. Lewis wrote: "The central miracle asserted by Christians is the Incarnation [. . .]. Every other miracle prepares for this, or exhibits this, or results from this."[101] If Christ's miracles are accepted as the unambiguous signs of his divine nature, post-Christic miracles (which almost without exception in the period involve a healing) require a more sceptical interpretation, once again because their status is of itself neutral, and as such is devoid of an inherently didactic, even less a doctrinal component. Their authenticity is therefore once again dictated by Pike's "Scripture-dogma test" whereby, in common with visions, their purpose is to affirm and enhance the understanding of the corpus of revealed truth. The individual affected is in this perspective once again a channel, and not an end; and the function of the miracle of which he or she is the beneficiary is to reinforce and not to circumvent the authority of Scripture, the Fathers, the Councils and the Holy See. As Pascal succinctly asserts, the didactic relationship can be understood as effective in one direction alone, whereby "miracles serve doctrine, and not doctrine miracles"[102]; he then cryptically invokes the archetype of the discovery of the True Cross[103] in order to illustrate the power of miracles in the discernment of truth, whereby the fundamental dogma of the Crucifixion was

[97] "[. . .] un cierge blanc, fort grand et fort gros et fort allumé" (*Relation*, p. 184).

[98] "Dieu a opéré plusieurs miracles par cette relique dont on pourrait faire un livre" (*Relation*, p. 187).

[99] Robin Briggs comments on how "Mère Jeanne des Anges, flaunting her dubious stigmata, was made welcome at the royal court in the course of a triumphant progress round France" (*Communities of Belief: Cultural and Social Tensions in Early-Modern France*, Oxford, Clarendon Press, 1989, p. 393).

[100] "A sensible fact [*opus sensibile*] produced by the special intervention of God for a religious end, transcending the normal order of things usually termed the Law of Nature" (*ODCC*).

[101] *Miracles: A Preliminary Study*, London, Collins (Fount Paperbacks), 1960, p. 112.

[102] "Les miracles sont pour la doctrine, et non pas la doctrine pour les miracles" (*Pensées*, L 840, S 428).

[103] *Pensées*, L 856, S 436 and L 901, S 449. The discovery of the True Cross (known as the Invention of the Cross, from the Latin verb *invenire*, to find, to come across) is attributed to St Helena, mother of Constantine. The Feast is celebrated on May 3.

subsequently endorsed by a further physical sign. Once right doctrine is established, it could be inferred from this, both visions and miracles have fulfilled their role.

Miracles, initially those worked by Christ, the Apostles and the early Saints, nonetheless have a central if disputed place in Pascal's apologetic project. One entire section of the *Pensées* is devoted to them,[104] containing in particular a questionnaire sent to his co-partisan Barcos[105] by Pascal, in which answers are provided (which are based in turn on the teachings of St Thomas Aquinas). In particular we note the examination of the status of post-incarnation miracles, illustrated as being such experiences as "the healing of an ill person achieved by the application of a holy relic, the healing of a possessed person by the invocation of the name of Jesus etc.".[106] Two additional points also arise, both concerning the question of discernment, and establishing a hierarchy of signs. First, Pascal asserts that the existence of miracles of the Antichrist should not deter the believer from according credence to those attributed to Christ, since "no sign has ever occurred from the devil without a stronger sign on the part of God. At least without it having been predicted that it would occur."[107] Second, that "a miracle [performed by] schismatics is not so much to be feared, because schism, which is more visible than a miracle, is a sure mark of their error".[108] More globally, therefore, and resuming these two examples, there is a reciprocal obligation established between God and man, whereby "men owe it to God to receive the religion that he sends them" and "God owes it to men not to lead them into error".[109]

The most disputed miracle in the period, and certainly the most enduring in its implications, was the recovery from a lachrymal fistula by Pascal's niece, Marguerite Périer, as a result of the application of a relic from the Crown of Thorns.[110] The antagonists in the Jansenist–Jesuit dispute, which was then in

[104] L 830–912, S 419–51. The section is subdivided in Sellier. Pol Ernst (*Les 'Pensées' de Pascal, géologie et stratigraphie*) shows convincingly that the fragments devoted to the evidence evinced from miracles was likely to have been superseded by those dealing with evidence from prophecy. Mesnard comments that "this reflection on miracles does not definitively amount either to a polemical or an apologetic text" ["cette réflexion sur les miracles n'aboutit en définitive ni à un écrit polémique ni à un écrit apologétique"] (*Les 'Pensées' de Pascal*, p. 39).

[105] Martin Barcos (1600–78) succeeded his uncle as Abbé de Saint-Cyran.

[106] "[. . .] la guérison d'une malade faite par l'attouchement d'une sainte relique, la guérison d'une démoniaque par l'invocation du nom de Jésus etc." (*Pensées*, L 830, S 419). Curiously, both Pascal's categories of miraculous beneficiary are marked by a feminine form of the noun.

[107] "[. . .] jamais signe n'est arrivé de la part du diable sans un signe plus fort de la part de Dieu. Au moins sans qu'il eût été prédit que cela arriverait" (*Pensées* L 903, S 450).

[108] "Un miracle parmi les schismatiques n'est pas tant à craindre, car le schisme qui est plus visible que le miracle marque visiblement leur erreur" (*Pensées*, L 903, S 450).

[109] "[. . .] les hommes doivent à Dieu de recevoir la religion qu'il leur envoie [. . .] ; Dieu doit aux hommes de ne les point induire en erreur" (*Pensées*, L 840, S 428). The specific applicability of these assertions to miracles is made clear from their context.

[110] The miracle of the Holy Thorn is recounted, *inter alia*, by Gilberte Périer in her *Life* of Pascal [*Vie*] (L p. 17–33, S p. 37–78). The healing allegedly took place on March 24, 1656.

full swing, were unsurprisingly quick to latch on to its ambiguous potential, with the outcome that each side read the phenomenon in the light of its own interests. Thus, for Port-Royal, the miracle was a sign of the justness of the Jansenist cause against its persecutors:

> When people no longer listen to tradition [. . .] and have thus excluded the true source of truth which is tradition, and forestalled the Pope who is its depository, [so that] truth is no longer free to manifest itself, then men no longer speak of truth, [and] truth must itself speak to men.[111]

For the Jesuits, on the other hand, the fact that the physical object to which miraculous powers were accorded was taken from a relic of the Passion served as a reminder of the universality of salvation, against the alleged predestinarianism of their opponents; and the fact that it was applied to an infection of the eye was irresistibly taken up as a taunt. Thus, for example, in the pseudonymous 1656 *Défense de la vérité catholique touchant les miracles*:

> God has wished, by a quite particular action of his mercy, to let the Passion of Jesus Christ burst forth, by using an instrument of this Passion in order to operate a miracle before the eyes of those very people who persist in impugning the merit and effects of the Passion [. . .] and so as to invite the Jansenists to reflect on their interior blindness.[112]

Yet both parties would also, paradoxically, have agreed that the supernatural can only be understood as authentic if it promotes, endorses or deepens the understanding of the corpus of doctrine which has been inherited. Whereas the devout understanding of the Incarnation might expand, therefore,[113] as we saw in the cult of the Sacred Heart, the period of transmission of the corpus of Christian dogma has, from whatever tradition it is approached, elapsed. And yet, as Pascal asserts in the *Preface* to his (unwritten) *Treatise on the Vacuum*, promoting scientific innovation and opposing theological speculation, "the error of our times is such that we see many new opinions in

[111] "[. . .] quand on n'écoute plus la tradition, [. . .] et ainsi qu'ayant exclu la vraie source de la vérité qui est la tradition et ayant prévenu le pape qui en est le dépositaire, la vérité n'a plus de liberté de paraître, alors les hommes ne parlent plus de la vérité, [et] la vérité doit parler elle-même aux hommes" (*Pensées*, L 865, S 439). The context of this fragment is again clear, since it is situated in the section "Miracles".

[112] "Dieu a voulu, par une conduite toute particulière de sa miséricorde, faire éclater la Passion de Jésus-Christ, en se servant d'un instrument de cette Passion, pour opérer un miracle devant les yeux de ceux-là mêmes qui s'obstinent à impugner le mérite et l'effet de la Passion [. . .] pour inviter les Jansénistes à faire réflexion sur leur aveuglement intérieur" (*Défense de la vérité catholique touchant les miracles*, p. 17–18).

[113] This was to be a central argument of Blessed J. H. Newman's 1845 *Essay on the Development of Christian Doctrine*.

theology, unknown to all antiquity, obstinately promoted, and greeted with applause".[114]

All these manifestations have something to do with the givenness, with the specificity, in other words, of the Incarnation itself; but they also open up the question as to how to interpret extraordinary events in the context of ecclesial authority, or, more globally, in that of a mediating Church. Just as the desire for the knowledge of good and evil was at the origin of the Fall, so the redeemed power of discernment becomes in turn a defining gift of the Spirit, as manifested in the Church and its ministers. What we have been looking at in these two chapters is the open question of how, and how far, individual enlightenment is bound to be subjugated to the discernment of those empowered to interpret it, in order to promote the primacy of Catholic doctrine over such phenomena as divine utterance, visions, possessions and miracles, of the kind I have considered. That is the role delegated within the Church to those empowered with the gift of *discretio spirituum*; and that, presumably, is both why Margaret Mary Alacoque is a Saint, and why she took so long to become one. In reading these lives we notice similar experiences in terms of extreme ascetic practices, physical and mental suffering, verbal and mental prayer, supernatural intervention, and the ensuing dilemma of obedience, all of which are common in varying degrees. Even a handful of biblical texts are recurrent, as is a group of common images.

Yet St Margaret Mary and Antoinette Bourignon stand in other respects at opposite ends of the spectrum of acceptance by the Holy See, the former meriting the ultimate accolade of canonization, the latter condemned and ostracized as a *visionnaire*. And the victims of the Loudun possessions seem to occupy some kind of middle ground in terms of (at least ecclesial) even-handedness. The issue at stake is the capacity (or its lack) of unmediated inspiration to affirm the revealed truth, to which end the individual, in this perspective, can never be more than a channel. What such individual *cas limites* as we have considered nonetheless illustrate is the Christian imperative to maintain some tangible, consistent, and rigidly imposed line between the divine, the deluded, and the diabolic.

[114] "[Le] malheur du siècle est tel, qu'on voit beaucoup d'opinions nouvelles en théologie, inconnues à toute l'Antiquité, soutenues avec obstination et reçues avec applaudissement" (*Sur le traité du vide. Préface* in L 230–2, p. 231, S 81–92, p. 86).

6

Particularity and Polemic (i): Jansenism

Christian authority is vested, as Bossuet unsurprisingly asserts, in "the decrees of the Councils, the doctrine of the Fathers and their holy unanimity, the ancient tradition of the Holy See and of the Catholic Church".[1] But, as Voltaire will equally unsurprisingly riposte a century later: "There is no article of faith that has not given birth to a civil war."[2] The Council of Trent may safely be taken to codify the essence of Catholic teaching both at the time of its activity and for centuries thereafter. As far as the Holy See was concerned, the tenets of Christian dogma had been established as clearly and fully and indeed faithfully as it lay within a human institution to achieve. As Mark Noll puts it, Trent offers "an official statement of Catholic teaching that gave the Church a more detailed definition of its own beliefs than it had ever had".[3] That is not however to say that no divergent or heterodox opinions were expressed at any later stage within the Roman communion; and it could indeed be argued that many of the ways in which Christian particularity was subsequently displayed and fought over lay in the constituent elements of the two major intra-Catholic disputes of the French seventeenth century, known respectively as Jansenism and Quietism. It could also be argued that both arose from two of the very points which constituted the strengths of the Catholic Reformation: a return to the teaching of the Fathers; and an emphasis on personal devotion, in the tradition of *devotio moderna*,[4] as embraced above all by the Society of

[1] "[. . .] les décrets des conciles, la doctrine des Pères, et leur sainte unanimité, l'ancienne tradition du Saint-Siège et de l'Église catholique" (*Oraison funèbre de Henriette-Marie de France*, in *Œuvres*, 57–81, p. 68). The context is, tellingly enough, a condemnation of the Reformation, delivered in the commemoration of the death of a French princess (the youngest child of Henri IV and Marie de Médicis), who had become Queen of England. An account of her eventful life, whose vicissitudes stem largely from the circumstances of her mixed marriage (to Charles I), is given in the same volume at p. 1206–7.

[2] "Il n'y a pas un article de foi qui n'ait enfanté une guerre civile" (*Eloge et 'Pensées' de Pascal*, p. 276).

[3] Mark Noll, *Confessions and Catechisms of the Reformation*, Leicester, Apollos, 1991, p. 166.

[4] This is the movement which spread from Northern Europe in the late fourteenth century, placing an emphasis on personal devotion, and which was marked above all by the influence of the *Imitation of Christ*.

Jesus, and as manifested in the practices of Christian humanism. What I shall attempt to determine in the two chapters on polemic that follow is not only what Jansenism and Quietism respectively represented in the period, but also to examine if and in what ways the two phenomena have any points in common.[5]

It is worth stressing at the outset the extent to which the specificity of the Christian revelation, its distance in antiquity, the early disputes over dogmatic formulations and the more recent upheavals of the Reformation all conspired to render conflicts probable. The likelihood is archetypally promoted by the intrinsic contradictions which have to coexist within orthodoxy, and which preoccupied the Church during the first millennium of its existence: God as one and three; Christ as God and man; Mary as virgin and mother. To some extent, to repeat, these mysterious contradictions are inherent to the definition of the faith, as we saw in the first chapter, although ideally, in the Church's conciliar definitions of dogma, they will be held within a credal formulation. Furthermore, different periods have been associated, for a variety of historico-theological reasons, with certain emphases in such a dogmatic coexistence, as actions, reactions, and counter-reactions have succeeded one another in what seems like a perennial debate. Most pertinent to our period, I would argue, are the tensions between inspiration and obedience, grace and free will, and transcendence and mediation.

What we shall see in both this chapter and the next, in addition, is how a relatively limited and erudite point of controversy is expanded into a whole range of tangential polemics and disputes. This has partly to do with the nature of polemic, which, certainly on the evidence of this material, tends to promote an exponential level of disagreement and acrimony, without there always being any additional substantive issues in play. That is not to say that these disputes were about nothing; it is rather to suggest that their social, political, and literary manifestations far transcended the precise points of theological divergence which gave rise to them. There is therefore in both cases a major disjunction between origins and developments; but there is also a sense in which the issues that exploded into conflict were themselves lying more or less dormant within Western orthodoxy. As René Pommier writes, in a highly provocative article, with respect to the subject of this chapter:

> From Pelagius and St Augustine, up to the progressive and traditionalist Christians of the present day, and by way of the Jesuits and Jansenists of the 17th century, it is always the same debate that is being pursued [. . .]. More or less

[5] A third highly problematic area, which was also productive of a substantial corpus of writing, was the so-called "Querelle du théâtre", in which the legitimacy of dramatic performance, and the motivation for theatrical attendance, both came under scrutiny. See on this subject Henry Phillips, *The Theatre and Its Critics in Seventeenth-Century France*, Oxford, Oxford University Press, 1980; and Jean Dubu, *Les Églises chrétiennes et le theatre (1550–1850)*, Grenoble, Presses universitaires de Grenoble, 1977.

> sharply focussed, according to whether society is evolving more or less rapidly, the conflict is nonetheless permanent: the Church is obliged to try to adapt to social evolution, but cannot do so without provoking rifts and protests, because it cannot do so without more or less denying its past and its traditions.[6]

As Pommier vitally suggests, the tensions within the doxa are definitional rather than circumstantial. Pascal puts it more brutally again:

> Grace will always be in the world, and so will [human] nature, so that [grace] is in some sense natural. And so there will always be Pelagians, and always Catholics, and always conflict.
>
> Because the first birth [that is natural birth] gives rise to the former [in his terminology, Pelagians], and the grace of the second birth [that is conversion] gives rise to the latter [that is, in his terminology, Catholics].[7]

In these terms, both the Jansenist tendency and the opposition to it were simply the latest in a series of articulations of an eternal sequence of action and reaction,[8] whose particular manifestation had its origins in a dispute about grace and free will that was grounded in Augustine's refutation of Pelagius in the fifth century. And then again, as Gemma Simmonds points out, elegantly transposing the problematics back to its originator, "the emphasis found in [Augustine's writings] depends [in turn] on the errors he was trying to refute".[9]

Such a tension is therefore consistent with the particularity of Christian doctrine, as Pascal makes powerfully clear in his defence of tradition. He writes in the *Pensées* (in what is in fact an anti-Jesuit fragment, but whose implications are far broader), using a telling verb: "All the religions and sects

[6] "Depuis Pélage et saint Augustin, jusqu'aux chrétiens progressistes et traditionalistes d'aujourd'hui, en passant par les Jésuites et les Jansénistes du XVIIe siècle, c'est toujours le même débat qui se poursuit [. . .]. Plus ou moins aigu selon que la société évolue plus ou moins vite, le conflit n'en est pas moins permanent : l'Église est bien obligée d'essayer de s'adapter à l'évolution d'une société, mais elle ne peut le faire sans provoquer des déchirements et des protestations, puisqu'elle ne peut le faire sans renier plus ou moins son passé et ses traditions" ("Jansénisme et noblesse de robe", in *Études sur le XVIIe siècle*, Paris, J & S éditeur (Eurédit), 2006, 99–113, p. 109).

[7] "La grâce sera toujours dans le monde, et aussi la nature, de sorte qu'elle est en quelque sorte naturelle. Et ainsi toujours il y aura des pélagiens, et toujours des catholiques, et toujours combat. // Parce que la première naissance fait les uns, et la grâce de la seconde naissance fait les autres" (*Pensées*, L 662, S 544). The Pelagian heresy, combatted by St Augustine during the fifth century, asserted that "man can take the initial and fundamental steps towards salvation by his own efforts, apart from Divine grace" (*ODCC*).

[8] Jean-Louis Quantin evokes the attempt to "reconcile a majority religion, with its necessary compromises and accommodations, and the requirement of a radical individual conversion" ["concilier une religion du grand nombre avec ses compromis et ses accommodements nécessaires, et une exigence de conversion invididuelle radicale"] (*Le Rigorisme chrétien*, Paris, Éditions du Cerf, 2001, p. 19).

[9] Gemma Simmonds, "Jansenism (1640–1713): an historico-theological account", unpublished PhD thesis, University of Cambridge, 2005, p. 117.

in the world have had natural reason for their guidance. Only Christians are *compelled* [*astreints*] to take their rules from outside themselves, and to find out what rules Jesus Christ left to the early church to transmit to the faithful."[10] The gradual codification of what the Western church now understands as orthodoxy bears witness therefore to the struggle to give expression to the multiple tensions which were present from the start of Christendom. Indeed Pascal again, now in the *Writings on Grace*, asserts that

> it is not only in [the dispute over grace and free will] that [the Church] suffers from opposing enemies. It has virtually never been without such a double conflict. And, just as it experienced this incompatibility in the person of Jesus Christ, its head, whom some made into man alone, and others into God alone, so it has felt it in almost all the other aspects of its belief.[11]

The strange givenness of Christianity, in other words, is precisely what perpetuates its potential for internal dissent; and both the Jansenist and Quietist disputes are simply imitative, in this perspective at least, of a well-established paradigm.

The label Jansenism[12] derives from the name of the Bishop of Ypres, latinized as Cornelius Jansenius, whose *Augustinus* was published posthumously in 1640. This was the point of reference, arguably more often symbolically than substantively, for the development of a movement within the French Church which sought to redress what it saw as the tendency manifested by Trent towards an overly free-will-dominated theology of grace. This neo-Pelagian position, as it was polemically described, was promoted, among others, by the Spanish theologian Luis de Molina (1535–1600) in 1588 in his

[10] "Toutes les religions et les sectes du monde ont eu la raison naturelle pour guide. Les seuls chrétiens ont été *astreints* à prendre leurs règles hors d'eux-mêmes, et à s'informer de celles que Jésus-Christ a laissées aux anciens pour être transmises aux fidèles." The fragment continues: "This constraint wearies these good Fathers, who want to be like other peoples, and have the freedom to follow their imagination" ["Cette contrainte lasse ces bons Pères, ils veulent avoir comme les autres peuples la liberté de suivre leurs imaginations"] (*Pensées*, L 769, S 634, my emphasis).

[11] "Ce n'est pas en cette seule rencontre qu'elle [l'Église] éprouve des ennemis contraires. Elle n'a quasi jamais été sans ce double combat. Et, comme elle a éprouvé cette contrariété en la personne de Jésus-Christ, son chef, que les uns ont fait homme seulement, et les autres Dieu seulement, elle en a senti presque en tous les autres points de sa créance" (*Écrits sur la grâce*, I, p. 313). The references derive rather generally from the range of early heresies which found expression in the attempt to define the nature of the personhood of Christ. More comprehensively again, Pascal writes: "The Church has three sorts of enemies: Jews, who have never been part of its body; heretics, who have withdrawn from it; and bad Christians, who tear it apart from within" ["L'Église a trois sortes d'ennemis: les Juifs qui n'ont jamais été de son corps; les hérétiques qui s'en sont retirés; et les mauvais chrétiens, qui la déchirent au-dedans"] (*Pensées*, L 858, S 437).

[12] A readable brief account of Jansenism is given by Louis Cognet, *Le Jansénisme*, Paris, Presses universitaires de France ("Que sais-je?"), 1964. See also the first part of Kolakowski, *God Owes Us Nothing*.

treatise on grace and free will (the *Concordia liberi arbitrii cum gratiae donis*) – and Molinist is the other label most frequently attached by Jansenists to their adversaries. The foundations associated with Jansenism were the two monasteries of Port-Royal – one in Paris, and one in the countryside just outside, at which a male sodality was founded, and to which there was also a school attached, at which Racine was famously a pupil. It was as spiritual director of Port-Royal that Jean Duvergier de Hauranne, Abbé de Saint-Cyran (1581–1643) exerted his influence, as a result of which he was imprisoned by Richelieu in 1638. The family most associated with the later stages of the movement was however the Arnauld dynasty; and it was indeed the condemnation in 1656 of Antoine Arnauld[13] on a relatively precise point of interpretation of the *Augustinus* by the Paris Faculty of Theology, the Sorbonne, which triggered the movement's most famous literary document, Pascal's *Provincial Letters*. Other literary manifestations of a climate of Augustinian pessimism were also in evidence including, on one reading at least, the whole corpus of Racinian tragedy, or the rigorously secular *Maximes* of La Rochefoucauld[14]; and the major apologetic work to be imbued with its theology was, as I proposed in the first chapter, the so-called *Pensées* of Pascal.[15]

The nature of the phenomenon has predictably elicited a good deal of debate. Probably the most famous critical work devoted to Jansenism in the twentieth century was by the Marxist philosopher Lucien Goldmann in *Le Dieu caché*,[16] in which he gives a socio-political origin to the movement, whereby the disempowered legal nobility sought under the absolutist regime of Louis XIV to reassert its autonomy by expressing its political divergence through the channel of religious dissent; and there is no doubt that both secular and religious forces of authority were the instrumental causes of its suppression. I shall neither endorse nor refute Goldmann's reading; I shall rather attempt to assess both why Jansenism elicited such a fervent and systematic campaign of persecution, and why it exerted such a powerful influence.

[13] Antoine Arnauld (1612–94) is known as "le grand Arnauld". In the year following his treatise on frequent communion (*De la fréquente communion*) of 1643, his defence of Jansenius in 1644 (*Apologie de M. Jansénius*) established irrefutably his support for the movement.

[14] The *Maximes* of the Duc de La Rochefoucauld (1613–80) nonetheless purport, in their deeply pessimistic view of humankind and its motives, to exclude from the blanket of opprobrium directed against human nature "those whom God protects by a particular grace" ["ceux que Dieu en préserve par une grâce particulière"] (*Maximes*, ed. Jacques Truchet, Paris, Librairie Garnier (Classiques Garnier), 1967).

[15] See on the literary manifestations of Jansenism Philippe Sellier, *Port-Royal et la littérature*, Paris, Champion, 1999; Tony Gheeraert, *Le Chant de la grâce: Port-Royal et la poésie d'Arnauld d'Andilly à Racine*, Paris, Champion, 2003.

[16] Lucien Goldmann, *Le Dieu caché*, Paris, Gallimard, 1959. A less tendentious socio-political reading of the period is afforded by Paul Bénichou in his *Morales du grand siècle*, Paris, Gallimard, 1948.

The polemical point at issue originally surrounded the condemnation of five technical formulations (the so-called *Five Propositions* ["*Cinq Propositions*"]), describing specific aspects of the interaction between grace and free will in the *Augustinus*.[17] Of course it could be argued that, according to the model of orthodoxy which I have been proposing (that it is defined by the binary coexistence of contradictory givens), it should in the end be no harder or easier to justify the coexistence of grace and free will than the coexistence of three and one, God and man, or virgin and mother, even if the debate in question is superficially likely to impinge more directly on human conduct than those of a more strictly definitional nature. Perhaps what ultimately needed to be transcended by Bossuet's "change of language" was the immanent concept of causality, in favour of a transcendent one of interdependence. This possibility is indeed entertained by Pascal in the first of his *Writings on Grace*, in which he makes room for "a single and dominant volition", even if specific actions can be "accorded or denied to the secondary volition", and he drives this back in turn to the Galatians verse: "I live, not I, but Jesus Christ in me."[18] In other words, he accepts the primacy of grace over free will, without fully accounting for the manner of their co-operation; and he does so without apparently going beyond the well-established scriptural formulation of a paradox.[19]

So what is it all about? One obvious answer, which I shall examine further in what follows, is that the *Augustinus*, by its countering of the Tridentine position, demonstrated a perceived leaning towards the Calvinist tendency, and *ipso facto* was likely to incur the condemnation of the Holy See; and that this was at risk of occurring, whether or not anyone could identify with any degree of textual precision the credal departures from orthodoxy of which it was accused. And a second point of conflict, to which I shall return in the final chapter, concerns the evidence which the movement irrefutably gave—not even of coming to a given answer to the question as to who was saved and who was damned and why, but of asking the question in the first place.

[17] A secondary and subsequent debate revolved around the issue of whether the statements were in fact heretical ("la question de droit") and, more straightforwardly again, whether or not they occurred *totidem verbis* in the *Augustinus* ("la question de fait").

[18] "Je ne vis pas moi, mais Jésus-Christ en moi" (*Écrits sur la grâce*, I, p. 324).

[19] "If then we ask why men are saved or damned, it can in one sense be said that it is because God wishes it and in one sense because men wish it. // But it is a matter of knowing which of these two wills, namely the will of God or the will of man, is the governing, the dominant, the source, the principle and the cause of the other" ["Si donc on demande pourquoi les hommes sont sauvés et damnés, on peut en un sens dire que c'est parce que Dieu le veut et en un sens dire que c'est que les hommes le veulent. // Mais il est question de savoir laquelle de ces deux volontés, savoir de la volonté de Dieu ou de la volonté de l'homme, est la maîtresse, la dominante, la source, le principe et la cause de l'autre"] (*Écrits sur la grace*, I, p. 311). Pascal variously uses "volonté dominante", "volonté maîtresse", and "volonté primitive" for the will of God; and more consistently "volonté suivante" for the will of man.

Let me first of all return to Pascal, and begin with two apparently contradictory remarks: that there is nothing in his writing to suggest that he seeks to deny the role of free will in the economy of salvation; and that there is ample evidence of his belief in some form of predestination. So how do we reconcile those two statements? The question is first of all asked in the *Pensées* as to whether those who fall away from faith are divinely predestined to do so, and certainly the tenor of two fragments incorporated in the same section supports such a reading: "We can understand nothing of the workings of God, if we do not take as a principle that he has wished to give blindness to some and enlightenment to others"[20]; or again, in a more complex play of *chiaroscuro*: "There is enough light to enlighten the elect and enough darkness to humiliate them. There is enough darkness to blind the damned but enough light to condemn them and to render them inexcusable."[21] There seems therefore to be in embryo a mysterious co-operation implied in a state that is already decided. On the other hand, in an unexpected gloss on the psychology of Christian hope in the *Pensées*, the apologist appears to promote the need to dissuade the believer from indulging his natural pessimism and thus believing himself damned, in an ironic and sententious fragment: "There are only two sorts of men: the righteous who believe they are sinners; and sinners who believe they are righteous."[22] Or, now more expansively:

> Only the Christian religion [. . .] teaches the righteous, whom it elevates to the point of participation in the godhead itself, that in that sublime state they still carry the source of all the corruption which makes them throughout their lives subject to error, to wretchedness, to death, to sin; and it cries out to the most impious that they are capable of the grace of their Redeemer.[23]

What we find in the single major work Pascal devoted to the question, the *Writings on Grace*,[24] and what is no doubt disturbing about it, is once again

[20] "On n'entend rien aux ouvrages de Dieu si on ne prend pour principe qu'il a voulu aveugler les uns et éclaircir les autres" (*Pensées*, L 232, S 264).

[21] "Il y a assez de clarté pour éclairer les élus et assez d'obscurité pour les humilier. Il y a assez d'obscurité pour aveugler les réprouvés et assez de clarté pour les condamner et les rendre inexcusables" (*Pensées*, L 236, S 268).

[22] "Il n'y a que deux sortes d'hommes : les uns justes, qui se croient pécheurs ; les autres pécheurs, qui se croient justes" (*Pensées*, L 534, S 469). This is essentially a summary of the parable of the Pharisee and the tax-collector (Luke 18: 9–14), evoked in the two words ("Pharisien, publicain") of fragment L 928, S 756.

[23] "La seule religion chrétienne [. . .] apprend aux justes qu'elle élève jusqu'à la participation de la divinité même qu'en ce sublime état ils portent encore la source de toute la corruption qui les rend durant toute la vie sujets à l'erreur à la misère, à la mort, au péché, et elle crie aux plus impies qu'ils sont capables de la grâce de leur Rédempteur" (*Pensées*, L 208, S 240).

[24] *Écrits sur la grâce*, in Pascal, *Œuvres complètes*, ed. Louis Lafuma, Paris, Seuil (L'Intégrale), 1963, p. 310–48. All references will be to this edition. The date of the work is given by Lafuma as 1657–8. On Pascal's theology, a good introduction is provided by Jan Miel, *Pascal and Theology*, Baltimore and London, Johns Hopkins University Press, 1969.

the intractability of the enquiry itself. This difficult and unfinished treatise is principally concerned to assert and defend the Augustinian position, presented as orthodoxy, and to place it in opposition to Molinists on the one hand (referred to as the residue of Pelagianism), and Calvinists on the other. This latter contrast allows Pascal to give a particularly affirmative view of the Augustinian position, defining the power of Christ's grace as "a delight ['suavité', once again] and a delectation in the law of God, poured into the heart by the Holy Spirit [. . .], [which] fills the will with a greater delectation for good than concupiscence affords it for evil".[25] This is in distinction to the view attributed to Calvinists, of whose perspective Pascal writes of "the grace of Jesus Christ [. . .] which leads their will to good (not which causes the will to be led to good, but which leads it to [good] in spite of its repugnance)".[26] The difference lies crucially in the manner of co-operation. But it is here, significantly enough, that we also find common ground with St François de Sales, in discerning the pleasure accorded to the will in gaining the desire to follow God: "When God gives us faith", François writes in the *Treatise on the Love of God*,

> he comes into our soul and speaks to our spirit, not in the manner of a discourse, but in the manner of inspiration, proposing what it is necessary to believe so agreeably to our understanding, that the will thereby receives a great sense of compliance, such that it incites our understanding to consent and acquiesce to the truth, without any degree of doubt or defiance.[27]

In this respect at least, we find a consonance in Pascal with the more accommodating theology of the Bishop of Geneva, and one expressed in terminology that is fundamentally thomist. As Moriarty comments, in an irenic interpretation of the period as a whole, "seventeenth-century French religious culture was not, as it sometimes appears, systematically divided between two parties each with radically opposed visions of human nature".[28]

But to move thus far is to overlook the fact that Pascal's *Writings on Grace* are themselves a polemical document; and his rhetorical situating of

[25] "La grâce de Jésus-Christ, qui n'est autre chose qu'une suavité et une délectation dans la loi de Dieu, répandue dans le cœur par le Saint-Esprit [. . .] remplit la volonté d'une plus grande délectation dans le bien, que la concupiscence ne lui offre dans le mal" (*Écrits sur la grâce*, II, p. 318).

[26] "La grâce de Jésus-Christ [. . .], qui porte leur volonté au bien (non pas qui fait que la volonté s'y porte, mais qui l'y porte malgré sa répugnance)" (*Écrits sur la grâce*, II, p. 319).

[27] "Quand Dieu nous donne la foi, il entre en notre âme et parle à notre esprit, non point par manière de discours, mais par manière d'inspiration, proposant si agréablement ce qu'il faut croire, à l'entendement, que la volonté en reçoit une grande complaisance, et telle qu'elle incite l'entendement à consentir et acquiescer à la vérité, sans doute ni défiance quelconque" (*Traité de l'amour de Dieu*, p. 450).

[28] *Fallen Nature, Fallen Selves*, p. 344.

Augustinianism as holding the central (and by implication the orthodox) ground between Calvinism and Molinism is as elegant as it is spurious, in that the identification of what is in the middle will depend, to put it simply, on what you place on either side. Thus the Holy See could well have argued back that it held the middle ground between Augustinianism and Molinism, within the intra-Catholic spectrum, and it could have done so without taking the controversial step of introducing a Reformed tradition into the dialectic. As Quantin pertinently remarks, Jansenists situated themselves between Molinists and Calvinists in order to conform to "the traditional image of orthodoxy as a *juste milieu*",[29] and to seek thereby to exemplify Catholic moderation. So what does Pascal's theology of grace amount to?

What is first of all clear is that, in conformity with his recurrent insistence on binary models, seeking, persevering in faith, and falling away from it are all double actions. Such an idea is implicit in the *Pensées*, in the apparently awkward phrase, following an enumeration of the proofs of the Christian religion: "It is indubitable that, in this light, we should not refuse, when considering what life is, and what this religion is, *to follow the inclination to follow it*, if it comes into our hearts."[30] On a closer inspection, however, this turns out not to be a stylistic inelegance, but rather a recognition, achieved by the emphatic repetition of the same verb in the same (infinitive) form, of the intimate link between seeking and finding. As we have seen, Pascal considers that there are only three sorts of people, "those who serve God, because they have found him; others who make it their business to seek God, because they have not found him; others who live without seeking him and who have not found him". The first are, in his formulation, "happy and reasonable", the last "unhappy and unreasonable". The privileged interlocutors of the apologetic project are those in the middle who are "unhappy yet reasonable", those, in other words, who follow the inclination to seek God, and for whom the apologist has only compassion.[31] As he writes more affirmatively again in the essay *On the Sinner's Conversion*: "[God] can only be taken away from

[29] "[...] l'image traditionnelle de l'orthodoxie comme juste milieu" (*Le Rigorisme chrétien*, p. 11).

[30] "Il est indubitable qu'après cela on ne doit pas refuser, en considérant ce que c'est que la vie et que cette religion, *de suivre l'inclination de la suivre*, si elle nous vient dans le cœur" (*Pensées*, L 482, S 717, my emphasis).

[31] "Il n'y [a que] trois sortes de personnes : les uns qui servent Dieu l'ayant trouvé, les autres qui s'emploient à le chercher ne l'ayant pas trouvé, les autres qui vivent sans le chercher ni l'avoir trouvé. Les premiers sont raisonnables et heureux, les derniers sont fous et malheureux, ceux du milieu sont malheureux et raisonnables" (*Pensées*, L 160, S 192). The apologist writes of "those in the middle" ["ceux du milieu"]: "I can have nothing but compassion for those who sincerely bewail their state of doubt" ["Je ne puis avoir que de la compassion pour ceux qui gémissent sincèrement dans ce doute"] (*Pensées*, L 427, S 681). The Scriptural resonances with Matthew 7: 7 (or in the Old Testament, Jeremiah 29: 13) are clear.

those who reject him, because to desire him is to possess him, and to renounce him is to lose him."[32]

Where we move onto the relatively more technical dimension of the enquiry is in the complementary exposition in the *Writings on Grace* of the theory of the "double abandonment"[33] of the man who leaves God. The terminology is attributed by Pascal to St Augustine and his disciple St Prosper of Aquitaine,[34] whereby "the first abandonment consists of God not holding him back, after which man leaves God, and gives rise to the second abandonment, whereby God leaves man".[35] But this first abandonment is already "entirely mysterious and incomprehensible"[36]; or, in the words of St Prosper: "*Why God retains some men and not others is a question to which it is not allowed to seek, nor possible to find, the answer.*"[37] We gain a strong sense, as a result, in this verbose and repetitive text, of Pascal struggling but failing to achieve the kind of synthesis which marks so much of his thought. Yet despite its tortuous nature, it does at length arrive at a succinct conclusion, all of whose terms have been analysed in what has preceded, as follows: "That God, in his mercy, gives whenever it pleases him, to the righteous, the full and perfect power to accomplish his precepts, but that he does not always give it, by a judgement that is just although hidden."[38]

The *Writings on Grace* essentially look at two questions, therefore: how grace co-operates with free will; and who is chosen and why; and certainly the specific answers given explicitly accord to God an element of pre-selection which is lacking, for example, in the universalism of St François de Sales, for whom "God has signified to us in so many ways and by so many means that he

[32] "Dieu [...] ne peut être ôté qu'à ceux qui le rejettent, puisque c'est le posséder que le désirer, et que le refuser c'est le perdre" (*Sur la conversion du pécheur* in L, 290–1, p. 291).

[33] Pascal's phrase is "double délaissement", and his argument is above all developed in the third piece.

[34] St Prosper of Aquitaine (c. 390 – c. 463) was a fervent supporter of St Augustine's stand against the Pelagian heresy.

[35] "Le premier délaissement consiste en ce que Dieu ne retient pas, ensuite de quoi l'homme quitte, et donne lieu au second délaissement par lequel Dieu le quitte" (*Écrits sur la grâce*, III, p. 325).

[36] "Mais le premier délaissement est tout mystérieux et incompréhensible" (*Écrits sur la grâce*, III, p. 325).

[37] "*Pourquoi Dieu retient ceux-ci et non pas ceux-là, est une chose qui est défendue d'être recherchée et qu'il est impossible de trouver*" (*Écrits sur la grâce*, III, p. 328).

[38] "[Que] Dieu par sa miséricorde donne quand il lui plaît, aux justes, le pouvoir plein et parfait d'accomplir les préceptes, et qu'il ne le donne pas toujours, par un jugement juste quoique caché" (*Écrits sur la grâce*, IV, p. 348). This summary, which closes the fourth *Écrit*, is in fact amplified in the third piece (*Écrits sur la grâce*, III, p. 326). Bossuet too, in the 1656 *Sermon on Providence*, reminds his hearers that since on the Day of Judgement alone the good will be separated from the wicked, so that, "in advance of this great day, they must necessarily remain mixed" ["en attendant ce grand jour, il faut qu'ils demeurent mêlées"] (*Sermon sur la Providence*, in *Œuvres*, p. 1046).

wanted us all to be saved, that no-one can be ignorant of it".[39] On the other hand, the whole of the corpus of writing we have considered so far (and indeed shall do) is unanimous in seeing the prevenient grace of God as the origin of all that is good in humankind, and humankind itself as the origin of all that is sinful.[40] What we might retain is the following: that there is a universal recognition of the coexistence of grace with free will, shared by Pascal, alongside a disagreement that is partly (but not entirely) methodological or linguistic as to the cause and mode of interaction. What we might note more concretely, in addition, is that the distance between Pascal and St François de Sales is far less great than that between the Catholic and the Reformed traditions, at least insofar as these are interpreted by writers in the Catholic tradition.[41] And finally, that even Pascal considers

> that all men in the world are obliged to believe, but with a belief mixed with fear, and that is not accompanied by certainty, that they are of that small number of the elect that Jesus Christ wishes to save, and not to judge any men that live on earth, however wicked and impious they might be, for as long as there remains a breath of life within them, that they are not among the number of the predestined, leaving to the impenetrable secrecy of God the discernment of the elect and the damned.[42]

[39] "Dieu nous a signifié en tant de sortes et par tant de moyens qu'il voulait que nous fussions tous sauvés, que nul ne le peut ignorer" (*Traité de l'amour de Dieu*, p. 721). Angers summarizes François's teaching on grace by two juxtaposed statements relative to finality and causality: "Man is made for God and directs himself towards him as towards his own good [. . .]. Man cannot go to God without God's help, but he is free to reject it or to collaborate with it" ["L'homme est fait pour Dieu et se dirige vers lui comme vers son bien [. . .]. L'homme ne peut aller à Dieu sans le secours de Dieu, tout en étant libre de le rejeter ou d'y collaborer"] (*Humanisme chrétien*, p. 2).

[40] Pascal gives an untranslated quotation from St Bernard in the *Pensées*: "Quo quisque optimus eo pessimus si hoc ipsum quod sit optimum ascribat sibi" ["The better one is, the worse one becomes, if one attributes to oneself that by which one is good"] (L 191, S 224).

[41] In the *Traité de l'amour de Dieu*, François describes compatibly with Pascal the impact of the Fall, but crucially emphasizes the good which has remained in man: "So, although the state of our human nature is not endowed with the original holiness and uprightness which the first man had at his creation, and that on the contrary we are gravely depraved by sin, *nonetheless the holy inclination to love God above all things has stayed with us, as has the natural light by which we know that his supreme goodness is loveable above all things*" ["Or, bien que l'état de notre nature humaine ne soit pas doué de la sainteté et droiture originelle que le premier homme avait en sa création, et qu'au contraire nous soyons grandement dépravés par le péché, *si est-ce toutefois que la sainte inclination d'aimer Dieu sur toutes choses nous est demeurée, comme aussi la lumière naturelle par laquelle nous connaissons que sa souveraine bonté est aimable sur toutes choses*"] (*Traité de l'amour de Dieu*, p. 399, my emphases).

[42] "Que tous les hommes du monde sont obligés de croire, mais d'une créance mêlée de crainte et qui n'est pas accompagnée de certitude, qu'ils sont de ce petit nombre d'élus que Jésus-Christ veut sauver, et de ne juger jamais d'aucun des hommes qui vivent sur la terre quelque méchants et impies qu'ils soient, tant qu'il leur reste un moment de vie, qu'ils ne sont pas du nombre des prédestinés, laissant dans le secret impénétrable de Dieu le discernement des élus d'avec les réprouvés" (*Écrits sur la grâce*, I, L, p. 313).

And it is indeed in the light of this belief that a Christian apology was able to be written by the same author, as the following phrase testifies: "This obliges [the disciples of St Augustine] to do what they can for [men] in order to achieve their salvation."[43] Pascal "did what he could" in what we now call the *Pensées*.

This simple injunction is far more telling in terms of how the believer lives than is any theory of grace, guarding as it does against both the sin of pride and the heresy of antinomianism. The emphases in Pascal's more technical attempts at a systematic assessment of grace and free will place him clearly at one end of the spectrum of possible orthodox opinion, more by what he does not say about God's universal desire to save humankind, than by what he does say about predestination. But they do not do more than that.

Yet to say as much is in some ways to miss the point; because the real battles of Jansenism were to be fought out on adjacent territory, and these concerned above all the question of Christian laxism, as promoted, in the perception of Pascal and his co-partisans, by the Society of Jesus, and as manifest in the sacramental issues of frequent communion and of penitential casuistry.[44] Because the perceived threat of Jansenism, I suggest (and without starting on socio-political causes), lay less in what it was trying to defend, and more in what it was determined to attack (and that was already the case for Arnauld). The constant tension between grace- and free-will-dominated theologies might well have triggered, in the aftermath of the Council of Trent, a reaction that was predicated on Augustinian pessimism. It is difficult historically to deny that point of departure. But the enduring impact of Jansenism came from its move onto two contingent areas of controversy, and I would argue that it was those areas of attack which placed it beyond the pale of orthodoxy, because they apparently placed it, despite all its disclaimers, in the line of Calvinism.

The work which made the impact of Jansenism into a literary phenomenon was Pascal's polemical sequence of *Provincial Letters*,[45] written purportedly by

[43] "Ce qui les oblige [les disciples de saint Augustin] de faire pour eux [les hommes] ce qui peut contribuer à leur salut" (*Écrits sur la grâce*, I, L, p. 313).

[44] The *DTC* gives the simple and global definition: "The application of theological conclusions to specific concrete cases, with the aim of making a decision as to what remains permitted [...] and what is prohibited" ["L'application des conclusions théologiques à des cas déterminés et concrets, dans le but de décider ce qui reste permis [...] et ce qui est défendu"].

[45] *Lettres provinciales*, or more fully: *Les Lettres écrites par Louis de Montalte à un provincial de ses amis et aux RR. PP. Jésuites*. I shall refer to the text edited by Philippe Sellier and Gérard Ferreyrolles in Pascal, *Les Provinciales, Pensées et Opuscules divers*, Paris, Le livre de poche/ Classiques Garnier (Pochothèque), 2004, p. 155–696. Another excellent edition is that of Michel Le Guern (Paris, Gallimard "Folio", 1987), which has the particular advantage that it contains both the *Avertissement* of Pierre Nicole and substantial extracts from the Jesuit replies. Among recent studies of the *Lettres provinciales*, see: Walter Rex, *Pascal's 'Provincial Letters': An Introduction*, London, Hodder and Stoughton, 1977; Roger Duchêne, *L'Imposture littéraire dans les 'Provinciales' de Pascal*, Aix-en-Provence, Publications de l'Université, 1985; Gérard

a Parisian, Louis de Montalte,[46] to a friend in the country in order to explain what was going on in the religious disputes that were engrossing the capital. Their trigger was the condemnation of Arnauld by the Sorbonne; and indeed the first four address, by means of a reductive caricature, the terminological questions of grace and free will at issue in the inaugural dispute. The quartet of pieces leads the reader to conclude that the whole episode was little more than a semantic and a tactical ruse, invented by the Sorbonne and its associates, and undertaken in order to inculpate Port-Royal and its spokesman. But defence is fatal to polemic; and it is hardly a coincidence if Pascal only spends a small amount of time on the business of heaping ridicule on the condemnation of Arnauld. What he moves rapidly towards doing, and what gives his letters their bite and their efficacy, is to attack the contemporary French Church's most powerful order, the Society of Jesus; and to do so on grounds which were to become in the process a landmark in the evolution of satirical deformation, that is the alleged abuse of probabilism. According to this practice, adopted by the largely Jesuit authorities on case ethics, it was alleged that where, in the case of a sin confessed, there was at least a probable lenient interpretation proposed as to its gravity, such an opinion might prevail over a more severe alternative; and so the fictive Jesuit interlocutor of the next sequence of letters (5 to 10) is cheerfully and willingly encouraged to list the most ingenious justifications for committing the most heinous of sins. Of course the whole point of casuistry is that it deals with the penitential grey areas; once it is taken out of that zone of operation, its fallibility becomes evident, and Pascal was to lose no opportunity to exploit such a potential in black and white terms. At the same time, as Robin Briggs judiciously notes, "it would certainly be most unwise to take Pascal and the other Jansenist polemicists as fair guides to what the Jesuits taught and practiced",[47] even, or especially, if "the Jansenist view held obvious advantages as a debating position".[48]

If we look for a moderate and party-line definition of what was required, we find it predictably enough in Bossuet's *Meaux Catechism*: first, in an exposition of the act of auricular confession itself, to the effect that pains should be taken to consider the circumstances of a sin in assessing its gravity; and second, that there is a double satisfaction required: of God, by penance; and of the wronged party by, for example, retribution or apology. But also, third,

Ferreyrolles, *Blaise Pascal: 'Les Provinciales'*, Paris, Presses universitaires de France, 1984; Richard Parish, *Pascal's 'Lettres provinciales': A Study in Polemic*, Oxford, Clarendon Press, 1989. There is a good translation by A. J. Krailsheimer, *The Provincial Letters*, London, Penguin Classics, 1976.

[46] The name is not used until the title of the collected series, published in 1657. It has however become common critical practice to use it to refer to the fictive first-person epistoler.

[47] *Communities of Belief*, p. 286. This is amply illustrated by Roger Duchêne in *L'Imposture littéraire*.

[48] *Communities of Belief*, p. 289.

that both are undertaken in view of the readmission of the penitent to the Christian community (and it was in this light that the Jesuits were accused *inter alia* of prioritizing absolution, and of disregarding both retribution and readmission). He then goes on to define the much-contested differentiation between contrition and attrition, to the effect that it is the proportion of love to fear which determines the distinction between the two: contrition arises from a true regret at the offence committed, born of the love of God and of the wish to repair the harm done; and attrition is purely the result of the fear of eternal punishment. At the minimum, he nonetheless concedes, imperfect contrition does not invalidate the efficacy of the sacrament; but, on the other hand, the coexistence of perfect contrition and the desire for the sacrament are of themselves the guarantors of grace.[49] As Fénelon compatibly asserts: "Contrition is more important than the exact confession of all our sins; good faith would be enough to ensure forgiveness provided that one was of a general disposition to hate [the] sin [confessed] and all other sins without exception."[50]

The dispute over sacramental absolution is symptomatic therefore of an enduring intra-Christian tension between laxism and rigorism, in which the Society of Jesus was perceived by its opponents to have erred too far on the side of human nature. So much is clear. But is that divergence in penitential practice sufficiently grounded in issues of Christian fundamentals to engage the believing—or *a fortiori* the non-believing—reader with the kind of visceral assault launched by Pascal in the persona of Montalte? It is tempting, as we have seen from Church history, from Pascal himself and from the reaction of an eighteenth-century *philosophe*, to assert that Christian doctrine is by definition prone to conflict; and indeed Voltaire would claim that all intra-Christian disputes simply demonstrate the inherent fallibility of revealed religions. Given (as its opponents would see it) the tenuous credibility of Christianity in the first place, surely the last thing that needs to happen is for its adherents to engage in public scraps over the finer points of penitential absolution. I want to suggest two possible reactions to that accusation: one on the side of Pascal; the other on the side of the Jesuits.

The first is to suggest that Pascal is entirely prepared to admit that the credibility of Christianity is tenuous. It is he who gave me the title of this book; and it is he who recoils in horror, albeit with a degree of rhetorical overstatement, at the doctrine of the Fall. We do not naturally believe in Christianity, our purely human perception does not find its teaching attractive, it is riddled

[49] These remarks are a brief summary of the fifth section of the *Catéchisme de Meaux*.

[50] "La contrition est bien plus importante que la confession exacte de tous nos péchés ; la bonne foi excuserait pourvu que l'on fût dans la disposition générale de détester ce péché et tout autre sans exception" (*Lettres et opuscules spirituels*, XLVIII (*Sur la confession générale*) in *Œuvres*, I, p. 771).

with dogmatic paradox, and so on. It is strange precisely in the sense of being unnatural, unexpected, and inconvenient. Furthermore, its applicability to the human condition in his writing is predicated on a far-from-flattering self-perception. But to reduce the sinfulness of humankind, for Pascal, is to deny and not to enhance that tenuous applicability. That for him is the central accusation against the Society of Jesus, and the point of junction between apologetics and polemics: the Jesuit tendency, as Pascal presents it, is to deform Christian doctrine to such a degree that it becomes inappropriate to the human condition which it purports to understand, explain, and indeed heal. In two of the most important of the *Provincial Letters*, therefore, each of which marks a turning point in the series, he makes two fundamental points. First, in the fifth piece, Montalte launches the accusation that the Jesuits "suppress the scandal of the Cross, and only preach Jesus Christ in his glory, and not in his suffering".[51] They deny, in other words, and in what amounts to a heretical spirit, those elements of human experience that are the very premisses of the Redemption—failure, sin, sickness, death. Second, now in the pivotal eleventh letter (which effects the transition from the satirical to the more openly polemical sequence), that they thereby make Christianity worthy of the kind of abuse which its opponents are only too ready to throw at it. If this is Christianity, Montalte implies, it is not believable. In this central document of the entire series, in which the tone shifts dramatically from the parodic to the evangelistic, he blisteringly counters the accusation that he has turned religion into a matter of ridicule by asserting that his scorn is reserved for the profaners of Christian doctrine; and that, whereas the truths of the faith are worthy of respect and love, their deformation is only suitable for the mockery and hatred to which he had subjected it. Furthermore Pascal's polemics are entirely in accordance with his apologetics in this respect. Montalte writes of the Jesuits in the eleventh letter, using the obligation *topos* which so frequently marks polemic attacks in the period: "For, Fathers, since you oblige me to enter into this discourse, I ask you to consider how, since Christian truths are worthy of love and respect, so the errors that are contrary to them are worthy of scorn and hatred."[52] It is to this that the apologist of the *Pensées* affords the positive correlative, as he declares his intention to show that the Christian faith is: "Worthy of respect because

[51] "[...] ils suppriment le scandale de la Croix, et ne prêchent que Jésus-Christ glorieux, et non pas Jésus-Christ souffrant" (*Lettres provinciales*, p. 331). The context of the accusation is the so-called "querelle des rites", whereby the Jesuit missions were accused of diluting the more unappealing doctrines of Christianity in their attempts to convert adherents of Far-Eastern religions. Its broader applicability is easy to discern.

[52] "Car, mes Pères, puisque vous m'obligez d'entrer en ce discours, je vous prie de considérer que, comme les vérités chrétiennes sont dignes d'amour et de respect, les erreurs qui leur sont contraires sont dignes de mépris et de haine" (*Lettres provinciales*, p. 442).

it has understood mankind. // Worthy of love because it promises the true good."[53]

The other side of the question, perhaps surprisingly, will take us to the same end point. In the vast, turgid, and highly technical volume entitled *The Summa of Sins* by Étienne Bauny,[54] one of the foremost Jesuit casuists and the principal target of Pascal's venom, a laborious attempt is made to examine what kinds of sub-divisions are available within the taxonomy of sins, and to advise the confessor on how to counsel the penitent. What Bauny does, however, is not to set out to exculpate all penitents pre-emptively, *pace* Pascal, but to explore the full range of morally ambiguous acts which constitute the experience of the majority; and, to some degree, to try and enter into what we would now call the psychology of the sinner. What Pascal was to parody in his polemic was of course the kind of exemplary material which, inevitably within its genre, is present in such a *summa*. In certain cases, Bauny undisputedly takes the search for a justification for absolution beyond not just what orthodoxy but what common sense can condone, in a kind of *amplificatio ad absurdum*; but that is by definition likely to occur in any work which aspires to comprehensiveness and which admits of moral hypotheses. What Bauny would no doubt argue in return, as did certain of the polemically feeble replies to Montalte's attack, is that it is Pascal who denies the place of the Redemption, by pretending that fallen humankind is capable of a consistency of holiness which is quite simply contrary to human nature; and that the sacrament of penance is nothing more or less than the means of recognizing that enduring fallenness.[55] And what is true of the penitent is of course also true of the priest, as Fénelon notes in a paraphrase of Hebrews 5: 3: "This is why St Paul recommends that the mortal priest, who represents Jesus Christ, being subject to human weaknesses, offers the sacrifice [of the Mass] for his own sins as well as for those of the people."[56]

It would be pertinent too at this stage to introduce another kind of counterpoint to perceived laxism, and that is the contemporary practice of hypothetical

[53] "Vénérable parce qu'elle a bien connu l'homme. // Aimable parce qu'elle promet le vrai bien" (*Pensées*, L 12, S 46).

[54] Père Étienne Bauny, SJ, *La Somme des péchés qui se commettent en tous états*, Cologne, [no pub.], 1633. See Richard Parish, "Le Père Étienne Bauny, SJ: *La Sommes de péchés qui se commettent en tous états* face aux *Lettres provinciales*", in *French Studies*, 63, 4, 385–98. On the history of penitential practice, see P. Rouillard, *Histoire de la pénitence des origines à nos jours*, Paris, Éditions du Cerf, 1996 and A. Jonsen and S. Toulmin, *The Abuse of Casuistry: A History of Moral Reasoning*, Berkeley, University of California Press, 1988.

[55] Substantial sections of the Jesuit replies are incorporated in the edition of the *Provinciales* by Michel Le Guern, p. 323–404.

[56] "C'est pourquoi saint Paul recommande que le prêtre mortel, qui représente Jésus-Christ, étant sujet aux faiblesses humaines, offre le sacrifice pour ses propres péchés en même temps que pour ceux du peuple" (*Exhortations, entretiens, sermons*, III (*De la prière*), in *Œuvres*, I, p. 870).

rigorism. Thus St Margaret Mary admits freely in her autobiography her tendency to confess sins which she had almost certainly not committed (throwing in turn a questionable light on other aspects of the veracity of her self-inculpation): "I wrote", she admits,

> everything I could find in books that dealt with confession; and I sometimes wrote things down that I was ashamed even to mention. But I said to myself: "Perhaps I did it without knowing, or perhaps I have forgotten it; so that it is appropriate for me to endure the humiliation of mentioning it, in order to satisfy divine justice." But it is [also] true that, if I had believed I had done the majority of the things of which I accused myself, I should have been inconsolable.[57]

Fénelon again gives a more balanced picture, when he notes how "little faults become greater and more horrible in our eyes as the pure light of God grows stronger within us".[58] Perhaps, conversely, that is also why Bauny recommends that the confessor does not enumerate hypothetical sins when questioning his penitent, in case he or she is given the idea of committing sins which they had not previously contemplated.

The second point at issue received a less dramatic literary treatment, although it is brought out strongly in the Jesuit replies to the *Provincial Letters*. But it chimes entirely with the rigorist sacramental ethos of the first; and that is the vexed question of frequent communion. If we try to situate it once again in the mainstream practice of the period, we find plenty of evidence that the frequent and devout reception of the sacrament was, more often than not, advocated as desirable. Bossuet, for example, proposes in his *Meaux Catechism* a criterion of results: "[The frequency of reception of the sacrament] depends on the disposition of each believer, and on the profit he makes of his communion by his application to living a good life."[59] St Margaret Mary is instructed by Christ to make her communion "'as often as obedience allows you to'",[60] the effect of which on her is immediate and devastating, albeit still within the mainstream of (more extreme) devotional practice: "Whenever I had made [my communion]", she writes, "I had no more desire to drink, to eat, to see or

[57] "J'écrivais tout ce que je pouvais trouver dans les livres qui traitent de la confession ; et je mettais quelquefois des choses que j'avais horreur même de prononcer. Mais je disais en moi-même : 'Je l'ai peut-être faite, et je ne la connais pas, ni ne m'en souviens pas ; mais il est bien juste que j'aie la confusion de la dire, pour satisfaire à la divine justice'. Bien est-il vrai, que si j'avais cru d'avoir eu fait la plupart des choses dont je m'accusais, j'aurais été inconsolable" (*Vie*, p. 52).

[58] "Les petites fautes deviennent grandes et monstrueuses à nos yeux à mesure que la pure lumière de Dieu croît en nous" (*Lettres et opuscules spirituels*, V (*Sur les fautes volontaires*), in *Œuvres*, I, 570).

[59] "Cela dépend de la disposition de chaque fidèle, et du profit qu'il fait de la communion par son application à mener une bonne vie" (*Catéchisme de Meaux*, p. 130). The element of discretion seems indeed to be the most frequent pastoral advice.

[60] "'[. . .] autant que l'obéissance te le voudra permettre'" (*Vie*, p. 72).

to speak, such were the consolation and the peace which I felt."[61] On the question of abstaining from communion on grounds of unworthiness, Bossuet is also absolutely clear: "There are those", he writes, "who make it a subject of pride not to make their communion, and who imagine that they are more virtuous than other people [. . .]. This is a pernicious illusion [. . .]. Jesus Christ is our bread that we should eat every day, as did the first Christians; and we should feel humiliated, when we are judged unworthy to receive him. [. . . Therefore] one may approach Holy Communion however unworthy one feels to receive it; for humble, repentant sinners are those whom Jesus Christ came to seek out"[62]; and Fénelon advocates it simply on the strength of the reference to "our daily bread" in the *Our Father*.[63] St François de Sales devotes a whole chapter of the *Introduction to the Devout Life* to the question (II, xx), in the course of which, in another of his memorable zoological images, he advises his (lay and female) addressee:

> Make your communion often, Philothée, and as often as you can, with the guidance of your spiritual counsellor; and, believe me, [just as] the wild mountain hares become white in winter because they only see and eat snow, so by worshipping and eating the beauty, goodness and purity of this holy sacrament, you will become fully beautiful, good and pure.[64]

All of this is clearly at odds with the 1643 treatise of Arnauld *On* [that is, against] *Frequent Communion*,[65] in which he calls for a return to the practices of the primitive Church. This scholarly and detailed reply to what was clearly little more than a sententious pamphlet devotes a good deal of attention to

[61] "[. . .] lorsque je l'avais faite [la communion], je n'aurais voulu ni boire, ni manger, ni voir, ni parler, tant la consolation et la paix que je sentais étaient grandes" (*Vie*, p. 50).

[62] "Il y en a qui se font un sujet d'orgueil de ne pas communier, et qui s'imaginent être plus vertueux que les autres [. . .]. C'est une illusion pernicieuse [. . .]. Jésus-Christ est notre pain que nous devrions manger tous les jours, comme faisaient les premiers chrétiens ; et nous devons nous confondre, quand nous sommes jugés indignes de le recevoir [. . .]. On peut s'approcher de la communion, quelque indigne qu'on se sente encore de le recevoir : car les pécheurs humbles et repentants sont ceux que Jésus-Christ est venu chercher" (*Prières ecclésiastiques* (1689), in *Œuvres complètes*, ed. Lachat, vol. V, 206–354, p. 336).

[63] "It is certain that when we ask God in the *Our Father* for our daily bread, that is the bread of each day, we are asking him for the Eucharist. So why do we not eat this daily bread each day, or at least very frequently?" ["Il est certain que quand nous demandons à Dieu dans le *Pater* notre pain quotidien, c'est-à-dire de chaque jour, nous lui demandons l'eucharistie. Pourquoi donc ne mangeons-nous pas chaque jour ou du moins très souvent ce pain quotidien ?"] (*Lettres et opuscules spirituels*, XLIII (*Sur la confession générale*), in *Œuvres*, I, p. 755).

[64] "Communiez souvent, Philothée, et le plus souvent que vous pourrez, avec l'avis de votre père spirituel ; et croyez-moi, les lièvres deviennent blancs parmi nos montagnes en hiver parce qu'ils ne voient ni ne mangent que la neige, et à force d'adorer et manger la beauté, la bonté et la pureté même en ce divin Sacrement, vous deviendrez toute belle, toute bonne et toute pure" (*Introduction à la vie dévote*, p. 121).

[65] Antoine Arnauld, *De la fréquente communion, où les sentiments des Pères, des Papes et des Conciles touchant l'usage des sacrements de Pénitence et d'Eucharistie sont fidèlement exposés*, Paris, A. Vitré, 1643.

eliciting the support of Tridentine authority alongside patristic evidence, and—perhaps unhelpfully in the context—of explicitly and somewhat defensively distancing itself from teaching in the Reformed tradition. But it is once again an area in which the Jansenist tendency through its spokesman situated itself in a position that was certainly at odds with the contemporary ethos, even if that did not axiomatically put it at odds with dogmatic fundamentals. There is, at the very least, a divergence in pastoral guidance, if not in sacramental theology; and it was this dimension which brought about some of the most scathing replies to the *Provincial Letters*. The crypto-Calvinist slur constituted the Jesuits' most powerful means of counter-attack and, as Briggs notes, "the likeness between Jansenism and Protestantism proved uncomfortably obvious even at the time".[66] Just because Port-Royal was professedly orthodox on the seminal doctrinal issue of transubstantiation, it did not follow that its conformity to contemporary Eucharistic discipline was impeccable; and this disparity was above all exploited in the title of a famous pamphlet published as a further attempt, now on the part of the Society of Jesus, to shift the arena of polemic, to the effect this time that "Port-Royal [that is, Jansenism] and Geneva [that is, Calvinism]" were united in a pact "against the Most Holy Sacrament of the altar".[67]

I want to finish with two more open-ended questions about Jansenism. First: why was the Church so exercised by the phenomenon? And, more fundamentally again, wherein lay the attraction of a revival of Augustinian pessimism?

Most Jansenist writers represent a series of emphases which lay within what orthodoxy had traditionally been able to absorb. The shifting towards extremes, as reaction and counter-reaction followed one another, necessarily accorded it a range of expressions which prioritized grace in the economy of salvation, and in so doing denied the kind of universalism which is to be found in a St François de Sales, for example.[68] At the same time, the element of co-operation in the process of sanctification and ultimately redemption is a constant in all the writing we have looked at. All that remain unknowable are the proportions and the causes. Jansenism's first movement away from the

[66] *Communities of Belief*, p. 362.

[67] *Port-Royal et Genève d'intelligence contre le Très-Saint Sacrement de l'Autel*, by the Jesuit Père Bernard Meynier, was published in May 1656. See André Gounelle, "Calvinisme et jansénisme: les grandes structures doctrinales", in *Port-Royal et les protestants*, Paris, Bibliothèque Mazarine, 1998, 9–19.

[68] Angers treats these arguments extensively and technically, but summarizes as follows: "Salesian optimism [. . .] is difficult to reconcile with the *massa damnata* [. . .], [but] if the concern to safeguard the predominance of grace still exists, it is substantially redressed by the concern to accord an appropriate place to free will" ["L'optimisme salésien [. . .] se concilie difficilement avec la *massa damnata* [. . .], [mais] si le souci de sauvegarder la prédominance de la grâce existe encore, il est largement compensé par celui de donner sa juste place au libre arbitre"] (*Humanisme chrétien*, p. 26).

Roman centre was rather on a question of discipline; it erred not only by conducting, but by popularizing, an enquiry into the mystery of salvation.

More disconcertingly, it tended by the totality of its practices and writings to situate itself in most respects on the rigorist wing of ethical and sacramental teaching. It might be possible to argue therefore that Jansenism was Catholic in the sense of Catholicism as orthodoxy; but not that it was catholic in the sense of Christian catholicity. And this is aggravated by the areas of polemic themselves—the reception of the Blessed Sacrament and, in particular, penitential rigorism—both of which, at least in some of Geneva's more fundamental articulations concerning the Mass and Confession, are instantly identifiable as key issues of historical differentiation between the Catholic and the Reformed traditions. The label of crypto-Calvinism might well have been unjustly applied by the Society of Jesus, but it was nonetheless the most damaging way of countering the apparent capture of public support for the cause of Port-Royal which had been achieved by the *Provincial Letters*. Indeed Pascal seems to come close to recognizing this himself in what is perhaps an unwise concession to his Jesuit adversaries, to the effect that "Jansenists resemble heretics by their wish to reform manners, [whereas] you resemble them in doing evil."[69] (Against this we should hold in tension his fervent statement of adherence to papal authority in the sixth letter to Mlle de Roannez: "The body is no more alive without its head than the head without its body [. . .]. We know that all virtues, martyrdoms, austerities and good works are of no use if separated from the Church, and from communion with the head of the Church, who is the Pope.")[70]

This is perhaps also one of the difficulties of the *Pensées* and of Pascal's scattered writings on ethics.[71] Insofar as he is dealing with those who are outside the believing community, Pascal is, at least rhetorically, a realist. He starts, as I have suggested, from fallen humankind in all its self-interested, distracted indifference, and he takes his material as he finds it. But his inspirational view of Christian belief tells us little about how the believer will behave after conversion, perhaps because he does not see there as being any enduring conflict beyond the overwhelming conviction which it betokens. Pascal, we might infer as a result, is very good at bringing people to belief; but he has little of practical use to say about the life of the Christian majority thereafter. As he writes in the first letter to Mlle de Roannez, citing an

[69] "Les jansénistes ressemblent aux hérétiques par la réformation des mœurs, mais vous leur ressemblez en mal" (*Pensées*, L 900, S 448).

[70] "Le corps n'est non plus vivant sans le chef, que le chef sans le corps [. . .]. Nous savons que toutes les vertus, le martyre, les austérités et toutes les bonnes œuvres sont inutiles hors de l'Église, et de la communion du chef de l'Église, qui est le Pape" (*Lettres aux Roannez*, VI, in L, p. 268).

[71] On this subject, see A. W. S. Baird, *Studies in Pascal's Ethics*, The Hague, Martinus Nijhoff, 1975.

unidentified female saint: "We should not examine whether we have a vocation to leave the world, but simply whether we have a vocation to stay in it, just as we would not give much thought as to whether we were called to leave a house that was infested or burning [down]."[72] It is as if, paradoxically, Pascal's rhetorically persuasive emphasis on the Fall ceases to pertain once the constituency he is addressing has made the shift to commitment; and yet, as the profusion of penitential manuals bears witness, the faithful are no less fallen than the unbelievers. It is perhaps that omission which betrays the temptation (and I use the word advisedly) of rigorism, and which gives a further clue to the reason for the Church's opposition to Jansenism. It is also, to return to my first chapter, why it is not a coincidence that a Jansenist should be such an eloquent apologist for Christianity. The tradition is marked by its capacity to promote an ideal, but to do so from the periphery, and not from the centre, of a community of believers which is trying, but by definition failing, to live up to it.

That still leaves one more question unanswered. If Jansenism was to some degree perceived as attractive, wherein lay this attraction? One obvious answer is in the success of the writing undertaken by certain of its adherents, but that is more of an *ex post facto* literary reply than an aprioristic socio-theological one. The other possible reply lies in a curious meeting of extremes which perhaps says a good deal about the prevalent ethos of the age, because Jansenism appeals to two opposing tendencies. The first, which is unsurprising and certainly unoriginal, is the tendency to want from within the Church to see it return to basics. As Quantin has remarked, the appeal to a primitive rigour is, it seems, an instinctive and recurrent feature of the individual believer's psychology.[73] Or, in Pascal's imperative formulation, in the persona of Montalte of the *Provincial Letters*, "I am not content with the probable, I want certainty."[74]

But it is also likely that it appealed to a desire which was present in an increasingly dechristianized Christian society to want those who practice the faith to be perfect. The Christian majority who live within the confines of their belief also live within an understanding of failure; and none more so, no doubt, than the confessors who heard day by day of their penitents' shortcomings and who were guided, *inter alia*, by Bauny's flawed precepts as to how to counsel them. Pascal memorably writes, quoting ironically, to judge from the context, a Jesuit position, that "people naturally want a religion, but they want one that

[72] "La parole d'une sainte est à propos sur ce sujet : Qu'il ne faut pas examiner si on a vocation pour sortir du monde, mais seulement si on a vocation pour y demeurer, comme on ne consulterait point si on est appelé à sortir d'une maison pestiférée ou embrasée" (*Lettres aux Roannez*, I, in L, p. 266).

[73] *Le Rigorisme chrétien*, p. 19.

[74] "Je ne me contente pas du probable, [. . .] je cherche le sûr" (*Lettres provinciales*, p. 338).

is soft".[75] I would suggest on the contrary that people naturally want a religion, but they want one that is hard. But I would go on to add that they do so on condition that it is others, and not themselves, who adhere to its strictures. The fictive reply to the second *Provincial Letter* notes, no doubt accurately, that it had appealed above all to men and women of the world; and the series as a whole was to continue to resonate with an increasingly sceptical readership throughout the following century.[76] By far the most rigorous of believers, it would seem from this evidence, are those who do not practice their belief. It is perhaps to them, by means of the ultimate irony, that Jansenism was enduringly able to appeal.

[75] "Le monde veut naturellement une religion, mais douce" (*Pensées*, L 952, S 788).

[76] Thus Voltaire, in 1751, considered the *Provincial Letters* to be "a model of eloquence and wit. The best comedies of Molière do not have more piquancy than the first provincial letters; Bossuet has nothing more sublime than the later ones" ["Ses *Lettres provinciales* [. . .] étaient un modèle d'éloquence et de plaisanterie. Les meilleures comédies de Molière n'ont pas plus de sel que les premières lettres provinciales; Bossuet n'a rien de plus sublime que les dernières"] (*Le Siècle de Louis XIV*, ed. René Groos, Paris, Librairie Garnier, 1947, vol. II, 201).

7

Particularity and Polemic (ii): Quietism

The second of the perceived departures from orthodoxy in the period which I shall consider was known as Quietism; and I want to begin rather surprisingly with a quote from the anti-hero of André Gide's experimental novel *The Counterfeiters* [*Les Faux-Monnayeurs*]: "The forest makes the tree", Édouard claims. "But each tree has so little room to grow! So many saplings are atrophied! Each one throws out its branches as best it can. The mystical branch, most frequently, is therefore the result of strangulation. It can only escape by growing upwards."[1]

The controversy surrounding Quietism must appear even more esoteric than that which concerned grace and free will.[2] It seems to develop into an arcane, clerical sort of debate, which the critics of Christian polemic can latch onto *par excellence* as encapsulating the nonsensical issues which the faithful argue about. On a reductive reading, it demonstrates nothing much more than the struggles within a male hierarchy to reconcile itself to the possibility that the writings of a female mystic might have some enlightenment to convey to other believers. The figure in question was Madame Guyon, an unhappily married laywoman, who endured a succession of what she saw as persecutions, finally spending a period in the Bastille in the years before her death.[3] I have in previous chapters taken some material from her posthumous autobiography; but it is the substantial corpus of mystical, didactic, and exegetical works that were written, and either published or known in manuscript form during her

[1] "La forêt façonne l'arbre. A chacun, si peu de place est laissée ! Que de bourgeons atrophiés ! Chacun lance où il peut sa ramure. La branche mystique, le plus souvent, c'est de l'étouffement qu'on la doit. On ne peut s'échapper qu'en hauteur" (André Gide, *Les Faux-Monnayeurs*, in *Romans*, Gallimard (Pléiade), Paris, 1958, 931–1248, p. 1153). A good general introduction is provided by Louis Cognet, *Les Origines de la spiritualité française au XVIIe siècle*, Paris, La Colomba, 1949.

[2] An excellent account is given by Louis Cognet, *Crépuscule des mystiques*, Tournai, Desclée de Brouwer, 1958. There is also a very clear summary and bibliography in Fénelon, *Œuvres*, I, 1530–46.

[3] In a previously unpublished addition to her autobiography these are recounted in the *Récits de captivité*, ed. Marie-Louise Gondal, Grenoble, Éditions Jérôme Millon, 1992. This text is also reproduced in the Champion edition of the autobiographical works at p. 881–979.

lifetime, which above all caused the controversy to escalate. The two best known of these are a treatise entitled *Les Torrents*,[4] in which the progress towards union with God is explored in a graduated sequence of water images, as the individual rivers make their way to the sea of self-abnegation; and, at the centre of the controversy, the *Brief Method* or *Moyen court*, whose full title says it all: *A brief and very easy method of mental prayer, that all can practice without difficulty, and arrive thereby in a short time at a high degree of perfection.*[5] The first and most striking thing that Guyon was responsible for, it follows from this, was a kind of democratization of the highest forms of prayerful union with God, to which, as she provocatively writes in the *Moyen court*, the humblest peasant in the French countryside would be able to aspire.

It is also more difficult to write about Quietism than about Jansenism because it was not to the same degree in any sense a movement. Ronald Knox describes it witheringly as "the error of a few incautious souls, trying to repeat the lesson they had learned from the saints of the counter-Reformation, and getting it wrong".[6] Where it most of all elicits the opposition of the hierarchy is in two respects: in the dangers of unmediated spiritual enthusiasm, first of all, of a kind which leads the individual to believe that he or she enjoys nothing less than the pure vision of God; and, more disconcertingly again, that he or she does so to the point at which they find themselves in conflict with the specificity of the core doctrines of the Incarnation, and with the conduct that arises from them. What it shares symptomatically with Jansenism is a set of polemical features which grow from a relatively precise point of doctrinal divergence; and indeed the secondary dispute, which merits all the opprobrium that Christian polemic can deserve, was between two prelates, Fénelon, Archbishop of Cambrai,[7] and Bossuet, Bishop of Meaux, who came to verbal blows over the way in which the condemnation of

[4] *Les Torrents et Commentaire au Cantique des Cantiques de Salomon*, ed. Claude Morali, Grenoble, Éditions Jérôme Millon, 1992.

[5] *Moyen court et très facile de faire oraison, que tous peuvent pratiquer très aisément, et arriver par là dans peu de temps à une haute perfection.* The most recent critical edition is by Marie-Louise Gondal, Grenoble, Éditions Jérôme Millon, 2001, to which I shall refer. There is a little-known corrective text by Bossuet, the *Manière courte et facile de faire l'oraison en foi et simple présence de Dieu*, which appeared in 1694. I have translated "oraison" as "mental prayer" in this context in preference to the archaic "orison", and in order to make the distinction with verbal prayer.

[6] Ronald Knox, *Enthusiasm : a chapter in the history of religion*, Oxford, Clarendon Press, 1950, p. 259.

[7] François de Salignac de La Mothe-Fénelon (1651–1715) was tutor to the Duc de Bourgogne (the grandson of Louis XIV) from 1689 to 1694. It was in that capacity that he composed his most famous work, the didactic novel *Télémaque*, published anonymously in 1699. He became Archbishop of Cambrai in 1695. There is a clear, brief introduction to his life and work by J. H. Davies, *Fénelon*, Boston, MA, Twayne Publishers, 1979.

Madame Guyon had been handled.[8] In distinction to the Jansenist controversy, there is no literary *succès de scandale* of the nature of the *Provincial Letters*. There is a satirical attack on Quietism by the *moraliste* La Bruyère, but, although I shall quote briefly from it later in this chapter for the purposes of entertainment, it was written essentially after the ecclesial dispute had run its course.

In another respect, however, the Quietist dispute is just as enduring as the Jansenist one, albeit more low profile, in that it has its origins in a symbolic biblical contrast, that between Martha and Mary in Luke 10: 38–42, of which it is in some ways simply a more technical elaboration: "It is Mary who has chosen the better part", Christ pronounces in favour of the apparently passive devotion of the woman who was sitting at his feet, "and it is not to be taken from her".[9] Furthermore, if the Jansenist controversy was predicated on a largely unread Latin theological treatise written by a dead bishop, the Quietist dispute was above all dominated by a single short work written in French by a living laywoman. In the *Moyen court*, we find an account of the series of stages by which the common believer progresses in a methodical manner towards the highest states of communion with God. The ascent is steep indeed, and the reader soon arrives at the second stage, in the form of a sub-section entitled "Abandonment" ["Abandon"], in which he or she learns that: "Abandonment is a letting go of every concern for ourselves, so as to let ourselves be led entirely by God. [. . .] Being indifferent to everything, as much for the body as for the soul, concerning the good of this world and that of the world to come."[10] The last stage of the manual then promises an experience of mental prayer which rejoices in the simple presence of God; and Guyon writes all this, as she reveals in her autobiography, in the conviction that: "We were created to participate, already in this life, in the ineffable happiness of the commerce of the [Holy] Trinity."[11] It is at this degree of passivity that the question of

[8] The later stages of the debate are constituted by three texts, Bossuet's *Relation on Quietism* [*Relation sur le quiétisme*], Fénelon's *Reply to the Relation* [*Réponse à la relation*] and Bossuet's *Remarks on the Reply* [*Remarques sur la réponse*]. All were published in 1698, and represent an increasingly personal campaign in which, as Le Brun concisely notes, "at this level of the quarrel, it is a matter of everything except spirituality" ["à ce niveau de la querelle, il est question de tout sauf de spiritualité"] (*Spiritualité*, p. 644).

[9] Fénelon comments at the beginning of the *Sayings of the saints* that "illusion has always followed closely on the heels of the most perfect ways [to God]" ["l'illusion a toujours suivi de près les voies les plus parfaites"] (*Maximes des saints*, in *Œuvres*, I, 1002). The biblical episode serves to illustrate a chapter by St François de Sales in the *Treatise on the Love of God* (*Traité de l'amour de Dieu*, VI, 8, p. 634).

[10] "L'abandon est un dépouillement de tout soin de nous-mêmes, pour nous laisser entièrement à la conduite de Dieu [. . .]. Être indifférent à toutes choses, soit pour le corps soit pour l'âme, pour les biens temporels et éternels" (*Moyen court*, p. 74–5).

[11] "Nous étions créés pour participer, dès cette vie, au bonheur ineffable du commerce de la Trinité" (*Vie*, p. 537). Fénelon, more ambiguously, asserts that "all of one's life is a preparation for that blessed peace of the saints, who say for all eternity : *Amen, amen*" ["la vie

sacraments and works also becomes controversial, however, since Guyon recommends that the soul, satisfied with what she calls the divine effusion ["l'effusion divine"], has no further recourse to confession, communion, action or prayer. She further advocates that such a condition is accessible to all; thus it is picturesquely asserted that if the rural clergy adopted her methods, then "shepherds, minding their flocks, would have the spirit of the early anchorites, and ploughmen, guiding their ploughshares, would be happily conversing with God". In this way, she reassures provincial *curés*, "all vices would soon be banished, and all [your] parishioners would become spiritual beings".[12] Quite apart from the practical unlikelihood of her proposal, the implied criticism of the diocesan hierarchy and its priests is not difficult to discern.

It is of course a poignant irony that this work is once again so intimately influenced by the writings of St François de Sales, whose *Introduction to the Devout Life* is a model of systematic, patient, and gradual enlightenment, and who stresses that "the practice of devotion must be accommodated to the strengths, circumstances, and duties of each individual".[13] In the *Introduction* we are made powerfully aware of the attempt to codify the spiritual progress of the majority as unambiguously as possible, and to construct a method to adopt, in order to advance towards the less ambitious stages of a prayerful communion with God. One chapter of the earlier work indeed consists of a "Brief method of meditation",[14] intended to be followed in the same way as a course of instruction might be (and Guyon at least borrows from her saintly model the tendency to make progress in such carefully enumerated steps). On the strength of François's instruction, therefore, the reader need never feel that spirituality is something abstract and impressionistic, but rather may take encouragement from the assurance that the following of certain procedures

entière est un commencement de la paix bienheureuse des saints qui disent éternellement : *Amen, amen*"] (*Lettres et opuscules spirituels*, XXXV (*Au Marquis de Blainville*), in *Œuvres*, I, p. 724).

[12] "[. . .] les bergers, en gardant leurs troupeaux, auraient l'esprit des anciens anachorètes, et les laboureurs, en conduisant le socle de leur charrue, s'entretiendraient heureusement avec Dieu [. . .]. Tous les vices seraient bannis en peu de temps, et tous les paroissiens deviendraient spirituels" (*Moyen court*, p. 113–14).

[13] "Il faut accommoder la pratique de la dévotion aux forces, aux affaires et aux devoirs de chaque particulier" (*Introduction à la vie dévote*, p. 36). At the same time, Angers notes of Salesian spirituality that it is marked by a "dynamism [. . .] which, under the inspiration of the spirit, is capable of flowering into a total giving and abandonment [of the self]" ["[un] dynamisme [. . .] qui, sous l'inspiration de l'esprit, est capable de s'épanouir dans un don et dans un abandon total"] (*Humanisme chrétien*, p. 45).

[14] II, ii: *Brève méthode pour la méditation*. This divides each meditation into four stages: Preparation; Consideration; Affections and Resolutions; Conclusion. The last part is then subdivided into actions of thanksgiving, offering, and prayer. More modest spiritual practices, known as exercises (again on the Ignatian model), are also proposed, to be practiced morning and night.

will lead to the desired results (with due account taken of the risk of backsliding). Even on the higher spiritual level of "inspirations", a clear tripartite division is proposed (inspiration, delectation and consent), in exact symmetrical contrast to the three stages of falling into sin. The last section in particular of the *Introduction to the Devout Life* contains striking examples of François's strict classification of some of the more apparently subjective and abstract of spiritual concerns; and even in his later and more ambitious *Treatise on the Love of God*, the reader is struck by the comprehensively ordered way in which this most apparently indefinable of subjects is treated.[15] Yet François is firmly pragmatic in his recognition that many souls will not progress beyond certain defined limits, and that these will legitimately revert to less ambitious devotional practices.

Such balanced, systematic, and indeed caveat-filled spiritual writings would seem to be the antithesis of enthusiasm; and yet, as Fénelon was to remark in the *Explanation of the Sayings of the Saints on the Inner Life* (a text which was explicitly triggered by the first stage of the Quietist controversy): "Nothing is so difficult as to properly convey those states which consist of operations that are so simple, so delicate and so abstracted from the senses, and to place at each stage all the necessary correctives in order to pre-empt illusions."[16] And, already in the earlier work, St François de Sales had written, as if presciently: "There are certain things which many people consider to be virtues, but which are not at all [. . .]: these are ecstasies or ravishings, insensibilities, impassivities, deific unions, elevations, transformations, and other such perfections about which certain books have been written."[17]

One of the background issues in play, however arcane it might seem to a modern reader, lies in the distinction between meditation and contemplation.

[15] Vermeylen traces the influence of St Teresa of Ávila (1515–82), a Spanish Carmelite mystic, canonized in 1622, in particular in Books VI and VII. See *Sainte Thérèse en France*, p. 136–88. Pertinently to this chapter, he remarks on "[the] general credit in which St Teresa was held by French spiritual writers, whatever their degree of personal receptiveness towards mysticism" ["[le] crédit général de sainte Thérèse auprès des écrivains spirituels français, quel que soit leur degré personnel d'ouverture à la mystique"] (*Sainte Thérèse*, p. 282).

[16] "Rien n'est si difficile que de faire bien entendre des états qui consistent en des opérations si simples, si délicates, si abstraites des sens, et de mettre toujours en chaque endroit tous les correctifs nécessaires pour prévenir l'illusion" (*Explication des maximes des saints sur la vie intérieure*, in Fénelon, *Œuvres* I, ed. J. Le Brun, Paris, Gallimard (Pléiade), 1983, 999–1095, p. 1003). The *Réponse à la relation* [*sur le quiétisme*] (1698) can be found in the same volume at p. 1099–1199.

[17] "Il y a certaines choses que plusieurs estiment vertus et qui ne le sont nullement [. . .] : ce sont les extases ou ravissements, les insensibilités, impassibilités, unions déifiques, élévations, transformations, et autres telles perfections desquelles certains livres traitent" (*Introduction à la vie dévote*, p. 131). As Cognet accurately remarks, "the position of St François de Sales [. . .] differs very profoundly from the *néantisme* of the abstract school" ["la position de saint François de Sales [. . .] diffère très profondément du néantisme de l'école abstraite"] (*Crépuscule*, p. 24). It is difficult to translate *néantisme* without a cumbersome periphrasis such as "doctrine of the annihilation of the individual".

Meditation, in all treatments of the term in the period, is considered to be a methodical, teachable, and unremarkable activity. If we start once more from François, we find a clear definition provided of both terms: meditation, he writes, is "nothing other than [a process of] attentive thought, either reiterated or voluntarily entertained by the mind, in order to excite the will to holy and salvific affections and resolutions".[18] Contemplation, on the other hand, is defined by him as "nothing other than a loving, simple, and permanent attention of the mind to divine things".[19] And these definitions already point, when examined carefully, to the crux of the matter. Meditation is essentially an activity which is appropriate for the soul that has not yet reached the complete disinterestedness which characterizes the final stages of its progress towards the perfect love of God. It is an activity suited to the majority, furthermore, and one which can and should be undertaken by them on a daily basis. Both Bossuet and Fénelon concur as well (adapting an image from 1 Corinthians 3: 2) that it is an activity which, if prematurely abandoned, is equivalent to "[snatching] the baby from its mother's breast before it is capable of digesting solid nourishment"[20]; and both prelates also agree that, in Bossuet's words, "without [any such] extraordinary acts of mental prayer, it is possible to become a very great Saint, and to attain to Christian perfection".[21] Even if it is tempting to argue that Bossuet is more easily seen as the disciple of the

[18] "La méditation n'est autre chose qu'une pensée attentive, réitérée ou entretenue volontairement en l'esprit, afin d'exciter la volonté à de saintes et salutaires affections et résolutions" (*Traité de l'amour de Dieu*, p. 613). See Christian Belin, *La Conversation intérieure : la méditation en France au XVIIe siècle*, Paris, Champion, 2002; and *La Méditation au XVIIe siècle: rhétorique, art, spiritualité*, ed. Christian Belin, Paris, Champion, 2006.

[19] "La contemplation n'est autre chose qu'une amoureuse, simple et permanente attention de l'esprit aux choses divines" (*Traité de l'amour de Dieu*, p. 616). The transition between the two is provided in this work by a typically extended Salesian metaphor involving bees. For Le Brun, François "[. . .] shows that everyone can and must work towards the practice of contemplative mental prayer, and in this respect the *Traité* complements the *Introduction*; for him the terminus of contemplation is the conformity of the human will to the divine will" ["[François] montre que chacun peut et doit tendre à une oraison contemplative et le *Traité* complète ainsi l'*Introduction* ; pour lui le terme de la contemplation est la conformité de la volonté humaine à la volonté divine" (*Histoire*, p. 251).

[20] "C'est arracher l'enfant de la mamelle avant qu'il puisse digérer l'aliment solide" (*Maximes des saints* in *Œuvres*, I, p. 1061). Madame Guyon uses the same metaphor in a diametrically opposite spirit. For her, "first of all [. . .], you have to move your lips out of affection. But once the milk of grace begins to flow, there is nothing more to do than to remain in peace, swallowing gently" ["il faut [. . .] d'abord remuer les lèvres d'affection. Mais lorsque le lait de la grâce coule, il n'y a rien à faire qu'à demeurer en repos, avalant doucement"] (*Moyen court*, p. 85–6).

[21] "Sans ces oraisons extraordinaires on peut devenir un très grand saint, et atteindre à la perfection du christianisme" (*Ordonnance et instruction sur les états d'oraison*, in *Œuvres complètes*, ed. Lachat, vol. XVII, 353–673, p. 361). Le Brun writes disparagingly of this text, referring as well to previous attempts to address the issue by Bossuet: "The *Instruction* [. . .] is a hasty and provisional work, which takes up pages from all these unfinished treatises, but does not fully succeed in making them into a coherent whole" ["Œuvre hâtive et provisoire, l'*Instruction* [. . .] reprend des pages de tous ces traités inachevés mais parvient mal à en faire un ensemble cohérent"] (*Spiritualité*, p. 583).

methodical *Introduction to the Devout Life*, and Fénelon of the more ambitious spiritual taxonomy of the *Treatise on the Love of God*, both prelates would concur with their episcopal predecessor on certain basic definitions; and, in Bossuet's words in the *Instruction on the States of Prayer* (a text also triggered by the Quietist dispute), both would acknowledge that the abuse of the higher forms of mental prayer amounts to "placing the perfection of this life in an act which only pertains to the life [of the world] to come".[22]

But it is François's term "salvific" that is crucial, because the semantic origins of meditation, and indeed its *raison d'être*, lie in its serving to prepare: to prepare for action, to amend one's life in other words; to prepare for death; but, above all, to prepare for salvation. It is thus, by definition, a soteriological activity. And what the episcopal hierarchy could not contend with was the kind of indifference towards salvation as it was defined by Guyon: "Abandonment is the letting go of every concern for ourselves, so as to let ourselves be led entirely by God. [. . .] Being indifferent to everything, as much for the body as for the soul, *concerning the good of this world and that of the world to come*."[23] As Bossuet writes, very concretely and clearly in the *Instruction on the States of Prayer*, in a paraphrase of the *Our Father*: "God [. . .] wants us to desire our salvation; to ask for his grace [. . .]; to ask [. . .] every day for [our sins] to be forgiven; and to pray that we might overcome the temptations that lead us to commit them."[24] Every meditation is thus a securing of the means of sanctification; every meditation is thus also a step towards salvation. Putting it very simply, meditation is a means to an end; contemplation, on the other hand, is an end in itself, but one which carries, if it is not properly focused, the risks of illusion, enthusiasm, and error.

The amplitude and sophistication of the writing to which this fairly basic opposition gave rise is in direct contrast to the kind of ingenuous universality

[22] "[. . .] mettre la perfection de cette vie dans un acte qui ne convient qu'à la vie future" (*Instruction sur les états d'oraison*, p. 397). The degree of consonance between the two prelates, at least initially, is indeed far more striking than their disagreements. Le Brun remarks that "there is in both cases a similar approach to the mystery of spirituality" ["c'est chez l'un et l'autre une approche semblable du mystère de la spiritualité"] (*Spiritualité*, p. 496). On the other hand, for Cognet, "Fénelon always considered his own thought as the extension of that of the great mystics" ["Fénelon a toujours considéré sa propre pensée comme le prolongement de celles des grands mystiques"] (*Crépuscule*, p. 9); and for Sanson, "the quarrel surrounding pure love is no doubt a quarrel between individuals and [. . .] between clans; at a deeper level, it expresses marked differences in the ways of conceiving the Christian life, and in particular the life of prayer" ["la querelle du pur amour est sans doute une querelle de personnes et [. . .] de clans ; plus profondément elle exprime des différences notables dans la façon de concevoir la vie chrétienne, et particulièrement la vie de prière"] (*Saint Jean de la Croix*, p. 25).

[23] "L'abandon est un dépouillement de tout soin de nous-mêmes, pour nous laisser entièrement à la conduite de Dieu [. . .]. Etre indifférent à toutes choses, soit pour le corps soit pour l'âme, *pour les biens temporels et éternels*" (*Moyen court*, p. 74–5, my emphasis).

[24] "Dieu [. . .] veut que nous désirions notre salut ; que nous lui demandions ses grâces [. . .] ; que nous lui [. . .] demandions tous les jours pardon à Dieu [de nos péchés], et le priions qu'il nous fasse vaincre les tentations qui nous y portent" (*Instructions sur les états d'oraison*, p. 440).

which caused it to be so controversial in the first place.[25] The picture is further complicated by the fact that we are able to infer from his letters of spiritual direction, among others of his non-polemical works, that Fénelon shared an affinity with the tendency, and probably with its exponent (and indeed would be condemned by the Holy See in 1699 for doing so). Thus we find him writing at various points: of the denial of any role for the will in the exercise of virtue;[26] of the practice of a "confused view" of God[27]; of the sacrifice of the self and the abandonment of individual gifts[28]; and of a hierarchization of all forms of love, so that in the state of pure love, the penitent "says nothing, and notices nothing. What does she do? She suffers. Is that all? Yes, that is all, she has only to suffer. Love lets itself be heard well enough without speaking and without thinking."[29] These assertions are periodically accompanied in addition by images of the individual as an empty vessel, a holocaust or a slave. On the other hand, it could be argued, and despite their superficial affinity with Quietism, such expressions of passivity are no more than an amplification of the Augustinian transition from *amor sui* to *amor Dei*, more globally and uncontroversially resumed when Fénelon writes that "all religion consists of nothing more than ridding oneself of selfhood and self-love and of turning to God".[30]

[25] The first anti-Quietist move took the form of the thirty-four *Articles d'Issy*, drawn up by the three men charged with the investigation of Madame Guyon (Bossuet, Bishop of Meaux, the Archbishop of Paris, and the Superior General of the Congregation of Saint-Sulpice, one Louis Tronson), following the 1694 "Issy Conversations" ["Entretiens d'Issy"]. They are included in *Œuvres*, I, at p. 1534–8. Le Brun comments in the same edition that: "Forthwith [. . .] each party will seek to give to this ambiguous and composite text the interpretation that seemed to him the best" ["Désormais [. . .] chaque parti cherchera à donner de ce texte ambigu et composite l'interprétation qui lui paraissait la meilleure"] (p. 1538).

[26] "Christian perfection lies in the detachment of one's free will" ["[C'est] dans le détachement de sa volonté propre que consiste la perfection chrétienne"] (*Lettres et opuscules spirituels*, XVI (*Conférences sur l'amour de Dieu*), in *Œuvres*, I, p. 634). Pascal also wrote: "Self-will will never be satisfied even when it has power over everything it wishes for. But we are satisfied from the very moment we renounce it" ["La volonté propre ne se satisfera jamais, quand elle aurait pouvoir de tout ce qu'elle veut. Mais on est satisfait dès l'instant qu'on y renonce"] (*Pensées*, L 13, S 394).

[27] "Be content, in the course of the day and in your specific occupations, with a confused view of God" ["Contentez-vous, dans le cours de la journée et dans le détail de vos occupations, d'une vue confuse de Dieu"] (*Lettres et opuscules spirituels*, VI (*Discours sur la dissipation et la tristesse*), in *Œuvres*, I, p. 575).

[28] "You find God alone purely in this loss of all his gifts, and in this real sacrifice of all of yourself, when you have lost all internal resources" ["On ne trouve Dieu seul purement que dans cette perte de tous ses dons, et dans ce réel sacrifice de tout soi-même, ayant perdu toute ressource intérieure"] (*Lettres et opuscules spirituels*, XI (*Nécessité de la purification de l'âme par rapport aux dons de Dieu, et spécialement aux amitiés*), in *Œuvres*, I, p. 604).

[29] "Elle ne dit rien, elle ne remarque rien. Que fait-elle ? Elle souffre. Est-ce tout ? Oui, c'est tout, elle n'a qu'à souffrir. L'amour se fait assez entendre sans parler et sans penser" (*Lettres et opuscules spirituels*, XXXII (*De la nécessité de connaître et d'aimer Dieu*), in *Œuvres*, I, p.717).

[30] "Toute religion ne consiste qu'à sortir de soi et de son amour-propre pour tendre à Dieu" (*Lettres et opuscules spirituels*, XII (*De la prière*) in *Œuvres*, I, p. 611).

The key text of Fénelon is his *Explanation of the Sayings of the Saints on the Inner Life*, in which he painstakingly explores in a series of enquiries how fine distinctions can be made between the orthodox and faulty interpretations of previous saintly utterance – most recently and influentially in the teaching of St François de Sales – concerning the progress of the Christian soul in its stages towards the pure love of God. The work is elegant, subtle to a fault, and authoritative[31]; but of course it thereby relegates the issues to which it addresses itself to a kind of theological élite of which Guyon was not herself a member, and indeed which she claimed to have rendered otiose. It is divided into a series of forty-five articles of varying length; it is characterized by circumspection and precision, above all in the more abstract domains of spiritual investigation; and, even if it is dense and nuanced (or perhaps because of these features), it is the most impressive and spiritually rigorous of the polemical documents to emerge from the Quietist controversy.

Fénelon in this work above all advocates caution and obedience in the matter of the higher spiritual experiences, even though he is powerfully aware of the shortcomings of language in the process, and indeed recognizes that to write critically of such questions at all is, in terms which have now become familiar, to "expose all that is most pure and most sublime in our religion to the derision of profane minds, in whose eyes the mystery of Jesus Christ crucified is already a scandal and a folly".[32] He nonetheless perseveres with his project, drawing his evidence, in accordance with the title, from the Saints of the Church, in order to combat the risk of what he terms illusion. It is therefore to his episcopal predecessor St François de Sales that he turns in order to resume the tension (which is also apparent in his own work), according to which "[François] has not escaped criticism, but his critics have failed to recognize how he combines an exact, precise theology with the pre-eminent enlightenment of grace."[33] It is in this light that he advances a preliminary but comprehensive desideratum: "These examples must make mystics sober and restrained. If they are humble and docile, they must leave to the pastors of the Church not only the absolute decision concerning

[31] Le Brun is less generous, describing the *Sayings of the Saints* as "an awkward book, that left room for criticism without first having seduced spiritual souls" ["un livre maladroit, qui laissait place à la critique sans séduire d'abord les âmes spirituelles "] (*Histoire*, p. 280).

[32] "[. . .] exposer ce qu'il y a de plus pur et de plus sublime dans la religion à la dérision des esprits profanes, aux yeux desquels le mystère de Jésus-Christ crucifié est déjà un scandale et une folie" (*Maximes des saints*, p. 1001).

[33] "Saint François de Sales n'a pas été exempt de contradiction, et les critiques n'ont pas su connaître combien il joint une théologie exacte et précise avec une lumière de grâce qui est très éminente" (*Maximes des saints*, p. 1003).

doctrine, but also the choice of all the terms which it is appropriate to use."[34] We are back, in other words, with discernment.

The tradition at issue for Fénelon is presented as one which promotes the attainment of what he calls "pure and disinterested love" ["l'amour pur et désintéressé"], by means of "holy indifference" ["la sainte indifférence"]. The detail of such a quest will lead inevitably into an acknowledged need for linguistic precision, realized in this text by the systematic interpretation of a series of statements, sub-divided into two parts (true and false), in which he will point out the precise place at which the practice of orthodoxy ends and the danger of illusion begins. He thereby affords, in his own analogy, a kind of dictionary of spirituality, moving, again in the Salesian spirit, from the least to the most disinterested forms of the love of God. At the same time, as Moriarty notes, "Fénelon's more elaborate taxonomy seems designed to create a steeper scale of purification from concern with one's own good [than that of St François de Sales]".[35] Or, in Krumenacker's helpful distinction, "the writings of François de Sales are those of a director of conscience more than a theoretician of the spiritual life".[36] What is quickly emphasized in this complex taxonomy of spiritual states, however, is the value of the lower forms of progress towards the pure love of God, to the point at which Fénelon remarks, fully chiming with Bossuet, that "such love [that is a love of God mixed with a motivation of self-interest] [...] has nonetheless formed a great number of Saints across the centuries".[37] Again, now employing the *chiaroscuro* imagery common to both St François de Sales and Pascal, he stresses, first, that what is required is not a miraculous or extraordinary degree of inspiration, but rather that "this darkness of pure faith does not admit of any extraordinary light";[38] and, turning to the distinction between contemplation and meditation, he defines the former, conventionally enough, as "a loving and simple vision, to distinguish it from meditation, which is full of methodical and discursive acts".[39]

[34] "Ces exemples doivent rendre les mystiques sobres et retenus. S'ils sont humbles et dociles, ils doivent laisser aux pasteurs de l'Église non seulement la décision absolue sur la doctrine, mais encore le choix de tous les termes dont il est à propos de se servir" (*Maximes des saints*, p. 1004).

[35] *Fallen Nature, Fallen Selves*, p. 212, n. 67.

[36] "Les œuvres de François de Sales sont celles d'un directeur d'âmes plus que d'un théoricien de la vie spirituelle" (*L'École française*, p. 88). Angers too reminds the reader: "It should at all events not be forgotten concerning [François] that he is not a theoretician who puts forward theses, but an apostle who aims to save souls, a director of conscience who wants to bring them to the perfection of love" ["Il ne faut toutefois oublier à son endroit qu'il n'est pas un théoricien qui expose des thèses, mais un apôtre qui veut sauver des âmes, un directeur de conscience qui veut les mener à la perfection de l'amour"] (*Humanisme chrétien*, p. 17).

[37] "[...] cet amour [mélangé du motif d'intérêt propre] [...] a fait néanmoins dans tous les siècles un grand nombre de saints" (*Maximes des saints*, p.1018).

[38] "[...] cette obscurité de la pure foi n'admet aucune lumière extraordinaire" (*Maximes des saints*, p. 1028).

[39] "[...] un regard simple et amoureux, pour la distinguer de la méditation, qui est pleine d'actes méthodiques et discursifs" (*Maximes des saints*, p. 1060).

The move to contemplation should take place therefore under the guidance of a spiritual director, even if, it is stressed in common with François, it is still possible to go back to the earlier state; and, in the event of a relapse, the penitent should be just as happy, as Fénelon puts it in a pair of similes, to "meditate like beginners as to contemplate like cherubim".[40] Pure contemplation indeed moves beyond the "images of the senses" ["images sensibles"] to "the purely intellective and abstract idea of the being who is without limits and without restrictions"[41]; but it is still possible in such a state, he stresses, to contemplate the three persons of the Trinity and the life of Christ. Even the exclusively intellectual contemplation of God by the blessed souls in heaven, Fénelon insists, may be devoted to the mysteries of Christ's humanity, or in other words, to the revealed specifics of the faith.[42]

The vexed question of passive contemplation is then resumed with characteristic elegance and moderation, and the Spanish mystics in particular are quoted in support of the state's compatibility with the exercise of free will, and against its identification as miraculous. Further, it does not exempt the practitioner from the exercise of particular virtues, to believe which is once again to "place a stumbling block in the path of the children of God".[43] The idea that a state of pure love is unalterable, once achieved, is also challenged; and the comparison of it with the hypostatic union between Christ and the Father is condemned as blasphemous.[44] Such privileged souls as enjoy it certainly have "a facility and simplicity of loving union [with God]",[45] but they can still sin, and must therefore be vigilant, obedient, and prayerful at all times. Even those united to God by a spiritual marriage, and who may go to

[40] "[. . .] méditer comme les commençants que de contempler comme les chérubins" (*Maximes des saints*, p. 1064). The debt in such remarks to St John of the Cross is considerable. Sanson considers that Madame Guyon was responsible for introducing Fénelon to his writing, and that "Fénelon comes closer to St John of the Cross than Bossuet, but in a way that [. . .] is awkward and incomplete" ["Fénelon s'approche plus de saint Jean de la Croix que ne le fait Bossuet, mais d'une façon [. . .] maladroite et incomplète"] (*Saint Jean de la Croix*, p. 108).

[41] "[. . .] l'idée purement intellectuelle et abstraite de l'être qui est sans bornes et sans restrictions" (*Maximes des saints*, p. 1067).

[42] Cognet summarizes the question thus: "The problem consists of knowing whether Christ's humanity should also be included among those created elements which have finally to be transcended in order to find the simple divine essence" ["Le problème se pose de savoir si l'humanité du Christ doit être comprise elle aussi parmi les éléments créés qu'il faut finalement dépasser pour trouver la seule essence divine"] (*Crépuscule*, p. 18–19).

[43] "[. . .] mettre la pierre de scandale dans la voie des enfants de Dieu" (*Maximes des saints*, p. 1080).

[44] Envy of the hypostatic union is also a feature of Surin's possession: "It occurred that he felt dreadful jealousies towards Jesus Christ because of the fact that he [Jesus] had been elected to the hypostatic union rather than [Surin]" ["Il se trouve qu'il avait des jalousies effroyables contre Jésus-Christ de ce qu'il avait été élu à l'union hypostatique plutôt que [Surin]"] (*Science expérimentale*, p. 187).

[45] "[. . .] une facilité et une simplicité d'union amoureuse [avec Dieu]" (*Maximes des saints*, p. 1083).

heaven without enduring purgatory, are not exempt from daily sins; they do not enjoy the primitive state of grace (what Fénelon calls "original integrity" ["l'intégrité originelle"]), and must remain obedient to the Church. The alternative, and a very recognizable danger in the light of some of the autobiographical texts which we have considered, is a "damnable sect of independents and fanatics",[46] comparable to the heretical Gnostics[47] or Manicheans.[48] Even the highest order of all, that of unmediated union, does not negate humbler kinds of progress and, as is appropriate to its exceptional status, "when it is false and imaginary, represents the very height of illusion".[49] In summary, Fénelon finally and most dogmatically distances himself from the antinomian heresy, which he virtually paraphrases in his assertion that "no interior perfection dispenses Christians from [those] real acts which are essential for the accomplishment of the whole of the law".[50]

The overall impact of this work is thus to convey the orthodoxy of its writer, his consonance in terms of dogmatic basics with his eventual episcopal adversary (Bossuet) and the precision which he brings to bear on the most intractable of spiritual distinctions. It could be argued that, whereas Fénelon admits the value of the lower forms of spiritual experience in the more rarefied context of the higher, Bossuet rather concedes the possibility of the higher in the more ordinary context of the lower. Yet such a statement does not disguise the openness of both men to the whole range of legitimate mystical experience, as indeed their often consonant definition of what constitutes it. Despite their similarity of aim, we could say that Fénelon deals with the theory, whereas Bossuet attends to its practical implications for spiritual writers and their readers; or that Bossuet starts from errors in contemporary texts, whereas Fénelon exposes the ideal as against hypothetical misapprehensions. But leaving aside considerations of emphases, of stylistics, and of unwritten agendas, the objective reader is more likely to be struck by the amount of common ground displayed by the co-prelates than by any written evidence of a radical disjunction of purpose.

As the dispute develops, however, it becomes clear that Bossuet's contribution to the debate stems from a figure for whom questions of authority and

[46] "[. . .] une secte damnable d'indépendants et de fanatiques" (*Maximes des saints*, p. 1091).

[47] See Chapter 3, n. 36.

[48] The Manichaean heresy was formulated in the third century by Manes (or Manichaeus), and promotes a dualistic view of the created world, to which St Augustine was attracted before his conversion to Christian orthodoxy (as related in the *Confessions*).

[49] "[. . .] quand il est faux et imaginaire, c'est le comble de l'illusion" (*Maximes des saints*, p. 1093). Compare Pascal, at a humbler level: "Men often confuse their imagination with their heart; and they believe they have been converted as soon as they start thinking of conversion" ["Les hommes prennent souvent leur imagination pour leur cœur ; et ils croient être convertis dès qu'ils pensent à se convertir"] (*Pensées*, L 975, S 739).

[50] "[. . .] nulle perfection intérieure ne dispense les Chrétiens des actes réels qui sont essentiels pour l'accomplissement de toute la loi" (*Maximes des saints*, p. 1094).

discipline were more familiar than those of spirituality. His writing is marked by an increasingly legalistic tonality even if he, like Fénelon, draws his authority from Scripture, the Fathers and the Saints of the Church, with the already canonized François de Sales once again standing as a central point of reference. His first individual contributions to the Quietist debate are entitled *Ordinance and Instructions on the State of Mental Prayer*;[51] and, in the opening remarks of the first part, he cites the Archbishop of Paris's warning to his clergy to guard against those "who seek out in mental prayer sublime things which God has not revealed, and which the Saints have not known".[52] The theological objections consist essentially of the accusation that Quietists negate the humanity of Christ as the way to the Father, in distinction to which they prefer, in a terminology borrowed from Guyon, a "confused, general and indistinct faith or view of God".[53] This leads in turn to a reluctance to ask God for any good (petition), as to give him praise (worship), in favour of "a single, perpetual and universal act" ["un seul acte perpétuel et universel"][54] which lasts for the whole of one's life, and in which all specific acts of devotion or mortification are deemed unnecessary. As Bossuet ironizes later in the work, if the "fiat voluntas tua" was sufficient, why did Christ add the rest of the *Our Father*?[55] Orthodox Christians for Bossuet are identified by four features in contradistinction: their beliefs, their actions, their desire for salvation, and their penitence. Furthermore the two seminal influences on Quietism, Molinos[56] and Malaval,[57] are quoted against themselves, and their evocation of "a general and confused faith and knowledge" ["[une] foi et [une] connaissance générale et confuse"], is pitted against a restatement of the basics of

[51] The title is a conflation of the *Ordonnance et instruction pastorale* and *Instruction sur les états d'oraison*, which had originally been published independently. They can be found in the *Œuvres complètes*, ed. Lachat, vol. XVII, 353–763.

[52] "[...] recherchent dans l'oraison des sublimités que Dieu n'a point révélées, et que les saints ne connaissent pas" (*Ordonnance*, p. 351). The Holy See had pronounced provisionally in 1687; the Archbishop of Paris wrote to his clergy in 1694.

[53] "[...] la foi ou vue confuse, générale et indistincte de Dieu" (*Ordonnance*, p. 353). In opposition to this, Le Brun notes Bossuet's insistence on an "intellectualist conception of the spiritual life that is always formed by distinct acts" ["une conception intellectualiste de la vie spirituelle toujours formée d'actes distincts"] (*Spiritualité*, p. 483).

[54] *Instruction sur les états d'oraison*, p. 408.

[55] *Instruction sur les états d'oraison*, p. 426.

[56] Miguel de Molinos (1640–97) a Spanish Quietist, was the author of the highly influential *La Guida espiritual*, Rome, 1675 (*La Guide spirituelle*, Paris, 1675), of whom Le Brun quotes the aim to "'attain peace by the way of annihilation [...] to God who is pure, ineffable, abstracted from all particular thought, in an internal silence'" ["'aller par l'anéantissement à la paix [...] à Dieu, pur, ineffable, abstrait de toute pensée particulière, dans le silence intérieur'"] (Fénelon, *Œuvres*, I, p. 1091). He was condemned by the Holy See in 1687.

[57] François Malaval was a blind mystic from Marseille. His best-known work, *The Easy Method for Lifting the Soul to Contemplation* [*La Pratique facile pour élever l'âme à la contemplation*], published in 1664, was re-edited and expanded in 1670.

incarnational theology, the loss of which, Bossuet asserts in parallel with Fénelon, will lead to deism.

The second major area of contention lies once again in the issue of vulgarization. Bossuet, in common with the aims of the Council of Trent, was explicitly anxious to promote the spiritual education of the laity, even if the terms in which this was couched were not exactly progressive to our understanding; and both prelates agreed that higher states of communion could be attained, in the widely used phrase "within us [but] without us": ["en nous sans nous"], itself once again a compression of the motivic Galatians verse ("I live, not I, but Christ in me"), of which *Les Torrents* is in effect a vast metaphorical amplification.[58] It was also accepted, even by Bossuet, that a kind of mental prayer might occur which involved the "suppression of every discursive act, of every individual effort, [and] of all personal striving", so that "one is moved by God with a blessed ease"[59]; and that both biblical and subsequent empirical examples had validated these states. But he is equally adamant that such experiences must be exceptional in time and, above all, that their practitioners must be few in number and far advanced on their spiritual journeys.

What the Christian mystic must accept therefore, in Bossuet's elegant phrase, is "an ardent desire joined to a perfect submission to delay".[60] Thus, despite the reality and indeed proximity of the transcendent world in all his writing and preaching, what Bossuet sees the Quietists as risking is, in a striking image, "[to make] heaven out of earth and a homeland out of exile".[61] Most of all, it is to believe that the mortal can possess God fully, whereas, in a further memorable (now Latin) formulation drawn from scholastic teaching in the tradition of St Augustine, he can only do so "in hope and not in fact: *spe non re*".[62]

[58] The final stage, when the river meets the sea, is thus expressed: "It is a *life in God*. It is a perfect life. It [the soul] no longer lives of itself; but *God lives*, acts and works, and this gradually increases" ["C'est une *vie en Dieu*. C'est une vie parfaite. Elle [l'âme] ne vit plus, par elle-même ; mais *Dieu vit*, agit et opère, et cela peu à peu va s'augmentant"] (*Les Torrents*, p. 132, emphases original). Similarly, Bérulle describes St Mary of Magdala as "living and not living, she is dying and living at the same time" ["vivante et non vivante, elle est mourante et vivante, tout ensemble"] (quoted in Krumenacker, *École française*, p. 164). The likelihood of this being a Teresan commonplace, in the light of the poem "Vivo sin vivir in mí", is convincingly established by Vermeylen, *Sainte Thérèse en France*.

[59] "[. . .] la suppression de tout acte discursif, de tout propre effort, de toute propre industrie [pour être] mû de Dieu avec une heureuse facilité" (*Instruction sur les états d'oraison*, p. 522).

[60] "[. . .] dans un ardent désir une parfaite soumission pour le délai" (*Instruction sur les états d'oraison*, p. 589).

[61] "C'est de la terre faire le ciel et de l'exil la patrie" (*Instruction sur les états d'oraison*, p. 397).

[62] "[. . .] en espérance et non en effet: *spe non re*" (*Instruction sur les états d'oraison*, p. 484–5). Sanson resumes the essence of the disagreement thus: "In the end, Bossuet and Fénelon offer two different types of spirituality. The first is above all attentive to man on his journey towards salvation [. . .]. The second, on the other hand, thinks of man as already made divine, of man as already in possession of the good things of the world to come" ["Au fond, Bossuet et Fénelon présentent deux types différents de spiritualité. Le premier est surtout sensible à l'homme en

It is in what follows that the worst light is shed on Christian polemics, as the two prelates engage in a more and more acrimonious and detailed exchange of publications;[63] and it is in the *Relation on Quietism*[64] that Bossuet adds the autobiography of Guyon to the texts which he attacks, in order, in his phrase, to "warn the faithful against [. . .] a woman who is capable of deceiving souls by these kinds of illusion".[65] Without using the term, Bossuet is here again involved in the business of discernment; and, again unsurprisingly, he takes issue with the acts of spiritual direction in which his subject was engaged. He then goes further into her autobiography (which he had read as a manuscript), and deals with Guyon's prediction of the forthcoming reign of the Holy Spirit, and with what she had labelled "the Martyrs of the Holy Spirit" ["les Martyrs du Saint Esprit"], among whom she had included herself. It is here that he introduces the crucial term of "enthusiasm" ["enthousiasme"] (and it is tempting at this stage to gloss it by the cumbersome but helpful synonym which Ronald Knox prefers, but eschews, of "ultrasupernaturalism").[66] Bossuet then finally moves on to Guyon's *Exposition of the Book of the Apocalypse* [*Explication sur l'Apocalypse*],[67] in particular to her visions of the woman crowned with stars, and to her belief that she had the apostolic power "to bind and to loose" ["de lier et de délier"]. To this is added her dream of two beds, one for her and one for the Blessed Virgin, on the strength of which she aspires to the individuated status of the spouse of Christ, and therefore implicitly to a comparable role to Mary as his mother. At this point, we might well feel that the rationality of Bossuet affords a welcome corrective:

marche vers son salut [. . .]. Le second, au contraire, pense à l'homme déjà divinisé, à l'homme déjà en possession des biens de la vie de l'au-delà"] (*Saint Jean de la Croix*, p. 26).

[63] Le Brun's remark resumes the differences between the prelates to the effect that "Fénelon tries to look at the person, [whereas] Bossuet considers the action in the abstract, with respect to a dogma, a philosophy, an anthropology" ["Fénelon essaie de regarder la personne, Bossuet considère l'acte abstraitement, par rapport à un dogme, à une philosophie, à une anthropologie"] (*Spiritualité*, p. 666), but concludes that "incomprehension has rarely been taken further, and the two men are speaking different languages" ["rarement l'incompréhension a été poussée plus loin, les deux hommes parlant des langages différents"] (*Spiritualité*, p. 544).

[64] *Relation sur le quiétisme*, in *Œuvres*, ed. Abbé Velat et Yvonne Champailler, Paris, Gallimard (Pléiade), 1961, 1087–1177. Le Brun describes it as "this brilliant and unfair work that the Bishop of Meaux would have done better not to have written" ["ce livre brillant et injuste que M. de Meaux aurait mieux fait de ne pas écrire"] (*Spiritualité*, p. 670).

[65] "[. . .] prévenir les fidèles contre [. . .] une femme qui est capable de tromper les âmes par de telles illusions" (*Relation sur le quiétisme*, p. 1107). Madame Guyon's own account of their incompatibility echoes that of Bossuet. She notes that "it was for him a jargon that he considered to be the effect of a hollow imagination, and whose terms were to him as unfamiliar as they were intolerable" ["c'était un jargon qu'il regardait comme l'effet d'une imagination creuse, et dont les termes lui étaient aussi inconnus qu'insupportables"] (*Vie*, p. 804).

[66] *Enthusiasm*, p. 2.

[67] The whole series of exegetical works was published in the early eighteenth century, in the case of the New Testament series in 1713.

> When I represented this conjugal bed to her as being separated from the bed of the mother, as if the Mother of God in the spiritual and mysterious sense was not so to speak also the spouse above all spouses, she would always reply: It was a dream. But, I pointed out to her, it is a dream which you present as a great mystery.[68]

He therefore takes issue with the indeed shocking inference (at least within the Roman tradition) that she henceforth could not invoke Mary or the Saints as intercessors since, as she arrogantly asserts, the spouse does not need the servants to pray for her.

It is Bossuet's last verdict concerning Guyon's indifference to salvation which is the most telling, consisting of "the exclusion of every desire and every request for oneself, abandoning oneself to the most hidden wishes of God, whatever they should be, either for damnation or for salvation",[69] since not to wish for salvation is a negation of the theological virtue of hope. It is on this, in particular, that she is questioned by Bossuet, and on which she replies, entirely in accord with the spirit of the texts that we have considered, that "every request for oneself is self-interested, contrary to pure love and to conformity with the will of God";[70] and it is on the strength of this that she is excommunicated.

One way of approaching the difficulty of Madame Guyon's spirituality and its written expression lies in returning to Bossuet's term of velleity, understood in her case as the attempt to convey the degree of the believer's passivity by means of hypothetical suppositions. The biblical precedent is provided by St Paul in Romans 9: 3, when he writes of the conditional sacrifice of his salvation: "I could pray that I myself might be accursed and cut off from Christ, if this could benefit the brothers who are my own flesh and blood." Questions of authority begin to occur, however, when the exploitation of such paradox goes beyond the stylistic in order to push at the limits of orthodoxy, and indeed to reach a kind of absurd reversal of any conventional theological (let alone common-sense) understanding. This occurs in the case of Madame Guyon, for example, when the hypothesis is erected of the effects of the primacy of the will of God in the afterlife whereby, given the need for it absolutely to prevail: "If the soul that dies in a state of mortal sin did not find

[68] "Quand je lui ai représenté ce lit pour une épouse séparé d'avec le lit de la mère, comme si la Mère de Dieu dans le sens spirituel et mystérieux n'était pas pour ainsi parler la plus épouse de toutes les épouses, elle a toujours répondu : C'est un songe. Mais, lui disais-je, c'est un songe que vous nous donnez comme un grand mystère" (*Relation sur le quiétisme*, p. 1111).

[69] "[. . .] l'exclusion de tout désir et de toute demande pour soi-même, en s'abandonnant aux volontés de Dieu les plus cachées, quelles qu'elles fussent, ou pour la damnation ou pour le salut" (*Relation sur le quiétisme*, p. 1112).

[70] "[. . .] toute demande pour soi est intéressée, contraire au pur amour et à la conformité avec la volonté de Dieu" (*Relation sur le quiétisme*, p. 1112).

itself in Hell, which is the proper place for it given its state, it would be in a state of greater torment than that which it would find in that place."[71] As Moriarty puts it:

> If I learn that Christianity promises supreme happiness after death to those saved, and come to believe that it is true, then I would be irrational *not* to desire salvation. There is no reason why I should conceal that desire from myself, except perhaps in the extreme case of attempting to make the impossible supposition.[72]

Equally shocking, at least superficially, is her wish for God to reign in her director, the Père La Combe, by means of suffering, incurring in turn as a consequence that "I had such a strong instinct for his perfection, and to see him die to himself, that I would have wished him all the ills imaginable"[73]; and indeed he is soon after described as "annihilated and reduced to the state which God wanted for him".[74]

Such expressions also abound in Guyon's other writings, such as in *Les Torrents*, where we read of the soul which has arrived at a state of pure love of God:

> This soul would be indifferent to spending the whole of eternity with the demons rather than with the angels. Demons are God for it like the rest, and it is no more possible for it to see a created being outside of the uncreated being, since the created being itself is God, and all God, in everything, just as much in a devil as in a saint, although in a different manner.[75]

She then goes on to assert, towards the conclusion of the work:

> I believe that if such a soul were carried off to hell, it would suffer the cruel pains [. . .] in a state of perfect contentment, caused not only by the sight of the good

[71] "Si l'âme qui meurt en péché mortel ne trouvait pas l'enfer, qui est le lieu propre à son état, elle serait dans les tourments plus grands que ceux qu'elle trouve en ce lieu" (*Vie*, p. 509). A variant, if divergently perverse expression of the same phenomenon occurs when the possessed Surin, believing himself to be damned, confesses to having done good, since "my greatest sin, and the one that weighed most heavily on my conscience, was to commit the actions of a good man, being damned as I was" ["mon plus grand péché, et qui me pesait plus sur ma conscience, était de faire des actions d'un homme de bien, étant damné comme je l'étais"] (*Science expérimentale*, p. 183–4). But it is significant that this and various similar expressions are always explained as being the result of demonic possession.

[72] *Fallen Nature, Fallen Selves*, p. 398.

[73] "J'avais alors un si fort instinct pour sa perfection, et pour le voir mourir à lui-même, que je lui eusse souhaité tous les maux imaginables" (*Vie*, p. 523).

[74] "[. . .] anéanti et réduit au point où Dieu le voulait" (*Vie*, p. 535).

[75] "Aussi cette âme serait aussi indifférente d'être toute une éternité avec les démons qu'avec les anges. Les démons lui sont Dieu comme le reste, et il ne lui est plus possible de voir un être créé hors de l'être incréé le seul être créé étant tout, et en tout, tout Dieu, aussi bien dans un diable que dans un saint, quoique différemment" (*Les Torrents*, p. 150). My translation is only an approximation to the bewildering syntax of the original; and a variant wording provided in the same edition is not a great deal clearer.

pleasure of God, but by an essential contentment caused by the beatitude of the transformed essence.[76]

On a more disruptive level again, the supposition that sins which are committed by the "annihilated" ["anéanti"] penitent can be attributed to the will of God shows how the progression towards deism has been overtaken by a progression towards antinomianism, and indeed towards blasphemy.

If we return to Bossuet's polemic, we find that it then moves on to the secondary question of the demonstrated error (as he sees it) of Fénelon's tolerant judgement of Madame Guyon, portrayed as he is as deeming her comparable to St Paul, following which he recounts the conclusion of their meeting: "I withdrew, astonished to see such a fine mind filled with admiration for a woman, whose enlightenment was so limited, whose merit was so little, whose illusions were so palpable, and who behaved as if she were a prophetess."[77] The ensuing, and progressively more trivial, internecine dispute between prelates is best left to oblivion; but the essence of their conflict seems once again to lie in issues of discernment. There is no doubt that the most advanced of Christian mystics achieve the highest form of spiritual communion with God, irrespective of how it is described—and let us settle for contemplation; but to teach it requires either the eminently cautious, systematic and progressive method of St François de Sales in the *Treatise on the Love of God*; or the dizzyingly precise taxonomy of Fénelon's *Explanation of the Sayings of the Saints on the Inner Life*. In either case, in the judgement of a whole range of orthodox voices, it requires the guidance of a disinterested spiritual director. Bossuet's instinctive pragmatism, we might feel, does not do it justice, even if he sees and addresses the credal and doctrinal dangers present in unmediated enthusiasm; yet Guyon's equally instinctive passivity is driven by its own logic to a perversion of both sound doctrine and of common sense. Whatever the Holy See was ultimately to decide, however, it remains arguable that only Fénelon's *ex post facto* rationalization of the phenomenon carries any enduring theological significance.

[76] "Je crois que si une telle âme était conduite en Enfer, elle en souffrirait les cruelles douleurs [...] dans un contentement achevé : non contentement causé seulement par la vue du bon plaisir de Dieu, mais contentement essentiel, à cause de la béatitude du fond transformé" (*Les Torrents*, p. 158). The reading "contentement" for the first two occurrences seems more likely than "consentement".

[77] "Je me retirai étonné de voir un si bel esprit dans l'admiration d'une femme dont les lumières étaient si courtes, le mérite si léger, les illusions si palpables, et qui faisait la prophétesse" (*Relation sur le quiétisme*, p. 1113). Pascal, in a fragment within the *liasse* that carries the same title, offers the definition: "To prophesy is to speak of God, not from external proofs, but by an interior and immediate feeling" ["Prophétiser, c'est parler de Dieu non par preuves du dehors, mais par sentiment intérieur et immédiat"] (*Pensées*, L 328, S 360). Such a definition, which appears to apply equally well to the fulfilment of the claims of the prophets of the Old Testament as to the visions of later believers, serves simply to reinforce the criterion of discernment.

I want to finish these remarks about Quietism with a couple of references to the satirical work to which it gave rise, La Bruyère's *Posthumous Dialogues on Quietism.*[78] I will begin with one of the exchanges that gives a very good caricature of the issues at stake, in which the imprecision of Quietist teaching is presented as a challenge to the physicality of the Incarnation, and is encapsulated with respect to the term "abandonment" (to the will of God) ["abandon"]. The true/false ordering of Fénelon's treatise is also, probably unconsciously, adopted, and the orthodox position is expressed first:

> I adhere [. . .] to a perfect resignation to divine Providence, an entire submission to the will of God, a religious attention to its discernment, either in the Gospels or in the Commandments or in those of his Church; [I pay] scrupulous attention to the conduct which makes me act, as to whether or not it is in conformity with the will of God. What other kind of abandonment can there be?[79]

The contrary, and by implication erroneous position is then caricatured:

> Our abandonment [. . .] consists of acquiescing to everything that goes on within us, whether it is good or evil, without any discernment, considering in everything virtues and crimes indifferently as being the order and will of God. What is born of this total resignation? [. . .] The death of the soul, its perfect annihilation, its burial; and it is by these stages that it rises to the sublime state of essential union.[80]

But this text also contains one of the best parodies in the period, in the form of a Quietist *Our Father*:

> God, who are no more in heaven than on earth or in the underworld, who are present in everything: I neither wish nor desire your name to be held holy, you know whether or not that is appropriate; and if it is, it will be so, whether or not

[78] Jean de La Bruyère et Louis-Ellies Du Pin, *Dialogues posthumes sur le quiétisme*, ed. Richard Parish, Grenoble, Éditions Jérôme Millon, 2005. Le Brun remarks, rather disparagingly: "La Bruyère, a friend of Bossuet, left the *Dialogues on Quietism* unfinished. They are interesting because they show the superficial antimysticism of worldly people" ["Ami de Bossuet, La Bruyère laisse inachevés les *Dialogues sur le quiétisme*, intéressants pour connaître l'antimysticisme superficiel des gens du monde"]. They were completed by Louis-Ellies Du Pin (1657–1719), a religious historian and controversialist. See Georges Mongrédien, *La Bruyère. Recueil des textes et des documents contemporains*, Paris, Éditions du CNRS, 1979, and Phillip J. Wolfe, "La Bruyère critique du quiétisme", in *Papers on French Seventeenth Century Literature* 15, 2, 1981, 255–66.

[79] "Je connais [. . .] une parfaite résignation aux ordres de la Providence divine, une soumission entière à la volonté de Dieu, une religieuse attention à la bien discerner, soit dans le livre de l'Évangile, soit dans ses Commandements, ou de ceux de son Église ; une scrupuleuse attention sur la conduite qui me fait agir, si elle est conforme à la Loi de Dieu ou non ; y a-t-il un autre abandon que celui-là ?" (*Dialogues sur le quiétisme*, p. 180).

[80] "Notre abandon [. . .] est un acquiescement à tout ce qui se passe en nous, de bon ou de mauvais, sans aucun discernement, regardant en toutes choses vertu ou crime indifféremment, comme ordre et volonté de Dieu. Que naît-il de cette totale résignation ? [. . .]. La mort de l'âme, son anéantissement parfait, son ensevelissement ; et c'est par degrés qu'elle monte au sublime état de l'union essentielle" (*Dialogues sur le quiétisme*, p. 180–1).

> I wish or desire it. May your Kingdom come or not, it is indifferent to me. Nor do I ask for your will to be done on earth as it is in Heaven, since it will be so without my input; I simply have to resign myself to it. Give all of us today [our] daily bread, which is your grace, or do not do so; I wish neither to have it nor to be deprived of it. Equally, if you forgive me my sins, as I forgive those who have sinned against me, all well and good: but if on the other hand you punish me by damnation, so much the better, since that is your good pleasure. Finally, my God, I am too abandoned to your will to pray that I should be delivered from temptations or from sin.[81]

I want to begin my conclusion to these two chapters with the same more open-ended questions which I asked of Jansenism, which are to wonder: first, why the Church was so exercised by the phenomenon of Quietism; and second, why Christians should aim to attain to such a state of passive spirituality in the first place.

I suggested in the last chapter that Jansenism was compatible with Catholicism, but not with catholicity. It seems to me that Quietism demonstrates the complementary phenomenon, in that it aspires to universality, but without dogmatic rigour; and that, in its most extreme formulations, it contains a potential to circumvent the Christic mediation that is the precondition of salvation. Mediation is the role that Christ fulfilled; the aspiration to an unmediated communion with God, to go back to the beginning of this survey, is promotive of deism; and deism has nothing to do with Christianity. As Pascal writes in the *Pensées*: "We only know God through Jesus Christ. Without this mediator, all communication with God is removed [. . .]. But by Jesus Christ, and in Jesus Christ, God is proven, and morality and doctrine are taught."[82]

One term that was flung about in the period was of course heresy, and one of the jobs of the Bampton Lectures, which form the basis of this book, is to

[81] "Dieu qui n'êtes pas plus au ciel que sur la terre et dans les enfers, qui êtes présent partout, je ne veux ni ne désire que votre nom soit sanctifié : vous savez ce qui vous convient ; si vous voulez qu'il le soit, il le sera, sans que je le veuille et le désire. Que votre royaume arrive ou n'arrive pas, cela m'est indifférent. Je ne vous demande pas aussi que votre volonté soit faite sur la terre comme au ciel : elle le sera malgré que j'en aie ; c'est à moi à m'y résigner. Donnez-nous à tous notre pain de tous les jours, qui est votre grâce, ou ne nous la donnez pas : je ne souhaite de l'avoir ni d'en être privée. De même si vous me pardonnez mes crimes, comme je pardonne à ceux qui m'ont offensé tant mieux ; si vous me punissez au contraire par la damnation, tant mieux encore, puisque c'est votre bon plaisir. Enfin, mon Dieu, je suis trop abandonnée à votre volonté pour vous prier de me délivrer des tentations et du péché" (*Dialogues sur le quiétisme*, p. 152–3). It is worth bearing in mind in conclusion the simple insight of Le Brun (written of Bossuet's *Instruction*, but more globally applicable), that "a work of polemic is not a theological treatise" ["une œuvre de polémique n'est pas un traité de théologie"] (*Spiritualité*, p. 626).

[82] "Nous ne connaissons Dieu que par Jésus-Christ. Sans ce médiateur est ôtée toute communication avec Dieu [. . .]. Mais par Jésus-Christ et en Jésus-Christ on prouve Dieu et on enseigne la morale et la doctrine" (*Pensées*, L 189, S 221).

combat it. Theoretically the antonym of orthodoxy is heterodoxy, which may be subdivided into heresy, as I shall shortly define it, and schism, that is separation from the body of the Church; but to all intents and purposes, in our period, the term of heresy is used polemically to cover the majority of opinions which are perceived to diverge from orthodoxy. Thus in Bossuet's *Meaux Catechism*, heresies are defined rather broadly as "poor doctrines in which human reasoning is stubbornly preferred to divine revelation, and individual interpretation to the judgement of the Church".[83] More narrowly, heresy, which derives crucially from the Greek noun *haeresis*, "a choice", is defined by St François de Sales in the *Treatise on the Love of God*, in contradistinction to orthodoxy, as follows:

> Heretics are heretics and carry this name, because among the articles of faith they *choose*, according to their taste and their preference, those which it seems right for them to believe, rejecting the others and disavowing them; and Catholics are Catholics because, without any choice or selection whatsoever, they embrace with equal firmness and without exception the whole faith of the Church.[84]

According to this definition, the heresy of Quietism would be to choose the Father, since to deny the mediating role of the Redeemer is, in turn, to deny the Son. And, to quote I John 2: 23: "Whoever denies the Son cannot have the Father either; whoever acknowledges the Son has the Father too."

So, to ask the same question I asked about Jansenism: if Quietism was to some degree perceived as attractive, wherein lay this attraction? And the answer seems to lie precisely in this hubristic temptation of the unmediated, but now at a human level; in the opportunity, in Édouard's words, for the mystical shoots that are strangled by the hierarchical Church to grow unstoppably upwards.[85] There is certainly a case in this perspective for seeing Madame Guyon as a revolutionary in the true spirit, even if not the letter, of the Gospel, seeking as she does to take the practice of contemplation out into

[83] "[. . .] de mauvaises doctrines où l'on préfère opiniâtrement des raisonnements humains à ce que Dieu a révélé, et son sens particulier au jugement de l'Église" (*Catéchisme de Meaux*, p. 177).

[84] "Les hérétiques sont hérétiques et en portent le nom, parce qu'entre les articles de la foi ils *choisissent* à leur goût et à leur gré ceux que bon leur semble pour les croire, rejetant les autres et les désavouant ; et les Catholiques sont Catholiques, parce que, sans choix ni élection quelconque, ils embrassent avec égale fermeté sans exception toute la foi de l'Église" (*Traité de l'amour de Dieu*, p. 840, my emphasis).

[85] Krumenacker perceives the whole phenomenon as a response to a crisis whereby "theological discourse does not manage to express God sufficiently vigorously to be understood by all Christians" ["le discours théologique ne parvient pas à dire Dieu de manière suffisamment vigoureuse pour être entendue de tous les chrétiens"]. As a result "the reply to this crisis can therefore be to renounce theology [. . .] and attain God directly without an ontological hierarchy" ["la réponse à cette crise peut alors être de renoncer à la théologie [. . .] et atteindre Dieu directement sans ontologie hiérarchique"] (*École française*, p. 93).

the world, and doing so in the teeth of a conservative, male episcopacy.[86] And there is certainly an equally credible view that Bossuet did not have any real understanding of the higher forms of mysticism, and even less truck with the exegetical experiments of female lay enthusiasts.[87]

We might next try to see whether there is any internal relationship between the two tendencies I have been looking at.[88] Both movements arguably go beyond the limits of fruitful enquiry about salvation: Jansenism asks questions about it which cannot be asked; Quietism, in its democratic promotion of the highest spiritual states, seeks to transcend it. Both tendencies, in the perception of their critics, deny elements of sacramental theology: Jansenism, by withholding the sacraments of penance and the Eucharist; Quietism, by promoting an exclusively spiritual union with God which transcends the physicality of the Christian revelation. Both also fail to resist the divergently rigorist temptations afforded by the perfection/despair dichotomy or, in other words, both fail to acknowledge their binary coexistence in human nature – in the case of Quietism by advocating perfection; in that of Jansenism by promoting despair. Both furthermore, for different theological reasons, run the risk of exempting the believer from immanent moral conformity, and so invite the heresy of antinomianism—either because the individual has been given no choice in the matter of salvation (Jansenism), or because he or she has knowingly rejected its desirability (Quietism). More affirmatively, both seem to open up spaces for the laity, and in particular the educated female laity, to engage in theological speculation; and both, in different ways, promote a wider access to those texts, both biblical and devotional, which serve as a trigger for such enquiry.

The real difficulty is encapsulated in Pascal's reminder that Christianity is enduringly constrained by certain beliefs and practices: physical, temporal, spatial, credal, and historical. And that is also because of two immensely obvious givens: first, that each member of humankind lives with its physical body in time and in space, just as it lives mentally with its beliefs, with its past

[86] Le Brun writes of an enduring conflict, whereby "the need for spiritual warmth and experience [. . .] comes up against the theological, philosophical and ecclesiological traditions of individuals and Churches" ["un besoin de chaleur et d'expérience spirituelles [. . .] se heurte aux traditions théologiques, philosophiques et ecclésiologiques des individus et des Églises"] (*Spiritualité*, p. 441).

[87] Again, for Krumenacker, "mysticism is [. . .] a taking into account of the needs of the laity" ["la mystique est [. . .] une prise en compte des besoins des laïcs"] (*École française*, p. 95). And Gondal remarks succinctly of the difference of perspective that "as is the case for many other mystics, she affords a timely reminder that we should not confuse the stammerings of love with the language of doctrinal definition" ["comme bien d'autres mystiques, elle rappelle opportunément qu'il ne faut pas confondre les balbutiements de l'amour avec un langage de la définition doctrinale"] (*Moyen court*, p. 24).

[88] It should be noted that the Jansenist Pierre Nicole wrote in 1695 a *Refutation of the Principal Errors of the Quietists* [*Réfutation des principales erreurs des quiétistes*]. There is thus, we can infer, no willing collaboration in the period.

and with its future; and second, that it is, as a result, similarly constrained—both by its potential and its aspirations and, in equal measure, by its limitations and its failures. The reluctance, on the part of the reforming adherent to any belief system, to recognize the necessary equation between the constraints and potentials of his or her convictions, and the constraints and potentials of that broader anthropology, is tacitly to throw into question, and indeed potentially to invalidate, the very theology which they seek to amend. Such departures from orthodoxy are condemned in the first instance theologically because they do not reflect the specifics of Christian dogma; but they are condemned just as much, empirically, because they do not apply to the common realities of life.

That is probably also the broader reason why the Church, for all the vindictiveness shown by many of its adherents, was unable to accept the presence within itself of either Jansenism or Quietism. We are back, in other words, with a simple challenge: the challenge of how the definition of Christian orthodoxy correlates with the capacity of the faith to describe, and indeed to resolve and heal, the simple but mysterious fact of being human.

Two more overarching issues will conclude my remarks. First, in the form of a brief parenthesis on the question of tolerance and intolerance. Tolerance may well have been an ideal which certain writers of the sixteenth century and *a fortiori* certain *philosophes* of the eighteenth, would have wished to propagate[89]; but it was not at any stage of the seventeenth century one with which a Catholic writer was concerned. In a writer such as St François de Sales, in particular, we might be surprised at the juxtaposition of great spiritual humility and of great confessional intolerance. In many respects he is regarded as being the figure in the period who most corresponds to subsequent developments in the Catholic Church. Angers, for example, writes: "We cannot say that the prince-bishop of Geneva died too soon; it is not for us to judge the workings of Providence. And yet it remains the case that Vatican II, with its constitution *Gaudium et spes*, is exactly in his wake."[90] And for Bremond, "the brief itinerary which he traced boldly and triumphantly has become the common way that, with the exception of a few retarded, obtuse, or timid souls, is eagerly followed by the majority in our day".[91] No doubt this influence is to some extent the result of a chronological accident, as Angers suggests; yet in another respect both the sheer range and accessibility of his writing, even to

[89] Culminating explicitly in Voltaire's *Traité sur la tolérance* in 1762.

[90] "Nous ne pouvons dire que l'évêque-prince de Genève soit mort trop tôt ; il ne nous appartient pas de juger la Providence. Toujours est-il que Vatican II, avec la Constitution *Gaudium et spes*, est exactement dans son sillage" (*Humanisme chrétien*, p. 47).

[91] "Le raccourci qu'il a tracé d'une main hardie et conquérante est devenu la route commune où sauf quelques attardés, revêches ou timides, la foule se presse aujourd'hui" (*Histoire littéraire*, I, p.115).

a modern reader, must suggest that he, as much as any of his contemporaries, has a status which both marks and transcends his century.

Yet this exceptionally forward-looking and democratic prelate makes an exception, for example, within his chapter in the *Introduction to the Devout Life*, of those of whom one may speak ill: "I except above all", he writes, "the declared enemies of God and of his Church; for such people, they should be decried as much as possible, as is the case for the sects of heretics and schismatics and their leaders"[92]; and he describes Protestantism in the *Treatise on the Love of God* as "[a] degrading litter of abomination".[93] Yet it is as anachronistic and inappropriate to expect him to tolerant as it is to expect him to be inhumane. As Michel notes, "François de Sales was in no respects a model of tolerance, but he was a model of gentleness."[94] For Madame Guyon too, François was "the scourge of heresy and innovation"[95] and although she does not herself like the atmosphere of the institute founded for "New Catholics" ["Les Nouvelles Catholiques" – that is converts from Calvinism], she nonetheless asserts her willingness (albeit in typically passive terms) to contribute to "the conversion of errant souls, since I had for their conversion as much impulse as I was capable of in my state of total death and self-annihilation".[96] Pascal equally begins a polemical fragment of the *Pensées* with the statement: "As the two principal concerns of the Church are the conservation of the piety of the faithful and the conversion of heretics [. . .]",[97] although he writes elsewhere against the use of coercion, playing on a reference to what Sellier refers to as Augustine's "regrettably famous [tristement célèbre] *Letter to Vincent*"[98]: "But to wish to instil [religion] in the mind and heart by force and by threats, is not to instil religion but terror."[99]

It is in the light of this tension therefore that I want to finish this pair of chapters with a broader consideration of Christian polemic in general: "In this combat, where two French prelates / Seem to be seeking the truth, / One says that it is hope which is destroyed, / The other that it is charity: / But it is faith

[92] "J'excepte entre tous les ennemis déclarés de Dieu et de son Église ; car ceux-là, il les faut décrier tant qu'on peut, comme sont les sectes des hérétiques et schismatiques et les chefs d'icelles" (*Introduction à la vie dévote*, p. 217).

[93] "[. . .] l'infâme litière de l'abomination" (*Traité de l'amour de Dieu*, p. 742).

[94] "François de Sales ne fut nullement un modèle de tolérance, mais il fut un modèle de douceur" ("La grandeur et l'humilité" in Armogathe, p. 430).

[95] "[. . .] le fléau de l'hérésie et des nouveautés" (*Vie*, p. 300).

[96] "[. . .] la conversion des âmes errantes, puisque j'avais pour leur conversion autant d'attrait que j'en étais capable dans un fond très mort et très anéanti" (*Vie*, p. 409).

[97] "Comme les deux principaux intérêts de l'Église sont la conservation de la piété des fidèles et la conversion des hérétiques [. . .]"(*Pensées*, L 991, S 812).

[98] *Pensées*, S p. 116, n. 4. The letter was nonetheless apparently used to justify both the Massacre of St Bartholomew (1572) and the Revocation of the Edict of Nantes (1685).

[99] "Mais de la [religion] vouloir mettre dans l'esprit et dans le cœur par la force et par les menaces, ce n'est pas y mettre la religion mais la terreur" (*Pensées*, L 172, S 203).

that is going to be the loser, and no-one is thinking about that",[100] as an anonymous commentator wrote of the Quietist dispute. The implication is inevitably that the believer and *a fortiori* the non-believer will be driven away from Christianity by all such warring factions. Bossuet himself admits as much, albeit with an anti-Protestant sub-text, in the *Funeral Oration of Henriette de France*: "[Some will be] unable to recognize the majesty of a religion torn apart by so many sects", he writes, "[and] will go and seek an ominous repose and a complete independence either in indifference to all religions or in atheism".[101] Fénelon too identifies the constituent factors which have led to the dispute becoming so bitter, and perfectly describes in so doing the features which are common to all Christian polemic:

> Ten people competent to talk about the matter trigger the contributions of ten thousand [who are not]. Simple, pious souls are [alarmed]. [. . .] The derision of profane spirits is [excited] (and that is not difficult in matters of spirituality and mysticism). And everything [contributes] at once to the rising storm: knowledge, ignorance, piety, politics, insinuation, dissent, tears, and threats.[102]

Yet both prelates would also argue that the faith will be lost if error is not combated. All Christian polemicists of our period on all sides of their disputes seem ironically to concur that deism, atheism, antinomianism, or blasphemy will be the inevitable terminus of the tendencies which they oppose. As Fénelon writes in the *Sayings of the Saints*, those who deny the Incarnation are "engaging in a fantasy contemplation which has no real object, and which cannot any longer distinguish God from the void. This", he writes, "is to annihilate Christianity under the pretext of purifying it."[103] More strongly

[100] "Dans ce combat où deux prélats de France / Semblent chercher la vérité, / L'un dit qu'on détruit l'espérance, / L'autre que c'est la charité : / C'est la foi qui se perd et personne n'y pense". The epigram was published in 1696. The anecdotal attribution to Racine seems unlikely.

[101] "Les autres [. . .], ne pouvant plus reconnaître la majesté de la religion déchirée par tant de sectes, iront enfin chercher un repos funeste, et une entière indépendance, dans l'indifférence des religions, ou dans l'athéisme" (*Oraison funèbre de Henriette-Marie de France*, in *Œuvres*, p. 68). The piece contains a long and wide-ranging denigration of the threat posed to the Christian faith by the instability caused by doctrinal innovation, of which the particular manifestation is evinced by the historical circumstances in which the subject was inevitably embroiled in her capacity as Queen of England.

[102] "Dix personnes accrédités en font parler dix mille. On [alarme] les âmes simples et pieuses. [. . .]. On [excite] (ce qui est facile en matière de spiritualité et de mystique) la dérision des esprits profanes. Tout [concourt] à la fois pour grossir l'orage, science, ignorance, piété, politique, insinuation, dispute, larmes et menaces" (*Réponse à la relation*, in *Œuvres* I, p. 1193). Davies remarks of this later work: "In comparison to Bossuet's *Relation* it is a calm, moderate, subtle statement [. . .], but like its sequels [. . .], it added nothing new, doctrinally or otherwise, to the debate" (*Fénelon*, p. 88).

[103] "C'est faire une contemplation chimérique qui n'a aucun objet réel, et qui ne peut distinguer Dieu du néant. C'est anéantir le christianisme sous prétexte de le purifier" (*Maximes des saints*, p. 1068).

again, it is to deny Christ as the privileged way to the Father, to believe that the *telos* has been reached; indeed, "it is to be the Antichrist who rejects the Word made flesh".[104] The conflicts arise, once again, from the strange particularity of the Christian Incarnation.

[104] "[. . .] c'est être l'Antéchrist qui rejette le Verbe fait chair" (*Maximes des saints*, p. 1070).

8

Particularity and Salvation

> Only think of one thing, it is the Son of God who said it: *Porro unum est necessarium*: 'Only one thing is necessary', only one thing is important, and that is our salvation.[1]

Thus Bossuet puts it, dramatically, biblically and unambiguously, in the *Funeral Oration of Nicolas Cornet*; and his episcopal adversary Fénelon is just as simple: "We believe we have a thousand concerns", he writes, "but we only have one."[2] In conformity with this imperative, the Christian way is understood as a means of sanctification and ultimately of salvation, the desire for which has been a constant of the voices of orthodoxy we have considered. Pascal sees the salvific dimension as that which differentiates Christianity from deism; and St François de Sales instructs his disciple Philothée to consider God's invitation at the Last Judgement, interrupting his biblical quotation with an exclamatory parenthesis as he does so: "*Come*, says the Judge; ah! this is the delightful word of salvation, whereby God draws us to himself and receives us into the bosom of his goodness; *blessed ones of my Father*."[3] In Bossuet's 1656 *Sermon on Providence* too, the theme of salvation is archetypally allied to that of discernment with regard to the Day of Judgement: "This great day on which the Son of God will descend from heaven, this is the day of general discernment."[4] It is the day, in other words, on which that ultimate discernment which governs all of its more local manifestations will occur; the day on which, in Pascal's phrase from the *Writings on Grace*, God

[1] "Ne pensez qu'à une seule chose, c'est le Fils de Dieu qui l'a dit : *Porro unum est necessarium* : 'Il n'y a qu'une chose nécessaire' il n'y a qu'une chose importante, qui est notre salut" (*Oraison funèbre de Nicolas Cornet*, in *Œuvres*, 41–55, p. 55).

[2] "Nous croyons avoir mille affaires, et nous n'en avons qu'une" (*Fragments spirituels*, XIX in *Œuvres*, I, p. 789). The text on which this is a commentary is, predictably enough, Luke 10: 41.

[3] "*Venez*, dit le juge; ah c'est le mot agréable de salut, par lequel Dieu nous tire à soi et nous reçoit dans le giron de sa bonté; *bénis de mon Père*" (*Introduction à la vie dévote*, p. 58, emphases original to denote biblical texts).

[4] "[. . .] cette grande journée en laquelle le Fils de Dieu descendra du ciel, c'est le jour du discernement général" (*Sermon sur la providence*, in *Œuvres*, p. 1046).

will operate the "discernment of the elect" ["le discernement des élus"].[5] Only the Quietists seem to place it in question, all the more ironically so since the Christic injunction, *Porro unum est necessarium*, concludes the Lucan account of Martha and Mary with words spoken in support of the passive exemplar, and with words, furthermore, which have traditionally been interpreted by the Church in soteriological terms.[6]

If there are two stages that are fundamental to this process, by more or less unanimous consent, they are conversion and perseverance. Pascal's brief essay *On the Sinner's Conversion* deals with the nature and, initially, difficulties of a change of heart, whereby "the first thing which God inspires in the soul that he deigns to touch truly is a quite extraordinary knowledge and perspective, whereby the soul considers all things and itself in an entirely different way".[7] It is precisely this transition which brings the soul to reject the transience of the values of the world, "whether gold, learning, or reputation" ["soit or, soit science, soit réputation"] on the one hand; and to work towards the promise of a happiness "as durable as itself" ["[qui] dure autant qu'elle"] on the other.[8] The further point to emerge from this brief work is that conversion, while depending initially on a gift from God, is a progressive, indeed an exponential process. Conversion, in the sense of a single act of metanoia, is therefore only the first stage towards salvation: it is the sanctification of this life which leads to salvation in the next, a proposition for which there is no shortage of salutary reminders in the period.

One perspective on this progression is provided in another short work by Pascal, his world-denying *Prayer to Ask God for the Good Use of Illness*. This is above all an appeal for the victim of illness to see his affliction as a means of correction and as a preparation for death, by virtue of being unavoidably deprived of the distractions of the world. Illness is both a foretaste of death therefore, itself the final denial of worldly things, but also the occasion to experience God's mercy, to amend one's life, and thus to moderate the final judgement. The implicit picture of the penitent here is important too. He is a figure who has been baptized, but is still attached strongly to the things of the world; he has led a life free of excess, but free also of religious engagement, so that illness is deemed to afford the catalyst for a life-changing experience. But what is above all stressed thereafter is the absolute dependence on the grace of

[5] *Écrits sur la grâce*, I, p. 313.

[6] "'Martha, Martha', he said, 'you worry and fret about so many things, and yet few are needed, indeed only one.'"

[7] "La première chose que Dieu inspire à l'âme qu'il daigne toucher véritablement, est une connaissance et une vue tout extraordinaire par laquelle l'âme considère les choses et elle-même d'une façon toute nouvelle" (*Sur la conversion du pécheur*, in L 290–1, p. 290). The work dates from 1653.

[8] *Sur la conversion du pécheur*, p. 290–1.

God, expressed in a particularly self-contained prayer, whose progression underlines both the divine origin and the divine end of all that is good, in a formula which once again draws attention, by its apparently circular argument, to the intimate interaction of God and the sinner: "I give you thanks, my God, for the good impulses that you give me, and indeed for the good impulse you give me in order to give you thanks."[9] But if such a sentence appears stylistically cumbersome, it conceals by its chiastic structure a profound Christian insight into the co-operation of man and God in an accretive theology of salvation. And Fénelon, in a more elegant chiasmus, makes a similar point: "It is God's love for us that accords us everything. But the greatest gift that God can endow us with is the love that we must have for him",[10] so that as a consequence "the law of prayer is reciprocal between God and ourselves".[11] Finally, in a third short work by Pascal, the *Comparison of the Christians from Early Times with Those of Today*, he contrasts, among other features, the importance of the sacrament of baptism, insisting on the extensive preparation which it involved, on the penitence and commitment which were required, and above all on what he calls the "outstanding signs of a true conversion of the heart and of [. . .] an ardent desire for baptism".[12] He does so in the context in order to make a contrast with the practice of infant baptism, as it was later to evolve; but also with the routine nature which it had subsequently acquired as a result.

It is to the theatrical treatment of the early Christian centuries that we next turn to find this moment exemplified and indeed dramatized. Baptism, in Corneille's *Polyeucte martyr*, is first of all accorded a revelatory function, and indeed serves as the dramatic trigger for the major elements of the stage action which will ensue. It is, consistently with Corneille's tragic ethos, the epiphanic moment which drives the martyr-hero to the single-minded pursuit of his *gloire*, and as such it is credited with inspiring an immediate and total

[9] "Je vous rends donc grâces, mon Dieu, des bons mouvements que vous me donnez, et de celui même que vous me donnez de vous en rendre grâces" (*Prière pour demander à Dieu le bon usage des maladies* in L 362–5, p. 363). The work was first printed in 1666, but may date from as early as 1659.

[10] "C'est l'amour que Dieu a pour nous qui nous donne tout. Mais le plus grand don qu'il nous puisse faire, c'est de nous donner l'amour que nous devons avoir pour lui" (*Lettres et opuscules spirituels*, XXXI (*Dieu*), in *Œuvres*, I, p. 696).

[11] "La loi de la prière est réciproque entre Dieu et nous" (*De la prière*, in *Œuvres*, I, p. 870).

[12] "[. . .] des marques éminentes d'une conversion véritable du cœur, et [. . .] un extrême désir du baptême" (*Comparaison des chrétiens des premiers temps avec ceux d'aujourd'hui* in L 360–2, p. 360). The work is dated by Lafuma as falling between 1655 and 1657. Further unflattering comparisons between the early Church and their own times are made both by Pascal in certain fragments of the *Pensées*, notably L 701, S 317, and by Bossuet in the *Panégyrique de saint Victor*, where he describes his contemporaries as "half-Christians" ["demi-Chrétiens"] (*Œuvres*, p. 389).

conviction, transforming, in Polyeucte's case, a previously lukewarm Christian commitment into a fully fledged dramatic dilemma.[13]

Two other theatrical treatments of conversion in the two martyr tragedies I have considered afford striking, and strikingly different models. The first is the sequence of conversions which constitute the dénouement of the same play, in which two of the key pagan figures of the *dramatis personæ* left on stage after the martyrdom (Polyeucte's wife Pauline and his father-in-law, a Roman official, Félix), are suddenly and miraculously drawn to Christian belief. This dénouement is appropriately anticipated by a dramatic prolepsis in which the martyr, on the threshold of death, envisages with a reasonable degree of confidence that he will soon be in a position directly to intercede with God. It follows that the conversions of those who remain alive are perceived to be the results of this intercession; and logically, therefore, that his martyrdom is pleasing to God. This is certainly in conformity with Corneille's tragic aesthetic, whereby the hero's action is frequently crowned with some objective sign of approbation; but it is also undertaken in imitation of the "acceptable sacrifice" of Christ, to whose precise exemplar Polyeucte is closely attentive. It is understood in turn, within the ethos of the play, first as the retrospective justification for his hubristic iconoclasm, but also as a means of proselytizing, as we have seen, and so of initiating the potential for a more widespread growth of allegiance to the Christian cause.

It is thus made clear that Polyeucte's martyrdom, by finding favour with God, has triggered the ensuing developments. Yet it is the act, as much as any putative intercession which Polyeucte had envisaged, that is deemed efficacious as the play ends: Polyeucte, the subject of an epiphanic conversion which follows on from a more provisional commitment before baptism, is driven by Christian zeal to his death, whereupon two other protagonists instantly receive the faith and take his place in the work of spreading the Gospel.[14] Furthermore, at the end of *Polyeucte martyr*, his now converted widow Pauline herself has a vision, in which she sees her recently martyred husband stretch out his arms to her, in a minor variant of the more exuberant vision accorded to Polyeucte in the historical account of his martyrdom, albeit not in the Cornelian play.[15] The idea is thus conveyed that, once the barrier between heaven

[13] As Street writes, "Polyeucte conceives Christianity and martyrdom initially as a means of attaining a heroic status which the mutability of the world cannot tarnish" (*French Sacred Drama*, p. 193). This would lead me to disagree with Prigent, for whom "the conversion is [...] more Cornelian than Christian, more heroic than supernatural" ["la conversion est [...] plus cornélienne que chrétienne, plus héroïque que surnaturelle"] (*Le Héros et l'État*, p. 69).

[14] As Street comments, "that Polyeucte's new faith is valid is shown by its ability to produce miracles" (*French Sacred Drama*, p. 193).

[15] The account is provided by the tenth-century Byzantine hagiographer Simeon Metaphrastes, reprinted in the sixteenth century by the Carthusian Laurent Sirius. Corneille provides a *Summary of the Martyrdom of St Polyeucte* [*Abrégé du martyre de saint Polyeucte*], reproduced in *OC* at p. 290–1.

and earth is removed, the fervent believer is accorded a privileged posthumous relationship with her (or his) precursors in the faith. It is also an appropriate climax to the tragedy in the work of a playwright who sought to elicit the response of *admiration* – that is astonishment – from his audience, as they wonder at the dramatic representation of exceptional feats of (in this case Christian) heroism.[16]

The treatment in Rotrou's play about the actor-martyr St Genesius, *Le Véritable Saint-Genest*, is necessarily more complex again. In this case, we are given to understand in an early scene that the actor is psychologically ready for conversion; but this understanding accompanies the suggestion that belief may be progressively acquired through habit enhanced by repetition—that is, in other words, by the playing of a role or, in a very literal sense here, by the imitation of Christ.[17] In addition to this, Rotrou's dramatic aesthetic distinguishes itself from Corneille's by proposing a miraculous intervention, in which the stage directions furthermore recall an amalgamation of two Gospel episodes, the Baptism of Christ and Pentecost: "The Heavens open, flames appear, and a voice is heard";[18] and what the voice says is critically important in terms of the theology of conversion as it is developed in the remainder of the play:

> Persevere, Genesius, in your role,
> You will not imitate in vain;
> Your salvation only depends on a little steadfastness,
> And God will lend you his support.[19]

The salvation of Genesius will be assured, we are led to infer, by the collaboration between imitation, on the one hand (that is learning, by acting a part, to become the person portrayed), and divine help on the other. This might seem superficial, metatheatrical, or even dishonest, and yet the resonances are strong here with other writing: with Bossuet's insistence on the value of the mechanical recitation of the *Angelus* as a daily practice; with the import of such writing as Pascal's "automaton" fragment: "For we should not be deceived about ourselves, we are automata as much as we are minds"[20]; and, above all, with the notorious sequence from the wager argument:

[16] The term is glossed in the *Examen de 'Nicomède'*, in *Œuvres complètes*, ed. Stegmann, 1963, p. 520–1.

[17] The same idea is exploited in the novel by Nikos Kazantzakis, *Christ Recrucified* (1954), made into an opera (*The Greek Passion*) by Martinů, completed in 1959.

[18] "Le Ciel s'ouvre, avec des flammes, et une voix s'entend" (*Le véritable Saint Genest*, II, 4). Cf. Matthew 3: 16–17; Acts 2: 3.

[19] "Poursuis Genest ton personnage, / Tu n'imiteras point en vain ; / Ton salut ne dépend que d'un peu de courage, / Et Dieu t'y prêtera la main" (*Le Véritable Saint Genest*, II, 4, 421–4).

[20] "Car il ne faut pas se méconnaître : nous sommes automate autant qu'esprit" (*Pensées*, L 821, S 661).

> You want to move towards faith, and you do not know how to start? [. . .] Learn from those who were bound like you and who now risk all they have. These people know the way you want to follow and have been cured of an ill you want to be rid of. Follow the way in which they began: it was by behaving just as if they believed.[21]

Yet the play-acting, it becomes clear, was the critical starting point, but no more than that, of the process of conversion in Rotrou's tragedy. Genesius's change of heart, on a closer reading, is not adequately perceived as a divine ratification of mimicry; rather it is a subtler process of learning by imitation, undertaken in co-operation with the working of the spirit, the "soft and sacred breath", and of moving towards the goal of salvation, as it is later proposed in the same scene:

> Soft and sacred breath, which comes to enflame me,
> Holy and Divine Spirit, which comes to enliven me,
> And which, desiring me, inspires me with steadfastness,
> Work for my salvation, complete your undertaking.[22]

Intimately connected to this is the criterion of perseverance, which leads us to discern a pattern which has been implicit in much of what I have been looking at, and which we might call a cyclical model of sanctification. The Scriptural and liturgical starting point is made explicit by Bossuet in the *Catechism of Feasts*, when he deals with the Feast of Pentecost. Christ is sent to earth at the Nativity; he ascends to heaven at the Ascension; the Holy Spirit descends to earth at Pentecost; its fruits are manifested in the worship of God; and God rewards those who worship him appropriately. The same model is enacted in the Mass: God gives the bread and wine to humankind; the gifts are sanctified by the Holy Spirit; the priest offers them to God in their consecrated state; and the faithful, filled with grace by the reception of the sacrament, praise God in thanksgiving. Early in his *Introduction to the Devout Life*, St François de Sales compatibly promotes "the use of the sacraments, by which [our] good God comes to us, and holy orisons, by which he draws us to himself".[23] In Bossuet's *Exposition of Catholic Doctrine*, the validity of saintly intercession is accounted for in similar terms: thus the Saint is glorified by God and honoured by the faithful, as a result of which his or her intercession promotes in turn the

[21] "Vous voulez aller à la foi, et vous n'en savez pas le chemin ? [. . .] Apprenez de ceux qui ont été liés comme vous et qui parient maintenant tout leur bien : ce sont gens qui savent le chemin que vous voudriez suivre et guéris d'un mal dont vous voulez guérir. Suivez la manière par où ils ont commencé : c'est en faisant tout comme s'ils croyaient" (*Pensées*, L 418, S 680).

[22] "Souffle doux et sacré, qui me viens enflammer, / Esprit Saint et Divin, qui me viens animer, / Et qui me souhaitant, m'inspires le courage, / Travaille à mon salut, achève ton ouvrage" (*Le Véritable Saint Genest*, II, 4, 426–30).

[23] "[L]'usage des Sacrements par lesquels ce bon Dieu vient à nous, et la sainte oraison par laquelle il nous tire à soi" (*Introduction à la vie dévote*, p. 25).

spiritual progress of the believer towards holiness; and, as we saw when we looked at preaching, the *Ave Maria* cadence extends this model, at the linguistic level, to the intercession of the Blessed Virgin as a contribution to the homiletic impact. All these examples, therefore, in distinction to the passivity of Quietism, presuppose an interactive relationship between God and humankind in the form of a co-operation between grace and free will. All good comes from God, but its practical realization by men and women, animated by prayer, fed by the Eucharist and supported by the intercession of Mary and the Saints, serves to glorify God in return. The fixed point is God; but the Church, militant and triumphant, remains active, not passive, in his service and, thereby, in the exponential sanctification of humankind.

Within this cycle, different degrees of apparent freedom are recorded. In the Jansenist tradition a greater emphasis is placed on its mysterious nature. Thus, as Pascal puts it, quoting Aquinas in answer to the question as to why God instituted prayer: "To communicate the dignity of causality to his creatures. But to retain his pre-eminence, he gives prayer to those to whom he pleases."[24] Or, in the *Writings on Grace*: "God never refuses what he is worthily asked for in prayer, and [. . .] God does not always accord perseverance in prayer: which is in no respect contradictory."[25] In the autobiography of St Margaret Mary, predictably, a more anguished version of this interaction is in evidence. She sees herself as little more than the plaything of Christ; and although she writes about her opposition to God, evoking her "resistance" ["résistance"] and "repugnance" ["répugnance"], we equally learn that such departures are in fact simply "allowed" to happen. Thus of the composition of her autobiography, she is told by God:

> "I want this from you, to show you that you are my plaything, by making useless all the precautions that I have allowed you to take, in order to conceal the profusion of graces with which I have been pleased to endow such a poor feeble creature as you are."[26]

The recorded manifestations of such resistance in her life are rare, however, despite recurrent references to them, and probably reflect a hyperbolic tendency to self-inculpation, rather than any real battle with the world. If the vicissitudes of her struggle against obedience form a major element in the composition of her autobiography, the account of her life overall conveys

[24] "Pour communiquer à ses créatures la dignité de la causalité. Mais pour se conserver la prééminence, il donne la prière à qui il lui plaît" (*Pensées*, L 930, S 757).

[25] "Dieu ne refuse jamais ce qu'on lui demande bien dans la prière, et [. . .] Dieu ne donne pas toujours la persévérance dans la prière : ce qui n'est en aucune sorte contradictoire" (*Écrits sur la grâce*, p. 322).

[26] "'Je veux cela de toi, pour te faire voir que je me joue, en rendant inutiles toutes les précautions que je t'ai laissé prendre pour cacher la profusion de grâces dont j'ai pris plaisir d'enrichir une aussi pauvre et chétive créature que toi'" (*Vie*, p. 35).

the consistent impression only of her being enabled feebly to combat the (in the end) overpowering force of the divine.

It is perhaps Fénelon who affords the most powerful extended metaphor with which to convey the trials and tribulations of the believer, in a sequence of material images which opens itself up to empirical interpretation. In this way, we are given to understand, each penitent Christian is able to identify his or her point of association with their suffering redeemer, and thus to embrace their opportunity for salvation:

> God is ingenious in his provision of crosses for us. He makes some of iron and lead, which are overwhelming in themselves; he might make some of straw, which seem to weigh nothing, yet are no easier to bear; he makes some of gold and jewels, which dazzle those who behold them, and which excite public envy, but which crucify no less than those which are most scorned.[27]

I have written in various contexts about the translation to a transcendent perspective, and about the guidance of a spiritual director in the progress of the devout soul; but it is also true that all the writers with whom I have been dealing see earth and heaven, at least in an eschatological understanding, as very closely proximate. The Church militant is only a part of the story; and the believer is constantly aware that his or her precursors in belief, now in some cases raised to a state of glory, constitute an exemplary and, vitally, an intimately contiguous community of faith. As Bossuet writes in the *Panegyric of St Teresa*, apostrophizing the Church triumphant: "[Oh] holy Jerusalem, blessed Church of the first-born, whose names are written in heaven, although the Church, your dear sister, that lives and fights on earth, cannot be compared to you, she does not lose the conviction that a holy love unites you"[28]; and all of our writers, with only the exception of certain of the more unorthodox opinions of Madame Guyon, insist on their dependency on the prayers of the Blessed Virgin and the Saints, and on the protection of the angels.

St François de Sales's *Introduction to the Devout Life*, in particular, is a work in which heaven is very close to earth, and the incarnate God to incarnate woman. The deeply felt experience of the love of Christ is powerfully evoked in the kind of language and with the kind of specificity we find both here and in

[27] "Dieu est ingénieux à nous faire des croix. Il en fait de fer et de plomb, qui sont accablantes par elles-mêmes ; il en sait faire de paille, qui semblent ne peser rien, et qui ne sont pas moins difficiles à porter ; il en fait d'or et de pierreries, qui éblouissent les spectateurs, qui excitent l'envie du public, mais qui ne crucifient pas moins que les croix les plus méprisées" (*Lettres et opuscules spirituels*, IV (*Des croix qu'il y a dans l'état de prospérité, de faveur, de grandeur*), in *Œuvres*, I, p. 566).

[28] "[Ô] sainte Jérusalem, heureuse Église des premiers-nés, dont les noms sont écrits au ciel, quoique l'Église, votre chère sœur, qui vit et combat sur la terre, n'ose pas se comparer à vous, elle ne laisse pas d'assurer qu'un saint amour vous unit ensemble" (*Panégyrique de sainte Thérèse*, in *Œuvres*, p. 394).

the later *Treatise on the Love of God*: "You see, Philothée," François writes to his lay addressee, "it is certain that the heart of our dear Jesus perceived your heart from the wood of the Cross, and that he loved it, and by that love he obtained for it all the good things that you will ever enjoy"[29]; and, to the cloistered Théotime of the later work, he offers an individualized paraphrase of Christ's dying words to the Father:

> Alas, oh my eternal Father, I take onto myself and carry for him all the sins of poor Théotime, and suffer agony and death so that he is exempted from them, so that he should not perish, but should live. May I die, so that he should live; may I be crucified, so that he should be glorified.[30]

Even Pascal, in a rare moment of intimacy in the *Mystère de Jésus*, attributes to Christ the words, in the form of a prosopopœia: "Console yourself [and here he uses the intimate 'tu' form in French], you would not be seeking me if you had not already found me. // I was thinking of you in my agony. I shed certain drops of my blood for you."[31]

More important again, in the *Introduction to the Devout Life*, is the emphasis placed on God's desire that Philothée should be saved as a result: "God [. . .] desires [. . .] with an unequal desire that you should choose Paradise", François writes; "and your good Angel urges you on with all his power, offering you on God's behalf a thousand graces and a thousand aids to help you in your [heavenward] climb."[32] Complementarily to this, an attitude of mind is instilled whereby heaven is made to seem desirable, as much as hell fearful. The first part of the *Introduction* deals with the great cosmic and eschatological themes of creation, heaven, hell, sin, death, and judgement; but it does not seek thereby to bludgeon the addressee, rather to make her supremely prefer the possibility of salvation, and induce in her the desire to lead the devout life. This is also presented, on both saintly and Christic authority, in the most alluring sequence of epithets (and is so presented without any of Pascal's polysemic contrivances): "The Holy Spirit, by the mouths of all the Saints, and Our Lord by his own mouth assures us that

[29] "Voyez-vous, ma Philothée, il est certain que le cœur de notre cher Jésus voyait le vôtre dès l'arbre de la Croix et l'aimait, et par cet amour lui obtenait tous les biens que vous aurez jamais" (*Introduction à la vie dévote*, p. 310).

[30] "Hélas, ô mon Père éternel, je prends à moi et me charge de tous les péchés du pauvre Théotime, pour souffrir les tourments et la mort afin qu'il en demeure quitte et qu'il ne périsse point, mais qu'il vive. Que je meure, pourvu qu'il vive ; que je sois crucifié, pourvu qu'il soit glorifié" (*Traité de l'amour de Dieu*, p. 970).

[31] "Console-toi, tu ne me chercherais pas si tu ne m'avais trouvé. // Je pensais à toi dans mon agonie, j'ai versé telles gouttes de sang pour toi" (*Pensées*, L 919, S 751).

[32] "Dieu [. . .], désire [. . .] d'un désir non pareil que vous choisissiez le Paradis ; et votre bon Ange vous en presse de tout son pouvoir, vous offrant de la part de Dieu mille grâces et mille secours pour vous aider à la montée" (*Introduction à la vie dévote*, p. 63–4).

the devout life is gentle, happy and agreeable",[33] François reassures his addressee. Likewise, and in similar ternary form, the love of God is "gentle, peaceful, and calm" ["douce, paisible et calme"]; and meditation on the life and death of Christ is "blissful, delectable, and profitable" ["suave, délectable et profitable"]. These terms all come together in the ninth meditation, which gives a particularly clear (and hierarchically ordered) sense of the reality of Christ, Mary, the Communion of Saints, and the Holy Souls, as the whole heavenly community is accorded words of compassion and encouragement, in a powerful mixture of the transcendent and the anthropomorphic:

> Jesus Christ, from high in the heavens, looks down on you in his kindness and gently invites you: Come, my dear soul, to the eternal rest in the arms of my goodness, which has prepared for you immortal joys in the abundance of its love. See with the eyes of your heart the Blessed Virgin who calls to you as a mother: Do not be afraid, my daughter; do not scorn the desires of my Son, nor so many sighs that I breathe for you, looking forward with him to your eternal salvation. See the Saints who exhort you, and a million holy souls who plead gently with you, wanting only to see your heart one day joined to theirs, to praise God for ever, and assuring you that the way to Heaven is not as difficult as the world would have you believe. Be brave, they say, dearest friend; whoever considers the path of devotion by which we have climbed will see that we have reached these joys by passing through joys that were incomparably more delightful than those of the world.[34]

At this critical moment of commitment, the Church triumphant is given an equal if more exuberant reality with the Church militant, as a joyful witness of the penitent's progress towards salvation.

Even in the more anguished tonalities of the autobiography of St Margaret Mary, where we find that much of what she encounters on earth seems to stand in the way of her relationship with God, the same is not true of heavenly intercession. The role of Mary and the Saints in Margaret Mary's youth is central: "The most holy Virgin, to whom I have always had recourse in my

[33] "[Le] Saint-Esprit, par la bouche de tous les Saints, et Notre-Seigneur, par la sienne même, nous assure que la vie dévote est une vie douce, heureuse et amiable" (*Introduction à la vie dévote*, p. 34).

[34] "Jésus-Christ, du haut du Ciel, vous regarde en sa débonnaireté, et vous invite doucement : Viens, ô ma chère âme, au repos éternel entre les bras de ma bonté, qui t'a préparé les délices immortelles en l'abondance de son amour. Voyez de vos yeux intérieurs la Sainte Vierge qui vous convie maternellement : Courage, ma Fille, ne veuille pas mépriser les désirs de mon Fils, ni tant de soupirs que je jette pour toi, respirant avec lui ton salut éternel. Voyez les Saints qui vous exhortent, et un million de saintes âmes qui vous convient doucement, ne désirant que de voir un jour votre cœur joint au leur, pour louer Dieu à jamais, et vous assurant que le chemin du Ciel n'est pas si malaisé que le monde le fait : Hardiment, vous disent-elles, très chère amie ; qui considérera bien le chemin de la dévotion par lequel nous sommes montées, il verra que nous sommes venues en ces délices, par des délices incomparablement plus suaves que celles du monde" (*Introduction à la vie dévote*, p. 64).

needs, has always taken great care of me", she writes; "and she has held me back from some very great perils"[35]; and her healings by and visions of Mary are the first steps in the development which leads her finally to do God's will. Other Saints figure too in a kind of hierarchy of accessibility, including the recently canonized François de Sales, as exemplars of the rewards she might expect. The intercession of Mary as of the Saints and angels, alongside earthly obedience to her Superior and her director, thus coexist and interact with the direct mediation of Christ in her calling; and we may surmise that this fundamental if at times reluctant recognition of both intercession and obedience must in turn have reinforced her own claims to canonization.

Even in the accounts of Sœur Jeanne des Anges or of Père Surin, we often find that their overcoming of the diabolic is achieved by virtue of God's very precise instructions to them as to how to proceed. Thus Jeanne des Anges, in the course of her diabolic tribulations, is instructed by God to seek the intercession of St Joseph; as a result of this he obtains for her the gifts of mental prayer and contemplation, thanks to which, she writes, "I received great enlightenment, and Our Lord communicated with my soul in a very special manner."[36] More physically, the final episode in the first part of her story occurs on the feast of St Teresa of Ávila, when at Holy Communion the names of Christ and St François de Sales are added to those of Mary and St Joseph which are already carved on the (left) hand of the nun, with all four being renewed by her guardian angel at regular intervals.[37] And a note of downright domesticity occurs when Surin, having suffered from a fear of eating, is enabled to eat by seeing Christ and the apostles or Mary eating at table with him.[38] This kind of practical physical interventionism inevitably strikes the modern reader as either comic or sinister or both, even if, in other respects, it constitutes no more than a desperately personal application of incarnational theology when it is taken to its logical, or maybe illogical, limits.

Moving back to the episcopal mainstream, Bossuet's *Funeral Orations* exploit the same contiguity. In the *Funeral Oration of Marie-Thérèse*, Bossuet likens the French Queen's fear of losing her son to that of Mary's suffering, justifying the apparently audacious parallel by means of a more universal understanding of the Incarnation: "Do not let us hesitate to say it", he writes,

[35] "La très sainte Vierge a toujours pris un très grand soin de moi, qui avais recours à elle en tous mes besoins : et elle m'a retirée de très grands périls" (*Vie*, p. 30).

[36] "Je recevais de grandes lumières et Notre-Seigneur communiquait à mon âme d'une manière particulière" (*Relation*, p. 148).

[37] *Relation*, p. 190–3.

[38] *Science expérimentale*, p. 293. Surin himself accepts that a sceptical reader will find it "ridiculous or indecent" ["ridicule ou indécent"]. As we have seen, a similar degree of familiarity informs his dealings with the diabolic.

"since a God was made man only in order to surround himself with examples appropriate to all [human] states."[39] Elsewhere, the Saints once again act as intermediaries between the scriptural and the actual, nowhere more appositely than in the case of the repentant sinner, with St Peter, St Paul, and St Augustine lined up as precedents in the *Funeral Oration of the Princess Palatine*. Such proximity is particularly exploited in these pieces at the moment of death, and a note of outright rejoicing is struck in the *Funeral Oration of Michel Le Tellier*, in which a whole kaleidoscope of images conjoin to make their impact: "O blessed moment when we shall leave the shadows and enigmas and see truth manifest! [. . .] That is the end of the journey; there the groans finish; there the travails of the Faith reach their end, when it will give birth, as it were, to sight"[40]; and a strong sense of direct continuity is afforded in the dying man's recitation of the *Misericordias domini*: "[He] began the hymn of divine mercy: *Misericordias Domini in æternum cantabo*: 'I will sing', he said, 'for ever of the mercy of God.' He expired with these words on his lips, and he continued this sacred canticle with the voices of the angels."[41] More ominously the same prelate, in his anti-theatrical *Maxims on the Theatre* (1694) evokes the death of the comic playwright Molière with a reminder of the Beatitudes: "He passed from the ribaldries of the theatre", Bossuet writes, "among which he [had] breathed almost his last breath, to the tribunal of him who said: *Woe to you who laugh, for you shall weep.*"[42] More affirmatively, Pascal explains in the *Letter on the Death of his Father* how

> the same things happen to the body and the soul, but at different times; and the changes to the body only happen after those to the soul have been completed, that

[39] "Ne craignons point de le dire, puisqu'un Dieu ne s'est fait homme que pour assembler autour de lui des exemples pour tous les états" (*Oraison funèbre de Marie-Thérèse d'Autriche*, in *Œuvres*, p. 124).

[40] "Ô moment heureux où nous sortirons des ombres et des énigmes pour voir la vérité manifeste ! [. . .]. Là est le terme du voyage ; là se finissent les gémissements ; là s'achève le travail de la Foi, quand elle va, pour ainsi dire, enfanter la vue" (*Oraison funèbre de Michel Le Tellier*, in *Œuvres*, p. 187).

[41] "[Il] commença l'hymne des divines miséricordes: *Misericordias Domini in æternum cantabo* : 'Je chanterai, dit-il, éternellement les miséricordes du Seigneur.' Il expire en disant ces mots, et il continue avec les anges le sacré cantique" (*Oraison funèbre de Michel Le Tellier*, in *Œuvres*, p. 187). The biblical reference is to Psalm 89: 1. The impact of the French use of the historic present here is difficult to convey in English.

[42] "[Il] passa des plaisanteries du théâtre, parmi lesquelles il rendit presque le dernier soupir, au tribunal de celui qui dit : *Malheur à vous qui riez, car vous pleurerez*" (*Maximes et réflexions sur la comédie*, in *L'Église et le théâtre*, ed. C. Urbain and E. Levesque, Paris, Bernard Grasset, 1930, p. 185, emphasis original). The same passage is cited in the *Oraison funèbre de Henriette-Marie de France* in *Œuvres*, p. 78. The biblical reference is to Luke 6: 25. For the context of this, see Henry Phillips, *The Theatre and Its Critics in Seventeenth-Century France*, Oxford, Oxford University Press, 1980; and Jean Dubu, *Les Églises chrétiennes et le théâtre (1550–1850)*, Grenoble, Presses universitaires de Grenoble, 1977.

> is to say at the hour of death; so that death is the culmination of the beatitude of the soul, and the beginning of the beatitude of the body.[43]

I looked in Chapter 6 at some of the debates surrounding the question of who is or might be saved, and of how we might or might not know. I want now to propose two perspectives from the period which will in some sense allow us to transcend, or at least to reassess, that enquiry.

The first is quite simply the injunction to incuriosity, destined to coexist with a sometimes desperate attempt rationally to codify this most universal of enigmas. Such incuriosity is first of all advocated for the here and now. Thus, for Fénelon, aware like his episcopal predecessor St François de Sales of the astonishing gratuity of life, "the creator must renew at every instant the benefit of his creation, and conserve it by the same power with which it was created"[44]; and the same prelate writes, in the same spirit, that "it would be faithless and guilty of a pagan defiance to try to enter into the future that God conceals from us".[45] St François de Sales, in the *Treatise on the Love of God*, stresses the "abundant wealth of graces" ["abondante suffisance de grâces"] that Providence distributes to humankind, but he too emphasizes in this context that

> one should be very careful never to enquire why the ultimate Wisdom has accorded a grace to one rather than to the other, nor why he lavishes his favours in one place rather than another. No, Théotime, never embark on this kind of curiosity; since we all have sufficiently, indeed abundantly, what is required for salvation, what reason can anyone in the world have to complain, if it pleases God to accord his graces more liberally to some than to others.[46]

He is more dogmatic again in a later chapter: "The human spirit is so weak", he writes, "that when it wants to enquire too curiously into the causes and reasons of the divine will, it soon becomes enmeshed and entangled in the nets

[43] "Ainsi les mêmes choses arrivent au corps et à l'âme, mais en différents temps; et les changements du corps n'arrivent que quand ceux de l'âme sont accomplis, c'est-à-dire à l'heure de la mort : de sorte que la mort est le couronnement de la béatitude de l'âme, et le commencement de la béatitude du corps" (*Lettre à Monsieur et Madame Périer à l'occasion de la mort de M. Pascal le père* in L, 273–5, p. 274).

[44] "[Il] faut que le Créateur renouvelle sans cesse le bienfait de sa création, en la conservant par la même puissance qui l'a créée" (*Lettres et opuscules spirituels*, XXIII (*Sur le pur amour*), in *Œuvres*, I, 656–71, p. 661). Compare the *Introduction à la vie dévote*, Part I, Chapters IX–XI.

[45] "On serait infidèle, et coupable d'une défiance païenne, si on voulait pénétrer dans cet avenir que Dieu nous dérobe" (*Lettres et opuscules spirituels*, VI (*Discours sur la dissipation et la tristesse*), in *Œuvres*, I, 573–81, p. 577).

[46] "Il se faut bien garder de jamais rechercher pourquoi la suprême Sagesse a départi une grâce à l'un plutôt qu'à l'autre, ni pourquoi il fait abonder ses faveurs en un endroit plutôt qu'en l'autre: non, Théotime, n'entrez jamais en cette curiosité; car ayant tous suffisamment, ains abondamment, ce qui nous est requis pour le salut, quelle raison peut avoir l'homme du monde de se plaindre, s'il plaît à Dieu de départir ses grâces plus largement aux uns qu'aux autres" (*Traité de l'amour de Dieu*, p. 430). Angers writes that "the great characteristic of this gratuitous redemption lies in nothing other than its abundance" ["le grand caractère de cette rédemption gratuite n'est autre que l'abondance"] (*Humanisme chrétien*, p. 16).

of a thousand difficulties."[47] It is stressed as well in the second part of Bossuet's *Meaux Catechism* (devoted to Feasts of the Church) that incuriosity in matters of dogmatic theology can often be the only appropriate response. In a rather charming exchange, after the catechist has replied to the question as to where Christ was between the Resurrection and the Ascension by: "It is not permitted to enquire", a further somewhat persistent "*Why?*" elicits the equally intransigent: "Because it has not pleased God to reveal it to us."[48] More sententiously, his insistence on the limits of what may be known is expressed in the same work by an impatient parody of the frailty of the human mind: "[Men] do not know themselves, they do not know how even the smallest things are made, a fly, an ant, an ear of corn; and yet they want to penetrate the secrets of God."[49]

The same theme is forcefully expressed in Bossuet's preaching. He deplores in 1663 the "dreadful storm [which] has blown up in our times concerning grace and free will"[50] (that is the Jansenist controversy), as a result of which "there was a risk that we would be unwittingly thrown into consequences which were ruinous to the freedom of man",[51] and implies that the whole problem is by definition insoluble when he writes that "this heavenly doctrine has become *necessarily* wrapped around by impenetrable difficulties".[52] Humankind must accept that certain things cannot be discovered, and that the desire to arrive at dogmatic conclusions independent of the authority of the Church and the Holy See leads to error, born of what he terms an "obsession for arguing about divine matters".[53] He therefore insists in the *Funeral Oration of Nicolas Cornet*, calling on the authority of St Gregory of Nazianzus, that "the first duty of a man who studies holy truths is to be able to identify those places where it is permitted to proceed further, and those where we must be brought up short, and remember the narrow limits within which our

[47] "L'esprit humain est si faible, que quand il vient trop curieusement rechercher les causes et raisons de la volonté divine, il s'embarrasse et entortille dans les filets de mille difficultés" (*Traité de l'amour de Dieu*, p. 545).

[48] "Il n'est pas permis de le rechercher. *Pourquoi* ? Parce qu'il n'a pas plu à Dieu de nous le révéler" (*Catéchisme des fêtes*, in *Œuvres complètes*, ed. Lachat, vol. V, 139–205, p. 173).

[49] "Ils ne se connaissent pas eux-mêmes, ils ne savent pas comment sont faites les plus petites choses, une mouche, une fourmi, un épi de blé ; et ils veulent pénétrer les secrets de Dieu" (*Catéchisme de Meaux*, p. 78).

[50] "[. . .] l'effroyable tempête [qui] s'est excitée en nos jours, touchant la grâce et le libre arbitre" (*Oraison funèbre de Nicolas Cornet*, in *Œuvres*, p. 48).

[51] "[. . .] il y avait à craindre qu'on ne fût jeté insensiblement dans des conséquences ruineuses à la liberté de l'homme" (*Oraison funèbre de Nicolas Cornet*, in *Œuvres*, p. 49).

[52] "Cette doctrine céleste s'est trouvée *nécessairement* enveloppée parmi des difficultés impénétrables" (*Oraison funèbre de Nicolas Cornet*, in *Œuvres*, p. 49, my emphases).

[53] "[. . .] la fureur de disputer des choses divines" (*Oraison funèbre de Henriette-Marie de France*, in *Œuvres*, p. 67).

understanding is constrained"[54]; and that those who go beyond are, in the words of the same Father, "excessive, insatiable, and carried away more ardently than they should be by matters of religion".[55]

If incuriosity is a common theme in the writings of the Bishop of Meaux, it is accompanied and vindicated by a further and yet more fundamental belief in divine providence. The two come together in his conviction that, although God's ordering of the world is absolute, nonetheless an element of mystery pertains, and that this is as true of the government of nations as of the destiny of individuals. The positing of God's ultimate desire to save his chosen people is as far as Bossuet ever penetrates into the mysteries of divine providence; and if grace is always at work, its operations in the end remain hidden. There is thus a myopic perception of disorder in the world, which constitutes the principal thrust of both of his *Sermons on Providence*. But it is in the later (1662) one that he explicitly underlines how "almost all ages have complained of seeing iniquity triumph and innocence afflicted",[56] with no means of discerning in an immanent perspective the existence of any underlying order or meaning; and notes how this fact will in turn run the risk of being interpreted as denoting the absence of any omnipotent God. On the other hand, seen in the correct perspective, "every inequality will be rectified, and you will see nothing but wisdom where you only expected disorder".[57] It is in this perspective that the Christian may make sense of (apparent) good and evil being distributed to the (apparently) just and unjust, and only with his sights on eternity that equilibrium may be kept, and that Bossuet may conclude that: "Such are the holy thoughts which a faith in Providence will inspire."[58]

It is, unsurprisingly, in the *Funeral Orations* that the primacy of the divine plan becomes a recurrent motif, confidently asserted now with particular regard to the salvation of each individual, and effecting in the process that translation to the transcendent perspective which is the hallmark of his preaching. In this respect, the sub-genre becomes for him, in Velat's phrase,

[54] "La première partie d'un homme qui étudie les vérités saintes, c'est de savoir discerner les endroits où il est permis de s'étendre, et où il faut s'arrêter tout court, et se souvenir des bornes étroites où est resserrée notre intelligence" (*Oraison funèbre de Nicolas Cornet*, in *Œuvres*, p. 50).

[55] "[Il] les appelle excessifs, insatiables, et portés plus ardemment qu'il ne faut aux choses de la religion" (*Oraison funèbre de Nicolas Cornet*, in *Œuvres*, p. 49). In the words of an anonymous nineteenth-century translator of Pascal, such problems are the predilection of "those who are more intent on prying into that which is secret, than on regarding that which is revealed" (*The Provincial Letters of Blaise Pascal with a Biographical Preface*, London, Griffith, Fanon, Oakenden and Welsh (The Ancient and Modern Library of Theological Literature), 1889).

[56] "[. . .] presque tous les siècles se sont plaints d'avoir vu l'iniquité triomphante et l'innocence affligée" (*Sermon sur la providence* in *Œuvres*, p. 1062).

[57] "[. . .] toutes les inégalités se rectifieront, et vous ne verrez que sagesse où vous n'imaginiez que désordre" (*Œuvres*, p. 1062).

[58] "Telles sont les saintes pensées qu'inspire la foi en la Providence" (*Œuvres*, p. 1071).

"a sermon whose idea is Death[,] [for] which the deceased Christian will only serve as the opportunity and the pretext".[59]

At the end of the last piece, that of the soldier and nobleman, the Prince de Condé, remarkable for its action-packed narrative of the battlefield, it is nonetheless the moment of death which affords the most precisely Christian tonality, since it is here that the whole preceding encomium is placed into an apocalyptic perspective, as Bossuet predicts: "Histories will be abolished alongside empires, and no more mention will be made of all these dazzling feats with which they are filled."[60] It is as if the sheer magnificence of the subject matter requires the Christian corrective, whereby the massive military achievements of the dead soldier are compared unfavourably to "a glass of water offered in [Christ's] name".[61] It is as Bossuet recalls the moment of Condé's pious death, therefore, that he offers the greatest paradox of all, apostrophizing his subject and recalling his greatest victories, only to conclude that "it is there that I will see you more triumphant than at Fribourg or at Rocroy".[62]

There is nothing vague, impersonal, or theoretical about Bossuet's writing on death, however, since it is the direct concomitant of writing about deaths and about the dead.[63] The individuals who are being mourned are the *raison d'être* for the orations; their deaths are depicted with as much variety and detail as was contained in their frequently eventful lives, and indeed afford (or are induced to afford) a variety of illustrations of Christian gifts and shortcomings. The evocation of the moment of death is rather exploited as a didactic opportunity, in which context Bayley writes of "that sense of the immediacy of death which precedes, in the meditative scheme, the resolution to amend one's life".[64]

If his subjects are as a result accorded some kind of quasi-allegorical status, it is not least because of the exceptional positions at the court of Louis XIV

[59] "[. . .] un sermon dont l'idée est la Mort et dont le chrétien disparu ne sera que l'occasion et le prétexte" (*Œuvres*, p. 4).

[60] "[. . .] les histoires seront abolies avec les empires, et il ne se parlera plus de tous ces faits éclatants dont elles sont pleines" (*Oraison funèbre de Louis de Bourbon*, p. 210).

[61] "[. . .] un verre d'eau donné en son nom" (*Oraison funèbre de Louis de Bourbon*, p. 217).

[62] "C'est là que je vous verrai plus triomphant qu'à Fribourg ou à Rocroy" (*Oraison funèbre de Louis de Bourbon*, p. 217).

[63] See Cécile Joulin, *La Mort dans les 'Œuvres oratoires' de Bossuet*, Saint-Étienne, Publications de l'Université de Saint-Étienne, 2002.

[64] *French Pulpit Oratory*, p. 136. Émile Vaucheret too comments of Bossuet's grim images of death: "This is only one panel of a diptych, of which the other represents the glorious image that is promised us provided that we are able to follow the salutary counsels of Christian doctrine" ["Il ne s'agit là que d'un volet du diptyque, l'autre représentant l'image glorieuse qui nous est promise à condition que nous sachions suivre les salutaires conseils de la doctrine chrétienne"] ("'L'honneur du monde': usurpation de la gloire de Dieu dans les œuvres oratoires de Bossuet", in *Bossuet: la prédication au XVIIe siècle*, ed. Thérèse Goyet and Jean-Pierre Collinet, Paris, Nizet, 1980, 217–43, p. 233).

which in many cases they occupied. Yet Bossuet treats rank in the same way that he treats earthly achievement, convinced in the divine perspective that humankind will be divided not into princes and paupers, but into the saved and the damned.[65] As Vaucheret points out, "the eulogies which Bossuet accords to the nobility are capable of being restrained [when necessary], and he never fails to situate their human greatness beneath the gaze of God".[66]

A conditional recognition is nonetheless accorded to their exceptional status in such rhetorical sequences as "*if* something could raise men above their natural infirmity; *if* our common origin tolerated some solid and enduring distinction between those whom God has formed from the same earth, what *would be* more elevated in the whole universe than the princess of whom I speak?"[67] God permits rank, and it is within the confines of birth and station that salvation is worked out. As Krumenacker remarks, "an egalitarian society in the period is impossible to imagine. Original equality was abolished by the first sin; since then, the only way in which humankind can keep order and grow closer to God is by means of a strict hierarchy".[68] And yet rank, like language or any other human given, is in the last analysis neutral, and only becomes a quality when it is properly used.[69] In the interim, however, both rank and language may serve the Catholic faith; and Bossuet's funerary oratory is a unique monument to that service.

Nor are these, despite their often dramatic quality, simply stage deaths, and Bossuet evokes the gradual loss of consciousness as well as the climactic

[65] Indeed a further paradox within Christian writing of the period lies in the insistence by Bossuet on the social obligations of the ruling monarch, as implicitly conveyed by the 1659 *Sermon sur l'éminente dignité des pauvres* [*Sermon on the Outstanding Dignity of the Poor*]. See on this question Cuche, *Une pensée sociale chrétienne.*

[66] "[. . .] les éloges qu'il décerne aux grands savent être mesurés, et ne cesse jamais de placer leur grandeur humaine sous le regard de Dieu" ("L'honneur du monde", p. 234).

[67] "[. . .] *si* quelque chose pouvait élever les hommes au-dessus de leur infirmité naturelle; *si* l'origine qui nous est commune nous souffrait quelque solide et durable distinction entre ceux que Dieu a formés de la même terre, qu'y *aurait*-il dans l'univers de plus distingué que la princesse dont je parle ?" (*Oraison funèbre de Henriette-Anne d'Angleterre*, p. 85, my emphases). Truchet points out of the earlier series that "there is no place to minimize the often *ad hominem* dimension to the sermons preached in the Louvre" ["il n'y a pas à minimiser le côté souvent *ad hominem* de ces sermons du Louvre"] (*Sermons*, p. 23).

[68] "Une société égalitaire est à l'époque impossible à penser. L'égalité originelle a été abolie par le premier péché ; depuis, l'humanité ne peut plus trouver d'ordre et se rapprocher de Dieu qu'au moyen d'une stricte hiérarchie" (*École française*, p. 74).

[69] Pascal was also to propose this in his *First Discourse on the Condition of Nobles* [*Premier discours sur la condition des grands*] in L 366–7. More pithily in the *Pensées* we read: "Sudden death alone to be feared, and that is why confessors are in residence in noble houses" ["Mort soudaine seule à craindre, et c'est pourquoi les confesseurs demeurent chez les Grands"] (*Pensées*, L 984, S 781). On broader political matters in both writers, see Jacques Truchet, *Politique de Bossuet*, Paris, Klincksieck, 1966 or, more succinctly, Thérèse Goyet, "D'une politique de la foi : la théorie et l'expérience de Bossuet", in *Bossuet: la prédication au XVIIe siècle*, ed. Thérèse Goyet and Jean-Pierre Collinet, Paris, Nizet, 1980, 19–31. On Pascal, see Gerard Ferreyrolles, *Pascal et la raison du politique*, Paris, Presses universitaires de France, 1984.

farewell, or what he calls "the fatal moment of an imperceptible decline".[70] Even so, he does not hesitate, in evoking the death of the Prince de Condé, to depict his son's grief in all its theatrical detail: "What colours would be bright enough to convey to you at once the constancy of the father and the extreme grief of the son? First with his face in tears, with more sobs than words, now with his mouth fixed to these once victorious and now enfeebled hands, now throwing himself into the paternal arms and onto the paternal breast, he seems, by such efforts, to want to detain this beloved object of his respect and his tenderness".[71] Yet the nature of the exercise uniquely ensures that the personal drama of the particular leads back to a dogmatic conclusion which is universal: "I want", Bossuet writes, "[. . .] in a single death to demonstrate the death and the nothingness of all human greatness".[72] It is in part for this reason too that we might be tempted, when reading the *Funeral orations*, to feel that Bossuet takes on the quality of an omniscient and indeed immortal commentator on the transitory lives of the men and women who are the dedicatees of his oratory.

Yet that impression is above all conveyed because Bossuet does not see events in the context of the duration of the life of one man or woman, but rather in the context of the divine plan, from a perspective which not only reduces human achievements to insignificance (in divine terms), but goes further, and reduces to insignificance the very criteria by which they might be deemed to have meaning. As he writes in the 1662 *Sermon on Providence*: "Let us leave the Eternal one to act according to the laws of his eternity and, far from reducing him to our scale, let us try rather to enter into his vastness."[73] Sellier offers an architectural image which is particularly appropriate to these grandiose pieces of writing: "You must make your way into the work of Bossuet as you do into the vaults of a cathedral", he writes. "Although you feel a little disoriented, so much splendour leaves you speechless. [. . .] His great funeral orations are born in cathedrals: they share their somewhat distant qualities of majesty and magnificence."[74]

[70] "[. . .] le fatal moment d'un insensible déclin"—an alexandrine, incidentally (*Oraison funèbre de Michel Le Tellier*, p. 171).

[71] "Quelles couleurs assez vives pourraient vous représenter et la constance du père et les extrêmes douleurs du fils ? D'abord le visage en pleurs, avec plus de sanglots que de paroles, tantôt la bouche collée sur ces mains victorieuses et maintenant défaillantes, tantôt se jetant entre ces bras et dans ce sein paternel, il semble, par tant d'efforts, vouloir retenir ce cher objet de ses respects et de ses tendresses" (*Oraison funèbre de Louis de Bourbon*, in *Œuvres*, p. 214).

[72] "Je veux [. . .] dans une seule mort faire voir la mort et le néant de toutes les grandeurs humaines" (*Oraison funèbre de Henriette-Anne d'Angleterre*, p. 84).

[73] "Laissons agir l'Éternel suivant les lois de son éternité, et, bien loin de la réduire à notre mesure, tâchons d'entrer plutôt dans son étendue" (*Sermon sur la providence*, in *Œuvres*, p. 1064).

[74] "Il faut entrer dans l'œuvre de Bossuet comme dans les voûtes d'une cathédrale. Bien qu'on s'y sente un peu étranger, tant de grandeur frappe d'étonnement [. . .]. Ses grandes oraisons funèbres sont nées dans les cathédrales : elles en ont la majesté et la magnificence un peu

There is thus no room for doubt, in this scheme of things, that God will, sooner or later, intervene and put an end to disorder and irreligion, as to rank and rhetoric, but there is no knowing the time. Bossuet affords thereby one mode of resolution to the coexistence between incuriosity and faith, and he does so essentially, as a prelate who has become a byword for orthodoxy, by a radical restatement of fundamentals.[75] The subject matter of the *Funeral Orations* places an inevitable emphasis on death, but it is an emphasis which does no more than reinforce the perspective from which Bossuet sees, and from which he would seek to persuade others to see, life, death, past, present, and future, that of eternity. That death begins each oration, and that providence ends it, is just one way of coming full circle; wherever we had started, the principles would have been the same, for it is only the end of human time which brings humankind face to face with eternity, only the recognition of annihilation which leads to a reality that transcends it, only the demise of human rank and language which leads to a new order of things.

Bossuet's teaching holds few if any surprises; there is none of the human realism of St François de Sales, none of the dramatic challenges of Pascal, and none of the world-denying mysticism of Fénelon or of Madame Guyon. He says exactly what we would expect him to say; and he advances the party line. Where he does give us an important understanding of Catholic Christianity is in his overall teleology.[76] He combines what seems an almost God-like assurance of what, in the course of universal history no less than of individual salvation, everything is all about with a deep humility, and with an acknowledgement of the impenetrability of God's will. He knows that all will be achieved to the greater glory of God in the fullness of time; but he does not know how, when, or why, and he does not seek to. The job of the believer meanwhile, to go right back to the basics of the *Meaux Catechism*, is to "profit from what one understands, believe or worship what one does not understand, and submit oneself in all matters to the judgement of the Church".[77]

lointaines" (Bossuet, *Oraisons funèbres*, ed. Philippe Sellier, Paris, Larousse (Nouveaux Classiques Larousse), 1967, p. 13).

[75] Truchet remarks: "[He is] a theologian by temperament more than a *moraliste* or a psychologist. It is by the vigour and cohesion of his doctrinal constructions that he reaches his hearers" ["[Il est] théologien de tempérament plus que moraliste ou psychologue. C'est par la vigueur et la cohésion de ses constructions doctrinales qu'il atteint ses auditeurs"] (*Sermons*, p. 26).

[76] As Truchet resumes it: "Everything for him radiates around doctrine, around the revealed truth" ["Tout, chez lui, rayonne autour de la doctrine, de la vérité révélée"] (*Prédication*, p. 54).

[77] "Profiter de ce qu'on entend, croire ou adorer ce qu'on n'entend pas, et se soumettre en tout au jugement de l'Église" (*Catéchisme de Meaux*, p. 80).

Conclusion

I proposed at the outset that my enquiry would seek to provoke a kind of constructive defamiliarization. I have tried to show the many ways in which the French texts of the seventeenth century that I have explored serve both to illustrate and to revitalize, within a Catholic understanding, the objective and material specificity of the Christian Incarnation; and, in so doing, to demonstrate in how many ways, in Pascal's phrase, "Christianity is strange" ["le christianisme est étrange"].

Three related features of Christian dogma have predominantly emerged as a result: specificity, paradox, and inclusivity. The historical givenness of the Incarnation, its detail, its improbability, and its physicality must be the starting point for any re-examination of its particularity. The paradoxical nature of much of the theology which stems from it then stretches human language to its limits, and beyond, in the process of articulating the corpus of dogmatic belief; and perhaps indeed the greatest challenge which this corpus of dogma affords lies in the incorporation of apparently incompatible doctrines into a formulation of orthodoxy. At one level, as the writers I have considered would concur, such a codification was achieved once and for all by Scripture, and by the creeds and councils of the early Church; but the enduring coexistence of such apparently divergent truths is still capable of leading, in later times, to the linguistic exploitation of, and indeed delight in, such bewildering oxymora of Christian dogma as the triune Godhead, the crucified King or the *felix culpa*, to say nothing of predestined freedom. It is nonetheless such a coexistence which defines orthodoxy and identifies heresy, because, to bring my three terms together, it is orthodoxy which renders the paradoxical specifics inclusive.

This inclusivity of orthodoxy has in turn allowed me to open out these paradoxes, and to show how the potential for optimism and pessimism, activity and passivity, obedience and inspiration, enthusiasm and moderation, or accommodation and rigorism is already present in Christian dogma. It has tended to be the issues which have divided the writers in question that have above all been the subject of historians of ideas. But the specificity of Christianity is strange and fertile enough for the common ground as well to need to be consistently evaluated, or perhaps in this case re-evaluated; and contrasts between the theological emphases of different writers, whilst to some degree chronological, is in other respects no more than a reflection of that enduring potential. Yet we have also seen how, if any of this tenuous inclusivity is threatened, the strangeness of coexistence turns rapidly into the scandal of division.

I have insisted a lot therefore both on what divides and what unites the writers and the texts I have considered; and I have tried to suggest that the flexibility available within a fixed and immutable corpus of dogma is circumscribed by its historical givenness. Perhaps Voltaire was right, and that the combination of (progressive) temporal distance, and of the precision of scriptural evidence, accords to the record of any revelation, in whatever tradition, the capacity to divide rather than unite its adherents; and, in the case of Catholic Christianity, to place it at odds with other Christian traditions, with the other Abrahamic religions, and with those who share none of the common material of those belief systems.

I have looked as well at a whole gamut of linguistic expressions of Christian doctrine, experience, advice, and conjecture, ranging from apologies and catechisms through manuals of devotion and sermons to autobiographies and polemics and, in the more strictly literary domain, to martyr tragedies and lyric poetry. In all these discourses, however, the primacy of God's plan is explored: the Old Testament predicts, and the New Testament enacts that prediction; thereafter, in Christian time, the Saints exemplify and the liturgy actualizes; and, finally, the imperative continues of the progressive and accretive sanctification of humankind, in accordance with God's will, as the common fulfilment is awaited at the end of time.

In the mean time, we might disingenuously ask three fundamental and interlinked questions. What is Christian belief? How do we acquire it? How do we behave once we have acquired it? And one answer to those questions might be provided by quoting for the last time from the magisterial *summa* of St François de Sales, the *Treatise on the Love of God*, which provides the simplest and yet most global definition of Christian doctrine and its ramifications which I have encountered in the period: "Christian doctrine", François writes,

> proposes clearly to us the truths which God wants us to believe, the good which he wants us to hope for, the punishments which he wants us to fear, the things which he wants us to love, the commandments which he wants us to obey and the desires which he wants us to follow: all that together is called the signified will of God.[1]

[1] "La doctrine chrétienne nous propose clairement les vérités que Dieu veut que nous croyions, les biens qu'il veut que nous espérions, les peines qu'il veut que nous craignions, ce qu'il veut que nous aimions, les commandements qu'il veut que nous fassions et les conseils qu'il désire que nous suivions : et tout cela s'appelle la volonté signifiée de Dieu" (*Traité de l'amour de Dieu*, p. 718).

Perhaps, at least in the hands of St François de Sales, Christianity isn't so strange after all.

But if we might be tempted as a result to conclude that such an assimilation of Christianity into certainty and into common sense is, at one level, reassuring, it is in other ways fatal to its impact. This is where, once again, the rhetorical objectivity of Pascal is so vitally challenging and so strikingly modern; where the manifestations of linguistic complexity, whether they are stylistically conscious or simply the outpourings of a troubled soul, ring true; and where the conflicts within both individual and sectarian witness force the believer into frequently anguished self-examination. The difficulty of bringing Christian doctrine into focus must always reside in the degree to which it is possible to introduce an element of objectivity into the manner of the adherent's assent to a series of credal tenets, which both work against and make sense of human experience. It is thus only through the disquieting prism of Pascal, through the linguistic aphasia of mystics and poets, or through the agonizing tensions between inspiration and authority of our visionary autobiographers, that the overarching belief in providence of Bossuet or the pragmatic humanism of St François de Sales may strike their note of reassurance. And that in turn, at least within the terms of reference of this corpus of writing, is because it is only through the unlikely act of divine solidarity that is the Incarnation that human life may acquire any meaning; and only through the despair of the Crucifixion that the Resurrection may in turn carry its full transformative potential.

Bibliography

PRIMARY TEXTS

Alacoque, St Margaret-Mary, *Vie de la bienheureuse Marguerite-Marie Alacoque écrite par elle-même*, in *Vie et œuvres*, ed. François-Léon Gauthey, Paris, Ancienne librairie Poussielgue, 1915, vol. II, 29–118.

Arnauld, Antoine, *De la fréquente communion, où les sentiments des Pères, des Papes et des Conciles touchant l'usage des sacrements de Pénitence et d'Eucharistie sont fidèlement exposés*, Paris, A. Vitré, 1643.

——and Nicole, Pierre, *La Logique ou l'art de penser*, ed. Pierre Claire and François Girbal, Paris, Presses universitaires de France, 1965.

Bauny, Étienne, SJ, *La Somme des péchés qui se commettent en tous états*, Cologne, [no pub.], 1633.

Bérulle, Pierre, *Discours de l'état et des grandeurs de Jésus*, in *Œuvres complètes*, vol. VII, ed. M. Join-Lambert and R. Lescot, Paris, Éditions du Cerf, 1996.

Bonnefons, Amable, *Les Vies des saints*, Paris, Sébastien Piquet, 1649–50.

Bossuet, Jacques-Bénigne, *Maximes et réflexions sur la comédie*, in *L'Église et le théâtre*, ed. C. Urbain and E. Levesque, Paris, Bernard Grasset, 1930, 169–276.

——*Œuvres*, ed. Abbé B. Velat and Yvonne Champailler, Paris, Gallimard (Pléiade), 1961.

——*Œuvres complètes*, ed. F. Lachat, Paris, Louis Vivès, 1875.

——*Oraisons funèbres*, ed. Jacques Truchet, Paris, Garnier Frères (Classiques Garnier), 1961.

——*Oraisons funèbres*, ed. Philippe Sellier, Paris, Larousse (Nouveaux Classiques Larousse), 1967.

——*Sermons* (*Le Carême du Louvre, 1662*), ed. Constance Cagnat-Debœuf, Paris, Gallimard (Folio classique), 2001.

——*Sermon sur la mort et autres sermons*, ed. Jacques Truchet, Paris, Garnier-Flammarion, 1970.

Bourignon, Antoinette, *La Vie de Damoiselle Antoinette Bourignon écrite par elle-même*, in *Œuvres*, vol. I, Amsterdam, R. and G. Wetstein, 1717.

Brive, Martial de, *Œuvres poétiques et saintes*, ed. Anne Mantero, Grenoble, Éditions Jérôme Millon, 2000.

Camus, Albert, *Le mythe de Sisyphe*, in *Œuvres complètes*, ed. Jacqueline Lévi-Valensi, vol. I, Paris, Gallimard (Pléiade), 2006, 217–304.

Corneille, Pierre, *Œuvres complètes*, ed. André Stegmann, Paris, Éditions du Seuil (L'Intégrale), 1963.

——*Défense de la vérité catholique touchant les miracles* [. . .] *par le sieur de Sainte-Foy*, Paris, 1656.

Descartes, René, *Œuvres et Lettres*, ed. André Bridoux, Paris, Gallimard (Pléiade), 1953.

Fénelon, François de Salignac de la Motte-, *Œuvres*, vol. I, ed. Jacques Le Brun, Paris, Gallimard (Pléiade), 1983.

Gide, André, *Les Faux-Monnayeurs*, in *Romans*, ed. Jean-Jacques Thierry, Gallimard (Pléiade), Paris, 1958, 931–1248.

Guyon, Jeanne-Marie Bouvier de La Mothe, Mme, *Moyen court et autres écrits spirituels*, ed. M.-L. Gondal, Grenoble, Éditions Jérôme Millon, 1995.

——*Récits de captivité*, ed. Marie-Louise Gondal, Grenoble, Éditions Jérôme Millon, 1992.

——*Les Torrents, et Commentaire du Cantique des Cantiques de Salomon*, ed. Claude Morali, Grenoble, Éditions Jérôme Millon, 1992.

——*La Vie de Madame Guyon écrite par elle-même*, ed. B. Sahler, Paris, Dervy-Livres (L'Arbre de Vie), 1983.

——*La Vie par elle-même et autres écrits biographiques*, ed. Dominique Tronc, Paris, Champion, 2001.

Hopil, Claude, *Les Divins Élancements de l'amour exprimés en cent cantiques faits en l'honneur de la Très-Sainte Trinité*, ed. Jacqueline Plantié, Paris, Champion, 1999.

Jeanne des Anges, Sister, *Autobiographie* [*Relation*], ed. G. Legué and G. de la Tourette, Grenoble, Éditions Jérôme Millon, 1990.

La Bruyère, Jean de, *Les Caractères, ou les Mœurs de ce siècle*, ed. Marc Escola, Paris, Champion, 1999.

——and Du Pin, Louis-Ellies, *Dialogues posthumes sur le quiétisme*, in *Œuvres complètes*, ed. G. Servois, Paris, Hachette (Les Grands Écrivains de la France), 1878–1912, vol. II, 527–710.

——*Dialogues posthumes sur le quiétisme*, ed. Richard Parish, Grenoble, Éditions Jérôme Millon, 2005.

La Ceppède, Jean de, *Les Théorèmes sur le Sacré Mystère de notre Rédemption*, ed. Jacqueline Plantié, Paris, Champion, 1996.

La Rochefoucauld, Duc de, *Maximes*, ed. Jacques Truchet, Paris, Librairie Garnier (Classiques Garnier), 1967.

Loyola, St Ignatius, *Personal Writings*, trans. Joseph A. Munitiz and Philip Endean, London, Penguin Classics, 1996.

Meynier, Bernard, SJ, *Port-Royal et Genève d'intelligence contre le Très-Saint Sacrement de l'Autel*, Poitiers, J. Fleuriau, 1656.

Molière, Jean-Baptiste Poquelin, known as, *Œuvres complètes*, ed. Georges Forestier, Gallimard (Pléiade), 2010.

——*Le Tartuffe*, ed. Richard Parish, Bristol, Classical Press, 1994.

Molinos, Miguel de, *La Guide* [*sic*] *spirituelle*, Amsterdam, Arles, 1688.

Pascal, Blaise, *Entretien avec Sacy sur la philosophie*, ed. Richard Scholar, Actes Sud (Les Philosophiques), 2003.

——*Lettres provinciales*, ed. Michel Le Guern, Paris, Gallimard (Folio), 1987.

——*Œuvres complètes*, ed. L. Lafuma, Paris, Éditions du Seuil (L'Intégrale), 1963.

——*Pensées*, trans. A. J. Krailsheimer, London, Penguin Classics, 1960.

——*Les Provinciales, Pensées, et opuscules divers*, ed. Philippe Sellier and Gérard Ferreyrolles, Paris, Livre de Poche / Classiques Garnier (Pochothèque), 2004.

——*The Provincial Letters*, trans. A. J. Krailsheimer, London, Penguin Classics, 1967.

——*The Provincial Letters of Blaise Pascal with a Biographical Preface*, London, Griffith, Fanon, Oakenden and Welsh, 1889.

Racine, Jean, *Esther* and *Athalie*, in *Œuvres*, vol. I, ed. Georges Forestier, Paris, Gallimard (Pléiade), 1999.

Ribadeneyra, P. de, *Les Fleurs des vies des saints*, Rouen, J. de La Mare, 1645–6.

Rotrou, Jean, *Le Véritable Saint Genest*, ed. José Sanchez, Le-Mont-du-Marsan, Éditions José Feijóo, 1991.

Sales, St François de, *Œuvres*, ed. André Ravier and Roger Devos, Paris, Gallimard (Pléiade), 1969.

Surin, Jean-Joseph, Father, *Lettres spirituelles*, ed. L. Michel and F. Cavallers, Toulouse, Éditions de la *Revue d'ascétique et de mystique*, 1928.

——*Triomphe de l'amour divin sur les puissances de l'Enfer* and *Science expérimentale des choses de l'autre vie*, ed. Jacques Prunair, Grenoble, Éditions Jérôme Millon, 1990.

Valéry, Paul, "Variation sur une pensée", in *Œuvres*, vol. I, ed. Jean Hytier, Paris, Gallimard (Pléiade), 1957, 458–73.

Voltaire, François-Marie Arouet, known as, *Éloge et Pensées de Pascal*, ed. Richard Parish, *Œuvres complètes de Voltaire* (*OCV*), vol. 80A, Oxford, Voltaire Foundation, 2008.

——*Lettres philosophiques*, ed. Frédéric Deloffre, Paris, Gallimard (Folio classique), 1986.

——*Le Siècle de Louis XIV*, ed. René Groos, Paris, Librairie Garnier, 1947.

REFERENCE WORKS

Dictionnaire de l'Académie Française (1694), re-edn Lille, University of Lille, 1901.

Dictionnaire de Port-Royal, ed. Jean Lesaulnier and Antony McKenna, Paris, Champion, 2004.

Dictionnaire de spiritualité, ascétique et mystique, Paris, G. Beauchesne, 1937–95.

Dictionnaire de théologie catholique [*DTC*], Paris, Letouzey et Ané, 1909–46.

New Catholic Encyclopaedia, McGraw-Hill, New York, 1967.

Oxford Companion to Literature in French [*OCLF*], ed. Peter France, Oxford, Clarendon Press, 1995.

Oxford Dictionary of the Christian Church [*ODCC*], ed. F. Cross and E. Livingstone, 3rd edn, Oxford, Oxford University Press, 1997.

Sacramentum Mundi, London, Burns and Oates, 1968–70.

SECONDARY TEXTS

Angers, Julien-Eymard, d', *L'Humanisme chrétien au XVIIe siècle: François de Sales et Yves de Paris*, The Hague, Martinus Nijhoff, 1970.

Armogathe, Jean-Robert (ed.), *Le Grand Siècle et la Bible*, Paris, Beauchesne, 1989.

——*Le Quiétisme*, Paris, Presses universitaires de France, 1973.

Baird, A. W. S., *Studies in Pascal's Ethics*, The Hague, Martinus Nijhoff, 1975.

Bayley, Peter, *French Pulpit Oratory 1598–1650*, Cambridge, Cambridge University Press, 1980.

——"Le raffinement et l'ellipse dans le style oratoire de Bossuet", in *Bossuet: la prédication au XVIIe siècle*, ed. Thérèse Goyet and Jean-Pierre Collinet, Paris, Nizet, 1980, 311–28.

Belin, Christian, *La Conversation intérieure: la méditation en France au XVIIe siècle*, Paris, Champion, 2002.

——(ed.), *La Méditation au XVIIe siècle: rhétorique, art, spiritualité*, Paris, Champion, 2006.

Bénichou, Paul, *Morales du grand siècle*, Paris, Gallimard, 1948.

Boisson, Didier, *Consciences en liberté? Itinéraires d'ecclésiastiques convertis au protestantisme (1671–1760)*, Paris, Champion, 2009.

Bowman, Frank, "Suffering, madness and literary creation", *French Forum*, I, 1, 1976, 24–48.

Bremond, Henri, *Histoire littéraire du sentiment religieux en France*, new expanded edn, Grenoble, Jérôme Millon, 2006.

Briggs, Robin, *Communities of Belief: Cultural and Social Tensions in Early-Modern France*, Oxford, Clarendon Press, 1989.

Brockliss, Lawrence, *French Higher Education in the 17th and 18th Centuries: A Cultural History*, Oxford, Clarendon Press, 1987.

Busson, Henri, *La Religion des classiques*, Paris, Presses universitaires de France, 1948.

Calvet, Jean, *Bossuet*, Paris, Hatier (Connaissance des Lettres), 1968.

——*La littérature religieuse de François de Sales à Fénelon*, Paris, del Duca, 1956.

Canons and Decrees of the Council of Trent (1545–1563), trans. and ed. H. Schroeder, St Louis, B. Herder, 1941.

Carraud, Vincent, *Pascal et la philosophie*, Paris, Presses universitaires de France, 1992.

Cave, Terence C., *Devotional Poetry in France, c. 1570–1613*, Cambridge, Cambridge University Press, 1969.

Certeau, Michel de, *La Possession de Loudun*, Paris, Gallimard, 1990.

Chadwick, Henry, *The Early Christian Church*, London, Penguin, 1967, 2nd edn 1993.

Chadwick, Owen, *The Reformation*, London, Penguin, 1964, 2nd edn 1968.

Chédozeau, Bernard, "Les grandes étapes de la publication de la Bible catholique en français du Concile de Trente au XVIIe siècle", in *Le Grand Siècle et la Bible*, ed. Jean-Robert Armogathe, Paris, Beauchesne, 1989, 341–60.

——*La Bible et la liturgie en français: l'église tridentine et les traductions bibliques et liturgiques (1600–1789)*, Paris, Éditions du Cerf, 1990.

Chilton, P. A., *The Poetry of Jean de La Ceppède*, Oxford, Oxford University Press, 1977.

Cognet, Louis, *Crépuscule des mystiques*, Tournai, Desclée de Brouwer, 1958.

——*Le Jansénisme*, Paris, Presses universitaires de France (Que sais-je?), 1964.

——*Les Origines de la spiritualité française au XVIIe siècle*, Paris, La Colomba, 1949.

Courcelle, Pierre, *L'Entretien de Pascal et Sacy. Ses sources et ses énigmes*, Paris, Vrin, 1960.

Cragg, G. R., *The Church and the Age of Reason, 1648–1789*, London, Penguin, 1960, 2nd edn 1966.

Cuche, François-Xavier, *Une pensée sociale chrétienne*, Paris, Éditions du Cerf, 1991.

Davidson, H., *The Origins of Certainty: Means and Meanings in Pascal's 'Pensées'*, Chicago, University of Chicago Press, 1979.
——and Dubé, P. H., *A Concordance to Pascal's 'Pensées'*, Ithaca, NY, and London, Cornell University Press, 1975.
Davies, J. H., *Fénelon*, Boston, MA, Twayne Publishers, 1979.
Descotes, Dominique, *L'Argumentation chez Pascal*, Paris, Presses universitaires de France (Écrivains), 1993.
——, McKenna, Antony, and Thirouin, Laurent (ed.), *Le Rayonnement de Port-Royal*, Paris, Champion, 2001.
Dhôtel, J.-C., *Les Origines du catéchisme moderne*, Paris, P. Aubier, 1967.
Dubu, Jean, *Les Églises chrétiennes et le théâtre (1550–1850)*, Grenoble, Presses universitaires de Grenoble, 1977.
——"Racine et la Bible", in *Le Grand Siècle et la Bible*, ed. Jean-Robert Armogathe, Paris, Beauchesne, 1989, 721–34.
Duchêne, Roger, *L'Imposture littéraire dans les 'Lettres provinciales' de Pascal*, Aix-en-Provence, Publications de l'Université, 1985.
Ernst, Pol, *Les 'Pensées' de Pascal: géologie et stratigraphie*, Paris, Universitas and Oxford, Voltaire Foundation, 1996.
Fayard, J., "Les structures de la phrase oratoire et la résolution des tensions chez Bossuet", in *Bossuet: la prédication au XVIIe siècle*, ed. Thérèse Goyet and Jean-Pierre Collinet, Paris, Nizet, 1980, 291–310.
Ferreyrolles, Gérard, *Blaise Pascal: 'Les Provinciales'*, Paris, Presses universitaires de France, 1984.
——*Pascal ou la raison du politique*, Paris, Presses universitaires de France, 1984.
Force, Pierre, *Le Problème herméneutique chez Pascal*, Paris, Vrin, 1989.
France, Peter, *Rhetoric and Truth in France*, Oxford, Clarendon Press, 1972.
Garapon, Robert, *Les 'Caractères' de La Bruyère*, Paris, SEDES, 1978.
Gheeraert, Tony, *Le Chant de la grâce: Port-Royal et la poésie d'Arnauld d'Andilly à Racine*, Paris, Champion, 2003.
Goldmann, Lucien, *Le Dieu caché*, Paris, Gallimard, 1959.
Gondal, Marie-Louise, *Madame Guyon, un autre visage*, Paris, Beauchesne, 1989.
Gounelle, André, "Calvinisme et jansénisme: les grandes structures doctrinales", in *Port-Royal et les protestants*, Paris, Bibliothèque Mazarine, 1998, 9–19.
Goyet, Thérèse, *L'Humanisme de Bossuet*, Paris, Klincksieck, 1965.
——"D'une politique de la foi : la théorie et l'expérience de Bossuet", in *Bossuet: la prédication au XVIIe siècle*, ed. Thérèse Goyet and Jean-Pierre Collinet, Paris, Nizet, 1980, 19–31.
——and Collinet, Jean-Pierre, *Bossuet: la prédication au XVIIe siècle*, Paris, Nizet, 1980.
Hammond, Nicholas, *Playing with Truth: Language and the Human Condition in Pascal's 'Pensées'*, Oxford, Clarendon Press, 1994.
——(ed.), *The Cambridge Companion to Pascal*, Cambridge, Cambridge University Press, 2003.
Hawcroft, Michael, *Rhetoric: Readings in French Literature*, Oxford, Oxford University Press, 1999.
Huxley, Aldous, *The Devils of Loudun*, London, Chatto and Windus, 1952.
Jantzen, Grace, *Power, Gender and Christian Mysticism*, Cambridge, Cambridge University Press, 1995.

Jonsen, A., and Toulmin, S., *The Abuse of Casuistry: A History of Moral Reasoning*, Berkeley, University of California Press, 1988.

Joulin, Cécile, *La Mort dans les 'Œuvres oratoires' de Bossuet*, Saint-Étienne, Publications de l'Université de Saint-Étienne, 2002.

Kolakowski, Leszek, *Chrétiens sans Église: la conscience religieuse et le lien confessionnel au XVIIe siècle*, Paris, Gallimard, 1969.

——*God Owes Us Nothing: A Brief Remark on Pascal's Religion and on the Spirit of Jansenism*, Chicago, University of Chicago Press, 1995.

Knox, Ronald, *Enthusiasm: A Chapter in the History of Religion*, Oxford, Clarendon Press, 1950.

Krailsheimer, Alban, *Pascal*, Oxford, Oxford University Press (Past Masters), 1980.

Krumenacker, Yves, *L'École française de spiritualité*, Paris, Éditions du Cerf, 1998.

La Broise, René de, *Bossuet et la Bible*, Paris, Retaux-Bray, 1890.

Labrousse, Elisabeth, *Conscience et conviction: études sur le XVIIe siècle*, Oxford, Voltaire Foundation and Paris, Universitas, 1996.

Laude, Patrick D., *Approches du quiétisme, Papers on French Seventeenth Century Literature*, (Biblio 17), Paris, Seattle, Tünbingen 1991.

Le Brun, Jacques, *Histoire spirituelle de la France*, Paris, Beauchesne, 1964.

——*La Spiritualité de Bossuet*, Paris, Klincksieck, 1972.

Legros, Philippe, *François de Sales: une poétique de l'imaginaire*, Tübingen, Narr (Biblio-17), 2004.

Le Guern, Michel, *L'Image dans l'œuvre de Pascal*, Paris, Colin, 1969.

——and Le Guern, Marie-Rose, *Les 'Pensées' de Pascal, de l'anthropologie à la théologie*, Paris, Larousse (Thèmes et textes), 1972.

Lejeune, Philippe, *L'Autobiographie en France*, Paris, Colin, 1971.

——*Le Pacte autobiographique*, Paris, Seuil, 1975.

Lemaire, Henri, *Les Images chez François de Sales*, Paris, Nizet, 1962.

Lewis, C. S., *Miracles: A Preliminary Study*, London, Collins (Fount Paperbacks), 1960.

McCulloch, Diarmaid, *A History of Christianity*, Oxford, Oxford University Press, 2009.

McKenna, Antony, *De Pascal à Voltaire: le rôle des 'Pensées' de Pascal dans l'histoire des idées entre 1670 et 1734*, Oxford, Voltaire Foundation, 1990.

Maire, Catherine, *De la cause de Dieu à la cause de la nation: le jansénisme au XVIIIe siècle*, Paris, Gallimard, 1998.

Mallet-Joris, Françoise, *Jeanne Guyon*, Paris, Flammarion, 1978.

Mantero, Anne, "Récits bibliques et poésie religieuse en France", in *Le Grand Siècle et la Bible*, ed. Jean-Robert Armogathe, Paris, Beauchesne, 1989, 455–80.

Marin, Louis, "'Pascal': text, author, discourse . . . ", in *Yale French Studies*, 52, 1975, 129–51.

Melzer, Sara, *Discourses of the Fall*, Berkeley, University of California Press, 1986.

Mesnard, Jean, *Les 'Pensées' de Pascal*, Paris, SEDES, 1976.

Michel, Alain, "La grandeur et l'humilité: la Bible dans l'esthétique littéraire en France", in *Le Grand Siècle et la Bible*, ed. Jean-Robert Armogathe, Paris, Beauchesne, 1989, 425–54.

Miel, Jan, *Pascal and Theology*, Baltimore and London, Johns Hopkins University Press, 1969.

Mongrédien, Georges, *La Bruyère. Recueil des textes et des documents contemporains*, Paris, Éditions du CNRS, 1979.

Morel, Jean, *Rotrou, dramaturge de l'ambiguïté*, Paris, Colin, 1968.

Moriarty, Michael, *The Age of Suspicion*, Oxford, Oxford University Press, 2003.

——*Fallen Nature, Fallen Selves*, Oxford, Oxford University Press, 2006.

Murphy, Ruth, *Saint François de Sales et la civilité chrétienne*, Paris, Nizet, 1964.

Nelson, Robert J., *Pascal Adversary and Advocate*, Cambridge, MA, Harvard University Press, 1981.

Noll, Mark, *Confessions and Catechisms of the Reformation*, Leicester, Apollos, 1991.

Parish, Richard, "Automate et sacrement: figures de l'Incarnation", in *Religion et politique: les avatars de l'augustinisme*, Saint-Étienne, Université de Saint-Étienne, 1998, 333–9.

——"'C'est la foi qui se perd, et personne n'y pense': polémique et dogme chez Bossuet", in *Bulletin des Amis de Bossuet*, 31, 2004, 5–23.

——"Mais qui parle?: voice and persona in the *Pensées*", in *Seventeenth-Century French Studies*, 8, 1986, 23–40.

——*Pascal's 'Lettres provinciales': A Study in Polemic*, Oxford, Clarendon Press, 1989.

——"Le Père Étienne Bauny, SJ: *La Sommes de péchés qui se commettent en tous états* face aux *Lettres provinciales*", in *French Studies*, 63, 4, 385–98.

Pérouse, Marie, *L'Invention des 'Pensées' de Pascal: les éditions de Port-Royal (1670–1678)*, Paris, Champion, 2009.

Phillips, D. Z., "Mysticism and epistemology: one devil of a problem", in *Faith and Philosophy*, 12 (2), 1995, 167–88.

Phillips, Henry, *Church and Culture in Seventeenth-Century France*, Cambridge, Cambridge University Press, 1997.

——*The Theatre and Its Critics in Seventeenth-Century France*, Oxford, Oxford University Press, 1980.

Pike, Nelson, "On mystic visions as sources of knowledge", in *Mysticism and Philosophical Analysis*, ed. Steven T. Katz, New York, Oxford University Press, 1978, 214–34.

Pintard, René, *Le Libertinage érudit dans la première moitié du XVIIe siècle*, Paris, Boivin, 1943.

Pommier, René, "Jansénisme et noblesse de robe", in *Études sur le XVIIe siècle*, Paris, J. & S. Éditeur (Eurédit), 2006, 99–113.

Prigent, Michel, *Le Héros et l'État dans la tragédie de Pierre Corneille*, Paris, Quadrige / Presses universitaires de France, 1986.

Quantin, Jean-Louis, *Le Catholicisme classique et les pères de l'Église: un retour aux sources (1669–1713)*, Paris, Institut d'études augustiniennes, 1999.

——*Le Rigorisme chrétien*, Paris, Éditions du Cerf, 2001.

Ravier, André, "St François de Sales et la Bible", in *Le Grand Siècle et la Bible*, ed. Jean-Robert Armogathe, Paris, Beauchesne, 1989, 617–26.

Rex, Walter, *Pascal's 'Provincial Letters': An Introduction*, London, Hodder and Stoughton, 1977.

Rouillard, P., *Histoire de la pénitence des origines à nos jours*, Paris, Éditions du Cerf, 1996.

Sanson, Henri, *Saint Jean de la Croix entre Bossuet et Fénelon*, Paris, Presses universitaires de France, 1953.

Sayce, R. A., *The French Biblical Epic in the Seventeenth Century*, Oxford, Oxford University Press, 1955.

Scott, Paul, “Rotrou et la comédie de dévotion”, in *Littératures classiques*, 63, 2007, 85–96.

Sellier, Philippe, “La Bible de Pascal”, in *Le Grand Siècle et la Bible*, ed. Jean-Robert Armogathe, Paris, Beauchesne, 1989, 701–19.

——*Pascal et saint Augustin*, Paris, Colin, 1970.

——*Port-Royal et la littérature*, Paris, Champion, 1999.

Simmonds, Gemma, “Jansenism (1640–1713): an historico-theological account”, unpublished PhD thesis, University of Cambridge, 2005.

Southern, Richard, *Western Society and the Church in the Later Middle Ages*, London, Penguin, 1970, 2nd edn 1988.

Spink, J. S., *French Free-Thought from Gassendi to Voltaire*, London, Athlone Press, 1960.

Straudo, Arnoux, *La Fortune de Pascal en France au XVIIIe siècle*, Oxford, Voltaire Foundation, 1997.

Street, J. S., *French Sacred Drama from Bèze to Corneille*, Cambridge, Cambridge University Press, 1983.

Szasz, Thomas, *The Second Sin*, London, Routledge and Kegan Paul, 1974.

Taveneaux, René, *Le Catholicisme dans la France classique 1610–1715*, Paris, SEDES, 1980.

Thirouin, Laurent, “La figure de saint Augustin dans *Les Provinciales*”, in *La campagne des ‘Provinciales’*, Paris, Chroniques de Port-Royal, 2008, 225–41.

Topliss, Patricia, *The Rhetoric of Pascal*, Leicester, Leicester University Press, 1966.

Trochu, F., *Saint François de Sales*, Lyons and Paris, Emmanuel Vitte, 1955.

Truchet, Jacques, *Bossuet panégyriste*, Paris, Éditions du Cerf, 1962.

——“La division en points dans les sermons de Bossuet”, in *Revue d'histoire littéraire de la France*, 52, 1952, 316–29.

——*Politique de Bossuet*, Paris, Klincksieck, 1966.

——*La Prédication de Bossuet, étude de thèmes*, Paris, Éditions du Cerf, 1960.

Varden, Erik, *Redeeming Freedom: The Principle of Servitude in Bérulle*, Rome, Studia Anselmiana, 2011.

Vaucheret, Émile, “‘L'honneur du monde’: usurpation de la gloire de Dieu dans les œuvres oratoires de Bossuet”, in *Bossuet: la prédication au XVIIe siècle*, ed. Thérèse Goyet and Jean-Pierre Collinet, Paris, Nizet, 1980, 217–43.

Vermeylen, Alphonse, *Sainte Thérèse en France au XVIIe siècle (1600–1660)*, Leuven, Bibliothèque de l'Université, 1958.

Walker Bynum, Caroline, *Holy Feast and Holy Fast: The Religious Significance of Food to Medieval Women*, Berkeley, University of California Press, 1987.

——*Jeûnes et festins sacrés: les femmes et la nourriture dans la spiritualité médiévale*, Paris, Éditions du Cerf, 1994.

Watt, Diane, *Secretaries of God: Women Prophets in Late Medieval and Early-Modern England*, Cambridge, Cambridge University Press, 1997.

Wetsel, David, *L'Écriture et le reste: the ‘Pensées’ in the exegetical tradition of Port-Royal*, Columbus, Ohio State University Press, 1981.

——*Pascal and Disbelief: Catechesis and Conversion in the ‘Pensées’*, Washington, DC, Catholic University of America Press, 1994.

Wolfe, Phillip J., “La Bruyère critique du quiétisme”, in *Papers on French Seventeenth Century Literature* 15, 2, 1981, 255–66.

Index